Ad'
Language Practice

Michael Vince

English Grammar
and Vocabulary

3rd Edition

MACMILLAN

Macmillan Education
Between Towns Road, Oxford OX4 3PP
A division of Macmillan Publishers Limited
Companies and representatives throughout the world

ISBN 978 0 2307 2704 5 without key
ISBN 978 0 2307 2703 8 with key

First published 1993
This edition published 2009

Designed by Macmillan
Layout and composition by Xen

Illustrated by:
Paul Daviz pp 3, 16, 43, 80, 117, 135, 176, 210, 260;
Julian Mosedale pp 10, 12, 24, 27, 56, 89, 110, 122, 124, 147, 153, 191, 195, 217, 220, 235, 236.

The author would like to thank the many schools and teachers who
have commented on these materials. Also special thanks to
Peter Sunderland who revised the previous edition.

The publisher would like to thank Helen Forrest for her editorial support.

Printed and bound in Spain by Edelvives

2013   2012   2011   2010   2009
10   9   8   7   6   5   4   3   2   1

Contents

CONTENTS

iv

Would not: unwillingness
Would have: events in the past which did not happen,
assumptions
Needn't have and *didn't need to*: unnecessary actions done
and not done
Adverbs and modals: *well, easily, obviously, really, just*

CONTENTS

Introduction

This book is designed to revise and consolidate grammar points
at the level of Cambridge ESOL Proficiency and CAE or Common
European Framework levels C1 and C2.

This revised edition updates the material in accordance with changes
to Cambridge Proficiency and CAE, but also provides a range of
practice formats for this level.

The grammar section includes additional revision and more
advanced points. Units on phrasal verbs, prepositions and linking
devices are also included. There are also sections on spelling and
punctuation

The grammatical information provided can be used for reference
when needed, or worked through systematically.

The vocabulary section includes topic-based vocabulary, collocations
and idiomatic phrases, as well as word formation and multiple
meaning. It also recycles work on prepositions, and phrasal verbs.

The book can be used as a self-study reference grammar and
practice book or as supplementary material in classes preparing for
the CAE and Proficiency exams. If used for classwork, activities can
be done individually or co-operatively in pairs or small groups.

There are regular consolidation units which include forms of testing
commonly used in both exams and the material covers a range of
difficulty appropriate to both exams.

1

GRAMMAR

Present time

Basic contrasts: present simple and present continuous

- Present simple generally refers to:
  Facts that are always true
    *Water **boils** at 100 degrees Celsius.*
  Habits
    *British people **drink** a lot of tea.*
  States
    *I **don't like** gangster films.*

- Present continuous (progressive) generally refers to actions which are in progress at the moment. These can be temporary:
    *I'm **staying** in a hotel until I find a flat.*
  They can be actually in progress.
    *The dog **is sleeping** on our bed!*
  Or they can be generally in progress but not actually happening at the moment.
    *I'm **learning** to drive.*

- State verbs and event (action or dynamic) verbs
  State verbs describe a continuing state, so do not usually have a continuous form.
  Typical examples are:
    believe, belong, consist, contain, doubt, fit, have, know, like, love, matter, mean, need, own, prefer, seem, suppose, suspect, understand, want, wish

- Some verbs have a stative meaning and a different active meaning. Typical examples are:
    be, depend, feel, have, measure, see, taste, think, weigh
  Compare these uses:

State	Event
*Jack **is** noisy.*	*Jill's **being** noisy.*
*Deirdre **has** a Porsche.*	*We're **having** an interesting conversation!*
*I **think** I like you!*	*David's **thinking** about getting a new job.*
*This fish **tastes** awful!*	*I'm just **tasting** the soup.*
*I **feel** that you are wrong.*	*I'm **feeling** terrible.*
*This bag **weighs** a ton!*	*We're **weighing** the baby.*
*It **depends** what you mean.*	*Bill, I'm **depending** on you to win this contract for us.*

  The differences here apply to all tense forms, not just to present tense forms.

1

Other uses of present continuous

- Temporary situations
    *Are you **enjoying** your stay here?*

- Repeated actions
    *My car has broken down, so I **am walking** to work these days.*

- Complaints about annoying habits
    *You **are** always **making** sarcastic remarks about my cooking!*
    Other possible adverbs are: *constantly, continually, forever.*

- With verbs describing change and development
    *The weather **is getting** worse!*
    *More and more people **are giving** up smoking.*

Other uses of present simple

- Making declarations
    Verbs describing opinions and feelings tend to be state verbs.
    *I **hope** you'll come to my party.*
    *I **bet** you don't know the answer!*
    *I hereby **declare** this hospital open!*

- Headlines
    These are written in a 'telegram' style, and references to the past are usually simplified to present simple.
    *Ship **sinks** in midnight collision.*

- Instructions and itineraries
    Instructions and recipes can be written in present simple instead of in imperative forms. This style is more personal.
    *First you **roll out** the pastry.*
    Itineraries are descriptions of travel arrangements.
    *On day three we **visit** Stratford-upon-Avon.*

- Summaries of events
    Plots of stories, films etc, and summaries of historical events use present (and present perfect) verb forms.
    *May 1945: The war in Europe **comes** to an end.*
    *… At the end of the play both families **realize** that their hatred caused the deaths of the lovers …*

- 'Historic present' in narrative and funny stories
    In informal speech, it is possible to use what we call the 'historic present' to describe past events, especially to make the narration seem more immediate and dramatic.
    *… So then the second man **asks** the first one why he **has** a banana in his ear and the first one says …*

1 Underline the correct word or phrase in each sentence.

1 I haven't decided yet about whether to buy a new car or a second-hand one. But *I think about it/I'm thinking* about it.

2 All right, you try to fix the television! But *I hope/I'm hoping* you know what you're doing.

3 Every year *I visit/I'm visiting* Britain to improve my English.

4 It's time we turned on the central heating. *It gets/It's getting* colder every day.

5 Of course, you're Mary, aren't you! *I recognize/I am recognizing* you now.

6 The film of 'War and Peace' is very long. *It lasts/It is lasting* over four hours.

7 I can see from what you say that your mornings are very busy! But what *do you do/are you doing* in the afternoons?

8 I'm going to buy a new swimming costume. My old one *doesn't fit/isn't fitting* any more.

9 That must be the end of the first part of the performance. What *happens/is happening* now?

10 What's the matter? Why *do you look/are you looking* at me like that?

2 Underline the correct word or phrase in each sentence.

1 I work in this office *all this year/all the time*.

2 Harry Potter is *currently/for long* top of the best-sellers' list.

3 I am not making much money *these days/so far this year*.

4 The food tastes even worse *now/presently*. You've put too much salt in.

5 *Normally/previously* we get in touch with customers by post.

6 Pete was ill but he is getting over his illness *soon/now*.

7 I'm feeling rather run down *lately/at present*, doctor.

8 I always stay on duty *since/until* six o'clock.

9 I'm *often/forever* tidying up the mess in your room!

10 Fortunately the baby *now/recently* sleeps all night.

3 Complete each sentence with the present simple or present continuous form of the verb in brackets.

1 I (hear) ....*hear*.......... that you have been promoted. Congratulations!

2 British people (drink) .... more and more wine, apparently.

3 I hope Sarah will be here soon. I (depend) .... on her.

4 Please be quiet, David. You (forever/interrupt) ....

5 Hey, you! What (you/think) .... you're doing?

6 Could you come here please? I (want) .... to talk to you now.

7 Jane is away on holiday so Linda (handle) .... her work.

8 To be honest, I (doubt) .... whether Jim will be here next week.

9 You've only just started the job, haven't you? How (you/get on) ....?

10 Pay no attention to Graham. He (just/be) .... sarcastic.

4 Complete the text with the present simple or present continuous form of the verbs in brackets.

I work in a large office with about thirty other people, most of whom I (1) ....*know*.......... (know) quite well. We (2) .... (spend) most of the day together, so we have all become friends. In fact, most of my colleagues are so interesting, that I (3) .... (think) of writing a book about them! (4) .... (take) Helen Watson, for example. Helen (5) .... (run) the Accounts department. At the moment she (6) .... (go out) with Keith Ballantine, one of the sales representatives, and they (7) .... (seem) very happy together. But everyone – except Helen apparently – (8) ....(know) that Keith (9) .... (fancy) Susan Porter. But I (10) ....(happen) to know that Susan (11) .... (dislike) Keith. 'I can't stand people who never (12) .... (stop) apologizing all the time!' she told me. 'And besides, I know he (13) .... (deceive) poor Helen. He (14) .... (see) Betty Wills from the Overseas department.' And plenty of other interesting things (15) .... (currently/go on). For instance, every week we (16) .... (experience) more and more problems with theft – personal belongings and even money have been stolen. When you (17) .... (realize) that someone in your office is a thief, it (18) .... (upset) you at first. But I (19) .... (also/try) to catch whoever it is before the police are called in. I'm not going to tell you who I (20) .... (suspect). Well, not yet anyway!

5 Complete the second sentence so that it has a similar meaning to the first sentence, using one of the words in **bold**. Do not change the word in **bold**.

1 Charles and his father are exactly alike in appearance.

looks/looking

Charles ....*looks just/exactly like*........................ his father.

2 Take all your possessions and walk slowly to the exit.

belongs/belonging

Take everything .... and walk slowly to the exit.

3 I'm finding it really enjoyable to work here.

enjoy/enjoying

I .... here.

4 I take work home regularly because of my new responsibility at work.

means/meaning

My new responsibility at work .... work home regularly.

5 In my cycling group there's George, Tom, Harry and me.

consists/consisting

My .... George, Tom, Harry and me.

6 In your opinion, who's going to win the Cup?

think/thinking

Who do .... win the Cup?

7 I'm seeing how wide the door is.

measure/measuring

I .... the door.

8 Neil always forgets his wife's birthday.

remembers/remembering

Neil .... his wife's birthday.

9 Its ability to catch fish is the key to the polar bear's survival.

depends/depending

The polar bear's .... to catch fish.

10 What's on your mind at the moment?

think/thinking

What .... at the moment?

6 Correct any errors in these sentences. Some sentences are correct.

1 I'm depending on you, so don't make any mistakes!
.................................✓.................................

2 Is this total including the new students?
.........................Does this total include the new students?..............

3 Excuse me, but do you wait for somebody?
....

4 These potatoes are tasting a bit funny.
....

5 How are you feeling today?
....

6 I look forward to hearing from you.
....

7 I have a feeling that something goes wrong.
....

8 What's that you're eating?
....

9 Are you hearing anything from Wendy these days?
....

10 I think you're being rather mean about this.
....

7 Complete each sentence with a word from the box.

coming	making	~~trying~~	asking
talking	listening	taking	shooting

1 I'm ....trying........ to concentrate.
2 Are you .... off now, or can we talk?
3 Go on, I'm ....
4 I think we're .... at cross purposes.
5 You're .... for trouble.
6 It's .... along nicely.
7 You don't seem to be .... much interest.
8 You're .... a fuss about nothing.

Which expression means one of the following?
a Are you in a hurry to leave?
b We're talking about different things without realizing it.
c If you say or do this you will get into difficulties.

2

GRAMMAR

Future time

Basic contrasts: *will*, *going to*, present continuous

- *Will* is normally known as the predictive future, and describes known facts, or what we suppose is true.
    I'll be late home this evening.
    The company will make a profit next year.
  This can also take the form of an assumption.
    That'll be Jim at the door. (This means that I suppose it is Jim.)

- *Will* is also used to express an immediate decision.
    I'll take this one.

- *Be going to* describes intentions or plans. At the moment of speaking the plans have already been made.
    I'm going to wait here until Carol gets back.
  Going to is also used to describe an event whose cause is present or evident.
    Look at that tree! It's going to fall.
  Compare the following with the *will* examples above:
    I'm going to be late this evening. I've got lots of paperwork to finish off.
    The figures are good. I can see the company is going to make a profit this year.
  Decisions expressed with *going to* refer to a more distant point in the future.

- Present continuous describes fixed arrangements, especially social and travel arrangements. A time reference is usually included. Note the strong similarity to the *going to* future. *I am having a party next week* and *I am going to have a party next week* are communicating the same message.

Future continuous

- This describes an event which will be happening at a future point.
    Come round in the morning. I'll be painting in the kitchen.

- It can also describe events which are going to happen anyway, rather than events which we choose to make happen.
    I won't bother to fix a time to see you, because I'll be calling into the office anyway several times next week.

- In some contexts future continuous also sounds more polite than *will*.
    Will you be going to the shops later? If you go, could you get me some milk?

- It can also be used to refer to fixed arrangements and plans.
    The band will be performing live in Paris this summer.

Future perfect

- This has both simple and continuous forms, and refers to time which we look back at from a future point.

    *In two year's time I'll **have finished** the book.*
    *By the end of the month, I'll **have been working** for this firm for a year.*

- It can also be used to express an assumption on the part of the speaker.

    *You **won't have heard** the news, of course.* (I assume you have not heard the news.)

Other ways of referring to the future

- *Is/are to be*
  This is used to describe formal arrangements.

    *All students **are to assemble** in the hall at 9.00.*
    See also Grammar 9 and 10 for uses expressing obligation.

- *Be about to, be on the point of, be due to, just/just about to*
  Be about to and *be on the point of* both refer to the next moment.

    *I think the play **is about to start** now.*
    Be due to refers to scheduled times.

    *Ann's flight **is due to arrive** at 6.20.* (or **is due** at 6.20)
    Just can be used to describe something on the point of happening.

    *Hurry up! The train **is just leaving/just about to leave**.*

- Present simple and present perfect
  Present simple is used to refer to future time in future time clauses.

    *When we **get** there, we'll have dinner.*
    Present perfect can also be used instead of present simple when the completion of the event is emphasized.

    *When we've **had** a rest, we'll go out.*

- Present simple is also used to describe fixed events which are not simply the wishes of the speaker.

    *Tom **retires** in three years.*
    Similarly, calendar references use the present simple.

    *Christmas **is** on a Tuesday next year.*

Other future references

- *Hope*
  This can be followed by either present or future verb forms.

    *I hope it **doesn't** rain.   I hope it **won't** rain.*

- Other verbs followed by *will*
  Most verbs of thinking can be followed by *will* if there is future reference. These include: *think, believe, expect, doubt.*

    *I **expect** the train will be late.   I **doubt** whether United will win.*

- *Shall*
  The use of *shall* for first person in future reference is declining in use in everyday informal speech. See Grammar 9 and 10 for other uses of *shall* and *will*.

1 **Complete each sentence using the cues in brackets.**

1 In twenty-four hours' time (I/relax) ...*I will be relaxing*. on my yacht.

2 'There's someone at the door.' 'That (be) .... the postman.'

3 By the time you get back Harry (leave) ....

4 It's only a short trip. I (be) .... back in an hour.

5 What (you/do) .... this Saturday evening? Would you like to go out?

6 By the end of the week we (decide) .... what to do.

7 It (not/be) .... long before Doctor Smith is here.

8 We'll go to the park when you (finish) .... your tea.

9 It's very hot in here. I think I (faint) ....

10 What (you/give) .... Ann for her birthday? Have you decided yet?

2 <u>Underline</u> **the most suitable verb form in each sentence.**

In July Gordon (1) *will be/will have been* at his company for 30 years and (2) *he's finally retiring/he'll finally retire* on his 65th birthday. We've decided to have a long holiday and (3) *we're going to take/we'll take* the opportunity to visit some old friends in Hungary, and then travel around in that region. (4) *We leave/We'll be leaving* towards the end of August, and our aim is to visit as many countries as we can. (5) *We're flying/We'll fly* to Budapest on the 25th and then (6) *we stop over/we'll be stopping over* with our friends – they've got a house on Lake Balaton. (7) *We'll have spent/We'll probably spend* a couple of weeks in Hungary and travel around. After that (8) *we're thinking/we'll think* of going to Romania, but we haven't planned anything definite. (9) *We'll know/we'll have known* a bit more this weekend when (10) *we'll research/we'll be researching* the whole thing on the Internet. We'd like to go on from there to Bulgaria or Ukraine, but I doubt whether (11) *we'll have/we're having* time. Money could be a problem too – I hope the whole trip (12) *won't be/won't have been* too expensive. From now on (13) *we are really having to/ we'll really have to* save as much as we can. We're really looking forward to it – I can hardly wait! Just think, in just over two months' time (14) *we'll be travelling/we'll have travelled* around Europe like a couple of old hippies! When we come back, (15) *you aren't recognizing us/you won't recognize* us!

3 Read each sentence and decide which ending (A, B or C) best fits each space.

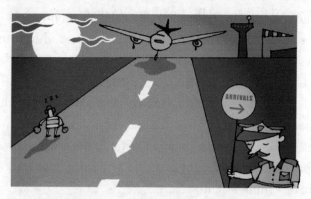

1   Paula's flight is bound to be late although ....B....
    A it arrives at 6.00.   **B** it's due at 6.00.   **C** it's arriving at six.

2   According to the latest forecast, the tunnel ....
    A will be finished next year.   **B** will have been finished next year.
    C is finishing next year.

3   It's no use phoning Bob at the office, he ....
    A will be leaving.   **B** is leaving.   **C** will have left.

4   Everyone says that this year City ....
    A are going to win the Cup.   **B** are winning the Cup.   **C** win the Cup.

5   I don't feel like visiting my relatives this year so ....
    A I won't go.   **B** I'm not going.   **C** I don't go.

6   You can borrow this calculator, I ....
    A am not going to need it.   **B** won't have been needing it.
    C am not needing it.

7   I'm sorry dinner isn't ready yet, but it ....
    A is going to be ready in a minute.   **B** will have been ready in a minute.
    C will be ready in a minute.

8   Can you send me the results as soon as you ....
    A hear anything?   **B** are hearing anything?   **C** will have heard anything?

9   You can try asking Martin for help but ....
    A it won't do you any good.   **B** it's not doing you any good.
    C it won't be doing you any good.

10 Don't worry about the mistake you made, nobody ....
    A is noticing.   **B** will notice.   **C** will be noticing.

4 Complete the second sentence so that it has a similar meaning to the first sentence, using the word given. Do not change the word given.

1 I don't suppose you have heard the news.

   won't

   You ......*won't have heard*..... the news.

2 The Prime Minister expects an easy victory for his party in the election.

   believes

   The Prime Minister .... the election easily.

3 I've been in this company for almost three years.

   will

   By the end of the month .... in this company for three years.

4 This book will take me two years to write.

   have

   In two years .... this book.

5 Scientists are on the point of making a vital breakthrough.

   about

   Scientists are .... a vital breakthrough.

6 Maria is pregnant again.

   have

   Maria is .... baby.

7 I'll be home late.

   until

   I .... late.

8 No one knows what the result of the match is going to be.

   who

   No one knows .... the match.

9 Don't worry; David won't be late.

   here

   Don't worry; David .... time.

10 Mary and Alan's wedding is next weekend.

   getting

   Mary and Alan .... next weekend.

5 Look at the three options (A, B and C) for each question. Decide which two are correct.

1 We've run out of fuel. .... *B, C* ....

 A What will we do now?   **B** What do we do now?

 C What are we going to do now?

2 You can't leave early, ...

 A we're having a meeting.   **B** we're going to have a meeting.

 C we will have a meeting.

3 Oh dear, I've broken the vase. ....

 A What will your mother say?   **B** What is your mother going to say?

 C What is your mother saying?

4 According to the weather forecast, ...

 A it'll rain tomorrow.   **B** it's raining tomorrow.

 C it's going to rain tomorrow.

5 I'd like to call round and see you. ....

 A What will you have done by the morning?   **B** What'll you be doing in the

 morning?   **C** What are you doing in the morning?

6 I've got nothing to do tomorrow so ....

 A I'll get up late.   **B** I am to get up late.   **C** I'm going to get up late.

7 It's my eighteenth birthday next month so ....

 A I'm on the point of having a party.   **B** I'm having a party.

 C I'll be having a party.

8 Why don't you come with us? ....

 A It'll be a great trip.   **B** It's going to be a great trip.   **C** It's a great trip.

9 When you get to the airport ....

 A someone is going to be waiting for you.   **B** someone is due to wait for you.

 C someone will be waiting for you.

10 Shut up, will you! ....

 A I'm getting really angry.   **B** I'm going to get really angry in a minute.

 C I'm getting really angry in a minute.

6 <u>Underline</u> the correct word or phrase in each sentence.

1 I'll be back *after a few minutes*/<u>*in a few minutes.*</u>
2 I'm sure that everything will be all right *at the end/in the end.*
3 Please call me *the moment/exactly* when you hear any news.
4 I should be back *by the time/at the time* the film begins.
5 I'm sure Fiona will be here *before long/after a while.*
6 I can't leave on Tuesday. I won't be ready *until then/by then.*
7 *By twenty four hours/This time tomorrow* I'll be in Bangkok.
8 Diana will be retiring *soon/already.*
9 There will be no official announcements *forthwith/from now on.*
10 Bye for now. I'll see you *in two weeks' time/two weeks later.*

7 Complete each sentence with a word from the box.

let	give	be	go	~~see~~	come	have	go	be	see

1 I'll ......*see*...... what I can do.
2 I'll .... a look and get back to you.
3 I'll .... it some thought.
4 I'll .... you know by tomorrow.
5 I'll just .... and get it.
6 I'll .... halves with you.
7 I'll .... to it.
8 I'll .... back in a minute.
9 I'll .... about five minutes.
10 I'll .... and show you.

Which expression means one of the following?
a I'll try and do this for you.
b I'll share it with you.
c I'll fix it/arrange it.

➜ **SEE ALSO**
Consolidation 1: Units 1–4
Grammar 7: Conditionals
Grammar 9 and 10: Modals

Past time

Basic contrasts: past simple and past continuous

- Past simple generally refers to:
  Completed actions
  > *I **got** up, **switched off** the radio, and **sat** down again.*
  Habits
  > *Every day I **went** to the park.*
  States
  > *In those days, I **didn't like** reading.*

- Past continuous (progressive) generally refers to:
  Actions in progress (often interrupted by events)
  > *I **was drinking** my coffee at the time.*
  > *While I **was opening** the letter, the phone rang.*
  Background description in narrative
  > *I entered the office and looked around. Most people **were working** at their desks, but Jane **was staring** out of the window and **pretending** to write something at the same time.*
  Changing states
  > *The car **was getting** worse all the time. One of the headlights **was** gradually **falling** off, and the engine **was making** more and more funny noises.*
  Repeated actions – criticism
  With a frequency adverb, this use is similar to the use of present continuous to express annoyance.
  > *When Jane was at school, she **was** always **losing** things.*

- Past continuous is not used to describe general habitual actions, without the sense of criticism mentioned above. Past simple is used for this meaning.
  > *When I **lived** in London, I **walked** through the park every day.*

Past perfect simple and continuous

- We use the past perfect when we are already talking about the past, and we want to go back to an earlier past time ('past in the past').
  > *By the time I got to the station, the train **had left**.*
  Compare this with:
  > *The train **left** five minutes before I got to the station.*
  When we talk about a sequence of past events in the order that they happened, we more commonly use the past simple, especially with quick, short actions.

- Past perfect continuous (progressive)
  The same contrasts between past simple and past continuous (see previous section)

can be made in past perfect verb forms for events further back in the past.

*I **had been living** in a bed-sitter up to then.*

*While I **had been talking** on the phone, Jimmy had escaped.*

*The whole place was deserted, but it was obvious that someone **had been living** there.*

*They'**d been cooking** in the kitchen for a start, and they hadn't bothered to clear up the mess.*

● Past perfect is also common in reported speech. See Grammar 13.

● Past perfect is not used simply to describe an event in the distant past.

Used to and *would*

● *Used to*

This often contrasts with the present. The contrast may be stated or understood. There is no is no present tense form 'use to'.

*I **used to go** swimming a lot* (but I don't now).

The negative form is either: *I didn't use to* or *I used not to* (rare for some speakers). The form *I didn't used to* may also be found. This is usually considered incorrect, unless we consider *used to* as an unchanging semi-modal form.

● *Would*

This describes repeated actions, not states. It describes a habitual activity which was typical of a person or a time period.

*Every week he'**d buy** his mother a bunch of flowers.* (habitual activity)

*I **used to like** cowboy films.*

Where we use *would* to describe a habitual activity, *used to* is also possible.

*Every week he **used to buy** his mother a bunch of flowers.*

Would is more common in written language and often occurs in reminiscences.

Unfulfilled past events

● These describe events intended to take place, but which did not happen.

*I **was going to phone** you, but I forgot.*

*I **was thinking of going** to Italy this year, but I haven't decided.*

*I **was about to do** it, but I started doing something else.*

*Jack **was to have taken part**, but he fell ill.*

● The contrasting past event is often understood, but not stated.

*How are you? I **was going to phone** you ...* (but I didn't).

Polite forms

These are common with *wonder*.

*I **was wondering** if you wanted to come to the cinema.*

See Grammar 9 and 10 for comment on this.

Contrasts with present perfect verb forms

See Grammar 4 for contrasts between past simple and present perfect verb forms. Past verb forms are also used to express unreal time. See Grammar 7 and 8.

1 <u>Underline</u> the correct word or phrase in each sentence.

1 When you passed the town hall clock, <u>*did you notice*</u>/*were you noticing* what time it was?

2 Last night my neighbours *were shouting*/*would shout* for hours and I couldn't get to sleep.

3 When you lived in London, *did you use to travel*/*were you travelling* by bus?

4 Everyone was having a good time, although not many people *danced*/*were dancing*.

5 Jill was really hungry because she *didn't eat*/*hadn't eaten* all day.

6 We decided to go to the cinema, but before that *we went*/*had gone* for a pizza.

7 It took a while for me to notice, but then I did. Everyone *stared*/*was staring* at me. What had I done wrong?

8 Nobody bothered to tell me that the school *decided*/*had decided* to have a special holiday on Friday.

9 I *was trying*/*tried* to get in touch with you all day yesterday. Where were you?

10 A: Excuse me, but this seat is mine.

B: I'm sorry, I *didn't realize*/*wouldn't realize* that you were sitting here.

2 <u>Underline</u> the correct word or phrase in each sentence.

1 *Once*/*Afterwards* I'd read the instructions, I found it easy to assemble the bookcase.

2 It was more than a month *before*/*until* I realized what had happened.

3 I managed to talk to Carol just *as*/*while* she was leaving.

4 It wasn't *until*/*up to* 1983 that Nigel could afford to take holidays abroad.

5 George always let me know *by the time*/*whenever* he was going to be late.

6 I was having a bath *at the time*/*that time*, so I didn't hear the doorbell.

7 We bought our tickets and five minutes *after*/*later* the train arrived.

8 According to Grandpa, people used to dress formally *those days*/*in his day*.

9 Everyone was talking but stopped *at that time*/*the moment* Mr Smith arrived.

10 The letter still hadn't arrived *by*/*until* the end of the week.

3 Decide if the verb form <u>underlined</u> is correct or not. If it is correct, write a tick
(✓). If not, correct it.

Text 1

> The train (1) <u>ground</u> to a halt at a small station miles from London, and it
> (2) <u>became</u> apparent that it (3) <u>had broken</u> down. Everyone (4) <u>was getting</u> their
> cases down from the luggage racks, and we (5) <u>were waiting</u> on the platform in the
> freezing wind for hours until the next train (6) <u>was turning up</u>.

1	......✓......	3	....	5	....
2	....	4	....	6	....

Text 2

> The mysterious disappearance of Professor Dawson (1) <u>was</u> on Inspector Gorse's
> mind. Six months before the Professor's disappearance, he (2) <u>was receiving</u> a letter
> from Jean Dawson, the Professor's wife. In the letter, Jean (3) <u>accused</u> her husband
> of plotting to murder her. Gorse (4) <u>considered</u> his next step when the phone rang. It
> was Sergeant Adams from the Thames Valley police force. A fisherman (5) <u>discovered</u>
> a body in the river, and it (6) <u>fitted</u> the description of the Professor.

1	....	3	....	5	....
2	....	4	....	6	....

4 Complete the text with a suitable past tense form of the verbs in brackets.

> This time last year I (1) ...was cycling... (cycle) in the rain along a country road in France with a
> friend of mine. We (2) .... (decide) to go on a cycling holiday in Normandy. Neither
> of us (3) .... (be) to France before, but we (4) .... (know) some
> French from our time at school and we (5) .... (manage) to brush up on the basics.
> Now we (6) .... (wonder) if we (7) .... (make) the right decision. We
> (8) .... (plan) our route carefully in advance, but we (9) .... (forget)
> one important thing: the weather. It (10) .... (rain) solidly since our arrival and that
> night we (11) .... (end up) sleeping in the waiting room at a railway station. Then the
> next morning as we (12) .... (ride) down a steep hill my bike (13) ....
> (skid) on the wet road and I (14) .... (fall off). I (15) .... (realize)
> immediately that I (16) .... (break) my arm, and after a visit to the local hospital I
> (17) .... (catch) the next train to Calais for the ferry home. Unfortunately my parents
> (18) .... (not/expect) me home for a fortnight, and (19) .... (go) away
> on holiday. So I (20) .... (spend) a miserable couple of weeks alone, reading 'Teach
> Yourself French'.

5 Complete the second sentence so that it has a similar meaning to the first sentence, using the word given. Do not change the word given.

I intended to call you yesterday, but I forgot.

going

I .... *was going to* .... call you yesterday, but I forgot.

2 Sylvia asked if I wanted more pudding, but I said I couldn't eat any more.

had

When Sylvia offered .... enough.

3 Owing to illness, Sally was unable to sing the solo, as arranged.

have

Sally was .... but she fell ill.

4 Carol wasn't always as rude as that.

be

Carol .... rude.

5 We've changed our minds about going to Rome, as originally intended.

intending

We .... we've changed our minds.

6 When I lived in London cycling to work was part of my daily routine.

used

When I lived in London I .... day.

7 I might possibly go to the theatre tonight.

wondering

I .... going to the theatre tonight.

8 I had to go past your house so I decided to drop in.

passing

I .... so I decided to drop in.

9 About 100 people were waiting for the late bus.

arrived

By .... about 100 people waiting.

10 What were you doing at the moment of the explosion?

occurred

When .... what were you doing?

6 **In each sentence decide whether one, or both, of the alternative verb forms given are appropriate. Write *O* for one or *B* for both.**

1 In those days, I always *used to get up/got up* early in the morning. ...B....

2 When I got to the cinema Jack *had been waiting/was waiting* for me. ....

3 We *would always have/were always having* breakfast in bed on Sundays. ....

4 Mary *was always falling/always fell* ill before important examinations. ....

5 My sister *used to own/would own* a motorcycle and sidecar. ....

6 Pay no attention to Dave's remarks. He *wasn't meaning/didn't mean* it. ....

7 I felt awful after lunch. I *ate/had eaten* too much. ....

8 Brenda *left/had left* before I had time to talk to her. ....

9 The explanation was simple. In 1781 HMS Sovereign, on her way back from India, *had sighted/sighted* an empty boat drifting off the African coast. ....

10 Pauline has changed a lot. She *didn't always use to look/wasn't always looking* like that. ....

7 **Complete the text by writing one word in each space.**

I once (1) ..spent.. a year in France, studying French at the University of Grenoble. Every Friday I (2) .... eat at the Alps café. I never (3) .... to spend much money, as I could not afford it, but it (4) .... my local café and I enjoyed sitting there. Anyway, the story I'm going to tell you is something that really (5) .... one day when I (6) .... eating there. Suddenly a beautiful girl (7) .... to my table and said, 'I was (8) .... if you'd like to take a walk with me in the park?' I (9) .... never seen her before, so I was rather shocked. I (10) .... about to follow her when I noticed a tough-looking man watching our every movement. Realizing that I (11) .... noticed him, the girl whispered to me, in English, 'Don't worry about him! Park — five minutes!', and then disappeared. Well, my bill (12) .... ages to arrive, and by the time I (13) .... to the park, there was no sign of the girl. I asked an old lady who was sitting there if she had (14) .... a young girl waiting around. I described the girl to her. The old lady said that the girl (15) .... had to rush off to the railway station. She had also left me a note. It said, 'I will explain everything. Meet me on platform 6.'

8 Complete each sentence with a suitable past tense form of the verbs in brackets.

1 I realized that someone (steal) ...was stealing... my wallet when I (feel) ...felt.. .... their hand in my jacket pocket.

2 When I (phone) .... Helen last night she .... (wash) her hair.

3 Peter (offer) .... me another drink but I decided I (had) .... enough.

4 Nobody (watch) .... , so the little boy (take) .... the packet of sweets from the shelf and (put) .... it in his pocket.

5 I (not/realize) .... that I (leave) .... my umbrella on the bus until it (start) .... to rain.

6 At school I (dislike) .... the maths teacher because he (always/pick) .... on me.

7 Wherever Marion (find) .... a job, there was someone who (know) .... that she (go) .... to prison.

8 Several years later I (find out) .... that during all the time I (write) .... to my pen friend, my mother (open) .... and reading the replies!

9 I (not/understand) .... what (go on) .... Several people (shout) .... at me, and one passer-by (wave) .... a newspaper in front of my face.

10 I (know) .... I (do) .... well in my exams even before I (receive) .... the official results.

➜ **SEE ALSO**
Grammar 4: Present perfect
Consolidation 1: Units 1–4
Grammar 7: Conditionals
Grammar 8: Unreal time
Grammar 9 and 10: Modals
Grammar 13: Reported speech

4

Present perfect

Present perfect simple

- Present perfect simple refers to:
  Recent events, without a definite time given. The recentness may be indicated by *just*.
  > *We've **missed** the turning. I've **just seen** a ghost!*

  Indefinite events, which happened at an unknown time in the past. No definite time is given.
  > *Jim **has had** three car accidents.* (up to the present)

  Indefinite events which may have an obvious result in the present.
  > *I've **twisted** my ankle.* (that's why I'm limping)

  With state verbs, a state which lasts up to the present.
  > *I've **lived** here for the past ten years.*

  A habitual action in a period of time up to the present.
  > *I've **been jogging** every morning for the last month.*

- Contrast with past simple
  Past simple is used with time expressions which refer to definite times. The time may be stated or understood. Compare:
  > *I've **bought** a new car.* (indefinite time)
  > *I **bought** a new car last week.* (definite time)
  > *I **bought** the car after all.* (implied definite: the car we talked about)

  Choice between past simple and present perfect for recent events may depend on the attitude of the speaker. This in turn may depend on whether the speaker feels distant in time or place from the event.
  > *I've **left** my wallet in the car. I'm going back to get it.*

  Here the speaker may be about to return, and feels that the event is connected with the present.
  > *I **left** my wallet in the car. I'm going back to get it.*

  The speaker may feel separated in time from the event, or be further away.

Present perfect continuous

- Present perfect continuous (progressive) can refer to a range of meanings, depending on the time expression used and the context.
  A state which lasts up to the present moment
  > *I've **been waiting** for you for three hours!*

  An incomplete activity
  > *I've **been cleaning** the house but I still haven't finished.*

  To emphasize duration
  > *I've **been writing** letters all morning.*

  A recently finished activity
  > *I've **been running**. That's why I look hot.*

A repeated activity
> *I've **been taking** French lessons this year.*

● Contrast with present perfect simple
There may be little contrast when some state verbs are used.
> *How long **have** you **lived** here?*
> *How long **have** you **been living** here?*

Some verbs (especially *sit*, *lie*, *wait* and *stay*) prefer the continuous form.
There may be a contrast between completion and incompletion, especially if the number of items completed is mentioned.
Completed: emphasis on achievement
> *I've **ironed** five shirts.*

Incomplete, or recently completed: emphasis on duration
> *I've **been ironing** my shirts.*

Time expressions with present perfect

● Meaning with present perfect verb forms is often associated with certain time expressions.
Contrast with past simple may depend on the choice of time expression.
Past simple: referring to a specific finished time.
> *yesterday, last week, on Sunday*

Present perfect: with 'indefinite' time expressions meaning 'up to now'.
> *since 1968, already*

Many time expressions are not associated with a specific verb form, since they refer both to finished time or time up to the present, depending on the speaker's perspective.
> *I **haven't seen** Helen recently.*
> *I **saw** Jim recently.*

Other examples:

*Sue **lived** in France for two years.*	*finished*
*Jim **has been working** here for three months.*	*unfinished*
*What **did** you **do** today?*	*finished*
*What **have** you **done** so far today?*	*unfinished*
*Peter never **knew** his father.*	*finished*
*I've never **eaten** Japanese food.*	*unfinished*

1 Underline the correct word or phrase in each sentence.

1 I can't believe it, Inspector. You mean that Smith *stole/has stolen/has been stealing* money from the till all this time!

2 You three boys look very guilty! What *did you do/have you done/have you been doing* since I *left/have left* the room?

3 Why on earth *didn't you tell/haven't you told* me about that loose floorboard? I *tripped/have tripped* over it just now and hurt myself.

4 It's a long time since I *saw/have seen/have been seeing* your brother Paul. What *did he do/has he done/has he been doing* lately?

5 I can't believe that you *ate/have eaten/have been eating* three pizzas already! I *only brought/have only brought* them in fifteen minutes ago!

6 Don't forget that you *didn't see/haven't seen* Mrs Dawson. She *has waited/has been waiting* outside since 10.30.

7 What *did you think/have you thought* of Brighton? *Did you stay/Have you stayed* there long?

8 I feel really tired. I *weeded/have weeded/have been weeding* the garden for the last three hours and I *didn't rest/haven't rested* for a single moment.

9 I'm having problems with David. He *has called/has been calling* me up in the middle of the night and *told/telling* me his troubles.

10 How long *did you have/have you had/have you been having* driving lessons? And *did you take/have you taken/have you been taking* your test yet?

2 Decide how many different endings (a–j) you can find for sentences (1–10). The sentences you make must be appropriate and meaningful.

1 I haven't been feeling very well … *e, h*   a time and time again.

2 I went to the dentist's … ……….   b all my life.

3 I've lived here … ……….   c so far.

4 Don't worry. I haven't been waiting … ……….   d for the time being.

5 I've written two pages … ……….   e for the past hour or two.

6 I waited outside your house … ……….   f yet.

7 I've warned you about this … ……….   g till half past eight.

8 I haven't made a decision … ……….   h for a while.

9 The repair worked … ……….   i the other day.

10 I've decided to believe you … ……….   j long.

3 Complete each sentence with a suitable perfect or past tense form of the verb in brackets.

1 So far we (not/notice) ......*haven't noticed*...... anything unusual, but we (not/pay) .
.... very close attention.

2 I'm sorry I (not/come) .... to class lately.

3 I (work) .... late in the evenings for the past fortnight.

4 I wonder if Mary (reach) .... home yet? She (leave)
.... too late to catch the bus.

5 Here is the news. The Home Office (announce) .... that the
two prisoners who (escape) .... from Dartmoor prison earlier
this morning (give themselves up) .... to local police.

6 (you/make up) .... your minds? What (you/decide)
.... to do?

7 Harry (leave) .... home rather suddenly and we (not/hear) ....
.... from him since.

8 Recent research (show) .... that Columbus (not/discover) ....
.... America, but that Vikings (land)
.... there five hundred years before him.

9 I think that people (become) .... tired of the poor quality of
television programmes, though they (improve) .... lately.

10 (something/happen) .... to the phone lines? I (try)
.... to get through to Glasgow for the past hour.

11 Bill (get) .... that new job, but he (complain)
.... about it ever since.

4 Complete the second sentence so that it has a similar meaning to the first sentence, using the word given. Do not change the word given.

1 This has been my home for thirty years.

lived

I .... *have lived here* .... for thirty years.

2 Eating Korean food is new to me.

never

I .... before.

3 Tony hasn't been to Paris before.

first

It's .... to Paris.

4 We haven't been swimming for ages.

since

It's .... swimming.

5 Mary started learning French five years ago.

has

Mary .... five years.

6 I am on the tenth page of this letter I am writing.

ten

So far I .... of this letter.

7 It's over twenty years since they got married.

for

They have .... than twenty years.

8 The last time I saw Dick was in 2007.

seen

I haven't .... 2007.

9 There is a definite improvement in your work.

has

Lately .... improved.

10 This is my second visit to Hungary.

visited

This is the .... Hungary.

5 Underline the correct phrase in each sentence.

1 The price of petrol _has risen_/_has been rising_ by 15% over the past year.

2 No wonder you are overweight! You _have eaten_/_You have been eating_ chocolates all day long!

3 _I've read_/_I've been reading_ a really good book this morning.

4 Doesn't this room look better? _I've put_/_I've been putting_ some posters up on the walls.

5 Don't disappoint me! _I've counted_/_I've been counting_ on you.

6 Don't forget your pill. _Have you taken it?_/_Have you been taking it?_

7 Who _has worn_/_has been wearing_ my scarf?

8 I think there's something wrong with your motorbike. _It's made_/_It's been making_ some very funny noises.

9 Jack _has asked_/_has been asking_ for a pay rise three times this year.

10 _I've been phoning_/_I've phoned_ Ann all evening, but there's no reply.

6 Complete the text with the past simple, present perfect simple or present perfect continuous of the verbs in brackets.

Three weeks ago I (1) ......moved...... (move) to London, full of enthusiasm, to start a new job, but ever since I (2) .... (arrive) in the capital, I (3) .... (wonder) whether this was the right decision. Before coming here, I (4) .... (hear) a lot of great things about life in London, but since arriving I can't really say that the city (5) .... (make) a favourable impression on me. It's so crowded and the people are so unfriendly, and I (6) .... (spend) hours every day on the underground going to and from work. You see, I (7) .... (grow up) in a small town in Wales and I (8) .... (not be) away from home before. Of course, I (9) .... (always/want) to see the world, so when my company (10) .... (offer) me a post in the London office, I (11) .... (jump) at the chance. The problem is that now I (12) .... (actually/start) living here, I can see that there are lots of reasons for being back in Wales! In fact, according to a piece I (13) .... (come across) in the paper the other day, a lot of large companies (14) .... (choose) to move away from the centre of London recently. I feel so miserable that I (15) .... (secretly/hope) my company might decide to move too, and that I'll be able to go back to Wales.

---

7 <u>Underline</u> the correct word or phrase in each sentence.

1 It's a long time *since/when* I last saw you.
2 I've seen Bill quite often *lately/from time to time*.
3 Have you spoken to the director *beforehand/already*?
4 I've lived in the same house *for years/for ever*.
5 I've read the paper *now/still*.
6 Jan has bought a computer *two years ago/since then*.
7 Nothing much has been happening *by now/so far*.
8 I've finished reading her new book at *last/this* evening.
9 Sue bought a CD player last week and she's been listening to music *ever since/for a while*.
10 Sorry, but I haven't got that work finished *already/yet*.

8 Match the expressions (1–10) with the explanations of when they might be said (a–j).

1 Have you heard the one about ... ? ....*d*....
2 I haven't seen you for ages! ....
3 I've had enough of this! ....
4 Sorry, you've lost me! ....
5 I've had a brainwave! ....
6 It's been one of those days! ....
7 I've had enough, thanks. ....
8 I haven't had a chance yet. ....
9 I've been having second thoughts. ....
10 Oh, haven't you heard? ....

a Saying you don't follow what someone is saying.
b Having doubts about a big decision.
c Having a brilliant idea.
d Introducing a joke.
e Declining more food.
f Spreading gossip.
g Seeing an old face from the past.
h Having a frustrating time, when everything is going wrong.
i Wanting to stop doing something because it's annoying you.
j Apologizing for not doing something you said you'd do.

→ SEE ALSO
Grammar 3: Past tenses
Consolidation 1: Units 1–4

Units 1–4

1 Complete the text with a suitable form of the verb in brackets.

Reporter Philip Taggart visits a farm where the sheep are super fit!

Farmers, as you may (1) ....*know*............ (know), (2) ....
(have) a hard time of it in Britain lately, and (3) .... (turn)
to new ways of earning income from their land. This (4) ....
(involve) not only planting new kinds of crops, but also some strange ways
of making money, the most unusual of which has got to be sheep racing.
Yes, you (5) .... (hear) me correctly! A farmer in the west of
England now (6) .... (hold) sheep races on a regular basis, and
during the past year over 100,000 people (7) .... (turn up) to
watch the proceedings. 'I (8) .... (pass) the farm on my way
to the sea for a holiday,' one punter told me, 'and I (9) ....
(think) I'd have a look. I (10) .... (not/believe) it was serious,
to tell you the truth.' According to a regular visitor, betting on sheep is more
interesting than betting on horses. 'At proper horse races everyone (11)
.... (already/study) the form of the horses in advance, and
there are clear favourites. But nobody (12) .... (hear) anything
about these sheep! Most people (13) .... (find) it difficult to tell
one from another in any case.' I (14) .... (stay) to watch the
races, and I must admit that I (15) .... (find) it quite exciting. In
a typical race, half a dozen sheep (16) .... (race) downhill over
a course of about half a mile. Food (17) .... (wait) for them at
the other end of the track, I ought to add! The sheep (18) ....
(run) surprisingly fast, although presumably they (19) .... (not/
eat) for a while just to give them some motivation. At any rate, the crowd
around me (20) .... (obviously/enjoy) their day out at the
races, judging by their happy faces and the sense of excitement.

2 Complete the second sentence so that it has a similar meaning to the first sentence, using the word given. Do not change the word given.

1 This matter is none of your business.

   concern

   This matter .... *is of no concern to/does not concern* .... you.

2 This bridge will take us three years to complete.

   completed

   In three years' time .... this bridge.

3 When is the train due to arrive?

   supposed

   What .... get here?

4 Today is Liz and John's thirtieth wedding anniversary.

   ago

   On this .... married.

5 To get to work on time, I have to get up at 6.00.

   means

   Getting to work on time .... at 6.00.

6 Whose watch is this?

   belong

   Who .... to?

7 Cathy hasn't been on holiday with her sister before.

   first

   This .... on holiday with her sister.

8 My dental appointment is for next Wednesday.

   see

   I have an .... Wednesday.

9 This will be the team's first match in the Champion's League.

   time

   This will be the first .... in the Champion's League.

10 The number of people who attended the fair exceeded our expectations.

   had

   More people .... expected.

11 I didn't receive the results of my test for a month.

   before

   It was .... the results of my test.

12 Quite a few books are missing from the class library.

   returned

   Several members of the class .... library books.

ADVANCED LANGUAGE PRACTICE

3 In most lines of this text there is one extra word. Write the extra word, or put a tick if the line is correct.

> *Our reporter, Sarah Hardie, goes to Otley Hall to experience a spooky weekend.*
>
> There have been signs of paranormal activity at Otley Hall at various times   1 ....✓.........
>
> over the last 200 years time. If tales of headless huntsmen and wailing nuns   2 ....
>
> don't spook you out, do get this for a ghostly tale: a young Victorian man in   3 ....
>
> a silver gown emerges himself from the garden, walks through the front door,   4 ....
>
> whether or not will it happens to be open, and walks upstairs with a lantern,   5 ....
>
> before vanishing in the library. If local folklore it is to be believed, he does   6 ....
>
> this without fail at midnight on 6 September every year, this is being the date   7 ....
>
> of the untimely death of one George Carpenter, the gardener of the hall,   8 ....
>
> who met his doom in the library, had burned by his own lantern. Otley Hall   9 ....
>
> stands 3 miles north of the town of Rugby, England, and that is reputedly the   10 ....
>
> most haunted house in England, a claim which few who have never visited it   11 ....
>
> would dispute. Even the approach to the Hall is not much a journey to be   12 ....
>
> undertaken by the faint-hearted; at one point an executioner emerges   13 ....
>
> from the trees, was brandishing an axe, although it must be said that this   14 ....
>
> practice ceases after September, when the Hall is closed to visitors.   15 ....
>
> My own visit revealed nothing more mysterious than such gimmicks,   16 ....
>
> laid on for an ever-gullible flow of tourists, cameras been at their sides,   17 ....
>
> eager to snap their buttons at the first sign of anything even remotely   18 ....
>
> unexplainable. But it was all having great fun, and the ghostly maze on   19 ....
>
> the final day was terrific, even if I never did get to see George Carpenter.   20 ....

4 Complete each sentence with a suitable word.

1 It's ....ages........ since I last had a good Chinese meal.

2 Funnily enough I saw Bob quite .... at the sports club.

3 I've loved you ever .... the first day I set eyes on you!

4 How long .... was it that you lived in Inverness?

5 I've .... to see anyone who can dance as well as Maria.

6 Could you phone me the .... you arrive at the hotel so I don't worry?

7 I promise to get everything ready .... eight o'clock at the latest.

8 I told Sue I .... already finished my essay.

9 I'm sorry you've been waiting so long, but it will be some time .... Brian gets back.

10 Just sit here, would you? The doctor will be with you ....

CONSOLIDATION 1

5 Complete each sentence with a suitable form of the verb in brackets.

1 This is my new boat. What (you/think) ......*do you think*...... of it?

2 A: Who are you?
   B: What do you mean? I (live) .... here.

3 I can't find the keys. What (you/do) .... with them?

4 Sorry I haven't fixed the plug. I (mean) .... to get round to it, but I just haven't found the time.

5 What (you/do) .... on Saturdays?

6 I don't know what time we'll eat. It (depends) .... when Helen gets here.

7 I supported you at the time because I (feel) .... that you were right.

8 Peter couldn't understand what had been decided because too many people (talk) . ... at once.

9 Jean, I'm so glad you've got here at last. I (expect) .... you all day.

6 Complete the text with a suitable form of the verbs in brackets.

Ask hundreds of people what they (1) ...*plan/are planning*.. (plan) to do on a certain day in August next year, or the year after, and there (2) .... (be) only one reply. Provided of course that the people you (3) .... (ask) (4) .... (belong) to the Elvis Presley Fan Club. Although the King of Rock and Roll (5) .... (die) over three decades ago, his fans (6) .... (meet) every year since then outside his home in Memphis, Tennessee, to show respect for the singer they (7) .... (love) so much. Fans like Jean Thomas, from Catford in South East London. Jean (8) .... (visit) Gracelands, the house where Elvis (9) .... (suffer) his fatal heart attack, twice in the past five years. 'The first time I (10) .... (borrow) the money from my Mum, as I (11) .... (not/work) then. But two years ago I (12) .... (get) married and since then I (13) .... (work) in my husband Chris's garage. Chris and I (14) .... (go) together last year, and we (15) .... (think) of spending two or three months in the USA next year. I (16) .... (always/want) to visit some of the places where Elvis (17) .... (perform). Like Las Vegas for example.' Jean says that Elvis (18) .... (be) her obsession ever since she (19) .... (be) ten years old, and she (20) .... (own) every single one of his records, good and bad.

31

7 Complete each sentence with a suitable form of the verb in brackets.

1 Sam ......*hadn't received*........ (not/receive) the parcel the last time I
   .... (speak) to him.

2 I .... (consider) buying a house but now I
   .... (change) my mind.

3 When you .... (feel) hungry, room service
   .... (bring) you whatever you want.

4 I .... (find) it difficult to convince the ticket inspector that I
   .... (lose) my ticket, but he believed me in the end.

5 Ever since I .... (be) a young child, I
   .... (die) to meet you.

6 As soon as I .... (have) a look at the designs, I
   .... (send) them to you. You'll get them by Friday.

7 Whatever .... (happen), I .... (meet)
   you here in a week's time.

8 By the time you .... (finish) getting ready, we
   .... (miss) the train!

9 Sally! I .... (not/expect) to see you here! What
   .... (you/do) in New York?

8 Decide whether each <u>underlined</u> phrase is correct or not. If it is correct, write a tick. If not, correct it.

1 <u>Will you be seeing</u> Rob Jones tomorrow? I wonder if you could give him a message
   from Sally Gordon? ....✓................

2 I had a great time in the Greek Islands. <u>We would rent</u> a small boat and <u>go</u> fishing
   every day. ....

3 Julie, hi! <u>I've been hoping</u> I'd see you. I've got some good news! ....

4 We had a terrible time looking after your dog. <u>It was constantly chasing</u> the cats
   next door. ....

5 We had a lovely time in Madrid. Every day <u>we were exploring</u> the city, and in the
   evening <u>we were going</u> to exciting bars. ....

6 The steam engine is usually thought of as a relatively modern invention, but the
   Greeks <u>had built</u> a kind of steam engine in ancient times. ....

7 I felt rather worried. <u>It was growing</u> darker and colder, and there was still no sign
   of the rescue helicopter. ....

8 Don't worry! All we have to do is wait here until someone <u>will find</u> us.
   ....

9 This meat <u>is really tasting</u> awful! Are you quite sure it was fresh?
   ....

5

Passive 1

Basic uses of the passive

- Agent and instrument
  The person who performs an action in a passive sentence is called the 'agent', introduced by *by*. The agent may or may not be mentioned.

  *My purse was found **by one of the cleaners**.*
  A new road has been built.

  An object which causes something to happen is called an instrument, introduced by *with*.

  *He was hit on the head **with a hammer**.*

- Verbs with two objects
  Verbs which have two objects can be made passive in two ways.

  ***I** was handed **a note**. **A note** was handed **to me**.*

  Other common verbs of this type are *bring, give, lend, pass, pay, promise, sell, send, show, tell*

- Verbs with object and complement
  Some verbs have a noun or adjective which describes their object.

  *We elected Jim **class representative**.*
  *Everyone considered him **a failure**.*

  When these are made passive, the complement goes directly after the verb.

  *Jim was elected **class representative**.*
  *He was considered **a failure**.*

- Verbs which cannot be passive
  Most verbs with an object (transitive verbs) can be made passive, e.g. *drive* is transitive because one can drive something (a car).

  However, a few transitive verbs may not be used in the passive. These include *become, fit* (be the right size), *get, have, lack, let, like, resemble, suit*.

  Verbs with no object (intransitive) cannot be passive, e.g. *sleep* is intransitive; you cannot 'sleep something'.

  Therefore it is not possible to say 'The baby was slept'. Instead the sentence must be active: *The baby slept*.

Using and not mentioning the agent

- Change of focus
  The passive can change the emphasis of a sentence.
  > *Jack **won** the prize.* (focus on Jack)
  > *The prize **was won** by Jack.* (focus on the prize)

- Unknown agent
  The agent is not mentioned if unknown.
  > *Two windows **have been broken**.*
  In this case, there is no point in adding an agent: 'by somebody'.

- Generalized agent
  If the subject is 'people in general' or 'you' the agent is not mentioned.
  > *Bicycles **are** widely **used** in the city instead of public transport.*

- Obvious agent
  If the agent is obvious or has already been referred to, it is not mentioned.
  > *Linda **has been arrested**!* (we assume by the police)
  > *The company agreed to our request and a new car park **was opened**.*

- Unimportant agent
  If the agent is not important to the meaning of the sentence it is not mentioned.
  > *I **was advised** to obtain a visa in advance.*

- Impersonality
  Using the passive is a way of avoiding the naming of a specific person who is responsible for an action.
  > *It **has been decided** to reduce all salaries by 10%.*
  In descriptions of processes, there is emphasis on the actions performed rather than on the people who perform them.
  > *Then the boxes **are packed** into crates.*

1 Correct any verb forms which are impossible or inappropriate.

1 A lot of homes in the area have been being broken into by burglars.
..........*have been broken into*.............

2 As I drove south, I could see that the old road was rebuilding.
....

3 I suppose the letter will have been delivered by now. ....

4 There is nothing more annoying than been interrupted when you are speaking. .....
....

5 Jim was been given the sack from his new job. ....

6 Somehow without my noticing my wallet had been disappeared.
....

7 The new shopping centre was opened by the local MP. ....

8 A lot of meetings have been held, but nothing has being decided yet.
....

2 Complete the second sentence so that it has a similar meaning to the first sentence.

1 The crowd was slowly filling the huge stadium.
The huge stadium ....*was slowly being filled*......... by the crowd.

2 The inventor of the computer simplified the work of accountants.
Since the computer .... the work of accountants
.... simplified.

3 Someone has suggested that the shop should close.
It .... that the shop should close.

4 'I'd take out some travel insurance if I were you, Mr Smith.'
Mr Smith .... take out some travel insurance.

5 The waitress will bring your drinks in a moment.
Your drinks .... in a moment.

6 Someone used a knife to open the window.
This window .... a knife.

7 You will hear from us when we have finished dealing with your complaint.
After your complaint .... you will hear from us.

8 An announcement of their engagement appeared in the local paper.
Their engagement .... in the local paper.

9 Nobody ever heard anything of David again.
Nothing .... David again.

10 They paid Sheila £1,000 as a special bonus.
£1,000 .... Sheila as a special bonus.

3 Rewrite each sentence in the passive, omitting the words <u>underlined</u>.

1 <u>Someone</u> left the phone off the hook all night.
The phone was left off the hook all night.

2 <u>The government</u> has announced that petrol prices will rise tomorrow.

3 <u>A burglar</u> broke into our house last week.

4 <u>People</u> asked me the way three times.

5 <u>The fruit-pickers</u> pick the apples early in the morning.

6 It's time <u>the authorities</u> did something about this problem.

7 Lots of <u>people</u> had parked their cars on the pavement.

8 The government agreed with the report and so <u>they</u> changed the law.

9 <u>You</u> have to fill in an application form.

10 <u>They</u> don't know what happened to the ship.

11 <u>Nobody</u> has seen the group's leader since his arrest last month.

4 Complete each sentence with a passive form of the verb in brackets.

1 The boxes (not/pack) *have not been packed* yet.
2 Your food (still/prepare) ....
3 The new ship (launch) .... next week.
4 Luckily by the time we got there the painting (not/sell) ....
5 We had to go on holiday because our house (decorate) ....
6 I'm afraid that next week's meeting (cancel) ....
7 If we don't hurry, all the tickets (sell) .... by the time we get there.
8 All main courses (serve) .... with vegetables or salad. At least that is what is written on the menu.
9 The second goal (score) .... by Hughes in the 41st minute.
10 The cathedral (build) .... in the fourteenth century.
11 There's a lot of noise outside because the road (repair) ....
12 I was promised that the parcel (deliver) .... by 10.00, but it still hasn't arrived.

5 Rewrite each sentence in a more formal style so that it contains a passive form of the word given in CAPITALS.

1 Sorry, but we've lost your letter.   MISLAY
            Unfortunately your letter has been mislaid.

2 The police are grilling Harry down at the station.   QUESTION

3 They've found the remains of an old Roman villa nearby.   DISCOVER

4 You'll get a rise in salary after six months.   RAISE

5 They stopped playing the match after half an hour.   ABANDON

6 They stopped traffic from using the centre.   BAN

7 They took Chris to court for dangerous driving.   PROSECUTE

8 You usually eat this kind of fish with a white sauce.   SERVE

9 I don't know your name.   INTRODUCE

6 Complete each sentence with a passive form of the verb in brackets.

1 Nothing (see) ....*has been seen*........ of Pauline since her car (find) .... abandoned near Newbury last week.

2 As our new furniture (deliver) .... on Monday morning I'll have to stay at home to check that it (not/damage) .... during transit.

3 The new Alhambra hatchback, which in this country (sell) .... under the name 'Challenger', (fit) .... with electric windows as standard.

4 For the past few days I (work) .... in Jack's office, as my own office (redecorate) ....

5 It (announce) .... that the proposed new office block (now/ not/build) .... because of the current economic situation.

6 A major new deposit of oil (discover) .... in the Arctic. It (think) .... to be nearly twice the size of the largest existing field.

7 Pictures of the surface of the planet Mars (receive) .... yesterday from the space probe 'Rover 3' which (launch) last year ....

8 A large sum .... (raise) for the Fund by a recent charity concert but the target of £250,000 (still/ not/reach) ....

9 No decision (make) .... about any future appointment until all suitable candidates (interview) ....

37

7 <u>Underline</u> any uses of the agent which are unnecessary.

1   My jewellery has been stolen <u>by a thief</u>!
2   It has been decided by the authorities that Wednesday will be a school holiday.
3   Harry was pushed over by someone standing next to him in the queue.
4   The goods are transported by rail to our warehouse in the Midlands.
5   I was told by someone that you have a vacancy for a computer operator.
6   Sue has been picked by the selectors for the national event.
7   The letter was sent by post on the 21st of last month.
8   The larger portrait was painted by a little-known Flemish artist.
9   It has been agreed by everyone that no smoking should be allowed.
10   As I arrived at the conference a note was handed to me by one of the delegates.

8 Complete the text with a suitable active or passive form of the verbs in brackets.

Dear Mrs Patel,

We are delighted to inform you that you (1) ....*have been selected*........... (select) for a free holiday.

According to our information, you (2) .... (answer) a telephone survey last

month, as a result of which your name

(3) .... (enter) in the holiday draw. Now our computer

(4) .... (choose) your name, so you and your family

(5) .... (invite) to spend a week in a European destination of your choice.

This offer (6) .... (make) on the condition that you attend a special

promotions day with other lucky families in your region who (7) .... (offer)

a similar deal. You (8) .... (ask) to attend on any Saturday next month

at the Royal Hotel, Manchester. If you (9) .... (interest) in attending and

taking up this offer, please (10) .... (detach) the slip below and return it

to us as soon as possible.

9 Complete the texts by writing a passive form of a verb in the box in each space.

~~announce~~	assume	call	destroy	discover
display	print	offer	take	write

Text A

It (1) ....*has been announced*........... that fossil remains of one of the largest ever sea

creatures (2) .... on an island in the North Sea. The 150 million year

old fossil, a type of pliosaur, (3) .... 'Big Boy' by scientists, as it is

over 15 metres long. The remains (4) .... to the Natural History

Museum in Oslo, where, after conservation work, they (5) .... in a

special section of the museum.

Text B

A bookseller has found a previously unknown poem by the English poet Shelley
nearly 200 years after it (6) .... The anti-war poem (7) ....
in a pamphlet first published in 1811 in Oxford when the poet was 20. It
(8) .... until the recent discovery that all copies of the poem
(9) ...., and experts are predicting great interest when the poem
(10) .... for sale in a book auction at the end of next month.

10 Rewrite each line with a passive verb form.

⟨◀⟩ ⟨▶⟩ ⟨⟲⟩ ⟨✕⟩ ⟨●————————————————⟩ ⟨⟨ ————⟩

FROM: The Managing Director   TO: All staff

1 We have decided to adopt a flexitime system for a trial period of three months.
   It has been decided to adopt a flexitime system for a trial period of three months.

2 The details are here below, and we'll send out a formal document in due course.
   ....

3 We'll consult all members of staff through their line manager,
   ....

4 and we'll seek feedback.
   ....

5 We'll collect and analyse comments
   ....

6 before we make a decision
   ....

7 as to whether we'll adopt the system permanently or not.
   ....

8 It's also possible that we may extend the trial period for a further month.
   ....

9 The new system will require all employees to arrive between the hours of 8.00 and
   10.00, and to leave after they have fulfilled their contractual obligations of eight hours.
   ....

10 We hope that this arrangement meets with your approval.
   ....

➜ **SEE ALSO**
Grammar 6: Passive 2
Consolidation 2: Units 5–8

Passive 2

Have and *get* something *done, need doing*

- *Have/get* something *done*
  This typically describes a service performed for us by someone else.
  > I've just **had/got** my car **serviced**. I **have/get** it **done** every winter.
  It can also describe something unfortunate that happens to someone.
  > We **had/got** our car **broken into** last month.
  Get is more likely to be used than have when:
  i) there is a feeling that something must be done.
  > I really must **get/have** my hair **cut**.
  ii) there is a feeling of eventually managing to do something.
  > I eventually **got/had** the car **fixed** at the Fast Service garage.
  iii) in orders and imperatives.
  > **Get** your hair **cut!**
  Note that *get* should not be used in the present perfect passive, where it would be confused with *have got*.
  > I've just **had** my hair **cut**. (possible)
  > I've just **got** my hair **cut**. (not possible)

- The need to have a service done can be described with *need doing*.
  > Your hair **needs cutting.**

Passive *get*

> *Get* can be used instead of *be* to form the passive in spoken language.
> > Martin **got arrested** at a football match.

Reporting verbs

- Present reference
  With verbs such as *believe, know, say, think*, which report people's opinions, a passive construction is often used to avoid a weak subject, and to give a generalized opinion. With present reference, the passive is followed by the present infinitive.
  > The criminal **is thought to be** in hiding in the London area.
  > Vitamin C **is known to be** good for treating colds.

- Past reference
  With past reference, the passive is followed by the past infinitive.
  > Smith **is believed to have left** England last week.

- Past reporting verb

  If the reporting verb is in the past, the past infinitive tends to follow, though not always if the verb *be* is used.

  > *People thought Sue had paid too much.*
  > *Sue **was thought to have paid** too much.*
  > *The police thought that the thief was still in the house.*
  > *The thief **was thought to** still **be** in the house.*

- Past reference with two objects

  In this case there are two ways of making a passive sentence.

  > *Everyone knows the portrait **was painted by** an Italian.*
  > *The portrait **is known to have been painted** by an Italian.*

- Continuous infinitive

  Past and present continuous infinitives are also used.

  > *Mary is thought **to be living** in Scotland.*
  > *The driver is thought **to have been doing** a U-turn.*

Verbs with prepositions

- Ending a sentence with a preposition

  It is possible to end a sentence with a preposition in a sentence where a prepositional verb is made passive.

  > *Somebody broke into our house.*
  > *Our house was broken **into**.*

- *By* and *with*

  With is used after participles such as *filled, packed, crowded, crammed.*

  > *The train **was packed with** commuters.*

  The difference between *by* and *with* may involve the presence of a person:

  > *Dave was hit **by** a branch.* (an accident)
  > *Dave was hit **with** a branch.* (a person hit him with one)

- *Make* is followed by *to* when used in the passive.

  > *My boss made me work hard.*
  > *I **was made to** work hard by my boss.*

- *Cover* and verbs which involve similar ideas, such as *surround, decorate,* can use *with* or *by. Cover* can also be followed by *in.*

  > *The furniture **was covered in** dust.*
  > *The living room **had been decorated with** flowery wallpaper.*

- Common contexts for the passive

  The passive is common in technical and scientific writing, and generally in spoken and written contexts where there is less use of personal reference, since the audience may be unknown, or the speaker wants to remain impersonal.

1 **Decide whether the sentences in each pair have the same meaning. Rewrite those which are different.**

1   I've just been to the hairdresser's. What do you think?

I've just cut my hair at the hairdresser's. What do you think?

............................*I've just had my hair cut.*............................

2   Someone is painting our house at the moment.

We are painting our house at the moment.

....

3   The dentist is going to take out two of my teeth tomorrow.

I'm having two teeth taken out tomorrow.

....

4   The teacher made us all tidy up.

We were made to tidy up by the teacher.

....

5   The car is thought to have been stolen by joy-riders.

Joy-riders are thought to have stolen the car.

....

6   Just a minute. I'll ask someone to wrap this for you.

Just a minute. I'll have to wrap this up for you.

....

7   The car hasn't been serviced for a long time.

We haven't had the car serviced for a long time.

....

8   They're coming to put in a new water-heater next week.

We're putting in a new water-heater next week.

....

9   Would you consider having plastic surgery to alter your nose?

Would you consider having your nose altered by plastic surgery?

....

2 <u>Underline</u> **the correct word in each sentence.**

1   The busy shopping street was thronged *by/<u>with</u>* people.
2   The emergency exit was concealed *by/from* a red curtain.
3   The price of excursions is included *in/with* the cost of the holiday.
4   All through January, the fields were covered *by/from* snow.
5   The room was crammed *by/with* furniture of all descriptions.
6   Two of the climbers were injured *by/with* falling rocks.
7   The island is inhabited *by/from* people of mainly Chinese origin.
8   The bank was quickly surrounded *from/with* armed police.
9   The window had been smashed *from/with* a hammer taken from the shed.
10   The stadium was packed *from/with* cheering fans.

3 Complete the second sentence so that it has a similar meaning to the first sentence, using the word given. Do not change the word given.

1 We think the treasure dates from the thirteenth century.

think

It .... *is thought to date* .... from the thirteenth century.

2 Your hair needs cutting.

get

You .... cut.

3 Jill's parents are making her study hard.

made

Jill .... her parents.

4 Apparently the ship did not sustain any damage.

appears

The ship .... any damage.

5 It is thought that the two injured men were repairing overhead cables.

have

The two injured men .... overhead cables.

6 There is a rumour that the escaped prisoner is living in Spain.

be

The escaped prisoner .... living in Spain.

7 We have agreed to meet again in a fortnight.

will

It has .... meet again in a fortnight.

8 We decided to try again later.

would

It was .... try again later.

9 There is confirmation of Mr Jackson's intended resignation.

that

It is .... to resign.

10 Most of the committee thought it was not a viable solution.

not

It was thought .... by most of the committee.

ADVANCED LANGUAGE PRACTICE

4 Rewrite each sentence so that it ends with the word <u>underlined</u>.

1 Another company has taken <u>over</u> our company.
   .... *Our company has been taken over.* ....

2 We are dealing <u>with</u> your complaint.
   ....

3 We have not accounted <u>for</u> all the missing passengers.
   ....

4 Someone had tampered <u>with</u> the lock of the front door.
   ....

5 We don't know how they disposed <u>of</u> the body.
   ....

6 I must insist that you keep <u>to</u> the rules.
   ....

7 We are looking <u>into</u> this allegation.
   ....

8 We will frown <u>upon</u> any attempts to cheat in the exam.
   ....

9 The youngest student complained that people were picking <u>on</u> him.
   ....

10 You haven't paid <u>for</u> the second pizza.
   ....

11 I think they have made <u>up</u> the whole story.
   ....

5 Complete each sentence with a suitable preposition.

1 The tree had been decorated ....*with*........ coloured balls.
2 The answers have been included .... the book.
3 After the rugby match, Jim's shorts were covered .... mud.
4 The victim was struck from behind .... a heavy object.
5 The house was built .... money that David borrowed from the bank.
6 The cat narrowly escaped being run over .... a car.
7 When the accident happened, Sue was struck .... flying glass.
8 The turkey was stuffed .... chestnuts, and was very tasty.
9 No one knew that Peter had been involved .... the investigation.
10 When I left the casino, my pockets were crammed .... money.
11 All the presents were wrapped .... yellow paper.
12 It turned out that the bridge had been damaged .... a lorry.

6 Complete the text by writing a verb from the box in each space.

was seen	were made to	was brought	was obliged to
are believed to have been	~~is known to have experienced~~		is not known
are thought to be	was packed	is thought to have been	

A plane carrying 15 members of the government to a conference in Brussels
(1) ....*is known to have experienced*...... a small-scale fire earlier this morning.
The plane (2) .... about 20 minutes into its
journey when the fire occurred in the luggage area. It (3) ....
how the plane caught fire, but initial eye-witness accounts confirm that a trail
of smoke (4) .... coming from the undercarriage. The fire (5) .... rapidly under control,
but the pilot (6) .... make an emergency
landing. Five people (7) .... treated for shock.
The plane (8) .... with business people flying to
Belgium. All 209 passengers (9) .... stay behind
for questioning after landing at a military airport in northern France. Police
(10) .... treating the incident as suspicious.

7 Rewrite the text using the passive where possible. Make sure the words
underlined do not appear.

Nobody knows exactly when someone invented gunpowder. People know for a fact
that the Chinese made rockets and fireworks long before people used gunpowder in
Europe, which occurred at about the beginning of the thirteenth century. We generally
believe that gunpowder brought to an end the 'Age of Chivalry', since anyone with a
firearm could bring down a mounted knight. In fact, people did not develop efficient
firearms until the sixteenth century. They used gunpowder mainly in siege cannon
when people first introduced it. Later they used it in engineering work and in mining,
but they found that it was extremely dangerous. Modern explosives have now replaced
gunpowder, but we still use it for making fireworks, just as the Chinese did.

.................................*It is not known exactly*...

....

....

....

....

....

....

7

GRAMMAR

Conditionals

Basic usage

- What is always true: present + present
    *If I **work** late, I **get** tired.*
    *If the water **is boiling/has boiled**, it **means** the food is nearly ready.*

- What was always true: past + past
    *We **went** home early if it **was** foggy.*
    *If it **was snowing**, we **stayed** at home.*

- Real situations: present + future
    Here we think that the outcome is really possible.
    *If you **keep** driving like that, you**'re going to have** an accident.*
    *If you see Mark, tell him I**'ll ring** him tomorrow.*

- Hypothetical situations: past + *would*
    These are unreal or imaginary situations.
    *If I **knew** the answer, I**'d tell** you.*
    *If I **was having** a party, I **wouldn't invite** Marcia.*
    The verb *be* usually takes the form *were* for all persons in these sentences, though *was* is used in everyday speech. Note that in the first person it is possible to use *should* instead of *would*.
    *If I **left** home, I think I **should** be lonely.*

- Hypothetical past situations: past perfect + *would have*
    These refer to past events.
    *If I **had known** you were coming, I **would have met** you at the station.*

- With modals
    Possible situations in the present
    *If you get wet, you **should** change your clothes immediately.*
    *If you come early, we **can** discuss the problem together.*
    Hypothetical situations
    *If I had the money, I **could** help you.*
    Hypothetical past situations
    *If you hadn't reminded me, I **might have** forgotten.*

Variations

- *If only*
    This adds emphasis to hypothetical situations. With past events it adds a sense of regret. The second part of the sentence is often left out.
    ***If only** I had enough time!*
    ***If only** I hadn't drunk too much, this wouldn't have happened!*

- *Unless* and other alternatives to *if*
  Unless means *only if not*.
  > *I'll go ahead and get the tickets **unless** you call me this afternoon.*
  (This means: If you call me this afternoon, I won't get the tickets.)
  If one situation depends on another, *if* can be replaced by *as/so long as*, *provided* or *only if*. See Grammar 11 for *only if*.
  > *I'll do what you say **provided** the police are not informed.*
  Even if describes how something will happen whatever the condition.
  > ***Even if** it rains, we'll still go for a picnic.*

- Past events with results in the present: past perfect + *would*
  > *If Jim **hadn't missed** the plane, he would be here by now.*

- *Should*
  After *if*, this makes the possibility of an event seem unlikely.
  > ***If** you **should see** Ann, could you ask her to call me?*
  (This implies that I do not expect you to see Ann.)

- *Were to*
  This also makes an event seem more hypothetical.
  > *If I **were to ask** you to marry me, what would you say?*

- *Happen to*
  This emphasizes chance possibilities. It is often used with *should*.
  > *If you **happen to see** Helen, could you ask her to call me?*
  > *If you **should happen to be passing**, drop in for a cup of tea.*

- *If it were not for/if it hadn't been for*
  This describes how one event depends on another.
  > *If it **weren't for** Jim, this company would be in a mess.*
  > *If it **hadn't been for** their goalkeeper, United would have lost.*

- *Will* and *would*: politeness and emphasis
  These can be used as polite forms.
  > *If you **will/would wait** here, I'll see if Mrs Green is free.*
  Will can also be used for emphasis, meaning 'insist on doing'.
  > *If you **will stay out late**, no wonder you are tired!* (insist on staying out)

Other ways of making a conditional sentence

- *Supposing, otherwise*
  Supposing or *suppose* can replace *if*, mainly in everyday speech.
  > ***Supposing** you won the lottery, what would you do?*
  Otherwise means 'or if not'. It can go at the beginning or end of the sentence.
  > *If you hadn't given us directions, we wouldn't have found the house.*
  > *Thanks for your directions to the house. We wouldn't have found it **otherwise**.*

- *But for*

  This can replace *if not*. It is used in formal language, and must be followed by a noun form.

  > *If you hadn't helped us, we would have been in trouble.*
  > ***But for your help***, *we would have been in trouble.*

- *If so, if not*

  These can refer to a sentence in a previous sentence.

  > *There is a possibility that Jack will be late.* ***If so***, *I will take his place.*

- Colloquial omission of *if*

  An imperative can be used instead of an if clause in everyday speech.

  > ***Sit down***, *and I'll make us a cup of tea. (If you sit down ...)*

- *If* and adjectives

  In expressions such as *if it is necessary/possible* it is possible to omit the verb be.

  > ***If interested***, *apply within.*
  > ***If necessary***, *take a taxi.*

- Formally *if* can mean 'although', usually as *if* + adjective.

  > *The room was well-furnished, **if** a little **badly decorated**.*

1 Complete each sentence with a suitable form of the verb in brackets.

1 Now we're lost! If you (write down) ....*had written down*............ Mary's directions, this (not/happen) ....

2 Why don't we emigrate? If we (live) .... in Australia, at least the weather (be) .... better!

3 I'm afraid that Smith is a hardened criminal. If we (not/punish) .... him this time, he (only/commit) .... more crimes.

4 Thanks to Dr Jones, I'm still alive! If it (not/be) .... for her, I (be) .... dead for certain.

5 I'm sorry I can't lend you any money. You know that if I (have) .... it, I (lend) .... it to you.

6 Don't be afraid. If you (touch) .... the dog, it (not/bite) ....

7 In those days, if you (have) .... a job, you (be) .... lucky.

8 It's always the same! If I (decide) .... to leave the office early, my boss (call) .... me after I've left!

9 What a terrible thing to happen! Just think, if we (not/miss) .... the plane, we (kill) .... in the crash.

10 Did you enjoy your meal? If you (finish) .... eating, I (clear away) .... the plates.

2 Correct any verb forms which are impossible or inappropriate.

1 If you haven't received a letter yet, you haven't got the job. ..*possible*..

2 If it isn't for David, we are missing the bus. ....

3 If it's raining, we go to the pub on the corner instead. ....

4 If you didn't lend us the money, we would have gone to the bank. ....

5 If you should happen to change your mind, drop me a line. ....

6 If it wasn't for the rain, we would have been home by now. ....

7 If you will drive so fast, no wonder the police keep stopping you. ....

8 If I knew you were coming, I would have met you at the airport. ....

9 But for you helped us, we would have taken much longer. ....

10 If Jack joins the team, I'm leaving. ....

ADVANCED LANGUAGE PRACTICE

3 Read each sentence and decide which ending (A, B or C) best fits each space.

1 If you'd told me you were coming
   A I can get some food in.
   B I'd have found us something to eat. ✓
   C I made a lovely dish.

2 If you're too ill to come
   A I'll come over and see you.
   B I wouldn't have done all this for you.
   C I asked someone else.

3 If I'd known you weren't coming
   A I wouldn't be very upset.
   B I would like to know why.
   C I wouldn't have gone to so much trouble.

4 If you're not coming
   A perhaps you'd have the courtesy to tell me.
   B we'd never have met.
   C you'd be so lucky.

5 If only you'd come
   A I'll be the happiest girl alive.
   B I'd have had a lovely time.
   C I would look forward to it.

6 If you do decide to come
   A the party's always a success.
   B I won't be coming either.
   C let me know.

7 If you really don't want to come
   A I'll understand.
   B I can't be sure.
   C tell me tomorrow.

4 Complete each sentence with a phrase containing a suitable form of the verb in brackets.

1 If I were (say) ....to say!........ loved you, what would you do?
2 If it (rain) .... I would have gone out for a walk.
3 If only you'd told me it was a surprise party, I (say) .... anything to Uncle Dave!
4 Thanks for your help with the garden; I (do) .... it without you.
5 If only Mick had come to the disco, then we (have) .... a great time!
6 (pay) .... the phone bill today, the phone will be cut off.
7 If I (had) .... your tools, I wouldn't have been able to fix the car.
8 Those wires look a bit dangerous; (touch) .... if I were you.
9 If (be) .... the goalkeeper's heroics, we would have lost the match.

5 **Rewrite each sentence three times so that it contains the word in CAPITALS.**

1 We won't go away if the weather is bad.

......*We'll go away unless the weather's bad.*............ UNLESS

.... ONLY

.... STAY

2 If you hurry up you won't be late.

.... DON'T

.... OR

.... WANT

3 If they offered you the job, would you accept?

.... WERE TO

.... SHOULD

.... HAPPENED

4 Without your help, I would have given up years ago.

.... HADN'T BEEN

.... BUT

.... HADN'T HELPED

5 I'll lend you the money on condition that you pay it back next week.

.... PROVIDED

.... LONG

.... ONLY

6 **Complete the text by writing one word in each space.**

Mr Jeffries, I have decided against a prison sentence in your case. You may walk free from this court on (1) ......*condition*...... that you report to Chesham police station every Friday for the next six months. Should you fail to (2) .... so, you will be given one warning; and if you persist (3) .... failing to meet this obligation, you will return to this court for a harsher sentence. (4) .... you can present good reason why you were unable to report to the station, you will (5) .... yourself in severe trouble. If you are (6) .... to attend because of illness, please note that a medical certificate must be produced, signed by your doctor, proving your state of health. You should realize that (7) .... for your previous good conduct, I would (8) .... had no hesitation in imposing a prison sentence. And I shall not forget that if your friend had (9) .... intervened in the fight, you might (10) .... seriously injured the defendant.

7 Complete the second sentence so that it has a similar meaning to the first sentence, using the word given. Do not change the word given.

1 I didn't have the money so I didn't buy a new suit.

   would

   If I .... *had had the money I would have bought* .... a new suit.

2 If you are in London by any chance, come and see me.

   happen

   If you .... , come and see me.

3 If you insist on doing everything yourself, of course you'll feel tired!

   will

   If you .... , of course you'll feel tired!

4 Please take a seat, and I'll inquire for you.

   will

   If you .... , I'll inquire for you.

5 If you do the shopping, I'll cook lunch.

   and

   You .... I'll cook lunch.

6 If Pauline hadn't been interested, the project would have been abandoned.

   interest

   But .... the project would have been abandoned.

7 The fire was brought under control thanks to the night-watchman.

   for

   If it hadn't .... got out of control.

8 Dick is in prison because a detective recognized him.

   if

   Dick wouldn't .... recognized him.

9 I am not tall enough to reach the shelf.

   taller

   If I .... reach the shelf.

10 But for Helen acting so wonderfully, the play would be a flop.

   wonderful

   If it .... the play would be a flop.

11 It won't make any difference if City score first; United will still win.

   even

   United .... City score first.

12 Getting up early makes me feel hungry.

   get

   If .... makes me feel hungry.

8 Complete each sentence using the cues in brackets.

1 That was a lucky escape! If I (fall/break leg) ....*had fallen*.... , I'd have broken my leg.
2 If you (finish/with my pen) .... , I'd like it back please.
3 Unless Pete (try/harder) .... , he won't win the competition.
4 f you took more time over your work, you (not make) .... so many mistakes.
5 But for Sally's bravery, Jim (drown) ....
6 If you'd told me you were coming, I (buy) .... more food.
7 If (it/not be) .... for Mary, the deal wouldn't have gone through.
8 If (I/be) .... late, you'd better start without me.
9 If Ann had known Tom wasn't coming, she (not/go) .... to so much trouble.
10 (finish/the painting) .... by Friday, and we'll pay you extra.

9 Complete the text by writing one word in each space.

Dear Sir or Madam,
We would like to remind you that your account is two months overdue. We are prepared to allow you another ten days to settle your account. However, (1) ....*if*.... you fail to pay your outstanding bills within ten days you leave us with no alternative but to take legal action. That is, (2) .... we receive full payment by 20th March, we will refer this matter to our legal department. If (3) ...., we are prepared to make a claim in the Small Claims court for the money owed plus interest.
(4) .... you be experiencing financial difficulties, please contact our Finance Department. (5) .... that you settle your account within the specified time period, we will (6) .... happy to continue to do business with you. However, we (7) ...., if necessary, take the regrettable step of closing your account.
We are sorry that this situation has arisen, but if you had paid your bills over the last two months, we (8) .... not be in this position now. On the other hand, you (9) .... have settled your account in the last two days. If (10) ...., please accept our apologies for this letter.
Yours faithfully

Brian Eccles
Customer Services
Wood View Office Supplies

→ **SEE ALSO**
Grammar 8: Unreal time
Consolidation 2: Units 5–8
Grammar 11: Inversion

8

GRAMMAR

Unreal time and subjunctives

It's time

- *It's time, it's high time*

  These are followed by past simple or continuous, though the time referred to is unreal. See Grammar 7.

  > *It's time we **left**. It's high time something **was done** about this!*

Wishes

- Present/future time

  Notice the past verb forms after *wish*.

  These are wishes where you want to change a present/future state.

  > *I wish I **had** a motorbike.* (I don't have one now.)

  > *I wish you **weren't** leaving.* (You are leaving.)

  > *I wish I **was going** on holiday with you next week.* (I am not going.)

- *Would*

  Would is used when the speaker wants somebody or something else to change.

  > *I wish he **would** change his mind and marry Jane.*

  > *I wish it **would** stop raining.*

  The use with *would* is often used to describe an annoying habit.

  > *I wish you **wouldn't make such a mess**.*

- Past time

  As with present wishes, the verb form after *wish* is one stage further back in the past.

  These are wishes referring to a past event, which cannot be changed.

  > *I wish I **hadn't eaten so much**.*

  This use of *wish* is common after *if only* to express regrets. See Grammar 7.

- *Hope*

  Wishes about simple future events are expressed with *hope*.

  > *I **hope** it doesn't rain **tomorrow**.*

  > *I **hope** you('ll) have a lovely time in Portugal (on your holiday **next week**).*

I'd rather/I prefer (followed by a clause)

- *I'd rather* is followed by past verb forms in the same way as wishes about the present. It expresses preference about actions.

  > *I'd rather you **didn't smoke** in here.*

  Both *I'd rather* and *I'd sooner* are used with infinitive without *to* when comparing nouns or phrases.

  > *I'd rather **be** a sailor than a soldier.* (present)

  > *I'd rather **have lived** in Ancient Greece than Ancient Rome.* (past)

- *I'd prefer* is used with *it + past verb form* to express preference about actions.

  *I'd prefer it if you **didn't** smoke.*

  I'd prefer is also used with *you/him/her* etc + infinitive without *to* to show what we would like a person to do. We can add *rather than* + infinitive without *to* as a comparison.

  *I'd prefer **you to sit** in your seat (**rather than sit** on the floor).*

  I'd prefer can also be used to show which thing we would like to have.

  *I'd prefer **tea to coffee.***

As if, as though

- Real and unreal

  The verb form here depends on whether the situation is true or unreal.

  *You look **as if you're having** second thoughts.* (True. You are having second thoughts.)

  *He acts **as if** he **were** in charge.* (Unreal. He isn't in charge.)

  *I feel **as if** an express train **had hit** me.* (It didn't hit me.)

  Note however, that the more colloquial *like* does not require this verb form change. This is not considered acceptable in formal and/or written English Compare:

  *You look **like you've** just **seen** a ghost*

  *You look **as if you'd** just **seen** a ghost.*

Suppose and *imagine*

- Understood conditions

  The conditional part of these sentences is often understood but not stated.

  *Suppose someone **told** you that I was a spy!*

  *Imagine we'**d never** met!* (We have met.)

  If the event referred to is a real possibility, a present verb form is possible.

  *Suppose it **starts** raining, what'll we do?*

Formal subjunctives

- Insisting, demanding, etc

  After verbs such as *demand, insist, suggest, require* which imply obligation, the subjunctive may be used in formal style. This uses the infinitive; there is no third person *-s* or past form.

  *They demanded that he **leave** at once.*

  *The school Principal suggested that he **be** awarded a scholarship.*

- Less formal usage

  Less formally, *should* can be used, and colloquially no verb form change is made, or an infinitive construction is used.

  *They demanded that he **should leave.***

  They demanded that he left. (informal)

Formulaic subjunctives

These are fixed expressions all using subjunctive. Typical expressions are:

Heaven help us!   *Be that as it may …*   *Come what may …*

1 <u>Underline</u> the correct word in each sentence.

1 I <u>*hope*</u>/*wish* I'll see you again soon.
2 I *hope*/*wish* the weather improves soon.
3 I *hope*/*wish* I knew the answer.
4 I *hope*/*wish* you didn't have to go.
5 I *hope*/*wish* you'd stop shouting so much.
6 I *hope*/*wish* nothing goes wrong.
7 I *hope*/*wish* it would stop raining.
8 I *hope*/*wish* you can come to my party.
9 I *hope*/*wish* you don't mind.
10 I *hope*/*wish* we could meet next week.

2 Complete each sentence with a suitable word or phrase.

1 I wish you ......*would stop*...... making so much noise late at night!
2 I'd rather the children .... on the television without permission.
3 Suppose .... half the money I owe you. Would that satisfy you?
4 I hope .... get into trouble on my account. What do you think they'll say?
5 This is an awful hotel. I wish we .... to the Grand instead.
6 It is absolutely .... you contact head office in advance.
7 I think it's high time we .... locking all the windows at night.
8 Would you rather I .... lunch, if you feel tired?
9 I wish my car .... as fast as yours.
10 I'd prefer you .... smoke in here, if you don't mind.

3 **Complete each sentence with a suitable form of the verb in brackets.**

1 I'd rather you (not/watch) ....*didn't watch*.... television while I'm reading.

2 It's high time you (start) .... working seriously.

3 I wish I (spend) .... more time swimming last summer.

4 Helen is bossy. She acts as if she (own) .... the place.

5 I wish you (not/keep) .... coming late to class.

6 Suppose a complete stranger (leave) .... you a lot of money in their will!

7 I wish I (go) .... to your party after all.

8 I'd rather you (sit) .... next to Susan, please.

9 The government demanded that the ambassador (be) .... recalled.

10 You are lucky going to Italy. I wish I (go) .... with you.

4 **Complete each sentence with one word.**

1 It's .....*high*...... time you learned to look after yourself!

2 I wish you .... try listening to me, just for once!

3 I .... rather not go by train, if possible.

4 .... that as it may, it doesn't alter the seriousness of the situation.

5 I wish Carol .... be here to see you all.

6 We both wish you .... staying longer.

7 You .... as if you had played in the match instead of watching it!

8 .... they offered you the job of managing director!

9 I really wish we .... married.

10 I .... you didn't mind my phoning so late.

5 **Correct the error(s) in each sentence.**

1 I wish I bought that old house. ....*I wish I had bought* ....

2 I'd rather you don't eat all the bread. ....

3 It's time I go. ....

4 I wish I own a motorbike. ....

5 I wish we are not leaving in the morning. ....

6 Sue would rather reading than watching television. ....

7 Come what comes, I'll be on your side. ....

8 I hope it would stop raining. ....

9 I'd prefer if you didn't wait. ....

10 I wish I didn't listen to you before. ....

6 Complete the second sentence so that it has a similar meaning to the first sentence, using the word given. Do not change the word given.

1 Do you ever regret not going to university?

wish

Do you ever .... *wish you had gone* .... to university?

2 I should really be going home now.

time

It's .... home now.

3 I'd rather not go by plane.

prefer

I'd .... go by plane.

4 Jack doesn't know all the answers, though he pretends to.

acts

Jack .... all the answers.

5 I'd love to be able to go with you to the opera.

wish

I .... go with you to the opera.

6 I wish I hadn't sold that old painting.

pity

It's .... that old painting.

7 I'd rather you didn't stay long at the party.

better

It .... stay long at the party.

8 The management said it was important for us to wear dark suits to the meeting.

insisted

The management .... dark suits to the meeting.

9 I've had enough of your constant complaining!

wish

I .... complaining all the time!

10 I'd love to be sitting on a beach in Turkey right now!

wish

I .... on a beach in Turkey right now!

7 Complete the second sentence so that the meaning is similar to the first sentence.

1 I wish you were a bit tidier.

I wish you would .... *put your things away.* ....

2 I wish you were more interested in your school work.

I wish you would ....

3 I wish I spoke more languages.

I wish I could ....

4 I wish I had enough money to buy a car.

I wish I could ....

5 I wish they had more chess books in the library.

I wish the library would ....

6 I wish there was some soap in the bathroom.

I wish the cleaners would ....

7 I just wish my partner was a bit more romantic!

I just wish my partner would ....

8 Complete the text by writing one word in each space. Contractions (*don't*) count as one word.

Dear Tom,

Well, this time next week you'll be somewhere in Europe. I'm sure any mum would worry! Actually, you're very lucky. I'd love to (1) .... *be* .... able to go off around the world.

I often wish I (2) .... travelled more when I was younger. I really hope you

(3) .... yourself, but you will be careful, won't you? You're only 18 after all. Do be careful

with your money too. And I'd rather you (4) .... spend too many nights in your tent alone.

It's so dangerous. I suggest you only (5) .... in your tent on a proper camp site. I wish you

(6) .... going quite so soon. It's a pity you (7) .... stay until after Dad's 50th

birthday. But never mind. I wish Dad had (8) .... here to see you off, but he had some

really important business that day. Suppose we (9) .... you at some nice seaside place in

June? Just a thought. Anyway, remember, if you get into any trouble, we're only a phone call away,

and come what (10) ...., we'll always be there for you.

Love, Mum

➜ **SEE ALSO**
Grammar 7: Unreal time
Consolidation 2: Units 5–8
Grammar 11: Inversion

Units 5–8

1 Complete the text with a suitable form of the verbs in brackets.

Employees protesting at the planned closure of the Magnet electronics factory have begun a protest outside the factory in Brook Road. It (1) ..was revealed.. (reveal) last week that production at the factory, where over 3,000 local people (2) .... (employ), (3) .... (transfer) to the existing Magnet plant in Luton next month. Only a few new jobs (4) .... (expect) to be created. 'Why (5) .... (we/not/inform) about this earlier? We (6) .... (only/tell) about this two days ago,' said Marjory Calder, representing the workforce. 'It's about time companies such as this (7) .... (start) thinking about how local communities (8) .... (affect) by their policies. Most of us here own our houses. How are we going to keep paying the mortgage and find a job? I wish I (9) .... (know).' Reg Reynolds, Director of Magnet was asked what was being done to help those who have (10) .... (make) redundant. 'Every effort (11) .... (make) over the past month to offer early retirement to those who qualify,' he told our reporter. When (12) .... (question) about why the workers (13) .... (not/tell) about the closure earlier, he revealed the company (14) .... (promise) a government loan to keep the factory open, but that at the last minute the government (15) .... (decide) not to provide the loan after all. 'So don't blame the company, we've done our best.'

2 Complete each sentence with a suitable word.

1 You are the person who ....gets........ things done around here!
2 The victim is thought to have been .... a bath at the time.
3 As I cycled along the lane I was hit .... an overhanging branch.
4 If the baby looked unhappy we .... her a toy to play with.
5 If .... you had asked me earlier, I could have helped you.
6 .... if I had got there in time, it wouldn't have made any difference.
7 I wouldn't be surprised if Patrick .... win.
8 .... for the bad weather, our holiday would have been perfect.
9 I .... rather you didn't stay any longer.
10 I wouldn't be surprised if Jack .... to call round this evening.

3 Complete the second sentence so that it has a similar meaning to the first sentence, using the word given. Do not change the word given.

1 It is thought that the escaped prisoner is back in custody.

been

The escaped prisoner is .... *thought to have been* .... recaptured.

2 The wind was bending the young tree to the ground.

bent

The young tree .... to the ground in the wind.

3 The police are interrogating Jim in connection with the break-in.

about

Jim is .... the break-in by the police.

4 I can't lift this table on my own.

won't

Unless I get .... to lift this table.

5 I won't stay in this job, not even for double the salary.

doubled

Even .... , I won't stay in this job.

6 It's a pity you aren't going to Ann's party.

wish

I .... to Ann's party.

7 If you found the missing money, what would you do?

were

What would you do if .... gone missing?

8 They suspended Jackson for the next two matches.

banned

Jackson .... in the next two matches.

9 Please come this way, and I'll see if Mr Francis is in.

will

If .... I'll see if Mr Francis is in.

10 New drugs are being discovered which are helping the fight against this disease.

discovery

The fight against this disease .... new drugs.

4 Rewrite each sentence in the passive, omitting the words <u>underlined</u>.

1 Mushroom-gatherers usually <u>work</u> in the early morning.
...... *Mushrooms are usually gathered early in the morning.* ......

2 It's time <u>the government</u> brought the economy under control.
......

3 <u>A thief</u> stole several coats from the cloakroom.
......

4 <u>The management</u> has decided to reduce the workforce by 10%.
......

5 The decorators only <u>took</u> a day to do our house.
......

6 <u>They</u> have no idea what caused the accident.
......

7 <u>You</u> have to make an application for a visa in advance.
......

8 Ticket collectors <u>work</u> on the train on this line.
......

9 Lots of <u>people</u> had left their luggage on the platform.
......

10 <u>A person</u> directed Sally to the wrong address.
......

5 Complete each sentence with a suitable word.

1 ...... *Be* ...... that as it may, it is still no excuse.
2 Graham ...... his car towed away by the police.
3 I am going to call the police ...... you leave at once.
4 I think it's high time you ...... taking yourself seriously.
5 If you ...... to think of moving, we could offer you a job.
6 I ...... you can come to my birthday party.
7 Just imagine! ...... they told you that you had won first prize!
8 I wish Harry ...... see the children now!
9 If only you ...... just stop talking for a moment and try listening!
10 It was not ...... necessary to call the fire brigade.

6 Complete each sentence with a suitable form of the verb in brackets.

1 I don't like this restaurant, I wish we had (go) ....had gone............ to the 'Taj Mahal'.

2 It's time something (do) .... about this problem.

3 The late Prime Minister is said (be) .... difficult to work with.

4 That was lucky! If I (catch) .... this bus, I (meet) .... you.

5 Your order (deal) .... with at the moment.

6 But for Pauline, I (not/pass) .... the exam.

7 All dishes (serve) .... with French fries and a green salad.

8 The house is thought to (sell) .... recently for a million pounds.

9 If only I (study) .... more when I was at school.

10 If I were (tell) .... you where the treasure is, what would you do?

7 Complete each sentence with a suitable form of the verb in brackets.

1 The second film we saw (direct) ....was directed.... by Tim Burton.

2 If I (know) .... that you .... (arrive) on that train, I (come) .... to meet you.

3 I wish you (not/eat) .... all the food! I'm hungry!

4 Be careful! If you (tease) .... the cat it (scratch) .... you!

5 Thanks very much! If you (not/help) .... me, we (not/finish) .... the work so quickly.

6 Hurry up, or all the best seats (take) ....

7 What a shame that it (decide) .... to cancel the school play!

8 Carol now wishes she (marry) .... in a church.

9 If it (not/be) .... for you, I (still/be) .... in prison today!

10 Unfortunately, tomorrow's match (call off) ....

8 Complete the second sentence so that it has a similar meaning to the first sentence, using the word given. Do not change the word given.

1 I'll get someone to press your trousers, sir.

pressed

I'll .... *have/get your trousers pressed* .... immediately, sir.

2 Everyone knows that taking exercise is good for your health.

known

Taking exercise .... good for your health.

3 Someone has suggested the resignation of the minister.

that

It .... the minister should resign.

4 They've asked me if I would chair the meeting.

to

I .... chair the meeting.

5 We have managed to account for all the missing papers.

successfully

All the missing papers .... for.

6 Since Sue left for Glasgow, nobody has seen anything of her.

of

Nothing has .... she left for Glasgow.

7 I'd rather you didn't sit at the back of the room please.

it

I'd prefer .... at the front of the room.

8 A traffic warden showed me how to get to the museum.

way

I was .... to the museum by a traffic warden.

9 John's school is making him sit his exams again.

made

John .... sit his exams again.

10 I should really be starting my homework.

time

It's .... starting my homework.

9

GRAMMAR

Modals: present and future

Don't have to and *must not*

- *Don't have to* refers to an absence of obligation.
    *You **don't have to** work tomorrow.*

- *Must not* refers to an obligation not to do something.
    *You **must not** leave the room before the end of the test.*

Should

Where **should* appears, *ought to* can also be used.

- Expectation
    *This film ****should** be really good.*

- Recommendation
    *I think you ****should** talk it over with your parents.*
    In writing, *should* can be used to express a strong obligation politely.
    *Guests **should** vacate their rooms by midday.*

- Criticism of an action
    *You ****shouldn't** eat so much late at night.*

- Uncertainty
    Should I leave these papers on your desk?

- *Should* and verbs of thinking
    Should is often used with verbs of thinking, to make an opinion less direct.
    *I **should think** that model would sell quite well.*

- With *be* and adjectives describing chance
    This group of adjectives includes *odd, strange, funny* (=odd) and the expression *What a coincidence.*
    *It's strange that you **should be staying** in the same hotel!*

- After *in case* to emphasize unlikelihood
    *In case I **should be out**, this is my mobile number.*
    See Grammar 7 for similar uses in conditional sentences.

Could

- *Could* is used to express possibility or uncertainty.
    *This **could** be the house.*

- *Could* is used with comparative adjectives to express possibility or impossibility.
    *The situation **couldn't** be worse.*
    *It **could** be better.*

- *Could* is used to make suggestions.
  *We **could** go to that new restaurant opposite the cinema.*

- *Could* is used to express unwillingness.
  *I **couldn't** possibly leave Tim here on his own.*

Can

- *Can* with be is used to make criticisms.
  *You **can** be really annoying, you know!*

- *Can* is also used with *be* to refer to capability.
  *Winter here **can** be really cold.*

Must and *can't*

These refer to present time only. (See *be bound to*.) In expressing certainty, they are opposites.
  *This **must** be our stop.* (I'm sure it is.)
  *This **can't** be our stop.* (I'm sure it isn't.)

May and might

- *May* can be used to express although clauses.
  *She **may** be the boss, but that is no excuse for shouting like that.*
  See also Grammar 12 for emphasis.

- *May/might as well*
  This describes the only thing left to do, something which the speaker is not enthusiastic about.
  *Nobody else is going to turn up now for the lesson, so you **may as well** go home.*

- *May* and *might* both express possibility or uncertainty. *May* is often used in formal language.
  *The peace conference **may** find a solution to the problem.*

- There is an idiomatic expression with *try*, using *may* for present reference, and *might* for past reference.
  *Try as I **might**, I could not pass my driving test.*
  (Although I tried hard, I could not pass my driving test.)

Shall

- *Shall* can be used with all persons to emphasize something which the speaker feels is certain to happen or wants to happen.
  *I **shall** definitely give up smoking this year.*
  *We **shall** win!* (*Shall* is stressed in this sentence.)

- Similarly, *shall* is used in formal rules and regulations.
  *No player **shall** knowingly pick up or move the ball of another player.*

Will

- *Will* can be used to express an assumption.
  A: The phone's ringing. B: That'll be for me.

- *Will/won't* can be used emphatically to tell someone of the speaker's intention, or to forbid an action, in response to a will expression.
  I'll take the money anyway, so there!
  You won't!
  I will!
  Similarly *I won't* can mean *I refuse*, and *I will* can mean *I insist*.
  A: I won't do it! B: Yes, you will!

Would

Would is often used in situations where a conditional sense is understood but not stated.
  Nobody would agree with that idea. (if we asked them)
  Life wouldn't be worth living without you. (if you weren't there)
  I think Jim would be the best candidate. (if he was under consideration for the job)
  Sue wouldn't do that, surely! (if you think she's capable of doing that)

Need and *need to*

- *Need to* is a modal auxiliary, and behaves like a normal verb.
  Do you need to use the photocopier?

- *Need* is a modal auxiliary, but mainly in question and negative forms.
  Need you make so much noise?
  See Grammar 6 for *need doing*.

Dare

- *Dare* can be used in two ways. It can be an intransitive verb followed by infinitive with *to*.
  I didn't dare to say anything.

- It can also be a modal auxiliary, mainly in questions and negatives.
  She dare not refuse.   *How dare you!*

Related non-modal expressions

- *Had better*
  This is a recommendation and refers only to the present or future.
  You'd better not phone her again.
  It can be reported in the past without change of form.
  He told me we'd better come back another day.

- *Be bound to*
  This makes a future prediction of certainty.
  It's bound to rain tomorrow.

1 <u>Underline</u> the correct word or phrase in each sentence.

1 I don't think you *could/<u>should</u>* tell anyone yet.
2 I *couldn't/shouldn't* possibly leave without paying.
3 That *mustn't/can't* be the hotel Jane told us about.
4 There are times when the traffic here *can/could* be really heavy.
5 We are enjoying our holiday, though the weather *could/must* be better.
6 You *couldn't/shouldn't* really be sitting here.
7 You *could/may* be older than me, but that doesn't mean you're cleverer.
8 You *might/should* like to look over these papers if you have time.
9 I'm afraid that nobody *should/would* help me in that kind of situation.
10 No member of the association *must/shall* remove official documents from these premises without written permission.

2 Complete the dialogue by writing one word in each space. Contractions (*can't*) count as one word.

Bill: This (1) ......*must*...... be the house, I suppose, number 16 Elland Way.

Jane: I pictured it as being much bigger, from the estate agent's description.

Bill: Well, we'd (2) .... go inside.

Jane: We (3) .... as well. Wait a minute. I (4) .... to just find my glasses. I (5) .... see a thing without them.

Bill: I don't think much of it from the outside, to be honest.

Jane: Yes, it (6) .... certainly do with a coat of paint or two.

Bill: Rather you than me! I (7) .... like to have to paint it all! And the gutters (8) .... replacing.

Jane: I (9) .... think they haven't been replaced since the house was built.

Bill: They (10) .... really be replaced every four years ideally.

Jane: And I don't like that big ivy plant growing up the side. Ivy (11) .... get in the brickwork and cause all sorts of damage.

Bill: I wonder if there's a lock on that big downstairs window? It looks very easy to break in to.

Jane: There's (12) .... to be one, surely.

Bill: Well, (13) .... we go inside?

Jane: Do we (14) .... to? I think I've seen enough already. I (15) .... possibly live here.

3 Complete the second sentence so that it has a similar meaning to the first sentence, using the word given. Do not change the word given.

1 I couldn't be happier at the moment.

could

I'm as .... *happy as could be* .... at the moment.

2 Although I tried hard, I couldn't lift the suitcase.

might

Try .... , I couldn't lift the suitcase.

3 I'm sure that Peter won't be late.

bound

Peter .... on time.

4 Fancy you and I having the same surname!

should

It's odd .... the same surname!

5 I think you should take up jogging.

were

If I .... take up jogging.

6 It's possible that this kind of snake is poisonous.

could

This snake .... the poisonous kinds.

7 You can't borrow my car!

won't

I .... borrow my car!

8 I'm sure this isn't how you get to Norwich!

can't

This .... way to Norwich!

9 It makes no difference to me if we call it off.

may

We .... call it off.

10 Although it's summer, the temperature is more like winter.

may

It .... the temperature is more like winter.

4 Choose the sentence (A or B) that is closest in meaning to the sentence given.

1 It's possible that we'll know the answers tomorrow. ....A....

   A We may know the answers tomorrow.

   B We should know the answers tomorrow.

2 I don't think you should ring him now. It's rather late. ....

   A You might not ring him now. It's rather late.

   B You'd better not ring him now. It's rather late.

3 You needn't come if you don't want to. ....

   A You won't come if you don't want to.

   B You don't have to come if you don't want to.

4 I think it's wrong for you to work so hard. ....

   A You don't have to work so hard.

   B You shouldn't work so hard.

5 Perhaps these are the keys. ....

   A These might be the keys.

   B These must be the keys.

6 It would be wrong for us to lock the cat in the house for a week. ....

   A We'd better not lock the cat in the house for a week.

   B We can't lock the cat in the house for a week.

7 It's possible that the decision will be announced next week. ....

   A The decision might be announced next week.

   B The decision will be announced next week.

8 Although I try hard, I can never solve 'The Times' crossword. ....

   A Try as I may, I can never solve 'The Times' crossword.

   B Try as I can, I may never solve 'The Times' crossword.

9 I know. Why don't we go out to eat instead? ....

   A I know. We must go out to eat instead.

   B I know. We could go out to eat instead.

10 Using Punter's Paints couldn't be easier. ....

   A You may as well use Punter's Paints.

   B You should find Punter's Paints easy to use.

11 Peter often really annoys people. ....

   A Peter can be really annoying.

   B Try as he might, Peter annoys people.

12 Jane wouldn't talk about people like that, surely! ....

   A Jane didn't want to talk about people like that.

   B Jane isn't the kind of person to talk about people like that.

5 Complete each sentence with a phrase from the box.

| couldn't be | wouldn't be | I might | ~~don't have to~~ | couldn't possibly |
| must be | must like | need to | may be | might as well |

1 The heating comes on automatically. You ....*don't have to*....... turn it on.
2 Of course I'll help! I .... let you do it on your own.
3 It's a lovely hotel. And the staff .... more helpful.
4 George .... it there if he has stayed there for so long.
5 You .... right, but I'm still not convinced.
6 We .... go in this museum. There's nothing else to do.
7 I love these trees. Without them the garden .... the same.
8 There's the phone call I was expecting. It .... George.
9 Thanks. And now you just .... sign on the dotted line.
10 Try as .... , I simply couldn't open the lid.

6 Complete the text by writing one word in each space. Contractions (*mustn't*) count as one word.

I (1) ......*might*... as well admit it – I'm one of those people who runs in marathons dressed as a duck. It's not normally something you (2) .... want to admit to your friends, but I (3) .... imagine life without running in my Donald Duck costume. You're probably thinking I (4) .... be an idiot who just wants to show off, and well, you (5) .... be right, I suppose! And you (6) .... think that running so far was hard enough, without the silly costume! I (7) .... to admit that I do enjoy the laughter as I run past, but that's only part of it. I (8) .... look silly, but it's all in a good cause, as I run to raise money for children's charities – people promise to give me money for running in the race. I (9) .... cheerfully run for hours in the rain because I'm doing something useful. Call me mad (10) .... you like, but I'd far (11) .... run through the streets dressed as a duck (12) .... sit at home and watch the race on television. Some of the other runners (13) .... be a bit mad too – I (14) .... be the only duck to be narrowly beaten in a race by three gorillas in bikinis. I (15) .... miss charity marathons for all the world!

➔ SEE ALSO
Grammar 6: Passive 2
Grammar 7: Conditionals
Grammar 10: Modals: past
Grammar 12: Emphasis

10

GRAMMAR

Modals: past

Had to

Had to is the past form of *must* and refers to a past obligation.

*Sorry I'm late, I **had to post** some letters.*

The negative form is *didn't have to* and refers to an absence of obligation.

Should have and ought to have

Where **should* appears, *ought to* is also possible.

- Expectation

  Should have refers to something which was supposed to happen.

  *The parcel I sent you ***should have arrived** by now.*

- Criticism of an action

  *You ***shouldn't have eaten** so much last night.*

- *Should have* and verbs of thinking

  The past form *knew* in the example is an unreal verb form, and the *should have* form is used according to 'sequence of verb forms'. See Grammar 8.

  *I **should have thought** you knew.*

- With *be* and adjectives describing chance

  *It was strange that you **should have been staying** in the same hotel last year.*

- As a polite expression of thanks on receiving a gift or a favour

  *I've done the washing up for you. – Oh, you really **shouldn't have**!*

Could have and couldn't have

- *Could have* refers to past possibility or uncertainty.

  *David **could have won** the race if he had tried.* (possibility/ability)

  *It **could have been** Sue, I suppose.* (uncertainty)

- *Couldn't have* can be used with comparative adjectives.

  *We **couldn't have been happier** in those days.*

- *Could have* can also express unwillingness.

  *She **could have gone** to the party with her friends.* (but she didn't)

Could

- *Could* refers to past permission or past ability.

  *When I was sixteen I **could stay** out till 11.00.* (I was allowed to)

  *Mary **could swim** when she was three.* (she actually did)

  Compare: *Mary **could have swum** when she was three.* (but she didn't)

May have and *might have*

- *Might have* refers to past possibility which did not happen.
    *You **might have** drowned!*

- *Might have* and *may* have refer to uncertainty.
    *I suppose I **may have been** rather critical.*

- Both can be used in the negative to express uncertainty.
    *They **might not have received** our letter yet.*

- *Might have* is used to express annoyance at someone's failure to do something.
    *You **might have told** me my trousers were split!*

- *I might have known + would* is an idiom by which the speaker expresses ironically that an action was typical of someone else.
    *I **might have known** that he **would** be late.*

Must have and *can't have*

- These refer to the speaker's certainty about a past action.
    *Someone **must have taken** it.* (I am sure they did)
    *You **can't have lost** it.* (I am sure you didn't)

- Both can also be used with *surely* in exclamations.
    ***Surely** you **can't have** eaten all of it! **Surely** you **must have** noticed it!*

Would not

- This expresses an unwillingness in the past.
    *Everyone was angry because Sam **wouldn't turn off** the television.*

Would have

- *Would have* can refer to events in the past which did not actually happen.
    *I **would have accepted** this job, but I didn't want to move house.*

- Assumptions about the past are also possible with *would have*.
    A: Someone called after you left but didn't leave a message.
    *B: That **would have been** Cathy, probably.*

Needn't have and *didn't need to*

Needn't have done refers to an unnecessary action which was actually done.
    *You **needn't have paid** all at once.* (you did pay)
Didn't need to refers to an unnecessary action which was not done.
    *I **didn't need to go** to the dentist again, luckily.*

Adverbs and modals

Adverbs such as *easily, just, really, well,* are often used to emphasize modal expressions, in both present and past time.
    *You could **easily** have been killed. I might **just** take you up on that.*
    *You couldn't **really** have managed without me. I might **well** decide to come.*

ADVANCED LANGUAGE PRACTICE

1 <u>Underline</u> the correct word or phrase in each sentence.

1 That <u>*can't have been*</u>/*shouldn't have been* Nick that you saw.
2 You *must have given*/*might have given* me a hand!
3 I caught a later train because I *had to see*/*must have seen* a client.
4 I suppose Bill *should have lost*/*might have lost* his way.
5 I didn't refuse the cake, as it *should have been*/*would have been* rude.
6 I don't know who rang, but it *could have been*/*must have been* Jim.
7 It was odd that you *should have bought*/*would have bought* the same car.
8 I asked them to leave but they *might not*/*wouldn't* go.
9 It's a pity you didn't ask because I *can't help*/*could have helped* you.
10 It's your own fault, you *can't have*/*shouldn't have* gone to bed so late.

2 Complete the text by writing a verb from the box in each space.

> can't have   must have   shouldn't have   may not have   may have
>
> shouldn't have   can't have   ought to have   didn't need to   ~~shouldn't have~~

1 You and your big mouth! It was supposed to be a secret. You ......*shouldn't have*...... told her!
2 The plane is late. It .... landed by now.
3 You .... met my brother. I haven't got one!
4 There is only one explanation. You .... left your keys on the bus.
5 You .... heard me right. I definitely said 204525.
6 The meat is a bit burnt. You .... cooked it for so long.
7 I'm sorry. I accept I .... been a little bit rude.
8 You really .... taken so much trouble over me.
9 Was it really necessary? You .... tell the police, you know.
10 Keep your fingers crossed! The traffic warden .... noticed the car's parked next to a No Parking sign!

74

3 Complete the second sentence so that it has a similar meaning to the first sentence, using the word given. Do not change the word given.

1 It wouldn't have been right to leave you to do all the work on your own.

couldn't

I ....*couldn't have left you to do*.......... all the work on your own.

2 Perhaps they didn't notice the tyre was flat.

might

They .... the tyre was flat.

3 All that trouble I went to wasn't necessary in the end.

needn't

I .... all that trouble.

4 Apparently someone has borrowed my laptop.

have

Someone .... my laptop.

5 I'm disappointed that you didn't back me up!

might

You .... me up!

6 Our worrying so much was a waste of time.

needn't

We .... so much.

7 It's just not possible for the cat to have opened the fridge.

possibly

The cat .... the fridge.

8 It would have been possible for Helen to take us in her car.

could

Helen .... us a lift.

9 It's possible that the last person to leave didn't lock the door.

might

The last person .... the door unlocked.

10 School uniform wasn't compulsory at my school.

wear

We .... school uniform at my school.

4 Complete each sentence by writing one word in each space. Contractions (*can't*) count as one word.

1 I ....*could*........ have become a millionaire, but I decided not to.

2 You .... have been here when Helen told the boss not to be so lazy! It was great!

3 Peter wasn't here then, so he .... have broken your vase.

4 I .... have bought that car, but I decided to look at a few others.

5 If you felt lonely, you .... have given me a ring.

6 Don't take a risk like that again! We .... have lost because of you.

7 It's been more than a week! You .... have had some news by now!

8 We were glad to help. We .... have just stood by and done nothing.

9 You really .... have gone to so much trouble!

10 I .... have thought that it was rather difficult.

5 Correct any errors in these sentences. Some sentences are correct.

1 Surely you mustn't have forgotten already! ....*can't*....

2 Even Paul couldn't have foreseen what was coming next. ....

3 Frances might not have understood what you said. ....

4 It was funny that she should have remembered me. ....

5 Harry may have won the match with a bit more effort. ....

6 You must have told me you had already eaten. ....

7 Look, there's £30 in my wallet. I shouldn't have gone to the bank after all. ....

8 You mustn't have been so unkind! ....

9 I couldn't have managed without you. ....

10 I have no idea who it was, but I suppose it would have been Ann. ....

6 Complete each sentence with a modal verb. Some are negative.

1 Pay no attention to what Jim said. He ....*can't have*.... been serious.

2 Fancy borrowing all my clothes like that! You .... asked me first!

3 The exam wasn't a problem at all. In fact, it .... been easier!

4 We should call Jack again, to be sure. He .... heard the phone the first time..

5 Phew, that was a lucky escape! We .... killed!

6 Hello, I'm home early. I .... stay late at work after all.

7 Thanks a lot! You .... told me that the meeting had been cancelled!

8 Ann didn't get home until 4.30 this morning. That party .... been good!

9 This bus is taking ages. We .... taken the metro, after all.

10 There were plenty of spare seats on the train. We .... booked in advance after all.

7 Underline the most suitable adverb for each space.

1 Someone *obviously/currently/fortunately* must have picked it up by mistake.
2 He could *really/cheerfully/easily* have stolen the painting without anyone knowing.
3 I may *surely/well/clearly* have made a mistake.
4 You *really/clearly/needlessly* shouldn't have spent so much on my present.
5 Bill *rarely/simply/certainly* wouldn't listen to anything we said.
6 I couldn't *just/yet/already* have left without saying a word.
7 *Certainly/Rarely/Surely* you can't seriously believe that I am guilty!
8 I opened the window, I *greatly/surely/simply* had to get some fresh air.
9 I *still/unfortunately/surely* couldn't have come to your party.
10 How dangerous! You could *still/strongly/well* have been injured!

8 Complete the text by writing a verb from the box in each space.

might have found	would have meant	must be	can't have been
~~might have heard~~	should have resigned	might have known	
must have thought	needn't have worried	would have had	

To: Katie　　　From: Tina

Hi Katie,

Just a quick update on my latest news. As you (1) ....*might have heard*.... from Paula, I won't be going to Australia after all. Basically, it (2) .... taking two months off, and I'm not sure whether I (3) .... a job when I came back. I really like my job at the hospital here, so I decided to play it safe. Maybe I (4) .... from the job and hoped for the best. After all, perhaps I (5) .... a really great job out there, or met the man of my dreams! Do you think I did the right thing? I kept changing my mind right up to the last minute. Bill and Sue in Sydney (6) .... I was really annoying. I thought they'd never speak to me again, but I (7) .... I got a call from them last week, and they were very sympathetic.

Paula told me you've decided to go back to university to study law – that (8) .... an easy decision! You (9) .... the world's coolest-looking lawyer! So no more working in the insurance company? I (10) .... you'd find it a bit dull! Good for you.

Keep in touch,

Love, Tina

➜ **SEE ALSO**
Grammar 8: Unreal time
Grammar 9: Modals: present and future
Consolidation 3: Units 9–12

11

GRAMMAR

Inversion

Inversion

The term inversion covers two different grammatical operations:

- Using a question form of the main verb

    *Not only **did he fail** to report the accident, but also later denied that he had been driving the car.*

    *Never **have I enjoyed** myself more!*

- Changing the normal positions of verb and subject

    *Along the street **came a strange procession**.*

    See Grammar 12 for an explanation of this example.

Inversion after negative adverbials

- This only occurs when the adverbial occurs at the beginning of a clause.

    All the examples below are used in formal language, usually for rhetorical effect, such as in political speeches. They are not usual in everyday spoken language. Compare:

    *Never **have I heard** a weaker excuse!*

    I have never heard a weaker excuse!

- Time expressions: *never, rarely, seldom*

    These are most commonly used with present perfect or past perfect, or with modals such as *can* and *could*. Sentences of this type often contain comparatives.

    ***Rarely can** a minister **have been faced** with such a problem.*

    ***Seldom has** the team **given** a **worse** performance.*

    ***Rarely had** I **had** so much responsibility.*

- Time expressions: *hardly, barely, scarcely, no sooner*

    These refer to an event which quickly follows another in the past. They are usually used with past perfect, although no sooner can be followed by past simple. Note the words used in the contrasting clause.

    ***Hardly had the train left** the station, **when** there was an explosion.*

    ***Scarcely had I entered** the room **when** the phone rang.*

    ***No sooner had I reached** the door **than** I realized it was locked.*

    ***No sooner was the team** back on the pitch **than** it started raining.*

- After *only*

    Here *only* combines with other time expressions and is usually used with past simple.

    ***Only** after posting the letter **did I remember** that I had forgotten to put on a stamp.*

    Other examples are *only if/when, only then, only later*.

    Note that when *only* refers to 'the state of being the only one', there is no inversion following it.

    Only Mary realized that the door was not locked.

78

- Phrases containing *no/not*

  These include *under no circumstances, on no account, at no time, in no way, on no condition, not until, not only ... (but also)*.

  > ***On no condition are they*** to open fire without a warning.
  > ***Not until*** I got home ***did I notice*** that I had the wrong umbrella.

- *Little*

  Little also has a negative or restrictive meaning in this sense.

  > ***Little does the government appreciate*** what the results will be.

Inversion after *so/such* with *that*

- This occurs with *so* and adjectives when the main verb is *be*. It is used for emphasis and is more common than the example with *such*.

  > ***So devastating were*** the floods that some areas may never recover.

- *Such* used with *be* means 'so much/so great'.

  > ***Such was*** the force of the storm that trees were uprooted.

- As in the examples with *such*, inversion only occurs if *so/such* is the first word in the clause.

Inverted conditional sentences without *If*

- Three types of *If-* sentence can be inverted without *If-*. This makes the sentences more formal and makes the event less likely.

  > If they were to escape, there would be an outcry.
  > ***Were they to escape***, there would be an outcry.
  > If the police had found out, I would have been in trouble.
  > ***Were the police to have found out***, I would have been in trouble.
  > If you should hear anything, let me know.
  > ***Should you hear*** anything, let me know.
  > If he has cheated, he will have to be punished.
  > ***Should he have cheated***, he will have to be punished.
  > If I had known, I would have protested strongly.
  > ***Had I known***, I would have protested strongly.

- Inversion after *as*

  This is more common in formal or written language.

  > We were short of money, ***as were most people*** in our neighbourhood.
  > I thought, ***as did my colleagues***, that the recession would soon be over.

- Inversion after *so, neither* and *nor*

  These are used in 'echoing' statements, agreeing or disagreeing.

  > A: I am going home. B: ***So am I***.
  > A: I don't like meat. B: ***Neither do I***.

  See Grammar 12 for ways of giving emphasis without inverting after *so*.

ADVANCED LANGUAGE PRACTICE

1 Correct any sentences which are inappropriate in the contexts given.

1 Guest to host: 'So nice was that pudding, that I would like to have some more.'
...............*That pudding was so nice that* ....

2 Witness to court: 'No sooner had I turned out the light, than I heard a noise outside.' ....

3 News reader: 'Such was the force of the earthquake, that whole villages have been devastated.' ....
.

4 Parent to child: 'Should you fancy a pizza, let's order one now.'
....

5 Friend to friend: 'Never before have I seen this film.'
....

6 Politician to audience: 'Seldom has the country faced a greater threat.'
....

7 Celebrity to interviewer: 'Were I to have the time, I'd go climbing more often.'
....

8 Victim to police officer: 'Scarcely had we been introduced when he punched me for no reason.' ....

9 Printed notice: 'Under no circumstances is this control panel to be left unattended.'
....

10 Colleague to colleague: 'Should you change your mind, just let me know.'
....

2 Complete the second sentence so that it has a similar meaning to the first sentence, using the word given. Do not change the word given.

1 It was only when the office phoned me that I found out about the meeting.
   find
   Not until ...... *the office phoned me did I find out* ...... about the meeting.

2 The facts were not all made public at the time.
   later
   Only .... all made public.

3 The response to our appeal was so great that we had to take on more staff.
   response
   Such .... to our appeal that we had to take on more staff.

4 Harry broke his leg, and also injured his shoulder.
   but
   Not only .... also injured his shoulder.

5 The police didn't suspect at all that the judge was the murderer.
   did
   Little .... as being the murderer.

6 The bus driver cannot be blamed for the accident in any way.
   held
   In .... responsible for the accident.

7 If the government increased taxes, they would lose the election.
   raise
   Were .... taxes, they would lose the election.

8 As soon as I got home, I realized I'd left my bag in the shops.
   had
   No sooner .... I realized I'd left my bag in the shops.

9 It was only when I asked a passer-by that I realized where I was.
   did
   Not until .... where I was.

10 The minister was interrupted just after starting his speech.
   when
   Hardly .... he was interrupted.

ADVANCED LANGUAGE PRACTICE

3 Complete each sentence with a phrase from the box.

> Rarely have   No sooner had   Under no circumstances are   Were you   Rarely have
> ~~Hardly had~~   Not only did   Under no circumstances will   as do   Little did

1 ....Hardly had............. we arrived at the hotel, when there was a power cut.
2 .... members of staff to accept gratuities from clients.
3 .... Detective Dawson realize what she was to discover!
4 .... to pay the full amount now, there would be a ten per cent discount.
5 I suppose, ... most people, that I will be retiring at 65.
6 .... the doctors seen a more difficult case.
7 .... Jean win first prize, but she was also offered a promotion.
8 .... late arrivals be admitted to the theatre before the interval.
9 .... one missing child been found, than another three disappeared.
10 .... so many employees taken sick leave at the same time.

4 Complete each sentence with a phrase containing a suitable form of the verb in brackets.

1 Should (need) ....you need............. anything, could you let me know?
2 Were the plane (take off) .... , everyone in it would have been killed.
3 Had (study) .... harder, I would probably have passed all my exams.
4 Should (be) .... in the neighbourhood, drop in.
5 Had (go) .... to the doctor immediately, your daughter would not be so ill.
6 Never before (spend) .... so much money on her daughter's birthday.
7 Should (feel) .... hungry, just call room service, and order a meal.
8 Were (offer) .... her the job, we couldn't be sure that she would accept.
9 Had (take) .... the necessary measures, this political crisis could have been avoided.
10 Scarcely (get) .... home when the police called us with news of Geoffrey.

5 <u>Underline</u> the correct word or phrase in each sentence.

1 Jim promised that <u>*he would never*</u>/*never would he* tell anyone else.
2 Not until it was too late *I remembered*/*did I remember* to call Susan.
3 Hardly had we settled down in our seats *than*/*when* the lights went out.
4 Only after checking three times *I was*/*was I* certain of the answer.
5 At no time *I was aware*/*was I aware* of anything out of the ordinary.
6 Only Catherine and Sally *passed*/*did they pass* the final examination.
7 Only when *Pete has arrived*/*has Pete arrived* can we begin the programme.
8 No sooner had it stopped raining *than*/*when* the sun came out.

6 Complete the text by writing a word or phrase from the box in each space.

little	such	not only	seldom	under no circumstances
along	as	~~no sooner~~	scarcely	had

Well, ladies and gentlemen, we've done it again – another election victory. The last four years of office have been a wonderful time for the party, a tale of adversity overcome. (1) ....No sooner........ had we come to office than the Stock Market crashed. But we survived that scare, and we came out of it stronger for the experience. The opposition claimed we were faltering. (2) .... have I heard such hypocrisy from a party which continued to squabble internally for the next four years. Then (3) .... came a fellow called David Rew, with his new breakaway Democratic party – but he didn't have much success in the opinion polls!
(4) .... did he claim he'd become Prime Minister within three years, he also reckoned that this party was now unpopular with younger voters. (5) .... did he realize that it would be the young voters who gave us an overwhelming vote of confidence in yesterday's election. (6) .... had the first votes rolled in when it was obvious that we would be re-elected with a huge majority. (7) .... was the extent of our victory that the New Democrats obtained a meagre five seats. (8) .... they known they would perform so poorly, I don't think they would have been quite so scathing in their criticism of our economic policy. But rest assured, ladies and gentlemen,
(9) .... will we rest on our laurels. There is no room for complacency in this government. And I am confident, (10) .... I'm sure are most of you, that the next four years will be a resounding success. Thank you.

7 Complete the second sentence so that it has a similar meaning to the first sentence, using the word given. Do not change the word given.

1 Please never ever interrupt me when I'm in a meeting.

am

On no account ...*am I (ever) to be interrupted*... when I'm in a meeting.

2 Nobody from this school has ever written a better composition.

anyone

Never .... written a better composition.

3 Such was the demand for tickets that people queued day and night.

great

The demand for tickets .... that people queued day and night.

4 The money is not to be paid under any circumstances.

no

Under .... to be paid.

5 Three days passed before we arrived at the first oasis.

had

Not until .... at the first oasis.

6 Little did Brenda know what she was letting herself in for.

no

Brenda .... what she was letting herself in for.

7 It was only when I stopped that I realized something was wrong.

did

Only .... that something was wrong.

8 The accused never expressed regret for what he had done.

time

At .... regret for what he had done.

9 Exhaustion prevented any of the runners from finishing the race.

were

So .... of them finished the race.

10 It's not common for there to be so much rain in March.

see

Seldom .... so much rain in March.

➔ **SEE ALSO**
Grammar 12: Emphasis
Consolidation 3: Units 9–12

12
GRAMMAR
Emphasis

Changing word order to change focus

- Passive

  Passive constructions vary the way information is given in a sentence, putting more emphasis on what comes first. See Grammar 5 and 6.

  *All roads to the north **have been blocked** by snow.*

- Fronting and inversion

  Inversion here refers to changing the normal word order in the sentence so that a prepositional phrase is emphasized before the verb. This also involves putting the verb before the subject.

  *Suddenly **down came** the rain!*

  ***Up in the air went** the balloon.*

  Fronting involves changing the order of clauses in a sentence and putting first for emphasis a clause that would usually not be first.

  I don't know where the money is coming from.

  ***Where the money is coming from**, I don't know.*

  Time phrases can vary in position, and are often put first because the time reference is important.

  ***At six o'clock** Monica decided to phone the police.*

  May clauses

  There is a type of *may* clause introduced by *although* which can be inverted. It is a highly formal expression.

  Although it may seem/be difficult, it is not impossible.

  ***Difficult as/though it may seem/be**, it is not impossible.*

- Cleft and pseudo cleft sentences

  These are sentences introduced by *it is/it was* or by a clause beginning *what.*
  Different parts of the sentence can be emphasized in this way. In speech, stress and intonation also identify the emphasis.

  With *it is/was*

  Sue borrowed my bike last night.

  ***It was Sue** who borrowed my bike.*

  ***It was last night** that Sue borrowed my bike.*

  ***It was my bike** that Sue borrowed.*

  Sentences with *because* are also possible.

  ***It was because** I felt ill that I left.*

  Modal auxiliaries are also possible.

  You can't have read the same book.

  ***It can't have been the same book** that you read.*

What clauses

These are common with verbs such as *need, want, like, hate*.

> *I hate rainy weather.*
> **What I hate** *is rainy weather.*
> *You need a holiday.*
> **What you need** *is a holiday.*

It is also possible to emphasize events, using auxiliary *do/did*.

> *Peter left the windows unlocked.*
> **What Peter did was** *(to) leave the windows unlocked.*
> *They are destroying the environment.*
> **What they are doing is** *destroying the environment.*

Clauses beginning all emphasize 'the only thing'.

> *I only need another €15.*
> **All I need** *is another €15.*

Adding words for emphasis

- *Own*

  This intensifies possessive adjectives.

  > *It was **my own** idea.*

- *Very* and *indeed*

  Very can be used emphatically to mean 'exactly/precisely'.

  > *At the **very** same moment, the telephone rang.*

  Very … indeed is another way of intensifying adjectives.

  > *It was **very cold indeed**.*

- Emphasizing negatives

  Ways of emphasizing not include: *at all, in the least, really*.

  > *It was **not at all** cold. It was **not** cold **at all**.*

  In the least/slightest usually adds *bit* if used before an adjective.

  > *I wasn't interested **in the slightest**.*
  > *I wasn't **the least bit** interested.*

  No and *none* can be emphasized by *at all* and *whatsoever*.

  > *There were **none** left **at all**.*
  > *There were **no** tickets left **whatsoever**.*

- *The*

  The can emphasize uniqueness. It is heavily stressed in speech.

  > *Surely you are not **the** David Beckham, are you?*

- Question words ending in *-ever*

  These add an air of disbelief to the question.

  > **Whatever** *are you doing?* **Whoever** *told you that?*

- Auxiliary *do*

  This can emphasize the verb, and is stressed in speech.

  > I **do** *like this film! It's really great!*

  It is also used in polite forms.

  > I **do** *hope you'll come again! Do sit down!*

- Adverbs and adjectives

  A large number of adverbs and adjectives are used to add emphasis.

  Common examples are:

  > *I **actually** went inside one of the Pyramids.*
  >
  > *It is **by no means** certain that the match will take place.*
  >
  > *Some people were **even** wearing two pullovers, it was so cold.*
  >
  > *Her performance was **sheer** magic!*
  >
  > *This book is **utter** nonsense!*

  The following examples are only possible with adjectives which express an absolute opinion (non-gradeable adjectives).

  > *It was **absolutely** fantastic!*
  >
  > *The third exam question was **quite (completely)** impossible.*
  >
  > *This guide book is **utterly** useless.*
  >
  > *You were **simply** wonderful!*
  >
  > *Don't cook the meat any more. It's **just** right!*

- Echoing phrases with *so*

  These express agreement.

  > *A: This is the book you are looking for.*
  >
  > *B: **So it is**!*

Other means

- Time phrases

  Common examples are *day after day*; *time and time again*; *over and over again*; *day in, day out*.

  > *David reads the same books **over and over again**!*

- Repetition of main verb

  > *I **tried and tried**, but it was no use.*

- In the repetition of a phrase with a possessive it is possible to omit the first mention of the noun and use a possessive pronoun.

  > ***Their marriage** was a successful marriage.*
  >
  > ***Theirs** was a successful marriage.*

ADVANCED LANGUAGE PRACTICE

1 Complete each sentence with a phrase from the box.

the least bit	waited and waited	as it may seem	by no means	not at all
what we did	time and time again	can't have been	none at all	~~do think~~

1 I know you're busy, but I ....*do think*.................. you could have
   helped me with the decorating.
2 It's .... certain that the president will be re-elected.
3 You may have lots of restaurants where you live, but there are
   .... in this part of town.
4 I told you .... about the leaking pipes, but you wouldn't
   listen.
5 You don't seem .... interested in my problems!
6 Strange .... , the bus is actually faster than the train.
7 In the end .... was to call a plumber.
8 We .... all day, but Chris never turned up.
9 Pauline was .... bothered by our turning up so late.
10 It .... Jim that you saw; he is in Germany at the moment.

2 Complete the text by writing a word from the box in each space.

whatever	whatsoever	why	all	as	again	what	is	utter	~~at~~

What really makes me furious is the sort of language used in official letters.
For example, I can't make any sense of this letter from the council
(1) ....*at*.......... all. It's (2) .... nonsense, if you ask me.
(3) .... the council can't write in plain English is beyond me.
(4) .... I really can't stand is this kind of long-winded, complicated
English. In my opinion, what they're doing (5) .... systematically
destroying the language with all this new jargon – 'input', 'time window',
'feasibility study' – (6) .... are they talking about?
(7) .... we get is the same meaningless drivel over and over
(8) .... Listen to this: 'Difficult (9) .... it may be for
all parties concerned, this is the most viable solution on offer.' I have no idea,
none (10) .... what that means. Can nobody write in plain English
nowadays? Or is there something wrong with me?

3 Complete the second sentence so that it has a similar meaning to the first sentence, using the word given. Do not change the word given.

1 The car doesn't need anything else except new tyres.

   needs

   All .... *the car needs is* .... new tyres.

2 Brenda didn't worry at all about her exams.

   bit

   Brenda wasn't the .... about her exams.

3 The person who told me about the hotel was Keith.

   who

   It .... told me about the hotel.

4 I had spent every last penny of my money.

   absolutely

   I had .... whatsoever.

5 Although the ticket may seem expensive, it is good value for money.

   though

   Expensive .... , the ticket is good value for money.

6 I really hate lukewarm food.

   stand

   What I .... lukewarm food.

7 In the end Martha went to the police.

   was

   In the end what Martha .... to the police.

8 I think you must have seen a ghost.

   that

   It .... you saw.

9 Her car was the last car you'd expect to be stolen.

   very

   Hers .... you'd expect to be stolen.

10 The accident happened because someone was very careless.

   caused

   Sheer .... happen.

4 <u>Underline</u> the correct word or phrase in each sentence.

1   Don't worry, I'm none at *all/<u>not at all</u>* tired.
2   I thought that speech was *utter/utterly* rubbish.
3   It was *because/why* the car broke down that we missed our plane.
4   A: You are sitting on my hat!
   B: *So am I/So I am*!
5   The sea was so rough that *actually/even* the experienced sailors were seasick.
6   *Whatever/Why* ever are you looking at me like that for?
7   I would like to make it *quite/simply* clear that we are just good friends.
8   This is my *very private/very own* computer.
9   On this course, we absolutely *expect/do expect* you to work hard.
10 There were warnings, but *nothing whatsoever/nothing simply* was done.

5 Read the dialogue and decide which option (A, B or C) best fits each space.

Jane: Well, did you see 'Western Warrior' at the cinema?

Ben: Yes, and I thought it was very good (1) .....B.... . A lot of people had warned me that the plot got a bit far-fetched, but I didn't notice anything like that (2) .... What about you?

Jane: No, I'm afraid I wasn't interested (3) .... I find these action films (4) .... unbelievable and over the top. Give me 'Love on the Danube' any day. I could watch that film (5) ....

Ben: Well, I (6) .... hope you'll come with me to see 'The Fall of Julian'.

Jane: It hasn't exactly done very well, has it?

Ben: (7) .... makes you think that? I heard it's been very popular. Some newspaper critics have (8) .... suggested it'll win several Oscars.

Jane: Well I think it's (9) .... not possible to predict these things. You never know what the judges will go for. Last year I was certain that 'The Leaping Lady' would sweep the board, but in the end it got no awards (10) ....

1 A certainly	B indeed	C surely
2 A at all	B by no means	C absolutely
3 A whatever	B slightly	C in the least
4 A very	B sheer	C utterly
5 A over and over again	B whatsoever	C at the very moment
6 A would	B do	C utterly
7 A Whatever	B Whatsoever	C Whoever
8 A quite	B utterly	C even
9 A completely	B simply	C utterly
10 A whatsoever	B at least	C indeed

6 Choose the most appropriate continuation (a–j) for each sentence (1–10).

1 All of the trains were delayed by fog. ....*d*....

2 It wasn't so much my qualifications that impressed them. ....

3 I found that I was spending more time staying late at the office. ....

4 I don't find that the buses are especially late, actually. ....

5 Actually my fridge is in quite good condition, considering its age. ....

6 I don't find watching television particularly relaxing. ....

7 I've decided to buy a new stereo after all. ....

8 This book didn't teach me everything I know about cooking. ....

9 The flight itself didn't really bother me at all. ....

10 Actually I wasn't in the office yesterday. ....

a Where I am going to get the money from is another matter.

b What I really need is a new washing machine.

c It must have been my assistant whom you dealt with.

d It was after 10.00 when I finally got home.

e What really gets on my nerves is people who push into the queue.

f It was when I got off the plane that I felt ill.

g What I did in the end was to ask for a pay rise.

h It was Sarah who taught me how to make bread.

i It was because I spoke well at the interview that I got the job.

j What I like most is a long walk in the country.

7 Complete each sentence with a suitable word.

1 You can't complain. It's your ....*own*........ fault, isn't it?

2 A: That looks like Janet.

   B: .... it is! My goodness, hasn't she changed.

3 I'm sorry to keep you waiting. I .... hope you haven't been here long.

4 It is by no .... certain that the Prime Minister will attend the meeting.

5 .... I really enjoy in winter is a bowl of hot soup.

6 I searched and .... for my keys but I couldn't find them.

7 .... you are all going to sleep I can't quite work out!

8 What the government then .... was to raise income tax.

9 There isn't much to eat. .... we've got is some leftovers.

10 Cathy wasn't the .... bit put out when I couldn't make it to her wedding.

➜ SEE ALSO
Grammar 6 and 7: Passive 1 and 2
Consolidation 3: Units 9–12

CONSOLIDATION 3

Units 9–12

1 Complete the text with a suitable modal verb in each space.

Some people always have good advice to give you, but only after the event. You
(1) ....*must*....... have come across the type, who somehow always know what you
(2) .... have done when it has become too late. By now I (3) .... spot
them a mile off. It (4) .... be because I have had so much practice. Last week, for
example, I (5) .... to take my car to the garage because the lights weren't working.
It was an expensive job, but I decided that I (6) .... as well pay, and get it over
quickly. 'You (7) .... have told me,' said a friend when I was telling him how much I
(8) .... to pay. 'I (9) .... easily have fixed it for you. Then you
(10) .... not have wasted so much money.' You (11) .... imagine how I
felt! Actually, he (12) .... probably have made a mess of the job, and I
(13) .... well have ended up paying more. But it does seem strange that everyone
else (14) .... know exactly what I (15) .... to do.

2 Complete each sentence with a suitable word.

1 Do you think I had ....*better*........ catch the earlier train?
2 .... have we eaten a more enjoyable meal!
3 Strange as it .... seem, I have never drunk coffee!
4 You .... have told me the meeting was cancelled!
5 Not .... I woke up did I realize that Sue had left.
6 .... I really need is a new motorbike.
7 You .... be Jane's mother. Pleased to meet you.
8 At the .... end of the film, she meets the murderer.
9 .... did we know what was in store for us later!
10 You know Steve, he's .... to be late, so don't bother waiting for him.

3 Complete the second sentence so that it has a similar meaning to the first sentence, using the word given. Do not change the word given.

1 You are not to leave the hospital under any circumstances.

   are

   Under ....*no circumstances are you to*........ leave the hospital.

2 Two weeks passed before the letter arrived.

   did

   Not until .... the letter arrive.

3 She was so popular that everyone voted for her.

   her

   Such .... that everyone voted for her.

4 Luckily it wasn't necessary for Jim to take the exam again.

   need

   Luckily Jim .... the exam.

5 In the end I had no choice but to get a lift with a colleague.

   could

   In the end all .... get a lift with a colleague.

6 The guests didn't finally leave until after midnight.

   before

   It .... the guests finally left.

7 Paul smashed a window and damaged the television too.

   but

   Not only .... damaged the television.

8 By law, all rear-seat passengers are obliged to wear seat belts.

   have

   By law, seat belts .... all rear-seat passengers.

9 Harry tells the same joke all the time!

   over

   Harry tells the same joke .... again!

10 It may seem strange but I like stale cake!

   as

   Strange .... , I like stale cake!

11 It was very kind of you to bring me chocolates.

   shouldn't

   You .... me chocolates.

12 There's nothing better to do, so go home.

   may

   You .... go home.

4 Complete each sentence with a suitable word or phrase so that the meaning stays the same. The new sentence must not contain the word or words underlined.

1 It <u>would</u> have <u>been a good idea</u> to take your umbrella.
 You .... *should have* .... taken your umbrella.

2 It's <u>certain</u> to rain tomorrow.
 It's .... to rain tomorrow.

3 <u>I know you're</u> tired, but that's no reason to be so irritable.
 You .... tired, but that's no reason to be so irritable.

4 The hotel <u>was as</u> comfortable as possible.
 The hotel could .... more comfortable.

5 <u>It's possible</u> that Ann is out.
 Ann .... out.

6 You <u>are quite wrong</u> to eat so much chocolate.
 You .... eat so much chocolate.

7 <u>I'm sure this isn't</u> the road to Canterbury.
 We .... on the road to Canterbury.

8 <u>It's typical of</u> Martin to get promoted!
 I .... Martin would get promoted!

9 Connie's mother <u>refused to</u> let the children watch TV.
 Connie's mother .... let the children watch TV.

10 I <u>don't think</u> anyone would agree with you.
 I .... whether anyone would agree with you.

5 Choose the sentence (A or B) that is closest in meaning to the sentence given.

1 He might have let me know! ....A....
 A I wish he had let me know.
 B I'm not sure whether he let me know.

2 It's quite the best film I've ever seen. ....
 A I have seen some that were better.
 B I haven't seen any that were better.

3 You must be joking! ....
 A I'm sure you are joking.
 B You are supposed to make people laugh.

4 I should like to invite her out. ....
 A People think it an obligation for me to do this.
 B I think it would be a good idea.

5 You mustn't work so hard. ....
 A It's not necessary to work so hard.
 B It isn't a good idea to work so hard.

6 Correct any errors in these sentences. Some sentences are correct.

1 Into the room three policemen came. ...*came three policemen*...

2 Never have I had such a good holiday. ....

3 Hardly I sat down, when there was a knock at the door. ....

4 Exactly where the boat leaves from, I'm not quite sure. ....

5 You must not leave the door locked under no circumstances. ....

6 Should you need me, I'll be in my office all day. ....

7 Strange as it may seem, but I enjoy hard work. ....

8 All I need is time. ....

9 Had the government acted more swiftly, the crisis might have been avoided. ....

....

10 Until you've completed this form, there's not much we can do. ....

7 Complete the text by writing one word in each space.

To: Carol   From: Margaret

Dear Carol

I have a little problem to say the least, and I (1) .... be grateful for your advice. Things have gone pretty badly this week here in Marketing. On Thursday I missed a really important meeting. I supposed, as we all (2) ...., that the meeting (3) .... been cancelled , as my boss, DW, had flu. (4) .... did I know that DW's boss, Mike Tranter (5) ...., was there in the meeting room waiting for us all, and nobody turned up! Apparently, Mike had sent me an email that morning asking me to tell everyone the meeting was still on, but that (6) .... be the day I was too busy to check all my e-mails, wouldn't it! Mike was absolutely livid, and accused me of having no common sense (7) .... I tried to apologize and suggested we (8) .... rearrange the meeting, but he wasn't the (9) .... bit interested. From his point of view, not (10) .... did I fail to attend a meeting, but also I failed to communicate a vital message from him which he'd entrusted me with. No (11) .... had I emerged from Mike's office after a dressing-down that must have lasted for a good fifteen minutes, (12) .... who (13) .... phone me but DW, wanting to know exactly what had happened at the meeting. He (14) .... have arranged for Mike to chair the meeting in his place. Well, I feel as if I (15) .... as well go and hand in my resignation now. Any advice will be more than gratefully received from a desperate friend!

Margaret

8 Complete each sentence with a phrase containing a suitable form of the verb in brackets. Some negatives are needed.

1 But I only lent you the book this morning! You (finish) .....*can't have finished*..... it already!

2 I don't know who phoned, but I suppose it (might) .... Sophia.

3 Strange (seem) .... , Harry has never been to London.

4 Never (see) .... a more boring film!

5 I told you we would miss the train! We (leave) .... earlier!

6 I was just thinking about you. It's strange that (should) .... phoned me!

7 Try (might) .... , I just can't understand how this computer works!

8 Seldom (snow/fall) .... here in winter, even when it is very cold.

9 It rained every day on my holiday in France, so I (need) .... the suntan lotion after all!

10 Well, I thought the food was awful. It (can) .... the same restaurant you went to.

9 Complete each sentence with a suitable word.

1 Jean must ....*hare*....... had a good time in Denmark.

2 I'm sure .... was last week that I paid the bill.

3 I think Phil .... better stay in bed today.

4 The meals in the hotel were .... awful.

5 Really the whole house .... painting.

6 Strange .... it may seem, Mary likes it here.

7 This restaurant is .... place to be seen in this town.

8 This is my .... own recipe, actually.

9 Hardly had I entered the office, ... the phone started ringing.

10 After we had been on the beach for an hour, ... came the rain!

13

GRAMMAR

Reported speech

Problems

This unit assumes that the basic rules for forming reported speech are already known.

● The most important rule is to use verb forms that are natural in the situation.

'I'm happy to help you,' she said.

*She told me she **is** happy to help us.*

In the above example, the verb has not been put one stage back in the past. In the following example, the same is true.

'I wanted to go to the cinema, but John wasn't so keen,' said Sue.

*Sue said that she **wanted** to go to the cinema, but John wasn't so keen.*

● Reported speech with modal auxiliaries

If the reporting verb is in a past verb form, modals change where there is a 'past' equivalent.

will – would   can – could   may – might

Could, would, and *might* do not change.

*'I might be late.' She said (that) she **might** be late.*

Should changes to *would* if it is used as a first person form of *would*.

*'I should love to come.' She said (that) she **would** love to come.*

Otherwise should remains unchanged.

*'You should rest.' They said (that) I **should** rest.*

Must can be reported as either *had to* or remain as *must*.

● Reported speech with conditional sentences

After a past tense reporting verb, real situations include verb form changes.

'If we leave now, we'll catch the train.'

*I **told** him that if we **left** then we'**d catch** the train.*

In reported hypothetical situations, verb form changes are not made if the event has reference to a possible future.

'If you came back tomorrow, I'd be able to help you.'

*She said that if **I came back** the next day, she'**d be able to** help me.*

If the event is clearly hypothetical and impossible, time changes are made.

'If I had a spanner, I could fix it.'

*He said that if **he had had** a spanner **he could have fixed** it.*

Hypothetical past conditional sentences do not change.

● *Don't think*

Statements reported with verbs of thinking such as think, expect, suppose can transfer the negative from the statement to the verb.

I suppose she won't come. (I don't suppose she'll come.)

Reporting verbs

There are numerous reporting verbs, which report the words of others, or our own words and thoughts. Only a selection is given here. Other examples are included in the activities. Only the most useful categories are given here. It is advisable to use a dictionary to check on how reporting verbs are used. See Grammar 16, 17 and 18 for prepositions or -*ing* forms following verbs.

- Verbs followed by *that* + clause (with * can be followed by a person)

add	confirm	feel	predict	say
admit	consider	hope	*promise	state
agree	decide	imply	*reassure	suggest
announce	deny	insist	reckon	suppose
argue	doubt	mean	remark	*tell
believe	estimate	mention	repeat	think
claim	*expect	object	reply	*threaten
complain	explain	persuade	*report	*warn

- Verbs followed by person + *to*

advise	forbid	invite	persuade	tell
ask	instruct	order	remind	warn

- Verbs followed by subjunctive or **should**

    Most of these verbs can also be used in the other ways given.

    As these verbs contain the sense that someone 'should do' something, *should* can follow them.

    > They **suggested that she should** apply again.

    More formally, the subjunctive can be used instead of *should*. This is formed from the base of the verb (without third person *s*).

    > They **suggested that she apply** again.

    Some other verbs of this type are:

    advise (also: someone to do/against something)
    agree (also: to do something, *that* + clause)
    demand (also: to do something)
    insist (also: on someone doing something)
    prefer (also: someone to do something)
    propose (also: doing something)
    recommend (also: doing something)
    request (also: someone to do something)
    suggest (also: *that* + clause)
    urge (also: someone to do something)

- Verbs which can be followed by *that* + clause containing *would*

    All these verbs report statements containing *will*. These verbs can also be followed by 'to do something'.

    > *I'll leave at 8.00.*
    > *She decided **to leave** at 8.00.*
    > *She decided **(that) she would leave** at 8.00.*

    Others are: *expect, hope, promise, threaten.*

Functions

● Many verbs describe a function, rather than report words.

Look, if I were you I'd leave early.

She advised me to leave early.

Examples are:

admit	*complain*	*request*	*suggest*
advise	*invite*	*remind*	*warn*
agree	*persuade*	*threaten*	

● Some verbs describe actions.

Hi, Dave, how are you?

He greeted me.

Examples are:

accept, congratulate, decide, greet, interrupt, introduce

Changes of viewpoint

Changes of time, place and person reference are assumed known at this level. In reported speech, there is no longer a clear reference which can be understood by two people in the same place.

*I left the parcel on **this chair**.*

In reported speech one would have to specify which chair:

*He said he had left the parcel on **the chair by the window**.*

Or the reference may be replaced by a more general one:

I love this town.

*She said that she loved **the town**.*

ADVANCED LANGUAGE PRACTICE

1 <u>Underline</u> the correct word or phrase in each sentence.

1 The government spokesperson *denied*/*refused* that there was a crisis.
2 Jane *said me*/*told me* there was nothing the matter.
3 Peter *persuaded me*/*insisted me* to stay to dinner.
4 The director of studies *advised me*/*suggested me* to spend more time in the library.
5 Sheila *explained me*/*warned me* not to leave the heater on all night.
6 The chairperson *mentioned us*/*reminded us* that time was extremely short.
7 Bill *answered them*/*replied them* with a detailed description of his plans.
8 Michael and Sarah *announced*/*reported* that they were going to get married.
9 Paul *accepted*/*expected* that he had made a mistake, and apologized.
10 The manager *confirmed*/*reassured* that our room had been reserved.

2 Rewrite each sentence in reported speech, using the verbs given in a suitable verb form. Some may be negative.

1 'I think I'll take the brown pair,' said the customer.
   ...*The customer decided to take the brown pair.*...... (decide)
   .... (decide) + (will)
   .... (say) + (will)

2 'Me? No, I didn't take Sue's calculator.' said Bob.
   .... (deny)
   .... (deny that)

3 'Don't forget to buy some milk, Andy,' said Clare.
   .... (remind)
   .... (say) + (should)
   .... (remind) + (need)

4 'I'm sorry I couldn't come on Saturday,' said David.
   .... (say) + (could)
   .... (say) + (be able to)
   .... (apologize for)

5 'Why don't you go back to Singapore, Brian?' I said.
   .... (ask) + (do)
   .... (suggest) + (should)
   .... (suggest)

6 'Be sure not to leave too late, Tim,' said Jack.
   .... (say) + (should)
   .... (warn)
   .... (warn against)

3 **Complete the second sentence so that it has a similar meaning to the first sentence, using the word given. Do not change the word given.**

1 'Helen, would you like to come to lunch on Sunday?' asked Mary.

if

Mary .....*asked Helen if she would like*...... to come to lunch on Sunday.

2 'You are not allowed to smoke in your room, Dick,' said his mother.

forbade

Dick's mother .... in his room.

3 Sue thought it would be a good idea for me to see a doctor.

advised

Sue .... see a doctor.

4 The minister proposed regular meetings for the committee.

suggested

The minister .... should meet regularly.

5 Jack demanded urgent action from the police.

do

Jack demanded .... something urgently.

6 My bank manager invited me to visit him at home.

could

My bank manager .... visit him at home.

7 'No, I really don't want to stay the night, Sophia,' Ann said.

staying

Ann insisted .... the night at Sophia's house.

8 'I'll call off the football match if you don't behave,' the teacher said.

threatened

The teacher .... the children's behaviour improved.

9 'Ok mum, I'll do my homework, I promise,' said Laura.

that

Laura .... do her homework.

10 'Congratulations on getting engaged, Sue,' said Harry.

congratulated

Harry .... engagement.

4 <u>Underline</u> the most suitable word in each sentence.

1 I thought Jim would say something about his new job. But he didn't *mention/state/ declare* it.

2 Sorry, I wasn't being insulting. I simply *offered/reassured/remarked* that you seem to have put on rather a lot of weight recently.

3 The police *requested/estimated/advised* that the crowd was under 50,000, although the organizers of the march put it at nearer 100,000.

4 The children *complained/threatened/persuaded* that their parents were always checking up on them.

5 It has been *objected/hoped/predicted* that by the year 2050 some capital cities will be almost uninhabitable because of the effects of air pollution.

6 During the months before Smith's transfer from City, it had been *rumoured/ doubted/threatened* that he and the manager had come to blows in the dressing-room, though this was denied by the club.

7 Brown *forbade/recommended/claimed* that the arresting officers had treated him roughly, and that one of them had punched him in the eye.

8 An army spokesman stressed that all troops patrolling the streets had been *denied/ ordered/announced* to issue clear warnings before firing any shots.

9 Although he didn't say so directly, the Prime Minister *told/ordered/suggested* that an agreement between the two sides was within reach.

10 The witness *suggested/insisted/gave* her name and address to the court before the cross-examination began.

5 Complete the text by writing one word in each space.

The case of the break-in at a Cambridge college entered its third day today. The accused's defence was based on the fact that he (1) ....*could*......... not have entered the building at 6.30. He claimed (2) .... have been playing football at the time, and stated that several witnesses could confirm this. At this point, the prosecution (3) .... him of changing his story, as he had previously stated that he had been at home at the (4) .... of the break-in. The defendant agreed that his memory (5) .... not in the best of shape, as he had been (6) .... from bouts of depression. The judge stepped in, reminding the defendant that he (7) .... taken an oath to tell the truth, and warning (8) .... of the severe consequences of lying in court. The defendant said that he had simply forgotten (9) .... the football match, and insisted (10) .... he was not changing his story.

---

6 Complete the second sentence as a report of the first sentence.

1 'I wouldn't stay out in the cold for too long,' Jill told Tom.

Jill advised ...... *Tom not to stay out in the cold for too long.*..

2 'Don't forget to buy some milk, Andy,' Carol told Andy.

Carol reminded ....

3 'Don't go back into the house,' the fire fighter told Jack.

The firefighter warned ....

4 'If I were you, I'd stay near the airport,' the travel agent told us.

The travel agent recommended us ....

5 'Don't worry, you'll make a complete recovery,' the doctor told me.

The doctor reassured ....

6 'It's not true that I am getting married to Ann Jones,' Prince Gary told us.

Prince Gary denied ....

7 'Why don't you come round to my house for a meal,' Alan told me.

Alan invited ....

8 'Yes, it's true, I am expecting a baby,' Mary Hawkins told the press.

Mary Hawkins confirmed ....

7 Complete the text by writing a verb from the box in a suitable form in each space.

advise	announce	anticipate	~~apologize~~	assure	confirm
estimate	mention	report	request		

Dear Mrs Henderson

Thank you for your letter of 21st August.

We would like to (1) ....*apologize*......... for the failure of our computer ordering system last week and (2) .... you that the system is now fully functional again. We (3) .... that the goods ordered will be delayed by two or three working days and we (4) .... the new arrival time for your order will be the week beginning September 6th. We are grateful to you for (5) .... the defect in the ZP200 model and we are happy to (6) .... that the defect has now been remedied. In your letter you (7) .... the possibility of taking goods from us on 'sale or return' at an exhibition you are organizing. We can certainly (8) .... our interest in this arrangement, but we would like to (9) .... further information before we commit ourselves to a decision. Please be (10) .... that as of 1 September our warehouse is now open seven days a week from 8.00am to 8.00pm.

Yours sincerely

David Smith

David Smith

➜ SEE ALSO
Grammar 16: Verbs + infinitive or -ing
Grammar 17: Verbs + prepositions
Grammar 18: Prepositions

Articles

Definite article

Basic uses of articles are assumed known.

● Classes

   This is one way to refer to classes, and is perhaps more formal than using a plural:

   The tiger is threatened with extinction.

● National groups

   Groups as a whole:

   The French eat in restaurants more than the English.

   Single examples are not formed in the same way:

   a Frenchman/woman, an Englishman/woman

● Other groups

   If these are clearly plural:

   the Social Democrats, the Rolling Stones

● Unique objects

   the moon, the sun

   Note that there are other suns and moons in the universe.

   This planet has a small moon.

● Titles

   These tend to be 'unique'.

   the director of studies

   If the title is post-modified (has a description coming after the noun), *the* is more likely, but not essential. Compare:

   She became President in 2008.

   She became (the) president of the country in 2008.

● Other titles

   The may be part of the title, and so is capitalized.

   Newspapers: *The Independent, The Sunday Times*

● Musical instruments

   Jane plays the flute. (in general)

   The guitar is my favourite instrument. (in general)

   It is, of course, still possible to use an article when we refer to an object.

   There was a small brown flute in the window of the shop.

● Emphatic use

   This is heavily stressed and emphasizes the following noun.

   This hotel is the place to stay.

   See also Grammar 12.

- Geographical names
  The following use *the*:
      Rivers: ***the*** *Thames*
      Mountain ranges: ***the*** *Alps*
      Oceans: ***the*** *Mediterranean*
      Unique features: ***the*** *Channel,* ***the*** *Arctic*
      Compass points/areas: ***the*** *East,* ***the*** *Middle East*
      Countries: collective or plural: ***The*** *United Kingdom,* ***The*** *Netherlands*
  This does not apply to:
      Mountain peaks: *Everest* (but ***The*** *Matterhorn*)
      Lakes: *Lake Geneva*
      Continents: *Asia*
      Countries: *France*
  The definite article is sometimes used before *Lebanon* and *Gambia*:
      The *Lebanon*   ***The*** *Gambia*

- Place names
  Post-modification, especially with ... *of* ... plays a role in place names.
  Compare:
      Leeds University/***The*** University of Leeds
      London Bridge/***The*** Tower of London
  If the first part of a place-name is another name, then normal rules about zero article apply.
  Brown's Restaurant
      The *Garden House Hotel*
  The same applies in geographical names:
      Canvey Island
      The Isle of Man

- *Most* and *the most*
      Most *hotels in England are very expensive.* (making a generalization)
      This is ***the most*** *expensive hotel in town.* (talking about a specific hotel)

- Importance of context
  The definite article refers to already mentioned items, and so its use depends on context.
      The Smiths had a son and a daughter. ***The*** *son was in the Army and* ***the*** *daughter was training to be a doctor.*
      On ***the*** *Saturday, there was a terrible storm.*
  Here, *the Saturday* refers to a day in an area of time already mentioned.
      On the Saturday ***of that week*** *...*

Indefinite article

- Jobs
  Compare: *Tony is **a** builder. Tony was **the** builder of that house.*

- In measuring
  *Three times **a** week. Fifty kilometres **an** hour.*
  *£3.50 **a** kilo. £15,000 **a** year.*
  Formally, *per* can replace *a/an*.
  *She was convicted of driving at more than 120 kilometres **per** hour.*

- Unknown people
  Use of *a/an* emphasizes that a person is unknown.
  ***A** Mr Jones called while you were out.*

Zero article

- Names
  Compare:
  Matthew Smith is one of my favourite artists. (a person)
  ***A** Matthew Smith hangs in their bedroom.* (a painting)

- Some unique organizations do not use *the*.
  Parliament, but The (House of) Commons

- Streets
  Most streets do not use an article.
  Green Road   Godwin Street
  Common exceptions are:
  The High Street   The Strand
  and street names without preceding adjectives. Compare:
  Holly Drive   The Drive

Translation problems

Study these sentences. Would you use an article in your language?
I really like rugby.
A pound and a half of cheese.
I was holding it in my hand.
It's a film about homeless people.
Terry has flu. I've got a headache.

1 Complete the text by writing *a/an* or *the* in each space, or leave the space blank.

It has been announced that for (1) ....the.......... third consecutive month
there has been (2) .... rise in (3) .... number of
(4) .... people unemployed, rather than (5) .... fall that
had been predicted. (6) .... rise was blamed on (7) ....
continuing uncertainty over (8) .... government economic policy,
and couldn't come at (9) .... worse time for (10) ....
Prime Minister, who is facing (11) .... growing criticism over
(12) .... way (13) .... present crisis is being handled.
(14) .... MPs are increasingly voicing (15) .... fears that
despite (16) .... recent reduction of (17) .... business
taxes and cuts in (18) .... interest rates, (19) ....
government still expects (20) .... recovery of the economy to take
three or even four years. To make (21) .... matters worse,
(22) .... number of small businesses going into (23) ....
liquidation is still at (24) .... record level, and (25) ....
housing market is showing no signs of recovery. Some backbenchers expect
(26) .... general election before (27) .... end of
(28) .... winter unless there is (29) .... rapid change of
(30) .... fortune.

2 <u>Underline</u> the most suitable option. A dash (–) means that no article is included.

1 Helen doesn't like *the*/– cream cakes sold in *a/the* local bakery.
2 *The*/– handball is fast becoming *a/the* popular sport worldwide.
3 We could see that *the*/– Alps were covered in *the*/– snow.
4 It's *a*/– long time since I met *a*/– lovely person like you!
5 Carol has *a*/– degree in *the*/– engineering from *the*/– University of London.
6 At *the*/– present moment, *the*/– man seems to have *the/an* uncertain future.
7 *The*/– problem for *the*/– today's students is how to survive financially.
8 *The*/– French enjoy spending holidays in *the*/– countryside.
9 Please do not turn on *a/the* water-heater in *a/the* bathroom.
10 Sue bought *a/the* Picasso I was telling you about *the*/– last week.

3 Correct any errors in these sentences.

1 It's not a first-class accommodation unless it has a private bathroom.
   It's not first-class accommodation unless it has a private bathroom.

2 On this record twins play piano duet.

3 The halfway through meal we realized what waiter had said.

4 If the Mrs Hillier phones, say I'm away on trip.

5 There is a wonderful scenery in eastern part of Turkey.

6 Cocker spaniel is one of most popular pet dogs.

7 There is going to be fog and a cold weather all the next week.

8 I spent very interesting holiday at the Lake Coniston in England.

9 We are against war in general, so of course we are against war like this between superpower and developing country.

10 The burglaries are definitely on increase.

4 Complete each sentence with *a/an* or <u>the</u>, or leave the space blank.

1 I'm going to stand for Parliament at ....*the*........ next election.

2 When I left .... station, I had to stand in .... queue for .... taxi for .... long time.

3 We took .... trip around London and saw .... Tower Bridge.

4 .... happiness of the majority depends on .... hard work for everyone.

5 .... most main roads in this part of .... country follow .... line of .... roads built by .... Romans.

6 Have you got .... the new album by .... *Anxious Frogs*?

7 If I had .... time, I would like to take up .... archery.

8 We spent .... pleasant evening having .... meal at .... Pizza Pan Restaurant.

9 .... Nile flows right through .... city.

10 .... summer I spent in .... USA was one of .... best in my life.

5 Complete each sentence with *a/an* or *the*, or leave the space blank.

1 She was ....*the*........ first woman to cross .... Atlantic in
.... canoe.

2 Go down .... High Street and turn right into .... Mill Road.

3 Please let me carry .... shopping. It's .... least I can do.

4 I don't like .... milk in .... coffee.

5 At .... end of .... busy day, ... sleep is
.... best tonic.

6 .... James Joyce I knew wasn't .... novelist and wasn't
.... Irish either.

7 We'll go for .... walk if .... sun comes out.

8 This is .... last time I do you .... favour for a while.

9 I'm staying in .... Hilton so you can leave me .... message.

10 Jim became .... furniture salesman after losing .... first job he
had.

6 There are ten extra appearances of *the* in the following text. <u>Underline</u> them.

Word processing and the calculator are without a shadow of doubt here to stay, and in <u>the</u> many respects our lives are the much richer for them. But the teachers and other academics are claiming that we are now starting to feel the first significant wave of their effects on a generation of the users. It seems nobody under the age of 20 can spell or add up any more. Even several professors at leading universities have commented on the detrimental effect the digital revolution has had on the most intelligent young minds in the country. At the root of one part of the problem, evidently, lies the automatic spellcheck now widely available on the word processing software. Professor John Silver of the Sydney University, Australia, said: 'Why should we bother to learn how to spell correctly, or for that matter to learn even the most basic of the mathematical sums, when at the press of a button we have our problem answered for us? The implications are enormous. Will the adults of the future look to the computer to make the decisions for them, to tell them who to marry or what kind of the house to buy? Are we heading for a future individual incapable of the independent human thought?'

7 Complete each sentence with *a/an* or *the*, or leave the space blank.

1   Please watch ....the........ cabin attendant as she demonstrates .... use of .... oxygen mask.

2   Paul spent .... half of his life in .... Far East.

3   You have to use at .... least .... pint and .... half of milk.

4   Dick has .... sore throat and is taking .... medicine.

5   We arranged .... accommodation on .... outskirts of .... city.

6   There is .... very difficult crossword in '...................... Times'.

7   Could you give me .... information I asked for in .... letter I sent you?

8   I bought .... jewellery for my sister but it wasn't .... kind she likes.

9   I always wanted to be .... astronaut but .... ambition wore off.

10 And .... last of all, don't forget to put .... cat out for .... night.

8 Underline the most suitable option. A dash *(−)* means that no article is needed.

1   Brenda is *the/−* ideal for *a/the* job. She has *a/−* wealth of *the/−* experience.

2   *The/−* safety at *the/−* work is *a/−* major concern for us.

3   *The/−* poorest people in *the/−* country live in this city.

4   Have you seen *a/the* new 'Hamlet' at *the/−* National Theatre?

5   There is *a/−* beautiful countryside within *an/−* easy reach of *a/the* hotel.

6   I have *a/−* terrible cold and am staying in *the/−* bed today.

7   I earn £3 *an/the* hour as *a/−* supermarket cashier on *the/−* Saturdays.

8   *The/−* charge for *an/−* excess luggage is £10 *a/the* kilo.

9   *The/−* most of *the/−* life is *a/−* matter of getting on with *the/−* others.

10 Britain is officially called *The/−* United Kingdom of *The/−* Great Britain and *The/−* Northern Ireland.

15

GRAMMAR

Relative clauses and non-finite clauses

Defining and non-defining

- Defining
  A defining clause specifies which person or thing we mean. It cannot be separated from the person or thing it describes.
  *By 4.30, there was only one painting **which hadn't been sold**.*

- Non-defining
  A non-defining clause contains extra information. In writing it is separated by commas, and in speech, if used at all, is usually indicated by intonation.
  *By 4.30, **which was almost closing time**, nearly all the paintings had been sold.*
  Some of the points given below depend on the type of clause.

Which and *that*

- These are alternatives in a defining clause, although *which* is felt to be more formal.
  *By 4.30, there was only one painting **that** hadn't been sold.*

- *That* is not normally used to introduce a non-defining clause.
  *The train, **which was already an hour late**, broke down again.*

- *That* cannot follow a preposition.
  *It was a service **for which** I will be eternally grateful.*

- *That* is often used instead of **who** in everyday speech in defining clauses.
  *Do you know the girl **that** lives next door?*

Who and *whom*

- *Whom* is the object form of *who* and is used formally in object clauses.
  *He was a person **whom** everyone regarded as trustworthy.*
  However, this is now felt to be excessively formal by most speakers and *who* is commonly used instead.

- *Whom* has to be used if it follows a preposition.
  ***To whom** it may concern.*
  ***To whom** am I speaking?*
  However, in everyday use, it is usual to avoid this kind of construction.
  Who am I speaking to?
  See *when* and *where* on the next page.

Whose

This means 'of whom'. It is used in both defining and non-defining clauses.

> *Several guests, **whose** cars were parked outside, were waiting at the door.*
>
> *Several guests **whose** rooms had been broken into complained to the manager.*

When and *where*

- Non-defining

Here they follow a named time or place.

> *Come back at 3.30, **when** I won't be so busy.*
>
> *I stopped in Maidstone, **where** my sister owns a shop.*

- Defining

When follows words such as *time, day, moment.*

> *There is hardly a **moment when** I don't think of you, Sophia.*

Where follows words such as *place, house, street.*

> *This is the **street where** I live.*

Omitting the relative pronoun

This is common in defining object clauses especially in everyday conversation.

> *I've found the keys (which/that) I've been looking for.*
>
> *That's the man (who/that) I was telling you about.*
>
> *He was a person (who/that) everyone regarded as trustworthy.*

Sentences ending in a preposition or phrasal verb

Another common feature of conversational English, as outlined in *who* and *whom* above, is to end a defining clause with a preposition.

> *That's the house I used to live **in**.*
>
> *I couldn't remember which station to get off **at**.*
>
> *He's not someone who I really get on **with**.*

Omitting *which/who* + *be*

It may be possible to reduce a verb phrase after *who/which* to an adjectival phrase in a defining clause, especially to define phrases such as *the only one, the last/first one.*

> *Jim was the only one of his platoon who had not been taken prisoner.*
>
> *Jim was the only one of his platoon **not taken prisoner**.*
>
> *By 4.30, there was only one painting which had not been sold.*
>
> *By 4.30, there was only one painting **not sold**.*

Which

A non-defining clause can comment on the whole situation described in the main clause.

> *There was nobody left on the train, **which** made me suspicious.*

Phrases with which, such as *at which time/point, in which case, by which time, in which event* can be used in the same way.

> *I watched the play until the end of the first act, **at which point** I felt I had seen enough.*
>
> *A warning sign 'Overheat' may come on, **in which case** turn off the appliance at once.*

Clauses beginning with *what* and *whatever*

● *What* meaning 'the thing' or 'things which' can be used to start clauses.

> I can't believe **what you told me** yesterday.
> **What you should do** is write a letter to the manager.

See Grammar 12 for emphasis.

● *Whatever, whoever, whichever* can be used in a similar way.

> You can rely on Helen to do **whatever she can**.
> **Whoever arrives first** can turn on the heating.

Non-finite clauses containing an *-ing* form

These are clauses without a main verb. The examples given here are non-defining. Note that the two clauses have the same subject.

● Actions happening at the same time

> **Waving their scarves and shouting**, the fans ran onto the pitch.

● One action happening before another

> **Opening the letter**, she found that it contained a cheque for £1,000.

This type of clause often explains the reason for something happening.

> **Realizing there was no one at home**, I left the parcel in the shed.

Both these types of sentence might begin with *on* or *upon*:

> **On** opening the letter …   **Upon** realizing …

● An event which is the result of another event

> I didn't get wet, **having remembered to take my umbrella**.

● Where a passive construction might be expected, this is often shortened to a past participle.

> *Having been abandoned by his colleagues, the Minister was forced to resign.*
> **Abandoned by his colleagues**, the Minister was forced to resign.

ADVANCED LANGUAGE PRACTICE

1 **There are ten extra appearances of *which* or *that*. Underline them.**

Having just spent three weeks of my life sitting on an uncomfortable saddle, pounding the roads of France, I am in no fit state <u>that</u> to do anything except sit and write, which suits me fine. For I have cycled some 1,500 kilometres, a figure which includes some extremely hilly routes, and frankly the thought of mounting a bicycle again which is not one that I can face for a good few days yet. The journey, which I undertook alone for most of the way, was all in the name of charity – Help the Aged, a cause which I support whenever that I can. Having organized my sponsorship, which I arrived in France armed only with a tiny map of the Tour de France route, which hastily removed from last month's 'Cycling World' magazine. My intention which was to try and follow the route that the professionals take, but after three days in which I pushed my body to extremes that it had never experienced before, that I rapidly abandoned this plan and returned to flatter ground. On the flat which I was able to keep to about 120 kilometres a day, which is respectable. I did have to rest my weary limbs at the weekends, though, which enabled me to recharge my batteries, by which I mean my bodily ones, not the ones that inside my bike lights. I am pleased to say that after three tortuous weeks which I ended up in Marseilles, but what pleased me all the more is that I managed to raise over £2,000 for Help the Aged.

2 **Complete each sentence with a suitable word.**

1 Midway through the second half City scored their fourth goal, at ......*which*...... point United gave up completely.

2 There is one person to .... I owe more than I can say.

3 It was the kind of accident for .... nobody was really to blame.

4 .... leaves last should turn off the lights.

5 Mary was late yesterday, ... was unusual for her.

6 At 6.00, ... was an hour before the plane was due, thick fog descended.

7 I don't know .... told you that, but they were wrong.

8 The first time I saw you was .... you answered the door.

9 Mrs Brown was the first owner .... dog won three prizes in the same show.

10 I've just spoken to Sally, ... sends you her love.

3 Complete the second sentence so that it has a similar meaning to the first sentence, using the word given. Do not change the word given.

1 I waited for him until 6.30 and then gave up.

which

I waited for him until 6.30, ...*at which point I*........................ gave up.

2 We suggested a lot of things, which were all rejected.

was

Everything .... rejected.

3 If anyone can understand this application form, they are cleverer than I am.

is

Anyone .... cleverer than I am.

4 I won't tell you this again, you naughty boy.

time

This .... tell you, you naughty boy.

5 The whole summer was sunny and warm, for a change.

made

The whole summer was sunny and warm, ... nice change.

6 I don't really approve of his proposal.

what

I don't really approve of .... proposing.

7 The police never caught the culprit.

committed

The police never caught .... the crime.

8 I have read all of her books but one.

that

There is only .... I have not read.

9 I can't remember the last heavy rain.

when

I can't remember .... heavily.

10 Do you get on with your next-door neighbour?

who

Do you get on with .... lives next door?

4 Make one sentence from the sentences given, beginning as shown. Make any other necessary changes. Omit any unnecessary relative pronouns.

1 We eventually caught a train. It was one that stops at every station.

The train ....*we eventually caught was one that stops*.................. at every station.

2 Carol slammed the door behind her. Her father had given her a car as a present. She drove off in it.

Slamming ....

....

3 At the end of the street was a building. The street was crowded with shoppers. Tom had not noticed the building before.

At the end of the street ....

....

4 Some people have just moved in next door. They have the same surname as some other people. Those other people have just moved out.

The people who have just moved in next door ....

....

5 I noticed that the door was open. I decided to go in. This turned out to be a mistake.

Noticing ....

....

6 Everyone expects the Popular Party candidate, Flora Benstead, to win the election. She has announced that she will cut income tax by 10% if elected.

Flora Benstead, ...

....

7 I listened to George patiently until he started insulting me. At that point, I told him a few home truths. He didn't like it.

I listened to George patiently until he started insulting me, ...

....

8 Pauline asked me a question. I had no reply to it.

Pauline asked me ....

....

9 He rushed out of the room. He was shouting at the top of his voice. This was typical.

Shouting ....

....

10 Some people wanted travel scholarships. The end of the week was the deadline. By then everyone had applied.

....

....

5 Correct the error in each sentence. Omit any unnecessary relative pronouns in your corrections.

1   To take my life in my hands, I walked to the very end of the high diving board. ......
.... *Taking my life in ...* ....

2   I wasn't sure what to address the letter to, so I put 'The Manager'.
....

3   Most of the guests turned up two hours early, that took us by surprise.
....

4   Whoever that he spoke to last was probably the person who murdered him.
....

5   The book I bought for his birthday is one where I enjoyed very much myself.
....

6   There's a chance that I may be late, in that case I'll phone you.
....

7   Everyone admires her. She's the kind of person whose everyone looks up to.
....

8   No one knows who she is. She is the only member of the gang who the identity
remained a secret. ....
.

6 Correct any errors in punctuation in these sentences.

1   Many people think that Saturn is the biggest planet which is wrong.
.... *... is the biggest planet, which ...* ....

2   That's the man, I used to live next door to.
....

3   I couldn't remember, which house I had to deliver the card to.
....

4   The coat she wore to the party, was similar to one I have at home.
....

5   Lynn is the only person in my circle of friends, who is married.
....

6   Whoever catches the ball, must come into the middle of the circle.
....

16

GRAMMAR

Verbs + infinitive or *-ing*

This unit focuses on problem areas.

Verbs followed by either *-ing* or infinitive with *to*

- *Can't bear, hate, like, love, prefer*
  Like to usually refers to habitual preferences.
  > We **like to** go out to lunch on Sunday.
  Not like to means 'think it is wrong to'.
  > I **don't like to** disturb colleagues at home.

- *Attempt, begin, continue, intend, plan, propose, start*
  There is no difference in meaning whether we use *-ing* or infinitive with *to*.
  Intend, plan, and *propose* can be followed by *that* + clause. This may include *should*.
  See Grammar 13 for reporting verbs.

- *Forget, remember*
  With *to* both verbs refer to an obligation.
  > I **had to** phone the office but I **forgot to** do it.
  With *-ing* both verbs refer to past events.
  > I don't **remember learning** to walk.
  Both can be followed by *that* + clause.
  > I **remembered that** I had to pay the phone bill.

- *Try*
  With *to* this refers to something attempted, which might fail or succeed.
  > I **tried to warn** him, but it was too late.
  With *-ing* this refers to making an experiment, or to a new experience.
  > **Try taking** an aspirin. You'll feel better.
  > **Have** you **tried windsurfing**? It's great!

- *Go on*
  With *-ing* this refers to the continuing of an action.
  > She **went on working** even though it was late.
  With *to* this refers to the continuation of a speech.
  > The Prime Minister **went on to praise** the Chancellor.
  (This means the Prime Minister continued his speech by praising the Chancellor.)

- *Mean*
  With the meaning *intend*, this is followed by *to*.
  > Sorry, I **meant to tell** you about the party.
  With *-ing*, and an impersonal subject, this refers to what is involved.
  > If we catch the early train, it will **mean getting up** at 6.00.
  That + clause is possible when meaning is being explained.
  > This **means that you have to report to the police station**.

● *Regret*

With *to* this refers to the speaker's regrets about what is going to be said. *It* often occurs in formal statements of this kind.

> We **regret to inform** you that your application has been unsuccessful.

With *-ing* this refers to a regret about the past.

> I **regret saying** that to him.

That + clause is also possible.

> We **regret that we didn't tell her earlier**.

● *Stop*

With *to* this refers to an intention.

> Jane **stopped to check** the oil level in the engine.

With *-ing* this refers to the ending of an activity.

> The baby has **stopped waking** up during the night now.

● *Hear, see, watch*

When followed by infinitive without *to*, the action is complete.

> We **watched** all the cars **cross** the finishing line.

With *-ing,* the action is still in progress.

> I **heard** someone **coming** up the stairs.

Verbs with an object, followed by either *-ing* or infinitive with *to*:

> Allow, forbid, permit

With an object and *to*:

> The school **forbids** students **to smoke** in the classrooms.

With an object *-ing* form:

> The school does not **allow/forbid/permit smoking**.

● *Consider*

With an object and *to* this refers to an opinion.

> She **is considered to be the finest pianist of her generation**.

With *-ing* this means 'think about'.

> At one point I **considered emigrating** to Canada.

With *that* + clause it refers to an opinion.

> We **consider that she has behaved badly**.

● *Imagine*

With an object and *to*:

> I **imagined** the castle to be haunted.

With *-ing,* an object is also possible.

> I couldn't **imagine (her) living** in a place like that.

With *that* + clause it means 'suppose'.

> I **imagine that you'd like** a cup of tea after your long journey!

● *Require*

With an object and *to*:

> They **required him to** fill out a form.

With *-ing*:

> These letters **require typing**.

See Grammar 6 for *needs doing*.

Verbs normally followed by infinitive with *to*

- Verbs marked * can also be followed by *that* + clause.

*agree	*demand	hurry	*pledge	*swear
*appear	deserve	*learn	*pretend	*threaten
*arrange	*expect	long	*promise	*vow
attempt	fail	manage	refuse	want
ask	grow	neglect	*resolve	*wish
choose	hasten	offer	seek	
dare	*happen	pay	*seem	
*decide	*hope	*plan	struggle	

- *Appear, (so) happen* and *seem* are only used impersonally with *that* + clause.
  It **appears that I've made a mistake**.
  It so **happens that he is my brother!**
  It seems **that Mary is going to win**.

- *Want* can be used colloquially with *-ing*, and has a similar meaning to *need*.
  The car **wants cleaning**.

Verbs normally followed by *-ing*

- Verbs marked * can also be followed by *that* + clause.

*appreciate	face	*suggest
avoid	*fancy	it's no good/use
contemplate	finish	feel like
delay	involve	give up
*deny	*mention	keep on
detest	mind	leave off
dislike	miss	look forward to
endure	postpone	put off
enjoy	practise	can't stand
escape	*resent	spend/waste time
excuse	risk	

- *Admit*
  This can be used with or without preposition *to* followed by *-ing*.
  They **admitted (to) being** members of the gang.
  That + clause is also possible.
  He **admitted that he was wrong**.

- *Appreciate* is often followed by possessive + *-ing*.
  I **appreciate your trying** to help.

- See Grammar 13 for *suggest*.

- *Involve* has an impersonal subject.
  Being an athlete **involves regular training**.

Verbs followed by infinitive without *to*

- *Help* can be used with or without *to*.
  I **helped** George **(to) carry** the bags.

- *Make*, and expressions with *make*
  They **made me leave**.
  We shall have to **make do**.
  In the passive, *to* is used.
  I was made **to leave**.

- *Let* and expressions with *let*
  They didn't **let me leave**.
  Let me go!

Verbs followed by an object and *to*

- Verbs marked * can also be followed by *that* + clause.
  *advise, assist, beg, bribe, command, dare, employ, enable, encourage, instruct, invite, lead, *order, *persuade, select, send, *teach, *tell, train, urge, *warn*
  See Grammar 13 for *advise, persuade, tell, warn*.

- *Dare* can be used without **to** when there is no object. Compare:
  They **dared** him to jump.
  I didn't **dare** (to) say anything.
  See Grammar 9 for *dare* as a modal verb.

ADVANCED LANGUAGE PRACTICE

1 <u>Underline</u> the word or phrase that is correct.

1 What do you mean *to do*/*doing* about the leaky pipes?
2 I never imagined the mountains *to be*/*being* so high!
3 Don't forget *to wake me*/*waking me* before you leave.
4 I regret *to tell you*/*telling you* that we cannot accept your offer.
5 Did you manage *to find*/*finding* the book you were looking for?
6 I tried *to take*/*taking* that medicine you gave me but I couldn't swallow it.
7 We have postponed *to tell*/*telling* anyone the news until after Christmas.
8 Have you considered *to buy*/*buying* a laptop?
9 Sorry I'm late, I had to stop *to pick up*/*picking* up the children from school.
10 Margaret was slow at school, but she went on *to be*/*being* Prime Minister.

2 Complete each sentence with a suitable form of a verb from the box.

look forward to	die	arrange	consider	~~do~~
grow	appear	intend	dare	face

1 It's too late to buy any food. We'll have to make ......*do*...... with what we've got.
2 I hardly .... ask how much it cost!
3 Have you ever .... taking a year off work?
4 I didn't like the town at first, but I .... to love it eventually.
5 What do you .... doing after this course has finished?
6 We are all .... our holiday in Australia this year. It's going to be such an adventure!
7 Jim and I .... to meet at 6.00 but he didn't turn up.
8 It .... that we won't need to pay so much after all.
9 I can't wait for Saturday! I'm really .... to see you!
10 I can't .... getting up at 6.30 tomorrow morning! I'll catch a later train.

3 Complete the second sentence so that it has a similar meaning to the first sentence, using the word given. Do not change the word given.

1 It's very kind of you to give me a lift.

   appreciate

   I ....*appreciate you giving*............... me a lift.

2 If I take the job I'll have to move to Paris.

   mean

   Taking .... moving to Paris.

3 Parking is not permitted here.

   park

   You are .... here.

4 'Shall I carry that bag for you, Pauline?' said John.

   offered

   John .... bag for her.

5 Winning the lottery meant we could buy a new car.

   enabled

   Winning the lottery .... buy a new car.

6 There is a risk that he will miss the plane if he waits.

   risks

   He .... if he waits.

7 I believed you were the murderer because of this clue.

   led

   This clue .... that you were the murderer.

8 Does using the hotel swimming pool cost extra?

   pay

   Do you have to .... the hotel swimming pool?

9 I think that this is the right street.

   appears

   This .... the right street.

10 Jean succeeded in finishing all her work on time.

   managed

   Jean .... all her work on time.

4 Complete the second sentence so that it has a similar meaning to the first sentence, using the word given. Do not change the word given.

1 They said they would like me to stay with them in Florida.

invited

They .... *invited me to* .... stay with them in Florida.

2 Calling Jim is pointless, because his phone is out of order.

use

It's no .... because his phone is out of order.

3 It is compulsory for all students to carry an identity badge.

required

All students .... carry an identity badge.

4 You waste time if you copy your work out again, so don't do it.

copying

Don't .... your work out again.

5 I bet you wouldn't ask David to come with you to the party!

if

I dare .... to the party with you!

6 'Please don't leave me on my own,' Martin begged us.

him

Martin begged us .... own.

7 Joe doesn't like it when people treat him like a child.

resents

Joe .... like a child.

8 It was resolved that the matter would be brought up at the next meeting.

bring

They resolved .... up at the next meeting.

9 The police were told that the use of unnecessary force was forbidden.

not

The police were instructed .... unnecessary force.

10 If you work for this company, you have to travel a lot.

involves

Working for this company .... of travel.

5 Complete each sentence with a suitable form of the verb in brackets.

1 Sorry, I meant (tell) ......*to tell you*...... I would be out, but I forgot.

2 That's all for now. I (hope) .... hear from you soon!

3 If I take the new job, it (mean) .... working a lot harder!

4 Are you still tired? Or do (feel) .... going out for a meal?

5 Jane is (say) .... the most outstanding player in the team.

6 I wish you (keep) .... complaining all the time!

7 How (suggest) .... that I would take a bribe! I've never been so insulted!

6 Complete the text with the gerund or infinitive of the verbs in brackets.

Yukie Hanue is considered by many (1) ......*to be*........ (be) the finest violinist of her generation – and she's still in her early twenties. When we visited her, in the music department of the University of New York, she was too busy practising (2) .... (talk), but she invited us (3) .... (have) a coffee with her in her mid-morning break. Astonishingly, she manages (4) .... (combine) her PhD at the university with international concerts and recitals, numerous public appearances and interviews. She evidently thrives on the workload, buzzing around the place with an industrious enthusiasm that leaves us all breathless. Her fame as a performer means (5) .... (make) regular appearances at high profile events. Last month, for example, she agreed (6) .... (appear) in a series of recitals organized by UNESCO. This involved (7) .... (travel) to far-flung places like Seoul, Oslo and Montevideo on successive days, a schedule which would have caused any normal person to wilt. 'I can't stand (8) .... (do) nothing,' she says. 'I happen (9) .... (have) a particular talent, and it would be wasteful not (10) .... (exploit) it to the full.' I encouraged her (11) .... (tell) me about her upbringing, but she was rather reticent to sing her own praises. I did, however, succeed in persuading her (12) .... (confess) to a secret desire. 'If I hadn't been a musician, I would have loved to train (13) .... (become) a martial arts expert,' she says. Certainly, she would have had the discipline, but I couldn't imagine someone so physically frail actually (14) .... (stand) there hitting someone. But it was an interesting revelation, and one that I was (15) .... (learn) more about during my day with her.

Units 10–16

1 Complete the second sentence so that it has a similar meaning to the first sentence, using the word given. Do not change the word given.

1 You haven't seen my pen anywhere, have you?

   happen

   You don't ....*happen to have seen*............ my pen anywhere, have you?

2 Everything I told you was true.

   all

   I told you a lot .... which were true.

3 According to reports, the President is in poor health.

   reported

   The President .... in poor health.

4 Julia's inheritance meant that she could give up work.

   enabled

   Julia's inheritance .... give up work.

5 Stupidly, I left my umbrella at home.

   which

   I left my umbrella at home, ... thing to do.

6 We received a warning to stay at home.

   should

   We were .... stay at home.

7 You could easily become ill unless you give up smoking.

   risk

   If you don't stop .... ill.

8 The decorators didn't leave too much mess when they did the job.

   without

   The decorators managed .... too much mess.

9 It's pointless to worry about someone else's problems.

   no

   There .... about someone else's problems.

10 According to Valerie, she is a relation of mine.

   be

   Valerie claims .... to me.

2 Complete each sentence with *a/an* or *the,* or leave the space blank.

1 That's ....the... last time that I go to .... horror film.

2 In .... circumstances I would say he hasn't .... chance.

3 I'd like to buy .... piano .... one day but I haven't got .... money.

4 Could you give me .... hand to take .... rubbish downstairs?

5 .... girl I told you about is .... one on .... left.

6 .... address is: .... Park Hotel, 42 .... Castle Road, ... Dover.

7 Mary spent .... year and .... half teaching .... children in .... Africa.

8 .... medicine .... doctor gave me makes me feel tired all .... day.

9 Dawson put .... ball in .... net early in .... second half but .... goal was disallowed.

10 .... teacher with .... best exam results in .... school was Mrs Anderson.

3 Complete each sentence with a suitable form of the verb in brackets.

1 I didn't know where (send) ....to send........... the parcel to, so I left it on the desk.

2 If you feel so tired in the morning, why (try) .... going to bed earlier!

3 The returning officer announced to the crowd that the Democratic candidate (win) ....

4 If I took a job like that, it (mean) .... earning less money.

5 Do you still feel ill? Or (fancy) .... coming shopping with me tomorrow?

6 I saw Harry arrive, but I don't remember (see) .... him leave.

7 All my family were sitting in the front row, which (make) .... nervous.

8 There is a rumour that the army is about to take power, though this (deny) .... by government sources.

9 Sandra trained (be) .... an architect but ended up as a rock star.

10 It's hard (believe) .... that Jim would be so brave.

4 Complete the second sentence so that it has a similar meaning to the first sentence, using the word given. Do not change the word given.

1 Does parking here cost anything?

pay

Do I need .... to pay for parking .... here?

2 After six months, Joe's search for a job was successful.

managed

After six months, Joe .... a job.

3 Jean was given permission by her boss to take a day off.

agreed

Jean's boss .... take a day off

4 Although Sue looked for the book for a long time, she couldn't find it.

spent

Sue .... , without success.

5 All visitors to the town fall in love with it.

those

All .... fall in love with it.

6 The manager warned Tom that they might dismiss him.

threatened

The manager .... dismissal.

7 I didn't expect to see you here!

last

This is .... to see you!

8 We haven't seen one another for a long time.

other

We stopped .... ago.

9 I don't know who did the washing up, but they didn't do it very well!

make

Whoever .... good job of it!

10 Janet came first, which surprised nobody.

when

Nobody .... Janet came first.

5 Complete the text with *the* where it is appropriate, or leave the space blank.

(1) ....The.... 6.45 train, which went from Winchester to Southampton, was already full of (2) .... commuters when Rale boarded it with fifteen minutes to go before its departure. He registered (3) .... vague annoyance at this, as it meant he had to actually communicate with a fellow passenger in order to find (4) .... one remaining window seat in his normal carriage, (5) .... carriage 3. Rale always made a point of travelling in the middle carriage for (6) .... safety's sake – about such things as (7) .... safety he was meticulous – and would only venture into (8) .... first four carriages, or for that matter (9) .... last four, in (10) .... extreme emergencies. Rale was nothing if not a creature of (11) .... habit; it bothered him intensely if he was unable to get a window seat or if (12) .... drinks trolley didn't come round, or worse still, it came but (13) .... hot water boiler wasn't working and so (14) .... coffee was not available. A brioche and a cup of coffee – black, one sugar – was Rale's early-morning indulgence. He found it sufficed for a breakfast, unless he was unusually hungry. Exactly ten minutes into (15) .... journey, Rale opened his briefcase and took out his copy of that morning's *Guardian* newspaper, neatly folded, and began (16) .... crossword. This was (17) .... time of day Rale liked best. He could immerse himself in (18) .... delightful challenge of teasing out words from his mind, and put off (19) .... thoughts of work in the administrative department of (20) .... Southampton Hospital. Today, however, Rale's neatly planned existence was to be well and truly turned on its head.

6 Complete each sentence with a suitable word.

1 There is nobody for ....whom....... we feel greater respect.
2 That's the couple .... house my sister bought.
3 .... buys the wardrobe will have to arrange to pick it up themselves.
4 Why don't you .... phoning Directory Inquiries? They might know.
5 Do you .... going out for a pizza later on?
6 That's an experience I .... rather forget.
7 The police officer .... us open the boot of the car.
8 It is recommended that all luggage .... bear a personal label.
9 The children always look .... to Christmas as they love all the parties and presents.
10 Charles is not the kind of person .... would help you.

7 Correct the error in each sentence.

1 My friends gave me a surprise party, it was good of them.
...... *party, which was good of them*

2 The inspector denied to say whether Peter was a suspect or not.
....

3 I afraid to say that your application has been unsuccessful.
....

4 Several people, which voices could be clearly heard, were waiting outside.
....

5 I don't know that you'd like another cat, would you?
....

6 The manager insisted that all the customers could be searched.
....

7 What you should do now means take a long holiday.
....

8 Whatsoever happens, I shall stand by you.
....

9 Sarah congratulated me with passing my driving test.
....

10 I left at 5.30 at that time they were still arguing.
....

11 The robbers forced the manager hand over the money.
....

12 I'm really looking forward to see you next Friday.
....

8 Complete the text by writing one word in each space.

It now seems clear that one of the most pressing problems (1) ...*which*... faces any large city during (2) .... first half of the twenty-first century, is that of water supply. While most cities were founded in places (3) .... water was plentifully available, no one could have foreseen the way (4) .... which some of these cities have expanded. Large numbers of people demand more and more water, which (5) .... that cities have to compete with other non-human water users, for water is not only a commodity needed for washing-machines and industrial processes. Many lakes (6) .... once served as breeding grounds for wild birds now face an uncertain future. As cities make greater demands upon the available water resources, we (7) .... losing more and more of our aquatic wildlife. And quite apart from this environmental problem, there is the economic issue to consider. Who owns the water, and how much should (8) .... consumer pay for it? The next time you decide (9) .... turn on the tap, you might (10) .... some of these problems, before you have wasted too much water.

17

GRAMMAR

Verbs + prepositions

This unit focuses on a selection of verbs, including their adjectival forms. Many verbs have other uses followed by *-ing* or infinitive (see Grammar 15, 16). Passive uses with *by* are not included. See also Grammar 19, 20, 21.

Verbs followed by *about*

argue about something
be concerned about something (*be worried about*)
boast about something
decide about something
protest about something
phase something *out*

Verbs followed by *against*

insure something *against* something
protest against something

Verbs followed by *at*

glance at something
guess at something
hint at something
marvel at something

Verbs followed by *for*

account for something
allow for something (to take into consideration)
apologize for something/someone (on their behalf: *Let me apologize for Jack.*)
blame someone *for* something
care for something/someone
cater for something/someone
charge someone *for* something (make them pay for it)
count for something (especially: *I count for nothing in this company.*)
earmark something *for* a particular use
pay for someone/something

Verbs followed by *from*

bar someone *from* a place
benefit from something
derive something *from* something
deter someone *from* something
differ from something
distinguish one thing *from* another thing (also: *distinguish between* two things)

distract someone *from* something
exempt someone *from* something
expel someone *from* a place
refrain from something
resign from something
result from something
stem from something
suffer from something
translate one language *from/into* another language

Verbs followed by *in*

absorbed in something (especially *absorbed in her work/a book*)
confide in someone
be engrossed in something
implicate someone *in* something (especially *be implicated in*)
involve someone *in* something
result in something
specialize in something
succeed in something

Verbs followed by *of*

accuse someone *of* something
convict someone *of* something
remind someone *of* something
suspect someone *of* something
take notice of something/someone

Verbs followed by *on*

base something *on* something (especially passive: *The film is based on a play.*)
blame something *on* someone
centre something *on* something (usually passive: *be centred on*)
concentrate something *on* something
decide on something
depend on someone/something
elaborate on something
impose on someone
insist on something/someone doing something
pride oneself on something

Verbs followed by *to*

answer to something (especially: *answer to a description*)
appeal to someone (beg)
It appeals to me. (I like the idea.)
apply something *to* something (*This rule doesn't apply to you.*)
apply oneself (to work hard and consistently at something)
attend to something said/heard
attribute something *to* someone

commit oneself *to* something (especially passive: *be committed to*)

confess to something

devote oneself *to* something (especially passive: *be devoted to*)

prefer one thing *to* another thing

react to something

refer to something (*This number refers to the next page.*)

refer someone *to* someone (*The doctor referred me to a specialist.*)

resign oneself *to* something (especially passive: *be resigned to*)

resort to something

see to something (make sure it is done)

subject someone *to* something (stressed: *sub<u>ject</u>*)

succeed to the throne

be used to doing something

Verbs followed by *with*

acquaint someone *with* something (also: *be acquainted with* something/someone)

associate someone *with* something

charge someone *with* something

clutter with something (especially passive: *The room was cluttered with boxes.*)

coincide with something

collide with something

comply with something

concern with something (usually passive: *be concerned with*)

confront someone *with* something

confuse someone/something *with* someone/something

cram with something (especially passive: *be crammed with*)

deal with someone/something

discuss something *with* someone

face with something (especially passive: *be faced with*)

ingratiate oneself *with* someone

meet with something (especially: *meet with an accident*)

pack with something (especially passive: *be packed with*)

plead with someone

provide someone *with* something

tamper with something

trust someone *with* something

ADVANCED LANGUAGE PRACTICE

1 Complete each sentence with a suitable preposition.

1 I really prefer just about anything ....*to*.......... watching television.

2 This year's conference coincided .... two other major conventions.

3 Is it possible to insure my bike .... theft?

4 The problem stems .... the government's lack of action.

5 When I asked Jean, she hinted .... the chance of a promotion for me.

6 Being rich doesn't count .... much on a desert island.

7 I pleaded .... John to change his mind, but he wouldn't listen.

8 I can't stand the way she is always boasting .... her wealthy parents.

9 My father always confuses Britney Spears .... Whitney Houston.

10 Could you please refrain .... smoking in the lecture hall.

2 Complete the text by writing a suitable verb in each space.

I had a difficult time last year with my health. For several months I was
(1) ...*suffering*... from severe headaches and almost constant nausea. I made several
visits to my GP, who finally (2) .... my headaches to migraine and prescribed
medication. When this failed to work he decided my nausea was the root cause and
(3) .... my headaches on the nausea. I was
(4) .... to five painful tests, none of which revealed anything significant.
I (5) .... my diet with the doctor at length while he made notes, and we
tried eliminating certain foods from my meals. Then he (6) .... that I
might (7) .... from a low-fibre diet. But still the symptoms persisted,
and I was starting to (8) .... myself to feeling ill for the rest of my life. I
was understandably concerned about the possibility of it being something serious,
even a brain tumour, but the doctor explained that this would not (9) ....
for my symptoms. After six months I was (10) .... to a consultant at
the hospital, who (11) .... in stomach disorders. She suggested that
I should (12) .... from eating late at night, and (13) .... at a
possible psychological cause. I think that she (14) .... me of not telling her
the complete truth about my symptoms. She prescribed mild tranquilizers, and this
treatment, I'm glad to say, (15) .... with complete success!

GRAMMAR 17 VERBS + PREPOSITIONS

3 Complete the second sentence so that it has a similar meaning to the first sentence, using the word given. Do not change the word given.

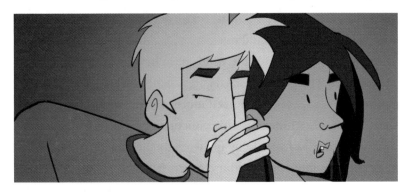

1   Peter always trusts me with his secrets.

   in

   Peter .... always confides in .... me.

2   A true story forms the basis of Mary's new novel.

   on

   Mary's new novel .... a true story.

3   I thought it was marvellous that Jane could jump so high.

   at

   I .... to jump so high.

4   A lot of people were packed on to the bus.

   with

   The bus .... people.

5   You were in my dreams last night.

   about

   I .... last night.

6   Danny was asked to leave the school for bad behaviour.

   from

   Danny was .... for bad behaviour.

7   This house makes me think of my own home!

   of

   This house .... my own home.

8   Tina rewrote the French book in Spanish.

   from

   Tina .... into Spanish.

9   Christmas and roast turkey go together in my mind.

   with

   Christmas .... roast turkey in my mind.

10 I think a rest would do you good.

   from

   I think you .... a rest.

4 **Complete each sentence with a suitable verb.**

1 The idea of marriage doesn't ....*appeal*........ to me.

2 We .... in finding Ann's house at the second attempt.

3 However poor I was I would not .... to stealing.

4 Have you .... for the wind speed in your calculations?

5 He confessed when he was .... with the evidence.

6 You need to .... yourself more to your work.

7 Alan .... himself on his punctuality.

8 I was .... from doing my work by the music.

9 I .... for breaking your electric drill.

10 Tina .... for everyone's lunch yesterday, as she'd just won some money on the lottery.

5 **Complete the text by writing a suitable preposition in each space.**

It never ceases to amaze me how little notice some people now take
(1) ....*of*.......... rules in public places. When I was a child, it would never
have occurred to me not to comply (2) .... the rules. If someone
smoked in defiance of a 'No Smoking' sign on a train, they would rapidly be
reminded (3) .... their transgression by several irate passengers,
who would refer the errant smoker (4) .... the sign in no uncertain
terms. What's more, the person accused would normally apologize
(5) .... his indiscretion, and would certainly refrain
(6) .... repeating his anti-social behaviour. These days reminding
someone (7) .... their public duty not to drop litter or swear on the
streets is likely to succeed only (8) .... unleashing a torrent of
verbal abuse (9) .... the wrongdoer. Many people seem blithely
unaware that, for example, the 'silence in the library' rule applies
(10) .... them, as much as to anyone else. Asking them is not
enough, pleading (11) .... them might still not deter them
(12) .... their noisy chat, resorting (13) .... physical
violence, an undesirable option, seems the only one likely to get a result. But,
in all seriousness, what really annoys me is that one is made to feel churlish
or old-fashioned just to insist (14) .... basic respect of everyday
manners. Truly, it seems polite behaviour and good manners count
(15) .... nothing in today's society.

6 Complete the second sentence so that it has a similar meaning to the first sentence, using the word given. Do not change the word given.

1 When he has to face a crisis, Tony panics.

 faced

 Tony panics .... *when faced with* .... a crisis.

2 Collecting stamps gives me a lot of pleasure.

 derive

 I .... collecting stamps.

3 The arrested man did not look the same as the wanted man.

 answer

 The arrested man did not .... the wanted man.

4 The facts of the case were familiar to the lawyer.

 acquainted

 The lawyer .... the facts of the case.

5 The deaths of over fifty people were caused by the storm.

 resulted

 The storm .... killed.

6 We have given winter equipment to all the soldiers.

 provided

 All the soldiers .... winter equipment.

7 It's just our luck that the wedding is at the same time as our holiday in Crete.

 coincide

 It's just our luck that .... in Crete.

8 You haven't really explained exactly how the money disappeared.

 account

 Your explanation .... of the money.

9 An ancient philosopher is supposed to have said these words.

 attributed

 These words .... an ancient philosopher.

10 I'm sure Brian won't mind looking after the baby.

 care

 I'm sure Brian won't object .... the baby.

➔ SEE ALSO
Grammar 15: Relative clauses
Grammar 16: Verbs + infinitive or -ing
Grammar 19–21: Phrasal verbs
Consolidation 5: Units 17–21

Prepositions

It is assumed that a wide range of prepositions and their general use to describe time, place and position are already known.

This unit focuses on a selection of expressions. See Vocabulary section for more work in this area. Note that there may be other possible meanings for verbs and phrases given here, with different prepositions.

Prepositions following adjectives

- About: *annoyed about, anxious about, certain about, excited about, pleased about, right about, serious about, sorry about, upset about, wrong about*

- At: *angry at* (a person), *annoyed at* (a person), *bad at, good at, surprised at*

- By: *baffled by, bored by, detained by, distressed by, plagued by, shocked by, surprised by*

- For: *early for, eligible for, famous for, grateful for, late for, liable for* (legally responsible), *ready for, responsible for, sorry for*

- From: *absent from, derived from, different from, safe from, missing from*

- In: *deficient in, experienced in, implicated in, interested in*

- Of: *afraid of, ashamed of, aware of, capable of, conscious of, fond of, full of, be good of* (someone to do something), *indicative of, irrespective of, jealous of*

- On: *keen on*

- To: *addicted to, apt to, attentive to, confined to, grateful to, kind to, immune to, impervious to, indifferent to, liable to* (likely to suffer from), *married to, prone to*

- With: *angry with* (a person), *annoyed with* (a person), *bored with, commensurate with, connected with, good at dealing with, happy with, incompatible with, obsessed with, pleased with, preoccupied with*

Prepositions following nouns

- For: *admiration for, craving for, credit for, cure for, desire for, disregard for, provision for, recipe for, respect for, responsibility for, room for, sympathy for*

- On: *an authority on* (expert), *ban on, comment on, effect on, influence on, restriction on, tax on*

- Over: *be in authority over, have control over, be in dispute over* something

- To: *access to, an alternative to, an attitude to, an exception to, a solution to, a threat to, a witness to*

- With: *contrast with, be in dispute with* someone, *encounter with, link with, quarrel with, have a/be in a relationship with*

Expressions beginning with prepositions

- After: *after all*

- At: *at any rate, at fault, at first sight, at the first/second attempt, at the end, at large*

- Beyond: *beyond belief, beyond a joke, beyond the shadow of a doubt*

- By: *by coincidence, by mistake, by the time, by rights, by surprise*

- For: *for fear of* (because something might happen), *for life, not for long, for the foreseeable future, for the time being, for ever*

- In: *in advance, in the balance, in all likelihood, in all probability, in answer to, in any case, in charge of, in the charge of, in collaboration with, in comparison with, in comfort, in decline, in demand, in dispute, in distress, in the early stages, in earnest, in the end, be in favour of* something, *be in favour with* someone, *in fear of* (being afraid of), *in (good) condition, in harmony, in high spirits, in jeopardy, in one way or another, in practice, in recognition of, in response to, in short, in theory, in time, in trouble, in turn*

- On: *on average, on approval, on a regular basis, on behalf of, on the contrary, on good terms, on loan, on the market* (for sale), *on (its) merits, on offer, on purpose, on the verge of*

- Out of: *out of breath, out of control, out of danger, out of doors, out of focus, out of luck, out of the ordinary, out of pocket, out of practice, out of all proportion, out of reach, out of stock, out of work*

- Under: *under age, under the circumstances, under control, under cover of, be under the impression that, under the influence of, under (a law), under an obligation, under pressure, under repair, under stress, under suspicion*

- With: *with the exception of, with intent to, with regard to, with a view to*

- Within: *within a day (week, month etc), within reach, within reason*

- Without: *without a chance, without delay, without exception, without a word*

ADVANCED LANGUAGE PRACTICE

1 **Complete the second sentence so that it has a similar meaning to the first sentence, using the word given. Do not change the word given.**

1   We get on very well with our next-door neighbours.

   terms

   We are ....*on (very) good terms with*.............. our next-door neighbours.

2   Everybody wants Pauline as an after-dinner speaker.

   demand

   Pauline .... as an after-dinner speaker.

3   After winning the match, the whole team was in a happy mood.

   spirits

   The whole team was .... because of their victory.

4   I realized I had said something wrong.

   conscious

   I .... having said something wrong.

5   You're not lucky today, I'm afraid.

   out

   You're .... today, I'm afraid.

6   You can't get to the village because of the snow.

   access

   There's .... the village because of the snow.

7   The meeting will probably be cancelled.

   probability

   The meeting will, ... , be cancelled.

8   The students are living temporarily in a caravan.

   being

   For .... the students are living in a caravan.

9   I intend to discover the truth somehow or other.

   or

   In one .... I intend to discover the truth.

10   The soldiers entered the castle while it was dark.

   cover

   Under .... , the soldiers entered the castle.

2 Complete each sentence with a suitable preposition.

1 Helen had great admiration ....*for*........ her history teacher.

2 I'm afraid I'm not very good .... animals.

3 The favourite dropped out of the race .... the early stages.

4 I was .... the impression that you liked Indian food.

5 The minister stated that no real alternative .... the plan existed.

6 This town is famous .... its hand-woven carpets.

7 In contrast .... its title, 'A Great Read' is actually a rather dull book.

8 Many young people become addicted .... drugs through ignorance.

9 Apparently a number of army officers were implicated .... the plot.

10 Carol doesn't have a very good relationship .... her mother.

11 Mary suddenly left the room .... a word.

12 I'm not .... favour of children staying up so late.

13 Unfortunately, most of the photos Terry took were .... of focus.

14 I don't think it was an accident. I think you did it .... purpose.

15 The bridge is .... repair, so we'll have to go a different way.

3 Complete the text by writing one word in each space.

Well, welcome to the swimming class everybody. I'm sure you're all dying to show me exactly what you're (1) ....*capable*........ of. I hope to see your faces at the pool a lot from now on. If you're (2) .... about learning to swim, you really need to be practising on a (3) .... basis, say two or three times a week – in addition to these teaching sessions. Now a bit about the course. In the early (4) .... , we'll be working on the basics – breathing, body position and so on. Today we're going to work on putting the head underwater, with a (5) .... to getting you all swimming correctly, with the head partly submerged. If you don't succeed at the first (6) .... , don't worry. And please don't be (7) .... of the water – just try and relax. Eventually we'll progress to the big pool, but for the (8) .... being, we're going to be in the small pool, where you can stand up and practise your techniques. Now, the warm-up exercises we're going to start with today may well be (9) .... from anything you're used to, as we'll be doing some jumping and hopping in the water. Yes, I know there are lots of you here today, but it's a big pool and there's (10) .... for all of you. So, in you go!

4 Complete the second sentence so that it has a similar meaning to the first sentence, using the word given. Do not change the word given.

1 Speaking for my colleagues, I would like to thank you.

of

On .... behalf of my colleagues .... , I would like to thank you.

2 I thought you had accepted his offer.

under

I was .... that you had accepted his offer.

3 Everyone was exhausted apart from Sally.

of

With .... , everyone was exhausted.

4 I like to spend most of my time in the open air.

doors

I like to .... most of the time.

5 I don't think you mean what you say about disliking me.

serious

I don't think you're .... disliking me.

6 Nothing unusual ever happens here.

ordinary

Nothing out .... ever happens here.

7 I wish I knew what to do about this problem.

solution

I wish I knew what .... this problem.

8 You can walk to the station easily from the hotel.

within

The station is .... of the hotel.

9 Karen received a medal for her services to the country.

recognition

Karen received a medal .... her services to the country.

10 You have to pay your son's debts, as he is under age.

liable

You .... your son's debts, as he is under age.

5 **Complete the text by writing a suitable preposition in each space.**

David Peters, the Scottish long-jumper, has been awarded a knighthood
in recognition (1) ....of.......... his services to charity and the world of athletics.
Sir David, as he will be known, will be knighted by the Queen in a ceremony next
week. David Peters, who retired from athletics last year, had a talent which was,
quite simply, (2) .... of the ordinary. All his performances were,
(3) .... exception, characterized by great effort and determination. He
seemed to thrive on difficult situations, and it was when (4) .... pressure
that he produced his greatest performances. In later years, he became increasingly
prone (5) .... injury, and last year, his talents evidently
(6) .... decline, he failed to regain his Olympic long-jump title and
promptly retired. At his best, however, his jumping was sometimes
(7) .... belief, and in his greatest year, 2000, he broke the world record
no fewer than four times. In the late 1990s he was single-handedly responsible
(8) .... bringing British athletics out of a severe slump with his
inspirational performances and personal charisma. Peters was capable
(9) .... great generosity, and once, famously, dropped out of a
competition in order to let his great rival, Aravan Sijipal, win on his farewell
appearance. When being interviewed, Peters was also an exception to the rule,
and he was famous (10)................ unselfishly praising his rivals. A deeply religious
man, he was (11) .... dispute with the athletics authorities on more than
one occasion for his refusal to compete on Sundays. His anti-drugs campaign had a
great effect (12) .... young athletes all over Britain, and throughout his
career, he remained very conscious (13) .... what he saw as his public
duty in this respect. Many charitable organizations have reason to be grateful
(14) .... him (15) .... the time he devoted to raising money
for their causes.

6 <u>Underline</u> **the correct word in each sentence.**
1 Diane showed a complete disregard <u>for</u>/with her own safety.
2 I was totally baffled *by/of* Tim's behaviour.
3 For Romeo and Juliet it was love *at/with* first sight.
4 They wouldn't let me in the pub because I was *below/under* age.
5 Our house has been *in/on* the market for months.
6 You are perfectly capable *for/of* making your own bed, I would have thought!
7 We walked on tiptoe *for/from* fear of being discovered.
8 This is one of the exceptions *of/to* the rule.
9 I am surprised *at/by* you, forgetting your briefcase like that.
10 We met at the hotel completely *by/from* coincidence.

Phrasal verbs 1

This unit (and Grammar 20 and 21) assume that a wide range of phrasal verbs, and their grammatical types, are already known. These units focus on multiple meaning, and other meanings of known phrasal verbs. Note that there may be other meanings for the verbs listed here.

Add up (make sense)
> His evidence just **doesn't add up**.

Ask after (inquire about)
> Jim **was asking after** you.

Back down (yield in an argument)
> Sheila was right, so Paul had to **back down**.

Bargain for (take into account)
> We **hadn't bargained for** there being so much traffic, and we missed the plane.

Bear out (confirm the truth)
> Helen's alibi **was borne out** by her sister.

Break down (lose control of the emotions)
> David **broke down** and wept when he heard the news.

Break off (stop talking)
> He **broke off** to answer the phone.

Break up (come to an end)
> The party **finally broke up** at 3.00 am.

Bring (something) about (cause to happen)
> The crisis **was brought about** by Brenda's resignation.

Bring (something) off (succeed in doing something)
> The team tried for years to win the competition and they finally **brought it off**.

Bring (something) on (cause the onset of an illness)
> Sitting in the damp **brought on** his rheumatism.

(cause trouble to happen to oneself)
> You have **brought this on/upon** yourself.

Bring (someone) round (influence someone to your point of view)
> After much discussion, I **brought** the committee **round** to my point of view.

Bring (something) up (mention)
> I feel I ought to **bring up** another small matter.

Carry (something) off (complete successfully – perhaps despite a problem)
> Jane had a difficult role to play, but she **carried it off**.

Carry out (complete a plan)
> The attack **was** successfully **carried out**.

Catch on (become popular – colloquial)
> This new hair style is beginning to **catch on**.

Come about (happen)

*Let me explain how the situation **came about**.*

Come down to (be in the end a matter of)

*It all **comes down to** whether you are prepared to accept less money.*

Come in for (receive – especially criticism, blame)

*The government has **come in for** a lot of criticism over the decision.*

Come off (take place successfully)

*I'm afraid that deal didn't **come off** after all.*

Come out (appear)

*All the flowers **have come out**.*

*When the news **came out**, everyone was shocked.*

*Kate's new book **comes out** next month.*

Come up (occur – usually a problem – colloquial)

*Look, something **has come up**, and I can't meet you.*

Come up against (meet a difficulty)

*We've **come up against** a bit of a problem.*

Come up to (equal – especially expectations, standard)

*The play didn't **come up to** expectations.*

Come up with (think of – especially an answer, a plan, a solution)

*We still haven't **come up with** a solution to the problem.*

Count on (rely on)

*Don't worry, you can **count on** me.*

Crop up (happen unexpectedly – colloquial)

*I can't come to your party, something **has cropped up**.*

Do away with (abolish – colloquial)

*Dog licences **have been done away with**.*

(murder – colloquial)

*What if they **do away with** the old man?*

Do (something) up (decorate – colloquial)

*We are **having** our living room **done up**.*

Draw up (come to a stop)

*A white sports car **drew up** outside the door.*

Draw up (organize – especially a document)

*The contract **is being drawn up** at the moment.*

Drop in (pay a visit – colloquial)

***Drop in** any time you're passing.*

Drop off (fall asleep – colloquial)

*The baby **has** just **dropped off**.*

End up (finish in a certain way, or place)

*We **ended** up staying there for lunch.*

*The car **ended up** in a ditch.*

Face up to (have courage to deal with – especially responsibilities)

*You have to **face up to** your responsibilities.*

Fall about (show amusement – especially laughing – colloquial)

*Everyone **fell about** when Jane told her joke.*

Fall back on (use as a last resort)

*If the worst comes to the worst, we've got our savings to **fall back on**.*

Fall for (be deceived by – colloquial)

*It was an unlikely story but he **fell for** it. (fall in love with – colloquial)*

*I **fell for** you the moment I saw you.*

Fall out with (quarrel with)

*Peter has **fallen out with** his boss.*

Fall through (fail to come to completion)

*The plan **fell through** at the last minute.*

Feel up to (feel capable of doing)

*Old Mr Smith didn't **feel up to** walking all that way.*

Follow up (act upon a suggestion)

*Thanks for the information about that book. I'll **follow** it **up**.*

(take more action)

*We'll **follow up** this lesson next week.*

Get (something) across (be understood – especially get an idea across)

*I had the feeling I wasn't **getting** my meaning **across**.*

Get at (imply – about personal matters – colloquial)

*What **are** you **getting at** exactly?*

Get someone down (make to feel depressed – colloquial)

*This cold weather really **gets me down**.*

Get down to (begin to seriously deal with)

*It's time we **got down to** some real work.*

Get off (with something) (avoid punishment)

*Susan was punished but Alice **got off**.*

*They were lucky to **get off with** such light sentences.*

Get on for (approach a certain age/time/number)

*He must be **getting on for** seventy.*

Get on (make progress – especially in life)

*Sue is **getting on** very well in her new job.*

Get over (be surprised)

*I **couldn't get over** how well she looked.*

Get over with (come to the end of something, usually unpleasant)

*I'll be glad to **get** this awful business **over with**.*

Get round to (find time to do – also around)

*Sorry, but I **haven't got round to** fixing the tap yet.*

Get up to (do something – usually bad when about children – colloquial)

*The children **are getting up to** something in the garden.*

*What **have you been getting up to** lately?*

1 <u>Underline</u> the correct word or phrase in each sentence.

1 Jim completely fell for my *joke/<u>story</u>*.
2 The *conversation/meeting* didn't break up until late.
3 It seems that we've come up against rather a tricky *idea/problem*.
4 It must be getting on for *six o' clock/extremely well*.
5 The witness's evidence bore out *what Peter had said/as Peter said*.
6 I really should get down to *my homework/the weather*.
7 Unfortunately my *plan/suggestion* didn't quite come off.
8 Mary's new novel doesn't come up to her usual *expectation/standard*.
9 Last night I dropped off *at 11.30/from 11.30* until 7.00 this morning.
10 When David started speaking everyone fell about *in laughter/laughing*.

2 Complete each sentence with a suitable word.

1 When I give an order I expect it to be ......*carried*..... out.
2 Getting up so early really gets me ....
3 It was a good idea, but I'm afraid it didn't quite .... off.
4 I'm afraid that your story doesn't really .... up.
5 I was so surprised when Harry got the job, I couldn't .... over it.
6 Terry's new book .... out next week.
7 Someone was .... after you in the club yesterday.
8 I tried to get an early night, but just as I was .... off, the phone rang.
9 Neil was too embarrassed to .... up the question of who would pay.
10 The police didn't .... up Bill's complaint about his neighbours.

3 **Read the text and decide which option (A, B, C or D) best fits each space.**

The Terrys were sitting calmly having afternoon tea in their lounge when the van (1) ...A.... up outside. The words 'Reliable Removals – you can (2) .... us' were printed on the side of the van in large blue capitals. Soon afterwards, an enormous man covered in tattoos appeared on the doorstep. Tim opened the door. 'Sorry we're late, guv,' said the tattoo man. 'We hadn't (3) .... all the traffic on the motorway, otherwise we'd have been here sooner. Isn't that right, Lester? His companion, an unshaven man roughly half his size, joined in: 'We didn't budge for a good half hour, and we (4) .... up coming off the motorway and going through the villages. We took a wrong turning and (5) .... up in a farmyard Anyway, we're here now, so let's (6) .... some serious work.' Tim said, 'Erm, I think there's been some sort of misunderstanding, gentlemen.'

1	A drew	B followed	C cropped	D called
2	A ask after	B bear out	C count on	D draw up
3	A got up to	B faced up to	C bargained for	D added up
4	A brought	B ended	C broke	D came
5	A added	B broke	C came	D ended
6	A do away with	B come up against	C fall out with	D get down to

4 **Read the text and decide which option (A, B, C or D) best fits each space.**

When I woke up, it was (1) ....C.... nine o'clock and I realized that I must have (2) .... , and missed my train. I couldn't (3) .... how stupid I had been. Now I was the only person on the station, there were no taxis outside, and it was snowing. I certainly didn't (4) .... carrying my heavy bags back to the hotel, and as the waiting room was well heated, and I couldn't (5) .... a better plan, I decided to stay there for the night and save money. Unfortunately, there was one thing I hadn't (6) .... That was the arrival of a large group of drunken soldiers.

1	A coming up with	B bringing off	C getting on for	D coming about
2	A dropped off	B fallen through	C followed up	D got across
3	A add up	B catch on	C get over	D fall for
4	A get round to	B feel up to	C bargain for	D come in for
5	A count on	B draw up	C get down to	D come up with
6	A come down to	B bargained for	C got over with	D brought about

5 Complete the second sentence so that it has a similar meaning to the first sentence, using the word given. Do not change the word given.

1 They didn't punish Karen, only gave her a warning.

got

Karen .... got off with .... a warning.

2 What sort of progress are you making in your new job?

getting

How are .... in your new job?

3 There were no taxis so in the end I had to walk home.

up

Because there were no taxis I .... home.

4 I didn't expect to be doing so much work.

bargain

I'm doing more work ....

5 Brenda doesn't get on with her next-door neighbour any more.

fallen

Brenda has .... her next-door neighbour.

6 I burst into tears when I heard the news.

down

I .... when I heard the bad news.

7 The best solution was thought of by Sally.

came

Sally .... the best solution.

8 Soon it will be time for lunch.

getting

It's .... lunch time.

9 What happened confirmed the truth of Jack's prediction.

borne

Jack's prediction .... by subsequent events.

10 Carol has trouble communicating her ideas to others.

her

Carol has trouble .... across.

➜ **SEE ALSO**
Grammar 20 and 21: Phrasal verbs
Consolidation 5: Units 17–21

20

Phrasal verbs 2

This unit (and Grammar 19 and 21) assume that a wide range of phrasal verbs, and their grammatical types, are already known. These units focus on multiple meaning, and alternative ways of expressing meanings of phrasal verbs. Note that there may be other meanings for the verbs listed here.

Give (someone) away (betray)
> *His false identity papers **gave** him **away**.*

Give off (send off a smell – liquid or gas)
> *The cheese had begun to **give off** a strange smell.*

Give out (be exhausted)
> *When our money **gave out** we had to borrow some.*

Give over (abandon, devote)
> *The rest of the time **was given over** to playing cards.*
>
> (stop – colloquial)
>
> *Why don't you **give over**! You're getting on my nerves.*

Give up (surrender)
> *The escaped prisoner **gave** herself **up**.*
>
> (believed to be dead or lost)
>
> *After ten days the ship was **given up** for lost.*

Go back on (break a promise)
> *The management has **gone back on** its promise.*

Go in for (make a habit of)
> *I don't **go in for** that kind of thing.*
>
> (enter competition)
>
> *Are you thinking of **going in for** the race?*

Go off (become bad – food)
> *This milk **has gone off**.*

Go on (happen – usually negative)
> *Something funny **is going on**.*

Go round (be enough)
> *There weren't enough life-jackets to **go round**.*

Go through with (complete a promise or plan – usually unwillingly)
> *When it came to actually stealing the money, Nora couldn't **go through with** it.*

Grow on (become more liked – colloquial)
> *This new record **is growing on** me.*

Hang onto (keep – colloquial)
> *I think we should **hang onto** the car until next year.*

Have it in for (be deliberately unkind to someone – also as have got)
> *My teacher **has (got) it in for** me.*

Have it out with (express feelings so as to settle a problem)
> *I put up with the problem for a while but in the end I **had it out with** her.*

Have someone on (deceive – colloquial)
*I don't believe you. You're **having me on**.*
Hit it off (get on well with – colloquial)
*Mark and Sarah really **hit it off** at the party.*
Hit upon/on (discover by chance – often an idea)
*They **hit upon** the solution quite by chance.*
Hold out (offer – especially with hope)
*We **don't hold out** much hope that the price will fall.*
Hold up (delay)
*Sorry I'm late, I **was held up** in the traffic.*
(use as an example – i.e. a model of good behaviour)
*Jack **was** always **held up** as an example to me.*
Hold with (agree with – an idea)
*I don't **hold with** the idea of using force.*
Keep up (continue)
*Well done! **Keep up** the good work!*
Lay down (state a rule – especially lay down the law)
*The company **has laid down** strict procedures for this kind of situation.*
Let (someone) down (disappoint, break a promise)
*Sorry to **let** you **down**, but I can't give you a lift today.*
Let in on (allow to be part of a secret)
*We **haven't let** Tina **in on** the plans yet.*
Let (someone) off (excuse from punishment)
*As Dave was young, the judge **let** him **off** with a fine.*
Let on (inform about a secret – colloquial)
*We're planning a surprise for Helen, but **don't let on**.*
Live (it) down (suffer a loss of reputation)
*If City lose, they'll never **live it down**.*
Live up to (reach an expected standard)
*The play quite **lived up to** my expectations.*
Look into (investigate)
*The police have promised to **look into** the problem.*
Look on (consider)
*We **look on** this town as our real home.*
Look someone up (visit when in the area)
*If you're passing through Athens, **look me up**.*
Make for (result in)
*The power steering **makes for** easier parking.*
Make off with (run away with)
*The thief **made off with** a valuable necklace.*
Make out (pretend)
*Tim **made out** that he hadn't seen the No Smoking sign.*
(manage to see or understand)
*I couldn't quite **make out** what the notice said.*
Make (someone) out (understand someone's behaviour)
*Janet is really odd. I can't **make her out**.*

Make (something) up (invent)

*I think you **made up** the whole story!*

Make up for (compensate for)

*Our success **makes up for** all the hard times.*

Miss (something) out (fail to include)

*You have **missed out** a word here.*

(lose a chance – colloquial)

*Five people got promoted, but I **missed out** again.*

Own up (confess – colloquial)

*None of the children **would own up** to breaking the window.*

Pack in (stop an activity – colloquial)

*John **has packed in** his job.*

Pay (someone) back (take revenge – colloquial)

*She **paid** him **back** for all his insults.*

Pick up (improve – colloquial)

*The weather seems **to be picking up**.*

Pin someone down (force to give a clear statement)

*I asked Jim to name a suitable day, but I couldn't **pin** him **down**.*

Play up (behave or work badly)

*The car **is playing up** again. It won't start.*

Point (something) out (draw attention to a fact)

*I **pointed out** that I would be on holiday anyway.*

Pull (something) off (manage to succeed)

*It was a tricky plan, but we **pulled** it **off**.*

Push on (continue with some effort – colloquial)

*Let's **push on** and try to reach the coast by tonight.*

Put across (communicate ideas)

Harry is clever but he can't put his ideas across.

Put down to (explain the cause of)

*Diane's poor performance **was put down to** nerves.*

Put in for (apply for a job)

*Sue **has put in for** a teaching job.*

Put oneself out (take trouble – to help someone)

*Please don't **put** yourself **out** making a meal. A sandwich will do.*

Put off (discourage, upset)

*The crowd **put** the gymnast **off**, and he fell.*

Put someone up (offer accommodation)

*We can **put** you **up** for a few days.*

Put up with (tolerate, bear)

*I can't **put up with** all this noise!*

1 Underline the correct word or phrase in each sentence.

1 Richard and I have never really hit _it_/ourselves off.
2 The manager promised to look into _my request/the matter_.
3 I am afraid I don't hold with _this kind of thing/people like you_.
4 Hang on to the tickets; _they might fall/we'll need them later_.
5 The team couldn't keep up _the pressure/the score_ in the second half.
6 This'll go off unless you _put it in the fridge/close the window_.
7 I think _the second paragraph/a great opportunity_ has been missed out.
8 Most of the meeting was given over _in the end/to Tom's report_.
9 Stephen eventually _confessed/owned up_ to sixteen murders.
10 Something odd is going on _behind my back/tomorrow afternoon_.

2 Complete each sentence with a suitable word.

1 We can't watch that programme if the television is ....playing.... up again.
2 This novel is beginning to .... on me.
3 It is quite clearly .... down that only amateurs can take part.
4 Sales were slow to start with, but now they're .... up.
5 I don't want to .... you off, but this type of plane has crashed quite often.
6 Two members of the gang eventually .... themselves up.
7 We .... out that we had forgotten Jane's birthday, though it wasn't true.
8 There should be enough plates to .... round.
9 What does that notice say? I can't .... it out.
10 Hilary told me to .... her up the next time I was in London.

3 Read the text and decide which option (A, B, C or D) best fits each space.

The small resort of Palama (1) ....B.... out rather in the 1990s, as the tourists flocked to the more obvious attractions of the nearby resorts of Calapo and del Mare. But now, thanks to a major new hotel development plan, business is (2) .... , and Palama is more than (3) .... its poor past showing and unfashionable image. The kindest thing one can say about Palama is that it (4) .... you if you've been staying there for long enough. It is being (5) .... up in many quarters as a shining example of the latest retro-style of modern hotel architecture, but as far as this observer is concerned, it only occasionally (6) .... its billing.

1	A held	B missed	C made	D gave
2	A picking up	B making out	C paying back	D giving over
3	A putting in for	B hanging on to	C hitting it off	D making up for
4	A grows on	B hold with	C puts up with	D pushes on
5	A played	B put	C held	D made
6	A lives up to	B holds out	C makes for	D puts across

4 Read the text and decide which option (A, B, C or D) best fits each space.

Jeremy Clark test drives the Vitesse Superb

You'd be hard-pushed to find a more comfortable drive – the superb suspension system makes (1) ....C.... an easy ride over bumpy roads, although the performance is somewhat let (2) .... by the handling round corners. Maybe I was just pushing it too hard! The instruction manual (3) .... that the Superb can hit a top speed of 240 kph: 200 would be nearer the mark – still not a figure to be sniffed at. The dashboard controls are a dream, although some of the electronics were a bit temperamental on my trial run – at one point, alarmingly, the windscreen wipers decided to (4) .... Also I did not (5) .... with the new Transtronic gearbox, which is a bit bizarre to say the least. But then I am the world's most demanding critic! Still, in the end you'll probably be (6) .... by the price, a cool £125,000.

1	A out	B off with	C for	D up
2	A off	B down	C in	D on
3	A puts up	B pulls off	C makes out	D holds up
4	A give away	B miss out	C put off	D play up
5	A hit it off	B pull it off	C have it out	D live it down
6	A missed out	B owned up	C put off	D hit upon

5 Complete the second sentence so that it has a similar meaning to the first sentence, using the word given. Do not change the word given.

1 I'm not really interested in sports.

go

I don't really ....*go in for*................................ sports very much.

2 Terry was rude but Anne got her revenge on him.

being

Anne paid Terry .... to her.

3 You can stay with us for a week.

up

We can .... for a week.

4 The police only warned Sally because it was her first offence.

off

Sally was .... warning because it was her first offence.

5 Sue drew attention to the flaw in the plan.

out

Sue .... plan was flawed.

6 The plain clothes officer's boots showed he was a policeman.

given

The plain clothes policeman's real identity .... his boots.

7 Hard work was what caused Jill's success.

put

Jill's success can .... hard work.

8 The box smelled faintly of fish.

gave

The box .... of fish.

9 I think my boss is prejudiced against me.

it

I think my boss .... me.

10 The holiday wasn't as good as we had expected.

up

The holiday didn't .... expectations.

➜ **SEE ALSO**
Grammar 19 and 21: Phrasal verbs
Consolidation 5: Units 17–21

21

Phrasal verbs 3

This unit (and Grammar 19 and 20) assume that a wide range of phrasal verbs, and their grammatical types, are already known. These units focus on multiple meaning, and alternative ways of expressing meanings of phrasal verbs. Note that there may be other meanings for the verbs listed here.

Rip someone off (charge too much – colloquial)
>   *You paid €50? They really **ripped** you **off**!*

Run (someone) down (criticize)
>   *She's always **running down** her husband.*

(lose power, allow to decline)
>   *I think the batteries **are running down**.*

Run into (meet)
>   *Guess who I **ran into** at the supermarket!*

Run to (have enough money)
>   *I don't think we can **run to** a holiday abroad this year.*

Run over (check – also run through)
>   *Let's **run over** the plan once more.*

Run up (a bill – let a bill get longer without paying)
>   *I **ran up** a huge telephone bill at the hotel.*

Run up against (encounter – usually a problem)
>   *We've **run up against** a slight problem.*

See someone off (go to station, airport, etc to say goodbye to someone)
>   *I went to the station to **see them off**.*

See through (realize the truth about)
>   *I **saw through** his intentions at once.*

Send (something/someone) up (make fun of by imitating)
>   *Jean **is** always **sending up** the French teacher.*

Set about (start working)
>   *We **must set about** re-organizing the office.*

Set in (establish itself – especially weather)
>   *I think this rain **has set in** for the day.*

Set out (give in detail in writing)
>   *This document **sets out** all the Union demands.*

(arrange)
>   *I've **set out** the refreshments in the hall.*

(start an action)
>   *Sue **set out** to write a biography but it became a novel.*

Set up (establish)
>   *An inquiry into the accident **has been set up**.*

Set on/upon (attack)

We were set upon by a gang of hooligans.

Sink in (realize slowly – colloquial, intransitive)

*Slowly the realization that I had won began to **sink in**.*

Slip up (make a mistake – colloquial)

*Someone **slipped up** and my application was lost.*

Sort (something) out (find a solution – colloquial)

*Don't worry, Mary will **sort out** your problems.*

Stand by (keep to an agreement)

*The company agreed to **stand by** its original commitment.*

Stand for (represent – initials)

*e.g. **stands for** exempli gratia, it's Latin.*

(tolerate)

*I **will not stand for** this kind of behaviour in my house!*

Stand in for (take the place of)

*Carol has kindly agreed to **stand in for** Graham at the monthly meeting.*

Stand up to (resist, bear stress)

*The engine **won't stand up to** the strain.*

Step down (resign – colloquial)

*The Chairman **has stepped down** after criticism from shareholders.*

Step up (increase)

*Production at the Leeds plant **has been stepped up**.*

Stick up for (defend – especially yourself, your rights – colloquial)

*You must learn to **stick up for** yourself.*

Take in (deceive)

***Don't be taken in** by her apparent shyness.*

Take (it) out on (make someone else suffer because of one's own sufferings)

*I know you are unhappy, but don't **take it out on** me!*

Take off (imitate – colloquial)

*Dave **takes off** the Prime Minister really well.*

Take on (acquire a new characteristic)

*My grandmother **has taken on** a new lease of life since her operation.*

(do something extra)

*She **has taken on** too much with a full-time job as well.*

Take out (insurance – sign an insurance agreement)

*Ann **has taken out** life insurance.*

Take over (gain control of)

*The army tried to **take over** the country.*

Take to someone (develop a liking for)

*You'll soon **take to** your new boss, I'm sure.*

Take up (time – occupy time)

*The meeting **took up** a whole morning.*

Talk out of or into (dissuade from, persuade into)

*Paul **talked** me **into** going skiing, against my better judgement.*

Tell someone off (scold – colloquial)

*Our teacher **told** us **off** for being late.*

Tie in with (be in agreement with)

*I'm afraid your party doesn't quite **tie in with** our arrangements.*

Track (someone) down (trace the whereabouts of)

*The police **tracked down** the killer and arrested him.*

Try out (test – a machine)

*Let's **try out** the new washing machine.*

Turn (something/someone) down (reject an offer)

*Another company offered me a job but I **turned** them **down**.*

Turn out (happen to be in the end)

*He **turned out** to be an old friend of Helen's.*

(come to a meeting or form a crowd)

*Thousands of fans **turned out** to welcome the team.*

Turn up (be discovered by chance)

*Don't worry about that missing book, it's bound to **turn up** sooner or later.*

(arrive – often unexpectedly)

*Not many people **turned up** for the lesson.*

Wear off (lose effect – especially a drug)

*These painkillers **wear off** after about two hours.*

Work out (calculate – also work out at for specific amounts)

*The hotel bill **worked out** at over £500.*

1 <u>Underline</u> the correct word or phrase in each sentence.

1 Tom asked Jane out, but she *turned down him*/<u>*turned him down*</u>.
2 *In the end*/*Initially* I set out to prove that such a voyage was possible.
3 If he treated me like that I wouldn't stand for *him*/*it*.
4 The government should set up *a committee*/*a minister* to sort the matter out.
5 Both teams stepped up *the pace*/*the rate* in the second half.
6 The dog didn't take to *its new owner*/*liking me*.
7 *The good news*/*The prize* hasn't really sunk in yet.
8 I *told her off*/*told off her* for leaving the office unlocked.
9 After a week on the ice the expedition ran into *difficulties*/*potholes*.
10 They really rip *the bill*/*you off* in this restaurant!

2 Read the text and decide which option (A, B, C or D) best fits each space.

Telesales Tantrum

Telesales have become the bane of my life. Recently I have been so inundated with them that I now refuse to answer the phone between 6 and 9 in the evenings. Friends and relatives understand, and don't bother calling at these times. Last week I was almost
(1) ....D.... taking out a contract with a different phone company, before I realized what I was doing, and slammed the phone down. If it's not advisers promising to (2) .... out your finances for you, or persuading you to (3) .... life insurance, it will usually be home improvement companies. My advice is, don't be taken (4) .... by the friendly chat at the beginning of the conversation. You can (5) .... all their charming chit chat with ease – all they really want is your custom and your money. So (6) .... them, and, preferably politely, just say 'no'.

1 A set in	B stuck up for	C worn off	D talked into
2 A try	B set	C sort	D take
3 A run into	B take out	C set about	D stand by
4 A in	B over	C up	D off
5 A turn out	B take to	C tell off	D see through
6 A stick up for	B run up against	C tie in with	D stand up to

3 Read the text and decide which option (A, B, C or D) best fits each space.

Meetings which (1) .....D..... too much of managers' time are being blamed for inefficiency and lost revenue, according to a report from the Institute of Managerial Affairs. The report concludes that a lot of business meetings are a waste of time: the decisions made in them could be arrived at by other means, or the manager's presence delegated, with a capable deputy standing (2) .... the manager. But it seems this message has not (3) .... in yet, for the number of hours devoted to meetings continues to increase annually. In-house meetings are bad enough, but some companies insist on lavish affairs in hotels or restaurants, (4) .... huge bills in the process. If this were not bad enough, one leading finance company has (5) .... a committee to investigate the new scourge of unnecessary meetings. The number of weekly meetings for the committee has just been (6) .... up from two to three!

1	A run over	B set in	C turn out	D take up
2	A by	B in for	C up to	D for
3	A sunk	B set	C taken	D stood
4	A taking on	B sending up	C working out	D running up
5	A run into	B sorted out	C taken out	D set up
6	A sent	B stepped	C run	D taken

4 Complete each sentence with a suitable word.

1 The government has allowed the coal industry to run ....*down*........ .

2 Robert was set .... by two masked men and robbed.

3 Why didn't you stick .... for me instead of saying nothing?

4 Let's run .... the details of the arrangements just once more.

5 Most of my time is taken .... with answering the phone.

6 I've run .... against a number of difficulties in this area.

7 The buffet was set .... on a number of low tables.

8 The next day, teams of local people set .... clearing up the damage.

9 No one expected the government to stand .... the agreement.

10 Hundreds of people turned .... in the rain to watch the marathon.

5 Complete the second sentence so that it has a similar meaning to the first sentence, using the word given. Do not change the word given.

1 I need someone to take my place at the ceremony.

    in

    I need someone to .... *stand in for me* .... at the ceremony.

2 In the end it was quite a sunny day after all.

    out

    It .... be quite a sunny day after all.

3 Members of the audience started making fun of the speaker.

    up

    Members of the audience started .... the speaker.

4 Janet persuaded me not to sell my house.

    out

    Janet .... my house.

5 Brian does a good imitation of the French teacher.

    off

    Brian .... the French teacher really well.

6 The effect of these pills only lasts for three hours.

    off

    The effect of these pills .... three hours.

7 Harry swore he would not go back on by his promise.

    by

    Harry swore that he .... his promise.

8 Terry has just insured her life.

    out

    Terry has just .... life insurance policy.

9 The detective found the thief and recovered the stolen jewellery.

    down

    The detective .... and recovered the stolen jewellery.

10 I need a calculator to arrive at the total.

    work

    I can't .... a calculator.

➜ **SEE ALSO**
Grammar 19 and 21: Phrasal verbs
Consolidation 5: Units 17–21

CONSOLIDATION 5

Units 17–21

1 Complete the text by writing a suitable preposition in each space.

Unlikely as it may seem, there has now been expert confirmation that wild pumas and lynxes are (1) ......*at*...... large in parts of Britain. Previous sightings of such large cats had been put down (2) .... exaggeration. (3) .... all, the argument went, some people are prone (4) .... seeing flying saucers and Loch Ness monsters, particularly when (5) .... the influence of one drink too many. Some newspapers were suspected (6) .... having made (7) .... stories such as that of the Beast of Exmoor, an animal which is responsible (8) .... the deaths of hundreds of sheep over the past ten years. But experts have now come (9) .... with proof that such stories were (10) .... earnest after all. The animals are (11) .... all likelihood pets missing (12) .... small zoos, or abandoned by their owners. Because the keeping of such animals is severely restricted (13) .... the terms of the Dangerous Wild Animals Act of 1976, owners of unlicensed animals might not report an escape (14) .... fear of prosecution. After examining hair samples, experts now say that the Beast of Exmoor in the South of England is (15) .... doubt a puma or lynx, both of which are normally native to the Middle East and Asia.

2 Complete each sentence with a suitable preposition.

1 My cousin George is obsessed ......*with*...... keeping fit.
2 Many frozen foods are deficient .... vitamins.
3 They say that there is an exception .... every rule.
4 It was very good .... Sue to drive us to the airport.
5 Breaking his leg put Peter's football career .... jeopardy.
6 The same rule applies, irrespective .... how much you have paid.
7 With total disregard .... her own safety, Ann jumped in to rescue the dog.
8 I'm afraid you are not eligible .... a pension until you are 65.

3 Complete the second sentence so that it has a similar meaning to the first sentence, using the word given. Do not change the word given.

1 You think I am someone else.

confusing

You are ....*confusing me with*.......... someone else.

2 Gary is proud of the fact that he is never late.

on

Gary prides .... being early.

3 On this ship passengers cannot get onto the bridge.

access

Passengers have .... the bridge of this ship.

4 What is the difference between nuclear fission and nuclear fusion?

differ

How exactly .... nuclear fusion?

5 An electrical failure was said to be the cause of the fire.

blamed

They .... an electrical failure.

6 It's all a matter of money, in the end.

comes

It all .... in the end.

7 His smooth manner didn't deceive us.

taken

We were .... his smooth manner.

8 The total came to just under £4,000.

worked

The total .... just under £4,000.

9 I haven't realized yet what winning this race means.

sunk

It hasn't .... won this race.

10 In the end we had to walk to the railway station.

up

We .... to the railway station.

4 Complete each sentence with a suitable word.

1 It looks as if the front door lock has been ....*tampered*.... with.

2 The people were protesting .... the closure of two local factories.

3 We are very .... to you for pointing out the mistake.

4 The hotel .... me €20 for phone calls I had not made.

5 I'd just like to consult my father before I .... myself to a decision.

6 The new television channel tries to .... for all tastes.

7 I couldn't .... from laughing at the President's remark.

8 I think that you would both .... from a few days holiday.

163

5 Complete the second sentence so that it has a similar meaning to the first sentence, using the word given. Do not change the word given.

1   A bus crashed into a lorry on the motorway.

with

A bus .... *collided with* .... a lorry on the motorway.

2   Don't make me suffer because of your problems!

on

Don't take .... just because you've got problems!

3   Sally persuaded me not to sell my car.

of

Sally talked .... my car.

4   A true story is the basis of the novel.

on

The novel .... a true story.

5   They said the accident was Mary's fault.

blamed

They .... Mary.

6   Joe gets on very well with his mother-in-law.

terms

Joe .... with his mother-in-law.

7   There is nothing strange about this.

out

There is nothing .... about this.

8   Ellen has been unemployed for six months.

out

Ellen has been .... for six months.

6 Complete each sentence with a suitable word.

1   It's safe to hide here. We won't give you .... *away* ....

2   My mum told me .... for coming home late from school.

3   Sorry I'm late. Something cropped .... at the office.

4   You can rely on her. She won't let you ....

5   Nick was taken to court but he got ....

6   It was surprising how quickly that fashion caught ....

7   Don't worry. I'll sort it ....

8   I don't really hit it .... with my new boss.

9   Don't eat that sausage. I think it's gone ....

10 She'll come round when the anaesthetic wears ....

7 Read each sentence and decide which option (A, B, C or D) best fits each space.

1 Jerry isn't fat at all. ......*away*......, he's quite skinny.

   A In any case   B By rights   C In practice   D On the contrary

2 We sent out lots of party invitations, but very few people ....

   A turned up   B came about   C hit it off   D looked us up

3 The old licensing system will have been .... by the end of the decade.

   A broken down   B set out   C phased out   D made off with

4 Fiona decided not to .... the exam in December.

   A take on   B go in for   C get round to   D make for

5 We hadn't .... such heavy traffic, and we were delayed for hours.

   A gone in for   B set about   C worked out   D bargained for

6 Whatever Carol ....to do , she achieves.

   A gets on   B sees to   C sets out   D looks for

7 This conservation project looks promising, but it's still ....

   A in the early stages   B in advance   D under stress   D at first sight

8 Has Tony's new book .... yet?

   A made up   B come out   C set about   D drawn up

9 The smell of paint from outside .... my breakfast, I'm afraid.

   A held up   B gave off   C came up against   D put me off

10 Charles was .... from military service on health grounds.

   A exempted   B barred   C earmarked   D resigned

8 Complete the sentence with one suitable word.

1 If this plan ...*comes*.... off, I promise you'll get the credit for it.

2 I just couldn't .... over how well the team played.

3 The policeman .... me off with a warning, as it was Christmas.

4 Please don't .... yourself out. A sandwich will do.

5 I hope there are enough glasses to .... round.

6 It's time you .... about organizing your revision programme.

7 Mark has .... for the same trick that I did.

8 I can't quite .... out what the sign says.

9 Half the meeting was .... over to reading the minutes.

10 We have .... up a huge bill at the shop on the corner.

9 Complete each extract by writing a verb from the box in a suitable form in each space, using the words in brackets as prompts.

abolish	attention	coincide	compensate	disappoint	establish
impression	obligation	place	~~reject~~	resign	specialize

Text 1

The three publishers who (1) ....rejected............... (turned down) this fantastic first novel must be kicking themselves. John Carter's 'Capital City' is a wonderful read and all the more amazing when one considers the author is just 23. What Carter may lack in experience he more than (2) .... (makes up) for in sheer enthusiasm. Read it and I promise you won't feel (3) .... (let down).

Text 2

I (4) .... (set up) my own business, 'Sarah Castle Photography Ltd,' two years ago, after (5) .... (stepping down) from my post as a TV camera person. I now (6) .... (do mostly) family portraits.

Text 3

Dear Mr and Mrs Sinclair,
I do apologize, but I am unable to come to your daughter's wedding on 21 May. Unfortunately, it (7) .... (happens at the same time as) a holiday I've already booked. When I booked it, I (8) .... (thought) that the wedding was to (9) .... (happen) in July.

Text 4

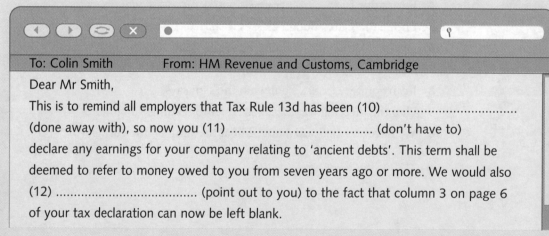

To: Colin Smith   From: HM Revenue and Customs, Cambridge

Dear Mr Smith,
This is to remind all employers that Tax Rule 13d has been (10) .... (done away with), so now you (11) .... (don't have to) declare any earnings for your company relating to 'ancient debts'. This term shall be deemed to refer to money owed to you from seven years ago or more. We would also (12) .... (point out to you) to the fact that column 3 on page 6 of your tax declaration can now be left blank.

22
GRAMMAR

Linking words and phrases

Text Organizers

This term covers a wide range of words and phrases which make text easier to understand. A selection is given here.

- Adding a point

  As well as the obvious dangers, there was the weather to be considered.
  In addition to the obvious dangers, there was the weather to be considered.
  Not only were there the obvious dangers, *but* there was *also* the weather to be considered.

- Developing a point

  Besides/Furthermore/In addition/Indeed/Moreover/What's more/On top of that/ To make matters worse, smoking has been directly linked to lung cancer.
  I quite often see Paula. In fact/As a matter of fact, she came round to see me yesterday.

- Explaining a point

  The exercise rate decreases n proportion to age. To put it another way, the older you are, the less exercise you tend to take.

- Contrast

  The identity of the attacker is known to the police. However/Nevertheless/All the same no name has been released.
  The identity of the attacker is known to the police. No name has, however/all the same, been released.
  (Al)though/While/Even though/Despite the fact that the identity of the attacker is known to the police, no name has been released.
  The identity of the attacker is known to the police. A name has nevertheless/none the less/still not been released.
  No, I didn't say the President got it wrong. On the contrary, I think he's handled the affair superbly.
  On the one hand, the new road would ease traffic congestion, but on the other hand, it would destroy Pratt Wood, a local beauty spot.
  I prefer city life as opposed to country life.
  I prefer city life, whereas John prefers country life.
  Donahue established his reputation as a novelist. In contrast, his new book is a non-fiction work.

- Explaining reasons

    The government does not intend to cause any further provocation. **As a result/ Accordingly/Thus/Hence/Consequently/For that reason,** *all troops have been withdrawn.*

    The employers have promised to investigate these complaints, and we **in turn** *have agreed to end the strike.*

    Owing to *the strike, some trains have been cancelled.*

- Making generalizations

    Broadly speaking/Generally speaking/On the whole/By and large/To a large/ some/a certain extent, *this has been an encouraging year for the company.*

- Starting

    That's absolute rubbish! **For a start/First of all/In the first place/For one thing/To start with,** *it was Rod who said that, not me. And secondly …*

- Giving new information

    She then turned to Henry, who **incidentally/by the way** *is now about two metres tall, and said …*

    By the way/Incidentally, *do you remember an old friend of ours called Ransom?*

- Concession/qualification

    OK, so you two have had a few problems. **Even so/All the same,** *I don't see why you need to split up.*

    Lancaster is a man of great personal integrity. **Anyway/At any rate/Having said that/Having said that/Even so/All the same,** *I don't think he'd make a good chairman.*

    The economic outlook is improving. **At least,** *it is beginning to show signs of doing so.*

- Giving a personal opinion

    What did you think of 'Death in Action'?

    To be (perfectly) honest/To tell the truth, *I can't stand films like that.*

1 Underline the correct word or phrase in each sentence.

1 A: Did you ring the hospital for me?
   B: I forgot *as a result/to be honest/to make matters worse*. I'll do it now.

2 A lot of adults are very wary of learning in a school situation. *For that reason/On the other hand/To tell the truth* they don't sign up for our courses.

3 *By and large/Despite the fact that/Owing to* I'm very pleased with their work on our home. *At any rate/Accordingly/Having said that*, I think they could have made a better job of the painting.

4 I missed two weeks' training because of flu last month. *To put it another way/As a result/To tell the truth*, I'm not expecting to run very well in today's race.

5 They've had a very difficult time. *On top of that/At any rate/To start with*, their home was burgled.

6 What a terrible experience! *Anyway/In contrast/By the way*, you're safe now – that's the main thing!

7 She's a sociable girl with lots of friends. *Even so/Furthermore/To some extent*, she can get lonely, like anyone else.

8 He comes across as being a bit difficult, *in contrast/broadly speaking/whereas* he's actually a very nice guy.

9 *Nevertheless/On the whole/Hence* I agree with what you're saying, but I'm not sure about your last point.

10 I seem to be giving the impression that I didn't enjoy my time in Norway. *After all/Having said that/On the contrary*, I had a wonderful time.

2 Underline the most suitable word or phrase to complete each sentence.

1 They've got a terrible record over tax and education. *Nevertheless/On the other hand*, I still think the Democrats will win the election.

2 Balding's 'People in the Sky' is a very disappointing painting. *At any rate/In contrast*, Rae's 'Beach Scene' really brings this exhibition to life.

3 I would like to complain about the way I was treated in your shop. *For one thing/Besides*, the assistant was rude …

4 Our dining room is a place which we keep strictly for eating, *as opposed to/whereas* the sitting room, which is for sitting, talking and watching TV.

5 We saw the Eiffel Tower, and went round the Louvre, *what's more/as well as* visiting Versailles.

6 The country's economy depends *to a large extent/for one thing* on the tourist industry.

7 I'm here on business *in addition to/as opposed to* pleasure.

8 The weather is likely to be dry and warm. In the far north-west of Scotland, *however/whereas*, it will be wet and windy.

9 The meeting went ahead, *nevertheless/despite the fact that* six members of the committee were unable to attend.

10 The government seems to be changing its policy on this issue. *At last/Even so*, there are signs that it is having second thoughts about the new legislation.

3 Read the interview and decide which answer (A, B or C) best fits each space.

Interviewer: The recent scandal involving your finance minister has done little to restore public confidence in the government.

Minister: (1) ....C...., I think the 'scandal', as you call it, has shown us to be a very moral party. The minister concerned resigned his post and showed great contrition for what he'd done.

Interviewer: (2) .... , a scandal is a scandal. (3) .... , a senior minister accepts a large donation on behalf of his party from the entrepreneur Robert Tivwell. Then, five weeks later, Tivwell's company, which (4) .... just happens to be nearly bankrupt, wins a contract with the government worth millions of pounds.

Minister: Well, as I say, the minister has resigned, (5) .... I should point out that there is technically nothing illegal about what he did.

Interviewer: Yes, there is, minister. It's called bribery.

Minister: Well you can call it that if you want. I prefer to call it 'sharp practice' (6) .... But it happens, it's always happened, and I'm sure it'll continue to happen. (7) .... , we will not condone this kind of financial dealing and will continue to stamp down on it.

Interviewer: This is pure double talk!

Minister: No that's not true. (8) .... we take such matters extremely seriously. But we are realistic enough to know that we can't eliminate them altogether. You see, there is nothing to stop people or companies making donations to parties – (9) .... if we didn't have such money, we wouldn't be able to survive. It's just that the timing of such payments can be unfortunate. So each case has to be investigated on its merits. But (10) .... , this practice is causing less controversy than it has done under previous governments.

	A	B	C
1	A Incidentally	B First of all	C On the contrary
2	A Even so	B As a matter of fact	C Hence
3	A By and large	B Consequently	C First of all
4	A in contrast	B incidentally	C at any rate
5	A despite	B although	C whereas
6	A anyway	B furthermore	C to be honest
7	A Having said that	B Moreover	C To make matters worse
8	A As a result	B As a matter of fact	C To some extent
9	A although	B thus	C indeed
10	A in contrast	B in addition	C broadly speaking

4 Read the text and decide which answer (A, B or C) best fits each space.

Starting your own business could be the way to achieving financial independence. (1).......B......... it could just as well land you in debt for the rest of your life. (2) .... , that is the view of Charles and Brenda Leggat, a Scottish couple, who last week saw their fish farm business put into the hands of the receiver. 'We started the business at a time when everyone was being encouraged by the banks to borrow money. (3) .... , we fell into the same trap, and asked for a big loan. (4) .... , at the time we were sure that we could make it into a going concern,' said Charles Leggat, a farmer from the Highlands. 'The bank analysed the proposals we put forward and they agreed that it would be a highly profitable business.' Sure enough, within five years the Leggats were exporting trout and salmon products to hotels all over Europe, and (5) .... they took on over fifty staff. (6) .... , with the advent of the recession, they began to lose ground as orders dried up. '(7) .... , said Brenda Leggat, 'the business has now been valued by the bank at a fraction of its true worth. If they had left us to work our way out of our difficulties, (8) .... virtually bankrupting us, I am sure that we could have gone back into profit. As it is, we have been left without a livelihood, and the bank has not recovered what it lent us.' The Leggats both felt that their banks had not treated them fairly. '(9) .... , they were falling over themselves to lend us the money initially, (10) .... now they are doing very little to keep the business going, and fifty local people in work.' A spokesman for the bank concerned refused to comment.

1	A Moreover	B On the other hand	C As well as
2	A At least	B However	C To make matters worse
3	A Incidentally	B At any rate	C As a result
4	A To put it another way	B Nevertheless	C In contrast
5	A what's more	B on the other hand	C to tell the truth
6	A Hence	B Consequently	C However
7	A In contrast	B Whereas	C To make matters worse
8	A as opposed to	B as well as	C in addition to
9	A However	B To tell the truth	C As a result
10	A as well as	B whereas	C on the other hand

Punctuation and spelling

Words commonly misspelled

● Common errors

Learners can benefit by making lists of the words they most frequently misspell. The words listed here are spelled correctly.

accommodation, address, advertisement, beginning, committee, conscience, curiosity, disappear, disappointed, embarrassed, faithfully, favourite, forbidden, government, guarantee, immediately, independent (adjective), *jealous, journey, manufacture, marriage, medicine, necessary, pollution, prefer, preferred, pronunciation, quiet, quite, receive, recommend, responsibility, separate, sincerely, successful, truly, unconscious, unfortunately, unnecessary, writing*

● Words with similar spelling but different meanings.

altogether	completely
all together	in one place(describes a group of things or people)
effect (verb)	ring about, make; noun: result
affect (verb)	have an effect on
lose (verb)	fail to have or find
loose (adjective)	not tight
specially	for a special purpose
especially	particularly
stationery	paper, envelopes, etc (collective noun)
stationary	not moving (used formally of vehicles)
principle	general truth or standard
principal	head of college or school

● Words with the same pronunciation but different spelling and meaning. This is a selection, as there are many of these.

allowed – aloud
bear – bare
fair – fare
hair – hare
pear – pair
piece – peace
practice (n) – practise (v)
stair – stare
their – there
weather – whether

Punctuation

- Commas

  Commas are used to separate items in lists (use before the final item in a list separated by *and* or *but* is optional), before question tags, to separate clauses, and after and around certain linking words. See Grammar 22.

  I've been to Dallas, New Orleans, Kansas(,) and Tampa Bay.
  Sue is a lovely girl, isn't she?
  If you see Kevin, tell him his photocopies are ready.
  Broadly speaking, I agree with what you are saying.
  I do not, however, agree with your last point.

  Note that commas are not used between a subject and its verb, or in defining relative clauses.

  The lady standing over there at the bus stop is my next-door neighbour.
  Will the pupil who threw that paper dart please stand up now.

- Apostrophes

  Apostrophes are used to indicate letters omitted, possession and plurals of letters and figures.

  Letters omitted: *It's warm today.*
  Possession: *Jack's car, the people's decision, the player's entrance*
  Possessive *its* does not have an apostrophe: *The dog sat in the corner licking **its** paws.*
  Plurals: *There are two **I's** in 'specially'. Are these 7's or 3's?* Note that many people regard this use as incorrect and prefer to use inverted commas: *Are these '7's or '3's?*

- Colons and semi-colons

  Colons introduce examples, lists, and statements which give in detail what has been stated in general.

  There were two possible courses of action: borrowing from the bank, or asking for more time to find the money elsewhere.
  There were two possible courses of action open to him; after some thought, he decided to ...

  Semi-colons divide parts of long sentences or long phrases in a list; it is usually possible to divide one sentence into shorter ones, so that semi-colons are unnecessary.

  There were two possible courses of action open to him. After some thought, he decided to ...

1 Add any necessary commas, (semi) colons and apostrophes to these texts.

Text 1

Ive been to the following Italian cities Rome Florence Genoa and Pisa. I thought Rome was incredible the food was great the views were fantastic and I will never forget the vivacious people. The Italians legendary hospitality was nowhere more evident than in the capital city. But my all-time favourite is probably Genoa with its fabulous hill-top houses and its dusty mountains reverberating to the sound of grasshoppers. I spent many a happy hour looking down on the seething city below and the sea beyond. Best of all the citys location at the heart of the Italian Riviera meant that fabulous resorts like Portofino and Camogli were only a train ride away.

Text 2

Water is becoming a more and more precious commodity so save as much as you can. Flushing the toilet accounts for a third of all household water use so dont flush wastefully. If you are only getting rid of a tissue for example resist the habit of reaching for the handle or chain. Take a shower rather than a bath it uses about a third of the water. And dont keep the water running all the time when you wash or clean your teeth. If you have a garden try to find ways of saving water outside such as using a water butt to collect rain water rather than using a hosepipe to water your flowers. A simple pipe connecting external gutters to a water butt can save an awful lot of water.

2 Complete each pair of sentences, using two words with the same sound but different spelling.

1 I cannot ......*bear*...... to see any animal suffering.
   The giant pulled the roof off the house with his ......*bare*...... hands.
2 As soon as the policeman was out of .... , one of the men broke a window.
   This spot you are standing on was once the .... of a great battle.
3 The dress showed off Maria's beautiful slender ....
   Quite frankly, this whole scheme has been a .... of time and money.
4 In the novel, Cruz is a clever servant who always .... through his master's plots.
   Armed police were sent to the house to .... the gang's weapons.
5 Mix the apples and almonds into a fine .... and pour it into a jug.
   The Inspector .... up and down the room, considering his next move.

3 Correct any errors in each line of the text. Some lines are correct.

It is an accepted part of everyday nostalgia to assume	1	.........✓..........
that in the past food was somehow better, than it is today.	2	better than
The fruit and vegetables were more naturaly grown and this	3	naturally
was not seen as an extra bonus which added ten per sent on to	4	....
the price. Most food was fresh, not frozen, and you had the	5	....
chance to examine it to see weather you wanted it. When you	6	....
went shopping you could ask for exactly what peace of meat you	7	....
wanted and see the butcher cutting, it instead of finding it	8	....
ready-wrapped in plastic. And your local tradesman soon got to	9	....
know what you wanted, and provided it for you, otherwise he	10	....
would have gone out of businness. Of course, unless we invent	11	....
time-travel we shall never know, whether this is all true.	12	....
Survivors from those distant days naturally tend to dislike	13	....
todays convenience foods, and to prefer the Good Old Days	14	....
when a joint of beef filled the oven, produced thick red juce	15	....
instead of water when cooked, and cost the same as a can of	16	....
Coke. What is always forgotten is that then as now the quality	17	....
of your food depended very much, upon who you were,	18	....
how well-off you happened to be, and where you lived.	19	....
Shopping then demanded considerable skill, and shopper's had	20	....
to be able to tell the fresh from the not-so-fresh. Their was	21	....
no sell-buy date to act as a guide. If you were hard up then	22	....
frozen meat and canned foods' would have been on the menu,	23	....
just as they are today.		

4 Correct any errors in the following sentences. Some are correct.

1 The sunlight shining on my desk is really effecting my concentration.
affecting

2 It's not necessary to do anything at this stage. ....

3 The doctor reccommended gargling with diluted aspirin. ....

4 I'm doing the stationery order now, if anyone's short of anything. ....

5 Mum and Dad went to see a marriage councillor. ....

6 The boxer was knocked unconscious. ....

7 My watch has a six-year gaurantee. ....

8 As far as I'm concerned, the marketing is a seperate issue. ....

9 As if by magic, the strange man dissappeared. ....

10 Too much sun can cause premature ageing of the skin. ....

5 **Correct any errors in each line of the text. Some lines are correct.**

The common cold, as it is technicaly known, still resists the   1   _technically._

efforts of science to control and cure it, and has given rise to a   2   ....✓.........

rich popular mythology. As the name suggests the assumption   3   _suggests,_

is that you catch a cold because you go out in the cold or get wet.   4   ....

As we now that a cold is a virus, and that we actually catch it   5   ....

from being in contact with others', this is not strictly true.   6   ....

Shakeing hands with people, kissing them, or just being in the   7   ....

same room can pass on the virus. It is now generally beleived   8   ....

that cold viruses; and there is more than one type, are always   9   ....

present in the throat, but only become active when the bodys   10   ....

resistence to infection is lowered. The activated cold virus then   11   ....

attacks the membranes in the nose and throat, who's tissues   12   ....

become weakened and thus suseptible to infection by types of   13   ....

bacteria which are generally also present in the body.   14   ....

Sudden chilling, or getting soked to the skin, promote   15   ....

conditions in nose and throat membranes that permitt the cold   16   ....

virus to invade the body, although some individuals seem to be   17   ....

resistant to this. Just being out in the cold is not enough, and   18   ....

studys conducted in wartime among troops living in the open   19   ....

found that the incidence of colds' was no greater. As far as   20   ....

prevention and cure are concerned, nearly everyone has there   21   ...,.............

own favourite remedy. Doctors have been unable to produse an   22   ....

affective vaccine against colds, although strong claims have been   23   ....

put forward for vitamin C.

6 Correct any errors in each line of the text. Some lines are correct.

A river in the west of England, made famous by the best-seller	1 ....✓........
'Tarka the Otter' has, once again become safe for otters after ten	2 _Otter', has_
years of what had been thought a loosing battle against pollution	3 _losing_
from chemicals. The River Torridge in North Devon was the	4 ....
setting for Henry Williamsons book, the success of which has	5 ....
led to the area calling itself 'Tarka Country', and becoming a	6 ....
popular tourist spot. Since 1927 when the book was written,	7 ....
the human population of the area has however increased	8 ....
three-fold, and increased use of pestisides and fertilizers	9 ....
lead to the river being declared 'dead' in the early nineteen	10 ....
eighty's. Otters are shy creatures and the river provides them	11 ....
with numerous places to hide along the river vallies, and the	12 ....
fear was that they had been elliminated because of the clearing	13 ....
away of undergrowth and trees, and the affects of chemicals on	14 ....
their breeding capabilities, not to mention otter hunting, though	15 ....
this has now ceased. However, a number of projects desined to	16 ....
cleanse the river area seem to have born fruit, despite a	17 ....
pesimistic announcement earlier this year. The Tarka Project,	18 ....
which includes local councils and environmental groups, now	19 ....
says that the otter poppulation is healthy and thriving in North	20 ....
Devon. Signs of otter habitation have been found in a number	21 ....
of places, and more and more sitings of otters have been	22 ....
recorded. But the otter is by no means widespred in other parts	23 ....
of the country.	

→ **SEE ALSO**
Grammar 22: Linking words and phrases
Consolidation 6: Units 22–23

Units 22–23

1 Complete the text by writing one word in each space.

Last summer my husband and I had two Italian students to stay at our house in London. It was a kind of exchange, with our two children off to Rome this summer, giving me, incidentally, an interlude of peace in (1) ......*which*...... to write this newspaper column, among other things. But back to the two Italians, two charming girls (2) .... English was a revelation to everyone in our family. I am not going to say that it was perfect or anything (3) .... that, simply that (4) .... used expressions that have either long ago died out in these islands, (5) .... are greeted when used with blank incomprehension. (6) .... example, when a day or two after their arrival Lucia made some coffee and handed it to my neighbour (who had come round to see (7) .... her husband kept popping over to brush up his Italian), she unmistakably said 'Here you are'. The shock was (8) .... great that we both nearly fell off our chairs. (9) .... the benefit of foreign readers, or for anyone who has just returned from a monastery or a few years on Mars, I should explain that this now quaint English expression has long (10) .... been replaced by the transatlantic 'There you go', an utterance which threw me into considerable confusion (11) .... first used by hairdressers, waitresses and barmen. The two girls also surprised us by asking intelligible questions (12) .... of making vague statements which were supposed to be taken as questions. And they had retained that ancient habit of addressing strangers by (13) .... surnames, preceded by a 'Mr' or 'Mrs', as in 'Good morning, Mrs Scott', rather than greeting me at the door on arrival with a 'Hello, Gloria, and have a nice day'. All in (14) .... , they were a delight, although I am sorry to report that by the time they left, they had absorbed (15) .... passes as the English language hereabouts, and had plunged downhill towards unintelligibility. Oh well, there you go, I suppose.

2 Complete the second sentence so that it has a similar meaning to the first sentence, using the word given. Do not change the word given.

1 I had only just arrived home when the phone rang.

sooner

No .... *sooner had I arrived home than* .... the phone rang.

2 Don't under any circumstances press this red button.

do

Whatever .... press this red button.

3 You can stay with us for a few days.

you

We can .... for a few days.

4 Apparently her ex-husband was a terrible gambler.

known

Her ex-husband is .... a terrible gambler.

5 Tony knew what the answer was after reading the book.

read

By the time Tony .... knew what the answer was.

6 Our MP demanded a police investigation.

should

Our MP .... a police investigation.

7 I think a change would do you good.

from

I think .... a change.

8 My passport needs renewing.

to

I .... my passport renewed.

9 Nobody there had heard of Miss Rutherford.

who

Nobody there .... was.

10 There is something on your mind, isn't there?

about

You're .... , aren't you?

3 <u>Underline</u> the 20 extra words in this dialogue.

Tina: Well Martin, pleased to meet <u>with</u> you, and congratulations on getting the job. I'm going to show you round the department, so that you know a bit more before you will start work next week. I gather you're coming with me to the Paris conference.

Martin: Yes, in two weeks' time. Is the job going to be involve a lot of travel to abroad?

Tina: A fair bit – Korea mainly. You'd better to get yourself a Korean phrasebook!

Martin: I've ever been to Korea once before, so I know a few words.

Tina: Good. We have contacts with most of Asian countries in fact. Well, here's the office you'll be working in. As you can see in this room has a photocopier, your computer … by the way, are you familiar with PowerPoint?

Martin: Well, to be perfectly honest, no. I've never really had needed it up to now.

Tina: You really need to spend a few hours in studying this book, then, if you don't mind. I'm sure it'll explain you how the system works.

Martin: May I ask who that man was who was leaving the office when we came in?

Tina: Oh that's Mike. I'm surprised he wasn't at your interview. He's probably the nicest one of the managers.

Martin: He looks like very cheerful.

Tina: As I say it, he's a very nice guy. He's my immediate boss. The only thing is, he does tend to make me to do more jobs than I can cope with. Still, he's letting me to go home early today, so I'm not complaining!

Martin: And on to the subject of leaving, I didn't really understand what they were saying about this 'finish your task' system.

Tina: Oh, well it's just one of the systems you can choose. Basically, it means that the sooner you do finish the sooner you can go to home. But if you finish your task, say, three hours over normal time, you can come in three hours of late the next day.

4 Complete each sentence with a suitable word.

1 That sister of yours! She ....*can*........ be really annoying, you know!

2 The crack in the beams resulted .... the collapse of the ceiling.

3 The block of flats was built .... money lent by the local authority.

4 The children are so .... forward to the party, they can hardly wait!

5 Have you insured the car .... fire?

6 I wish grandfather .... be here to see all the children.

7 I wouldn't be surprised if Mary .... come first after all.

8 .... this really be the right address? The house is for sale.

9 The spokesperson refused to elaborate .... the plans any further.

10 If you .... see Judith, would you give her my love?

5 In most lines of this text there is one extra word. Write the extra word, or put a tick if the line is correct.

A study into family of health conducted in California comes	1 .... *of* ......
up with some interesting conclusions, though these might not be	2 .... ✓ ......
acceptable to everybody. The main conclusion is so that for a	3 .... *so* ......
family to remain healthy, both the relationship between husband	4 ....
and wife plays a major role. The family perhaps surprising	5 ....
aspect of this research, however, is that statistically the	6 ....
healthy family is as optimistic, church-going, and led by a	7 ....
traditional male. And perhaps not so much surprisingly, what	8 ....
promotes the health of the husband and does not necessarily	9 ....
promote the health of the wife either, and vice versa. For	10 ....
example, when it comes to expressing emotions, thus it is	11 ....
generally assumed that giving up an outlet to feelings is healthy.	12 ....
But according to the study, there may be benefits for one party	13 ....
but not for the other. If the wife talks to more than the husband	14 ....
does in these situations and gives him feelings of guilt, then he	15 ....
is likely to become a depressed, whereas if the wife lets the	16 ....
husband dominate on the argument, then she in turn will be the	17 ....
one of whose mental state will suffer. The study also found that	18 ....
when men dominate in the domestic arguments, they often end	19 ....
up trying to avoid from the real issue, or become silent and	20 ....
withdrawn. This has the effect of making the wife feel anxious	21 ....
and depressed. As a person's mental state there is closely linked	22 ....
to their physical well being, it is as clear that the dynamics of	23 ....
family relationships help to determine health in general.	

24
GRAMMAR
Further practice

1 In most lines of this text there is one extra word. Write the extra word, or put a tick if the line is correct.

The term 'drugs' covers many of kinds of chemical substance	1	......*of*......
which they are absorbed by the body, the majority being	2	......*they*......
medicines designed to cure illnesses. They are manufactured	3	......✓......
from a variety of sources which include animal and products,	4	....
plants and minerals. In the recent years it has become possible	5	....
to synthesize in the laboratory many drugs which previously	6	....
obtained from plants and animal products. A small number of	7	....
drugs can become addictive if taken excessively, as that is either	8	....
too frequently, or in doses larger than they recommended for	9	....
medical to use. Drugs intended as painkillers, or drugs with a	10	....
hypnotic effect are used as sleeping pills, can both become	11	....
addictive if abused. It is important to make emphasize the fact	12	....
that it is the abuse of drugs which has once become a widespread	13	....
social problem in many societies, and not that the drug itself	14	....
may have many of beneficial effects when used medically. This is	15	....
why many drugs are obtainable only through prescription from	16	....
a doctor. Some people would argue that if addiction to drugs	17	....
involves both psychological and social factors, since those are	18	....
people who become addicts may do so as in order to find some	19	....
relief from personal or social inadequacies. This argument	20	....
implies that it is somehow the addict's fault if not he or she	21	....
becomes addicted, and this is it to ignore the powerful physical	22	....
effects of many drugs. Any temporary effects of the well-being	23	....
soon wear off, leading to severe physical discomfort.		

2 Choose the best answer.

What can the average family do to create a home environment which is eco-friendly? Well, (1) .... bear in mind that (2) .... half the average home's energy bill is spent on heating rooms, but (3) .... a typical house loses nearly half its heat through the walls and roof. So (4) .... number one priority is to ensure that your house is adequately insulated. Get advice (5) .... double glazing and loft insulation. Have your heating system inspected, and you might be surprised at how much energy it is (6) .... wasting. (7) .... you may not be able to afford a replacement, you should (8) .... consider lowering the temperature of the system. The next important point to consider is (9) .... of household waste. Even if you are lucky enough to have a recycling rubbish collection, you can (10) .... reuse things rather than putting them in the bin. The amount of packaging is an obvious (11) .... Try to reuse containers (12) .... glass jars and plastic cartons instead of wrapping food in foil or cling-film. Take bottles to bottle banks, and only shop in supermarkets which use recyclable packaging. (13) .... people are refusing to buy goods packed in plastic. The garden too is an area where waste can be recycled. Start a compost heap using food scraps and garden weeds (14) .... putting them in the dustbin. And it is surprising (15) .... can be done with some other things we throw away. For example, try papering your bedroom walls with pictures from magazines.

1 A the first point	B one could hardly	C first of all	D what is to
2 A the	B over	C one and a	D in
3 A similarly	B at the same time	C nevertheless	D besides
4 A the	B all of	C with this	D point
5 A from	B for	C with	D about
6 A only	B merely	C purely	D simply
7 A While	B Besides	C However	D Unless
8 A further	B at least	C thus	D more and more
9 A that	B instead	C in spite	D still
10 A utterly	B all in all	C still	D moreover
11 A one	B example	C task	D advantage
12 A with	B as	C such as	D or
13 A More and more	B All	C Increasing	D The
14 A before	B despite	C instead of	D for
15 A it	B what	C this	D in any case

ADVANCED LANGUAGE PRACTICE

3 Complete the second sentence so that it has a similar meaning to the first sentence, using the word given. Do not change the word given.

1 I am not to be disturbed under any circumstances.

no

Under .... *no circumstances am I* .... to be disturbed.

2 I didn't expect to see Tim there, of all people!

last

Tim was .... to see there!

3 This is none of your business!

doesn't

This .... , I'm afraid.

4 I really should be going now.

time

It's .... go now.

5 Foolishly, I paid all the money before collecting the goods.

which

I paid all the money before collecting the goods, ... to do.

6 Robert had no idea of his next move.

do

Robert had no idea .... next.

7 It was only when I checked that I noticed the tyre was flat.

notice

Only when I checked .... a flat tyre.

8 This problem cannot be solved instantly.

no

There .... this problem.

9 My friends persuaded me to go to the party in fancy dress.

talked

My friends .... to the party in fancy dress.

10 The garden party won't take place if the weather stays bad.

picks

Unless .... the garden party won't take place.

4 In most lines of this text there is one extra word. Write the extra word, or put a tick if the line is correct.

Letter 1

Can I add some comments to your to debate about the	1 to (second)
value of television? Your readers may find that some of my	2 ✓
views reflect exactly of their own experience in this matter.	3 ....
First of all, I heartily agree with your reader Mrs Goldwood who	4 ....
she wrote that she has decided to abandon her television set in	5 ....
protest at the mind-boggling boredom of medical dramas, soaps	6 ....
and fly-on-the-wall documentaries. Six months ago I decided	7 ....
that enough was that enough, and took my set to the rubbish tip	8 ....
where it belongs. I can assure to Mrs Goldwood that she will not	9 ....
miss with hers. Since getting rid of mine, I have discovered that	10 ....
there are far more than interesting serials on the radio. I think	11 ....
that she will also find herself is reading more, and at least with	12 ....
books you can choose what a kind of story you want to follow,	13 ....
instead of being at the mercy of the programme for planners.	14 ....
I am sure that other readers can confirm that life after The Box is	15 ....
richer and more rewarding.	

Letter 2

Was I the alone in detecting the note of superiority	16 ....
in the letter from Mr Hackett about giving up television? What is	17 ....
a lot of fuss about nothing! Mr Hackett seems not to think that if	18 ....
you have a television you have to look at it. Surely it is a rather	19 ....
question of choosing programmes carefully enough, and turning	20 ....
the TV off when there is nothing worth it watching. If he is so set	21 ....
against soaps, one wonders why on earth did he watched them?	22 ....

5 Complete the text by writing one word in each space.

Recently there have been doubts about the proper functioning of the English legal system, after several well-publicized cases in (1) ......*which*...... police evidence was eventually shown to be suspect, but only after the wrongful conviction of the accused. In several of (2) .... cases, the crimes involved acts of terrorism, and the police were (3) .... considerable pressure to discover (4) .... had been responsible. Although this in (5) .... way excuses the actions of police officers (6) .... may have falsified evidence, or suppressed evidence which worked against their case, (7) .... underlines the ways (8) .... which publicity in the press and on television exercises an enormous influence, (9) .... the supposed guarantees under the law designed to prevent a jury (10) .... becoming unduly influenced. The specific details of a criminal case are not discussed in the press before a case reaches the courts, and the names of those involved (11) .... often withheld. (12) .... , as many recent murder trials make clear, the press all too often reaches its (13) .... verdict to suit its taste for sensationalism and members of the police might be accused of enlisting the aid of the press by 'leaking' details of a prosecution. Unfortunately, far too few press reports of court cases examine the evidence (14) .... the defence in the same spirit as (15) .... for the prosecution.

6 Complete each sentence with a phrase containing a suitable form of the verb in brackets.

1 Don't be silly! It (can) ......*can't have been*...... Sally. She's in Scotland.
2 But for your help, (win) I .... the prize.
3 By the end of this year, we (marry).. for half a century!
4 Never before (see) .... such heavy snow in April.
5 Be that (may) ...., your behaviour is unacceptable.
6 If you'd said you were ill, I (go) .... the chemist's for you.
7 Try (might) .... , I just couldn't get the car started.
8 How kind of you! But you really (should) .... brought me a present.
9 Not until I looked at my watch (realize) .... how much time had passed.
10 Philip agreed to rob the bank, but then found he couldn't (go) .... it.

7 **Complete the text by writing one word in each space.**

The relationship between the British royal family and the popular press is curious, to (1) ....say........ the least. In many respects the press has yet to realize that the royals are indeed the goose that lays the golden egg. Royal scandals and royal divorces illustrated with tasteless photographs and supported by the worst kind of journalistic excess have proved to be just the thing (2) .... raising newspaper circulations. The same papers that oozed sentimentality over royal weddings, (3) .... drooled over idealized princesses, later went out of their way to hound various royals into separation or divorce. Every photograph became a contribution to (4) .... new rumour or other; even private telephone conversations were printed on the front page. (5) .... the press has yet to realize is that (6) .... intrusions into the privacy of members of the royal family have also helped to create an atmosphere in (7) .... the very existence of the monarchy has been called into question. The prestige of the royal family has undoubtedly suffered. And how could this not (8) .... so when their lives have been turned (9) .... some absurd soap opera? Just (10) .... the press feeds the illusion that the characters on television, those awful creeps in 'Eastenders' and 'Neighbours', are somehow 'real people', so it has reduced the royal family to the status of (11) .... series of cardboard characters. And if you are secretly thinking, 'Well, that's what they are, anyway,' perhaps you are yet (12) .... victim of the illusion. There are real issues still (13) .... be debated about the role, and indeed the survival, of the royal family, issues to which the popular press has hardly contributed. If the monarchy (14) .... lose its constitutional role, the press will be largely to blame. And ironically it will then (15) .... lost one of its main circulation boosters, and killed off its golden goose for good.

VOCABULARY

Leisure activities

1 **Read the text and decide which option (A, B, C or D) best fits each space.**

It is now generally recognized that stress is a major (1) ....C.... of heart disease, and contributes to many other illnesses. Stress is increased by (2) .... such as worry, overwork and lack of exercise or relaxation. For it is just as important from a psychological point of (3) .... to relax as it is to (4) .... physical exercise. Relaxing does not necessarily mean just lazing about and doing nothing. The benefits of a weekend away or the diversion of sporting activities are considerable. If you are suffering from high stress (5) .... , or wish to (6) .... after a trying day, it is generally advisable to have a change of (7) .... Although there are some individuals who (8) .... on stress, for most of us, it can lead to exhaustion, mood swings and even severe depression.

1 A reason	B motive	C cause	D purpose
2 A factors	B aspects	C elements	D items
3 A fact	B departure	C view	D return
4 A make	B have	C undergo	D take
5 A rates	B layers	C ratios	D levels
6 A hold up	B wind down	C draw back	D peter out
7 A scene	B location	C sight	D place
8 A bloom	B prosper	C thrive	D flourish

2 **Choose two items from the box which are used in each activity.**

rod   flippers   goggles   ~~horse~~   helmet   lens   hammer   rucksack
armbands   spanner   bait   mask   tripod   pump   compass   ~~bars~~

1 Gymnastics	horse	bars
2 Scuba Diving	....	....
3 Fishing	....	....
4 Walking	....	....
5 Photography	....	....
6 Do-It-Yourself	....	....
7 Swimming	....	....
8 Cycling	....	....

VOCABULARY 1 LEISURE ACTIVITIES

3 Both options make sense. <u>Underline</u> the one which forms a common collocation.

> Last week well over a thousand people (1) took place *in/<u>took part in</u>* our local round-the-city 10-kilometre fun run. This kind of race doesn't normally (2) *appeal to me/amuse me*, as, frankly, I'm not really (3) *cut out for/right for* long distance running. But I've got two friends who are dead keen runners and who keep going on about the (4) *beneficial/positive* effects of running. So I decided to run, partly for that reason and partly to (5) *earn/raise* money for charity. Friends and colleagues agreed to (6) *sponsor/support me*, and pay for each mile I completed. Well, I hadn't done much training for the big event, and after two kilometres I was (7) *gasping/panting* for breath, so I settled down to a slow jog and resigned myself to plodding along with the (8) *strugglers/ stragglers* at the back of the race. At least I finished, and was very pleased with myself, as I didn't need to stop. I timed myself with a stop-watch, and reckon I (9) *crossed/arrived* at the finishing line in 43 minutes – not bad for a novice. The heat proved too much for a few people who'd gone off too fast for their capabilities and ended up (10) *suffering from/showing* exhaustion. Apparently, the course was very fast, and both of my friends ran a (11) *personal best/ personal record*. The winner (12) *surpassed/broke* the course record. I was actually very impressed with the whole event; the organization was first-class, with medical volunteers (13) *on duty/on standby* throughout, and drinks (14) *stops/stations* every few kilometres of the route. So now the charity of my choice is £150 the richer, and as for me, I'm well and truly bitten by the running bug. I go running with my friends regularly now, and I'm actually starting to (15) *catch up with/get near to* them!

4 Complete each sentence with a word formed from the word in CAPITALS.

1 The new leisure centre doesn't quite come up to my ...expectations... . EXPECT
2 There was a bare .... of people at the youth club. HAND
3 Helen's solo crossing of the Pacific was a .... feat. REMARK
4 We .... go to the pub before lunch on Sunday. VARY
5 All the runners, with the .... of Mark, were exhausted. EXCEPT
6 Our club has just purchased new sports .... EQUIP
7 Our city has some open spaces but they are not very .... ACCESS
8 Is it possible to .... between a hobby and an interest? DISTINCT
9 Nowadays .... numbers of people are taking up jogging. INCREASE
10 Leisure habits won't change much in the .... future. SEE

189

5 Read the text and decide which option (A, B, C or D) best completes each collocation or fixed phrase.

Very few popular (1) ....C.... sports today remain amateur in any sense of the word. In the past, even in cases where payment to players or athletes was forbidden, many (2) .... tolerated what became known as 'shamateurism', and even the sports governing (3) .... turned a blind eye to such (4) .... as the paying of 'expenses'. More recently, sport has become, in effect, a (5) .... of the entertainment industry, and the elite (6) .... in sports such as swimming, tennis, football and track (7) .... can expect to become very rich. This worries some people, who complain that the old Olympic ideal has been lost, but the fact is, sport has become more and more (8) .... in the wider sense, not only requiring total dedication from (9) .... champions, but also expensive facilities, training and nutritional advice. As it is simply no longer possible to combine a career in sport with one elsewhere, shouldn't (10) .... sportsmen and women be able to earn as much as they can from sport?

1	A audience	B watching	C spectator	D viewing
2	A contests	B matches	C games	D sports
3	A associations	B confederations	C authorities	D bodies
4	A practices	B occurrences	C acts	D operations
5	A branch	B division	C wing	D limb
6	A doers	B players	C makers	D performers
7	A running	B athletics	C activities	D racing
8	A scientific	B part-time	C trained	D professional
9	A hopeful	B aspiring	C striving	D wishful
10	A faithful	B loyal	C dedicated	D whole hearted

6 Complete each sentence with a word from the box.

board	draw	lap	referee	runner-up
dive	fan	~~oar~~	round	whistle

1 While I was rowing across the lake I lost one ....*oar*........ .
2 Neither team deserved to lose and the match ended in a ....
3 Ruth was well out in front by the end of the fifth ....
4 After the rugby match David was attacked by an angry ....
5 Brian impressed everyone with his .... into the pool.
6 Our gym teacher used to make us stop by blowing a ....
7 During the chess game Carol knocked all the pieces off the ....
8 Our team was knocked out of the competition in the second ....
9 During the match one of the spectators offered the .... his glasses.
10 Denise won the race and her sister was ....

7 Complete each sentence with one word which fits in all three sentences.

1 Later in the programme we have highlights of two big matches played earlier today: Ajax met Juventus while Barcelona ......*took*........ on Porto.

The weightlifter who allegedly ....*took*....... performance-enhancing drugs has been named today.

On my doctor's advice, I ....*took*....... up yoga in order to relax.

2 The transfer of Mario Rossi has been approved by the club's .... of directors.

The new pool has a slide, water chute and diving ....

In any game of chess, the queen is the most powerful piece on the whole ....

3 Right now Evans is very .... in confidence; she needs to start winning a few races again.

There was a disappointingly .... turnout for the youth club's open day.

When you're cycling up a steep hill you will need to be in a .... gear.

4 .... the earth down around the roots after you've planted the flower.

Jim's Dad took him out into the middle of the pool and showed him how to .... water.

I've got my photos drying out on the kitchen floor, so whatever you do, don't .... on them!

5 Unbelievable – what an amazing .... of events! Smith has come from behind to take the gold medal!

As I'd never played this card game before, the others let me have another ....

… and Walton showed a .... of speed that left his opponents for dead.

2
VOCABULARY

Travel and movement

1 Read the text and decide which option (A, B, C or D) best completes each collocation or fixed phrase.

Most big cities were built long before the heyday of the private car. As a result they rarely have enough space for moving traffic or parked vehicles, and long queues of (1) .... C.. vehicles are a common sight. Indeed some cities end up being almost permanently (2) .... during the day. Those that have a relatively free (3) .... of traffic at non-peak periods of the day do not escape either. The (4) .... hour of early morning or early evening can easily see traffic brought to a (5) .... The effects of exhaust (6) .... on air pollution in cities has been well documented. Buses might be seen as the solution, but they move slowly because of the sheer (7) .... of other traffic, thus encouraging more commuters to abandon (8) .... transport.

1	A standing	B settled	C stationary	D static
2	A stuffed	B saturated	C crammed	D congested
3	A flow	B current	C tide	D flood
4	A push	B rush	C hasty	D hurry
5	A standstill	B hold-up	C jam	D freeze
6	A smells	B odours	C fumes	D stinks
7	A size	B volume	C breadth	D depth
8	A civic	B mass	C public	D popular

2 Match each person from the box with one of the sentences.

hitchhiker	cyclist	passenger	driver	traffic warden
commuter	steward	passer-by	pedestrian	~~rambler~~

1 I love wandering through the countryside along deserted footpaths. ..*rambler*..

2 I'll bring you your drink in just a minute, madam. ....

3 I've been waiting all morning at this roundabout for someone to stop. ....

4 I was just walking down the street opposite the bank when I saw it happen.
....

5 I've spent the last half an hour looking for a spot. It's hopeless. ....

6 I rang my bell and braked. but one of the pedals hit a post and I fell off. ....

7 The sign clearly says two hours only and you've been here all day. ....

8 It's impossible getting across the road here. We need an underpass. ....

9 Do you think you could go a little more slowly? I'm a bit nervous. ....

10 This train is late every morning. It has been for years. ....

192

3 **Complete the text by writing a form of the word in CAPITALS in each space.**

The Manager

Transworld Air

Portugal Street

London

Dear Sir or Madam,

I travelled last week on a Transworld Airbus from London

Gatwick to Copenhagen. This was the (1) ...*outward*......   OUT

journey of a holiday in Denmark, a (2) ....   PACK

tour arranged through a company called 'Sunset'. My

(3) .... was due to leave at 8.20 am on Tuesday   FLY

25th November, but did not in fact leave until 20.30, a delay

of more than eight hours. The reason given was that vital

(4) .... work had to be carried out. Although all   MAINTAIN

passengers were given a free meal, no other offer of

(5) .... was given. Such a long delay is totally   ASSIST

(6) .... , and I feel justified in the circumstances   ACCEPT

in requesting some form of financial (7) ....   COMPENSATE

I have written to the tour (8) .... , who denied   OPERATE

responsibility and advised me to write to you.

I look forward to hearing from you.

Yours faithfully,

Charles Rogers

4 **Both options make sense. <u>Underline</u> the one which forms a common collocation.**

1 We managed to complete our journey <u>*ahead of*</u>/*in front of* schedule.
2 On our way to York, we *divided*/*broke* our journey in Peterborough.
3 As I wasn't coming back by train, I asked for a *single*/*simple* ticket.
4 The two coaches *collided*/*bumped*, but luckily no one was *injured*/*wounded*.
5 There has been widespread public *enmity*/*opposition* to the plan for a new road.
6 My car *skidded*/*slipped* off the road and hit a tree.
7 The train was packed, and there was standing *place*/*room* only.
8 Look at that enormous *goods*/*industrial* train – it must have 20 or 30 wagons!
9 The police accused Donald of breaking the speed *limit*/*restriction*.
10 The Chairman made a *brisk*/*flying* visit to the company's new office in Brussels.

5 Read the text and decide which option (A, B, C or D) best fits each space.

Anyone who has gone on a skiing holiday at a ski (1) ....D.... of any size will be familiar with the age-old problem – the eternal wait for ski lifts and cable cars. Well, there is an alternative. If you feel like something just a little different why not try heli-skiing in Canada? Somewhere in the snowy wastes of the Rocky Mountains the helicopter will deposit you and your group onto a slope of virgin snow that you have all to yourselves. It is all a (2) .... cry from the busiest slopes of, say, Switzerland, France and Italy. You are fifty miles from the nearest town and there is nothing remotely (3) .... a ski-lift, so you have to (4) .... on legs, skis and the chopper. You might see the (5) .... mountain-goat or grizzly bear, but there won't be (6) .... of other skiers. There are one or two disadvantages. Your friendly helicopter pilot might just put you down in a five-metre snow (7) .... And freezing weather might ground your helicopter and leave you (8) .... in the wilderness.

1 A spot	B haunt	C refuge	D resort
2 A different	B strange	C far	D long
3 A resembling	B appearing	C seeming	D looking
4 A count	B trust	C rely	D reckon
5 A occasional	B sometime	C incidental	D irregular
6 A bunches	B hordes	C throngs	D swarms
7 A dune	B pile	C mound	D drift
8 A deserted	B stranded	C wrecked	D aground

6 Replace the words <u>underlined</u> in each sentence with a form of one of the verbs from the box.

accelerate	ascend	collide	~~dismount~~	fasten
alight	endanger	reverse	board	disembark

1 Ann <u>got off her horse</u> and picked up her riding hat. *dismounted*

2 As the plane <u>went faster</u> down the runway, David began to sweat nervously.
....

3 Without realizing it, Jim <u>drove backwards</u> into a lamp post. ....

4 All the visitors to the ship must <u>get off</u> immediately as we are about to sail.
....

5 Passengers who wish to <u>get off</u> at Hove should travel in the front coach ....

6 Please <u>do up</u> your safety belt before we begin the journey. ....

7 The captain refused to <u>put at risk</u> the safety of the crew. ....

8 The balloon <u>rose up</u> gracefully into the summer sky. ....

9 In thick fog, the two <u>ships ran into each other</u> outside the harbour. ....

10 The sooner the passengers <u>get on</u> the aircraft, the sooner it can take off. ....

7 **Complete the spaces with one word which fits in all three sentences.**

1   It only takes one small accident to ....*hold*........ up the traffic for several hours.
The new Atlantic airbus will ....*hold*........ about 700 passengers.
Like it or not, it is the train and not the car which will ....*hold*........ the key to the future of domestic travel.

2   Why don't you just get the goods delivered to your house, and .... yourself a two-hour car journey into the city-centre?
By driving at 70 km/h instead of 100, you can .... a lot of petrol.
I'm trying to .... up for a trip to Canada, so I can't afford to buy much at the moment.

3   The Department of Transport have .... a deadline of 1 June for completion of the new motorway.
Because of the strike by air traffic controllers, delays are .... to continue well into next week.
The trains in Switzerland are so punctual you can .... your watch by them.

4   The train was delayed because of ice on the ....
After the accident there was a solid .... of cars stretching back for several miles.
In a new initiative announced today, police are to take a harder .... on speeding motorists.

5   Sorry, I've rather lost .... of my argument.
Right, now, I want you to run twice around the .... for a warm-up.
After a while the .... we had been following became thick undergrowth.

News events

1 Read the text and decide which option (A, B, C or D) best fits each space.

Reports that the government is about to (1) ....c.... the go-ahead to plans for the building of a new runway at London's Heathrow airport have angered local (2) .... and raised fears of increased noise and exhaust pollution. The (3) .... plans also include a new sixth terminal building, and (4) .... the disappearance of a whole village, (5) .... the demolition up to 700 other homes. According to sources close to the Ministry of Transport, the government is known to be concerned by the increasing (6) .... of traffic at London Heathrow. At Gatwick, London's second airport, there are no plans for further runways in the foreseeable (7) .... and Heathrow is widely (8) .... as a better (9) .... for expansion. Although the planned building work would not take place until 2020, local people have already raised strong (10) .... A spokesperson for the Keep West London Quiet association, (11) .... up of local residents, accused the government of (12) .... back on promises made before the General Election. 'We were told then that the airport authority had no (13) .... of building another runway, and we believe that the government has a duty to (14) .... its pledges.' Prominent figures in the government are also believed to be concerned at the news, although the Prime Minister is (15) .... as saying that reports were 'misleading'. However, he would not give an assurance that plans for building a runway had definitely been rejected.

1 A sign	B make	C give	D approve
2 A inhabitants	B dwellers	C occupants	D residents
3 A controversial	B debatable	C notorious	D doubtful
4 A involve	B concern	C contain	D need
5 A further to	B as well as	C moreover	D what's more
6 A sum	B size	C volume	D length
7 A years	B period	C time	D future
8 A regarded	B believed	C felt	D held
9 A potential	B outlook	C prospect	D likelihood
10 A oppositions	B protests	C demonstrations	D objections
11 A made	B set	C brought	D taken
12 A getting	B falling	C going	D turning
13 A desire	B intention	C wish	D objective
14 A bear out	B count on	C pull off	D stand by
15 A quoted	B known	C thought	D written

2 Both options make sense. <u>Underline</u> the one which forms a common collocation.

1 The two men, <u>*disguised*</u>/*transformed* as security guards, overpowered staff at the bank and escaped with £150,000.

2 The pilot was the *one/sole* survivor of the crash.

3 The fire *extensively/widely* damaged the 500-year-old building.

4 Mr Johnson was taken to Maidstone General Hospital where his condition was described as '*critical/perilous*'.

5 The government spokesperson declined to *speak about/comment on* the matter.

6 A woman and a man were later *detained/arrested* for questioning.

7 The *findings/results* of the committee are due for publication this week.

8 The government agreed that the problem must be *removed/tackled* at once.

9 We must be very careful with *sensitive/difficult* issues such as this, to avoid giving offence.

10 A police spokesperson admitted that detectives were *baffled/upset* by Mr Day's disappearance, but were hoping to come up with an explanation.

3 Complete each sentence with a word from the box.

conditions	evidence	knowledge	place	responsibility
confidence	incident	opinion	~~prospect~~	verge

1 With Smith out injured, there is little ....prospect........ of City reaching the next round.

2 After heavy rain, ... during the race were hazardous.

3 It is common .... that Douglas intends to retire at the end of the season.

4 Two French and two English forwards were involved in an ugly .... just before half-time.

5 Miss Schmidt easily secured her .... in the next round with a confident display of power tennis.

6 The final day begins with the Australian team on the .... of victory.

7 Whether Rooney was offside is a matter of .... , in my view.

8 I have every .... that Jack Wood is the man to lead our team to victory.

9 There is no concrete .... that anyone in the team has taken drugs.

10 The club has disclaimed .... for the damage, blaming it on supporters from London.

4 Complete the collocation or fixed phrase in sentences (1–10) using endings (a–j).

1 The union is drawing up … ……f….
2 The managing director said that recent events had put … ……….
3 No one holds out … ……….
4 He went on to say that the company prided … ……….
5 Both sides have agreed to meet on a regular … ……….
6 The union has since challenged … ……….
7 Others believe that both sides would jump at the … ……….
8 It is unlikely that the union will moderate … ……….
9 The management stated that the problem had been exaggerated out of … ……….
10 The minister said that he put himself at the … ……….

a … basis from now on, he added.
b … all proportion, and that an agreement was close.
c … a strain upon everyone employed by the company.
d … its demand for a shorter working week.
e … the figures given to the press by the financial director.
f … new proposals to put to the employers.
g … disposal of both sides in the dispute.
h … itself on its good relations with all its employees.
i … chance to resume negotiations without delay.
j … much hope for the success of the discussions.

5 Replace the words underlined in each sentence with one of the phrases from the box.

argue that there should be	have no intention	raised fears
brought about	it is common knowledge	explained the cause as
little prospect of success	say for certain	

1 I am not thinking of resigning at the moment. *have no intention*
2 Everybody is aware that Smith has a criminal record. ……………………………
3 We all know what caused the closure of the factory. ……………………………
4 The report has made people afraid that others may be at risk from the disease. …………………………………
5 We shall try hard, although there is not much chance of winning. ……………………………
6 A hospital spokesperson refused to confirm that the injured man had been shot. ……………………………
7 Some conservationists advocate an immediate ban on hunting. ……………………………
8 Commenting on the weekend travel chaos, the rail company attributed this to a combination of snow and high winds. ……………………………

6 Replace the word or words underlined In each headline with one of the 'headline' words from the box.

bid	clash	held	toll	boost	cleared	looms	set	~~vows~~

1 Miners' union <u>promises</u> to fight over local pay deals. ......*vows*......
2 Change to school funding aims to <u>increase</u> teacher numbers. ....
3 Newspapers and union <u>going</u> to clash over pay claim. ....
4 Man <u>found innocent</u> in bank robbery case. ....
5 British <u>attempt</u> to aid refugees turned down. ....
6 Woman <u>arrested</u> by police after pub shooting. ....
7 Hotel fire <u>number of victims</u> rises to six. ....
8 Rail strike <u>approaches</u>. ....
9 Ministers <u>in disagreement</u> over pay rises. ....

7 Complete the text by writing a form of the word in CAPITALS in each space.

Press (1) ......*speculation*...... continues over whether the Prime Minister is on the point of calling a General Election. An (2) .... is expected shortly from government headquarters. Political (3) .... believe that the timing of an election is crucial to the (4) .... of the government. Michael Lee of the 'Independent' commented: 'We've had repeated (5) .... from the Prime Minister that no election would be called this year, but present circumstances may just cause him to change his mind.' Six months ago this would have been (6) .... An election would have been (7) .... suicide, and would certainly have led to the (8) .... of the government. The government was coming in for severe (9) .... for its foreign policy. It was also widely attacked for its (10) .... involvement in the arms export scandal, and for its (11) .... to address the problem of (12) .... But according to recent opinion polls, the electorate is impressed at the way the PM has restored party (13) .... and overcome the internal (14) .... which were threatening to rip the party apart. Michael Lee commented: 'There would be some (15) .... in calling an election pretty soon. In fact, I wouldn't be at all surprised if it happens within the next day or two.'

SPECULATE
ANNOUNCE
ANALYSE
SURVIVE
ASSURE
THINK
POLITICS
DOWN
CRITICIZE
DISASTER
FAIL
EMPLOY
UNITE
DIVIDE
JUSTIFY

Places

1 Read the text and decide which option (A, B, C or D) best fits each space.

When I first arrived here to take up my new job, I stayed in a hotel, but I soon started looking for a permanent (1) ...C.... , a place to (2) .... my own. The first flat I came (3) .... was cold and uninviting, and had large (4) .... of damp on the walls. The flat (5) .... onto a factory, so the view was not exactly inspiring. Then I had a look at a small flat in a modern apartment (6) .... It had a parking (7) .... and was fully (8) .... , but the rent was far too high for me. I didn't want to end up in a tiny place, so I answered an ad for house-sharing. The house was in a quiet (9) .... , and as soon as I saw it I fell in love with it. There was a high overgrown (10) .... around the front garden, and (11) .... to park cars in the drive. The room to (12) .... looked out over the back garden, and had a big bay window. (13) .... it meant sharing the kitchen and living room, I did have my own bathroom, really just a shower and washbasin (14) .... into what must have once been a cupboard. There was, however, quite a lot of (15) .... space.

1	A household	B accommodation	C residence	D habitation
2	A refer	B be	C call	D say
3	A over	B across	C up	D by
4	A patches	B pieces	C stretches	D stains
5	A showed up	B saw through	C gave over	D looked out
6	A tower	B skyscraper	C block	D column
7	A bit	B spot	C location	D space
8	A furnished	B provided	C supplied	D prevented
9	A surroundings	B neighbourhood	C vicinity	D premises
10	A fence	B bush	C hedge	D lawn
11	A space	B capacity	C area	D place
12	A let	B rent	C hire	D lease
13	A But for	B Despite	C Nevertheless	D Although
14	A cramped	B crowded	C cluttered	D crammed
15	A storage	B stocking	C saving	D accumulation

2 Complete each sentence with one word which fits in all three sentences.

1 It took us three hours of hard climbing to reach the ...*summit*.... .

   Being promoted to manager is undoubtedly the ...*summit*.... of my career to date.

   A special ...*summit*.... of the leading economic countries has been called.

2 When the agreement is finally signed by all parties, you will receive the .... to the house.

   The self-study edition of the book comes with a .... so you can check all your answers.

   His ability to persuade people is the .... to his success.

3 The second flat I saw was in a terrible ....

   His physical condition is improving, but I'm not sure about his .... of mind.

   The funeral of former President Jones was attended by heads of .... from all over the world.

4 The road out of the city affords a spectacular .... of the lake.

   I would like to look at the house again, with a .... to moving in shortly.

   You won't find a better house than that one; that's my .... anyway.

5 OK, let's .... on and try to reach the top by lunchtime.

   These trousers are specially designed so that you don't need to iron and .... them.

   If you .... this button here, you'll activate the alarm system.

6 From here you can see the river as it begins to .... its way towards Woodchester.

   Once a month, someone has to climb the tower and .... the clock.

   The car plant has decided to .... down production of 4 x 4 vehicles.

3 Both options make sense. <u>Underline</u> the one which forms a common collocation.

1 The room was *lightly/<u>sparsely</u>* furnished, with just a table and a chair.

2 I sat down with the landlady and signed the *tenancy/lodging* agreement.

3 At the dump, huge metal skips were crammed full with people's *household/domestic* rubbish.

4 A group of homeless people entered the unoccupied house and claimed squatters' *possession/rights*.

5 You can't come in here, as it's private *land/property*.

6 They are going to put up a ten-*floor/storey* building opposite my house.

7 Groups with guides should go to the side *access/entrance*.

8 There's been a *sharp/heavy* rise in the price of property in the south-east.

9 The rooms are dark and smelly, and the heating is *barely/hardly* adequate.

10 From the cliff top, it was a *vertical/sheer* drop to the rocks below.

4 Complete each sentence with a word from the box.

bay	horizon	pass	slope	strait
cliff	landscape	plain	~~spring~~	tide

1 This water comes from a .....spring...... near the bottom of the mountain.
2 The hills could be seen faintly outlined against the ....
3 The ship won't be able to sail until the .... comes in.
4 There was a rocky .... rising a hundred feet above the beach.
5 The two islands are divided by a narrow ....
6 There is only one .... through the mountains.
7 Many small boats could be seen moored in the wide curving ....
8 The children amused themselves by rolling down the grassy ....
9 The whole .... had turned white after the overnight fall of snow.
10 At the foot of the mountains was a wide, well-cultivated ....

5 Complete each sentence (1–10) with one of the endings (a–j).

1 I paused at the top of the stairs on the ... .e....
2 The walls of the bathroom were covered in ... .
3 I chained my bike to the ... .
4 There was a clock on the ... .
5 I left my umbrella in the ... .
6 After the storm we had to replace several ... .
7 I decided to oil the front door ... .
8 There was no heat coming from the ... .
9 You should try to remember to wipe your feet on the ... .
10 We stored our old books upstairs in the ... .

a ... railings at the front of the house.
b ... hinges, which were rather rusty.
c ... loft, in case we needed them again.
d ... mantelpiece over the fireplace.
e ... landing and wondered which was my room.
f ... doormat outside the back door.
g ... slates which had fallen off the roof.
h ... radiator under the window.
i ... tiles with a pattern of fruit and flowers.
j ... porch and opened the front door.

6 Complete each sentence with a word from the box.

architecture	desert	estuary	range	~~scenery~~
summit	site	shore	square	valley

1 One advantage of travelling by train is that you can forget about traffic jams and crowded roads, and sit back and admire the ..scenery... .

2 The area around George Square was first developed in the eighteenth century, and includes fine examples of the .... of that period.

3 We began climbing the narrow mountain path just before dawn, and by the time we reached the ...., the whole of the plain below lay revealed in the sunshine.

4 Away from the sea, the landscape becomes increasingly bare until the rocky slopes give way to the rolling dunes of the ....

5 My eye followed the course of the river, winding down through its green .... towards the distant town of Woodchester.

6 The towering waves rolled in towards the ...., finally crashing upon the rocks in clouds of spray.

7 At the end of the village, take the track on the right just past the petrol station (impassable for cars). The .... of the temple lies 3km to the east of the village

8 The island is divided by a .... of mountains running approximately north to south, the highest of which is Mount Ash, 3,230 metres.

9 Further along the coast, many diving and wading birds nest in the .... of the River Bourne, mainly in the marshes to the west of the railway bridge.

10 The narrow medieval street, now a pedestrian zone, leads away from the cathedral and brings you eventually to a .... in front of the Town Hall.

7 Replace the words <u>underlined</u> in each sentence with an expression from the box.

focus exclusively on	undecided	reach the highest point
~~large number~~	situation has changed	was much taller than
managed to get	puzzled	gathering of national leaders

1 We have had a <u>flood</u> of applications. ....large number....

2 John <u>towered</u> above his opponent. ....

3 Mary is still <u>sitting on the fence</u>. ....

4 Both presidents are due to attend a <u>summit meeting</u>. ....

5 Jones is <u>streets</u> ahead of all his rivals in this respect. ....

6 I was completely <u>floored</u> by the question. ....

7 We expect output to <u>peak</u> at around 150,000 cars a year. ....

8 Jack has decided to <u>channel all his energy into</u> politics. ....

9 Harry has <u>landed</u> a new job in sales and marketing. ....

10 Some experts believe that the economic <u>tide has now turned.</u> ....

5

VOCABULARY

Media and advertising

1 Complete the collocations in each sentence with a word from the box.

broadcast	bulletin	coverage	forecast	media
brochure	campaign	edition	~~booklet~~	novel

1 Read the instruction ....*booklet*......... before using your new digital camera.
2 'David Copperfield' is an autobiographical ....
3 What did it say on the weather .... ?
4 This is a party political .... on behalf of the Democratic Party.
5 What time is the next news .... ?
6 This channel doesn't have very good sports ....
7 A first .... of this book is worth a fortune.
8 The mass .... in most countries is dominated by advertising.
9 When does our new advertising .... begin?
10 I spent all of yesterday evening looking at this holiday ....

2 Read the text and decide which option (A, B, C or D) best completes each collocation or fixed phrase.

After more than seventy years of television, it might seem only too obvious to conclude that it is (1) ....D.... to stay. There have been many objections to it during this time, of course, and on a variety of grounds. Did it cause eye strain? Did the advertisements contain subliminal (2) .... , persuading us to buy more and telling us who to vote for? Did children turn to violence through watching it, either because so many programmes taught them how to shoot, rob, and kill, or because they had to do something to (3) .... the hours they had spent (4) .... to the tiny screen? Or did it simply create a vast passive audience, drugged by glamorous serials and inane situation comedies? On the other hand, did it increase anxiety by (5) .... the news and (6) .... our living rooms with war, famine and political unrest?

1	A around	B there	C ready	D here
2	A information	B messages	C data	D communications
3	A make up for	B negate	C deny	D compensate
4	A attached	B fixed	C glued	D adhered
5	A scandalizing	B hyping	C dramatizing	D sensationalizing
6	A filling	B loading	C stuffing	D packing

3 Read the text and decide which option (A, B, C or D) best completes each collocation or fixed phrase.

These days it's not just television which is (1) ....C.... the blame for turning the nation into mindless couch potatoes. According to a recent report, the nation's 11- to 15-year-olds now spend (2) .... 52 hours a week in front of a screen, whether it's the TV or the computer, and doctors and teachers are (3) .... worried about the effects. Sitting about watching TV or video games, instead of taking exercise, has clearly played its (4) .... in the rise in the number of seriously overweight children. Experts also believe that as a result of their exposure to fast-moving visual images, many children no longer (5) .... it possible to focus on reading, or sit still and pay attention in the classroom. Now these experts are saying that it is (6) .... parents to help teenagers cut down on TV and computer use, and make sure that they spend equal amounts of time on other activities.

1	A having	B setting	C taking	D making
2	A for the time being	B at any rate	C on average	D in time
3	A further	B excessively	C over	D increasingly
4	A part	B cards	C joke	D system
5	A make	B find	C believe	D concentrate
6	A in for	B down with	C up to	D back to

4 Complete each sentence with a word from the box.

fiction	illiterate	literature	outline	shorthand
gist	illegible	manuscript	prose	unprintable

1 The first chapter is based on fact, but the rest of the book is complete ....fiction.... .

2 David was unable to read the postcard because the writing was ....

3 I understood the .... of the article, but I didn't read it in detail.

4 Brenda's comments were so insulting they were ....

5 Bill decided to study French .... at university.

6 I managed to make notes of the speech in ....

7 Old Mrs Brown never went to school and is ....

8 Some people feel that Davis's .... is better than his poetry.

9 Sheila left the .... of her novel on a train by mistake.

10 Just tell me the .... of the story, don't go into too much detail.

5 Read the text and decide which option (A, B, C or D) best completes each collocation or fixed phrase.

One of the groups of consumers targeted by advertisers is, oddly enough, a group with very little money of its own, but which has a huge (1) ....ᶜ.... the way others spend their money. And in some ways, children and advertisers could have been made for (2) .... After all, it is easy to fool younger children into believing (3) .... anything and if an advertisement shows them how Biffo Breakfast Cereal will help them run faster than their friends, then (4) .... they are concerned, that is the truth. They also have strong feelings of admiration for action heroes or cartoon characters or sports stars, and will want to be (5) .... their favourite star, and drink the same cola or eat the same sweets. And when children want something badly enough, they won't stop nagging their parents until they (6) .... it. Advertisements will even (7) .... them with the arguments they can use when they are told that a water-firing robot or a giant chocolate bar is not good (8) ...., or too expensive, or not available in the supermarket. This is why most EU countries place (9) .... upon television advertising aimed at children. Some countries have (10) .... ban on ads promoting toys during children's programmes. Others restrict the advertising of unhealthy food, or ads involving anything dangerous. This seems to be a sensible way of preventing advertisers from taking (11) ....of children, but in some ways it also helps to make a more damning (12) .... If it is generally agreed that children need (13) .... from some kinds of advertising, then this (14) .... to definite proof that advertising strongly influences children's behaviour. In that case, why should any advertising aimed at children be allowed? After all, isn't it just another form of brain-washing? Adults may (or may not) resist the (15) .... claims of advertisers, but children clearly have not yet learnt to do this. This is why an EU-wide ban on advertising targeting children, or depicting children, is being called for in some quarters.

	A	B	C	D
1	A cause of	B reason why	C influence upon	D outcome which
2	A each other	B the worst	C ever	D the time being
3	A more and more	B all in all	C as good as	D just about
4	A unless	B whatsoever	C as far as	D supposing
5	A just like	B exactly the same	C as is	D in imitation
6	A stop	B achieve	C gain	D get
7	A offer	B explain	C fill	D supply
8	A at it	B for them	C with them	D to it
9	A handicaps	B rules	C restrictions	D conditions
10	A a total	B an utter	C a sheer	D a thorough
11	A advantage	B pity	C an interest	D responsibility
12	A change	B profit	C point	D contribution
13	A care	B preservation	C safeguards	D protection
14	A comes	B amounts	C indicates	D refers
15	A sceptical	B suspicious	C doubtful	D questioning

6 Both options make sense. <u>Underline</u> the one which forms a common collocation.

1 I do like Channel 4's *reporting/<u>coverage</u>* of the big sporting events.
2 We do not have the book in stock. It is *out of circulation/out of print*.
3 This report comes from our political *correspondent/journalist*, Edward Ross.
4 The 'Sunday News' has the highest *circulation/output* of any newspaper in Britain.
5 They are bringing out Sue's book in a new *edition/publication* soon.
6 Are books subject to *banning/censorship* in your country?
7 Through market research the advertising company identified their *intended/target* customer.
8 They are very concerned with the image that the advert *projects/gives*.
9 At least 50 members of the *population/public* wrote in to complain about the ad.
10 He sits there for hour after hour, staring *calmly/blankly* at the screen.

7 Complete the text by writing a form of the word in CAPITALS in each space.

A man takes a single (1) ....*spoonful*.... of a substance and puts it in his mouth. Instantly he is transported to another world, a place of surreal visions and swirling colours. He rushes (2) .... into this parallel universe. What is this (3) .... compound with the power to induce such a mind-blowing trip? Is it some kind of drug that makes the user hallucinate? No, it's just a humble cereal ad on TV. The Fruity Wheat ad is the latest in a long line of (4) .... ads whose imagery appears to draw on the effects of mind-altering substances. Colin Rees of the 'Stop TV Advertising' group, said: 'I find this and other such ads totally (5) .... Take this stuff and you will experience something out of this world – the (6) .... of the ad seems clear to me. The companies who make them will say that any relation to drugs is just one (7) .... of the advert, and not one that they (8) .... When I complained about this ad, I was told that it didn't contain any (9) .... messages. I thought that was a bit rich – I think the message in it is blatantly obvious! And I don't think we should be giving TV viewers any (10) .... in that respect.'

SPOON
HEAD
TERRIFY
CONTROVERSY
ACCEPT
IMPLY
INTERPRET
INTENTION
CONSCIOUS
ENCOURAGE

6

VOCABULARY

The natural world

1 Read the text and decide which option (A, B, C or D) best completes each collocation or fixed phrase.

Whenever we read about the natural world nowadays, it is generally to be given dire predictions about its (1) ....c.... destruction. Some scientists go so (2) .... as to assert that from now on, the world can no longer be called 'natural', insofar as future processes of weather, climate and all the interactions of plant and animal life will no longer carry on in their time-honoured way, unaffected by humans. There will never be such a thing as 'natural weather' again, say such writers, only weather affected by global warming. It is hard to know whether to believe such (3) .... of doom, possibly because what they are saying seems too terrible to be true. There are other equally influential scientists who argue that climate, for example, has changed many times over the (4) .... , and that what we are experiencing now may simply be part of an endless (5) .... of change, rather than a disaster on a global (6) ....

1	A coming	B close	C imminent	D nigh
2	A much	B deep	C long	D far
3	A prophets	B champions	C warriors	D giants
4	A generations	B millennia	C centuries	D eras
5	A revolution	B circle	C round	D cycle
6	A measure	B scale	C proportion	D extent

2 Both options make sense. <u>Underline</u> the one which forms a common collocation.

1 Could you close the window? There's a bit of a *current/<u>draught</u>*.
2 I'm soaked, I got caught in a *downpour/torrent*.
3 Through my binoculars I watched a tiger stalking its *food/prey*.
4 Many species of wildlife could become *extinct/defunct* if left unprotected.
5 I feel hungry. Could you *peel/skin* an apple for me?
6 Don't be afraid of the monkey, it's quite *tame/trained*.
7 Our country has many natural *resources/sources*.
8 Marcia is very much into environmental *facts/issues* at the moment.
9 Local people are concerned about pollution from *sea-located/off-shore* oil wells.
10 That's an unusual dog. What *breed/race* is it?

3 Choose four items from the box which are associated with each creature.

scratch	blind	flock	hole	ivory	lead	nocturnal	spray	kitten	tusks
bark	squeak	purr	buzz	kennel	stripe	roar	~~stable~~	trap	wing
whine	cub	hive	~~hoof~~	lamb	net	~~saddle~~	sting	trunk	wool

1 horse ....hoof....... ....stable....... ....saddle.......
2 bee ....
3 tiger ....
4 mosquito ....
5 dog ....
6 sheep ....
7 elephant ....
8 mouse ....
9 bat ....
10 cat ....

4 Complete each sentence with a word formed from the word in CAPITALS.

1 Kapo the gorilla was born and bred in ......captivity.... .   CAPTIVE
2 In the wild Kapo's chances of .... would   SURVIVE
   be slim.
3 The river cleaning project is run by conservation .... VOLUNTARY
4 The white rhino is now an .... species.   DANGER
5 .... claim that the virus among seals was   ENVIRONMENT
   caused by pollution.
6 She may look fierce but the lioness has .... instincts   MOTHER
   like any other female animal.
7 The fish in the river provide an .... supply of fish   ABOUND
   for the young bears.
8 The whale shark reaches .... at the age of 30.   MATURE
9 Nowadays only a .... of wild crocodiles remain there.   HAND
10 Nowhere epitomizes the wonderful ....   DIVERSE
   of nature better than the jungle.

5 **Complete each sentence with one word which fits in all three sentences.**

1 Glaciers provide vital evidence of climate ......*change*.... .

What you need is not pills but a simple ......*change*.... of scene.

If you need money, there's some spare ......*change*.... in my coat pocket.

2 Grassland and savannah .... a substantial part of Southern Africa.

It's a long journey – let's take some books to .... the children.

The protesting students intend to .... the Holman Building.

3 The vet said the .... on the dog's face was not cancerous.

She had a .... in her throat and a tear in her eye when she said goodbye.

Get up and do some work, you lazy .... !

4 Many of the wildebeest didn't make it and .... half-way across the river.

My voice was .... out by the sound of builders drilling.

I .... my meal in sauce to hide the bitter taste.

5 The falconer trained the hawk to fly in a perfectly .... line.

So let's get this .... ; you say you saw the man break in through the window.

Why can't you just give me a .... answer for once in your life?

6 <u>Underline</u> **the most suitable option in each sentence.**

1 Last year this tree was struck by *lightning/thunder/a storm*.

2 I like spring best, when the apple trees are in *blooming/blossom/flowers*.

3 Something must be done to protect *wild/wilderness/wildlife*.

4 When I want to relax, I go for a walk in *the countryside/the nature/the outside*.

5 In this part of the country, *the earth/the land/the soil* is quite expensive.

6 Suddenly we saw a ship appear on the *atmosphere/horizon/sky*. We were saved!

7 Most animals will attack you to protect their *babies/litters/young*.

8 Julia recently discovered a new *category/make/species* of fruit-fly.

9 We got soaked to the skin in the torrential *drizzle/downpour/snow*.

10 While I was eating cherries I accidentally swallowed a *nut/pip/stone*.

Work

1 Complete the text by writing one word from each column to form a collocation in each space.

Column A
working, sick, promotion, pension, covering, trial, career, job, claims, travel

Column B
description, letter, conditions, scheme, path, pay, prospects, expenses, form, period

Dear David,

You'll never guess what's happened – I've only got a job! I saw an advert in the press for an administrative assistant at London Insurance, and sent in my CV and a (1) ......*covering letter*........ , more out of curiosity than anything else. Well, to my surprise, I got an interview, and I managed to convince them that insurance is the (2) .... I intend to pursue. Apparently, they were impressed with my ambition, especially when I said I was looking for a job with good (3) .... , and a week later I was offered the job.

They seem to look after you well – for example, I was told to send in a (4) .... so that they could reimburse my (5) .... to the interview. It's little things like that which make all the difference.

I was also impressed by the (6) .... at the office when I went for the interview. So I'm actually starting work on Monday! I've received my (7) .... now, and it all seems very favourable. After a (8) .... of one month, I'll be on a permanent contract with (9) .... and paid holiday. There's even a company (10) .... which I can join.

David, why don't you apply? They take on 20 new graduates each year. It would be right up your street.

Best wishes,

Fiona

2 Read the text and decide which option (A, B, C or D) best completes each collocation or fixed phrase.

1   We're very busy this week. Can you work ....*c*..........?

   A extra time   B supplementary time   C overtime   D double time

2   Jane succeeded in her job through sheer hard ....

   A work   B labour   C industry   D effort

3   Catherine works for a .... advertising agency.

   A main   B forefront   C principal   D leading

4   Tom's employment .... would be better if he had a clean driving licence.

   A prospects   B opportunities   C odds   D likelihood

5   Bill has a real .... for caring for the elderly.

   A career   B post   C inspiration   D vocation

6   Ruth is looking for a new .... at the moment.

   A vacancy   B position   C work   D employment

7   I have a/an .... in computer aided design and three years' experience.

   A lesson   B course   C qualification   D examination

8   In some companies there is little .... to work hard.

   A inspiration   B advantage   C gain   D motivation

9   It's not very interesting work, but at least it's a .... job.

   A constant   B continuous   C nonstop   D steady

10 After the takeover, the Managing Director was forced to hand in his ....

   A resignation   B notification   C retirement   D dismissal

3 Complete the text by writing a form of the word in CAPITALS in each space.

This year, (1) ......productivity...... in the factory has suffered	PRODUCT
because of a lack of expert technical knowledge. As a result	
we have made very substantial (2) .... in sending	INVEST
employees on training courses. The fact remains that it is	
becoming increasingly difficult to get skilled labourers with	
the right (3) .... , experience, and above all,	QUALIFY
(4) .... The company has also suffered this year	EXPERT
from the industrial (5) .... in November, which	ACT
saw 340 union members walk out in a pay dispute. Union	
(6) .... eventually sat down with management	REPRESENT
and negotiated a four per cent pay rise and five working days were lost.	
We also now recognize the need to (7)	ECONOMY
in some areas, and our management (8) .... , Prior	CONSULT
and Young, have identified the need for at least three departments	
to be (9) .... It is thought that this will mean	STREAM
the loss of between six and ten jobs, though the exact figures will	
be (10) .... in the next report.	CLEAR

4 Complete each sentence with a word from the box.

agent	competitor	~~executive~~	industrialist	manufacturer
client	dealer	foreman	labourer	trainee

1 Nowadays you often find that the top ....executive........ in a company is a woman.
2 If you have any problems with your work, talk to the ....
3 'Happy Chips' is the number one .... of potato crisps in the country.
4 I'm starting next week as a .... chef in a large hotel.
5 Our company is the .... for several large insurance companies.
6 David was not content until he had become a rich ....
7 Our firm is quite a long way ahead of our nearest ....
8 With mechanization it is difficult to find work as an unskilled ....
9 I have been working as a used car .... for the past six months.
10 A company should make every .... feel important.

5 Match each sentence (1–10) with an explanation (a–j).

1 Jane was headhunted by a multinational company. ......e......
2 Pam is at the end of her tether. ....
3 Mary's assistant was given the sack. ....
4 Jean really has her nose to the grindstone. ....
5 Sue was given a golden handshake. ....
6 Helen took on a new secretary. ....
7 Ann is on the go all day. ....
8 Brenda was overlooked. ....
9 Judith has made good. ....
10 Pauline's boss keeps her on her toes. ....

a She is always busy.
b She doesn't have the chance to become complacent.
c She's working hard.
d She didn't get promoted.
e She was offered a better job.
f She has become successful.
g She was dismissed.
h She received a cash bonus on leaving her job.
i She has run out of patience.
j She gave someone a job.

6 Complete the second sentence so that it is a more formal version of the first sentence. Each space is one word.

1 You can join the company pension scheme

   You are ....*eligible*........ for the company's pension scheme.

2 You get 25 days' paid holiday.

   You are .... to 25 days' holiday.

3 The salary is fixed.

   The salary is not ....

4 You must wear smart clothes.

   All employees must be smartly ....

5 The hours are 9 to 5.

   The .... day will commence. at 9.00 and finish at 5.00.

6 You don't get paid for any extra work in the evening or at weekends.

   No .... payments are made in respect of this position.

7 If you're off sick for more than three days, get something written by a doctor.

   Any .... of more than three days must be explained by a doctor's

   ....

8 Tell us one month in advance if you want to end your employment with us.

   This contract may be .... at any time by you, but one month's ....

   must be given in writing of your intention to do so.

7 Complete the text by writing one word in each space.

Have you ever asked yourself why it is that we (1) .....*work*......? If it is, as some people say, just a question of money, would you be prepared to do any job as long as you (2) .... a lot, even if it involved working for long hours in appalling (3) ....? Or are you perhaps more interested in the (4) .... you get when you feel that you are good at your job? It's true that there is a great sense of (5) .... behind, for example, the creation of a well-made product, or the clinching of an important deal, though this might not be the (6) .... if you were serving in a shop or delivering letters. Still, as long as the customers are satisfied, then you can (7) .... yourself on a job well done, and feel that you have (8) .... to the success of the company that (9) .... you. On the other hand, would you feel that your work was more worthwhile if you received more praise from your employers? Would you feel happier if they paid you a (10) .... or sent you to a sales conference in Tahiti? Or is praise unnecessary, as long as the job (11) .... you with the company of other people, and the feeling that you belong to the group? Most of us are probably too (12) .... working to wonder too much about this. One day perhaps we'll find that ideal job which gives life meaning, but until then we'll just get up every morning and keep on working.

8

VOCABULARY

Business and money

1 Read the text and decide which option (A, B, C or D) best fits each space.

Ours is a vanishing world, one in which the familiar is constantly disappearing and technological change is often difficult to cope with. So it should come (1) ....B.... no surprise to most of us to hear that yet another part of everyday life is about to go for ever. Apparently, within the next decade, money as we (2) .... it will probably (3) .... to exist in technologically advanced countries. (4) .... Professor Gerry Montague of the Institute for (5) .... Reform, the familiar coins and banknotes will soon be replaced entirely by credit cards of various kinds. And the shop of the future will be (6) .... directly to the network of banking computers. The assistant will simply key in your bank account code number and the amount you have spent, and thank you politely. You won't have to dig (7) .... in your pockets for change. You may not even have a number for your account as such, as the computer may by then be able to read your handprint. So no more instances of credit card (8) .... But I am afraid that I shall miss money. I have felt (9) .... attached to it, ever since I received my first pocket (10) .... when I was five, and kept it in a money-box. Even if my credit card of the future will be able to tell me exactly how much spending (11) .... I have left, even if it lights up and plays a happy (or sad) tune at the same time, nothing will be able to replace the (12) .... pleasure I gained from rattling the coins in my money-box.

1	A with	B as	C to	D in
2	A have	B see	C know	D believe
3	A cease	B stop	C fail	D conclude
4	A With reference to	B Further to	C According to	D Owing to
5	A Economical	B Economics	C Economic	D Economy
6	A united	B fixed	C combined	D linked
7	A far	B long	C tall	D deep
8	A deceit	B trickery	C pretence	D fraud
9	A heavily	B strongly	C widely	D largely
10	A cash	B coins	C money	D gold
11	A capacity	B potential	C capability	D power
12	A sheer	B complete	C entire	D downright

2 Match each sentence (1–9) with a sentence from (a–i) which has a similar meaning.

1 We have to haggle. .....*e*.....
2 We have a nice little nest-egg. ....
3 We spend a lot. ....
4 We are in debt. ....
5 We don't waste money. ....
6 We are paid on commission. ....
7 We want a rise. ....
8 We lend money. ....
9 We earn a lot. ....

a We have a high expenditure.
b We are very thrifty.
c We let people borrow from us.
d We earn according to what we sell.
e We argue about the price.
f We have a high income.
g We need higher wages.
h We owe money.
i We have some savings.

3 Complete the text by writing one word from each column to form a collocation in each space.

Column A
stock, tax, raise, monthly, savings, down, household, current, earns, business

Column B
capital, venture, account, market, instalments, account, return, interest, bills, payment

Adviser: ... and what about your bank details?

Mr Lumley: Well, I have a regular (1) ......*current account*......
from which we pay all our (2) .... such as gas
and water, and also a (3) .... which
(4) .... at a rate of 4½ %.

Adviser: I notice you have a regular monthly payment of £200 going out to JCS.
What's that?

Mr Lumley: Oh yes, that'll be the sofa. We made an initial
(5) .... of £400; then we're paying the rest in
(6) .... of £200.

Adviser: Right, and do you have any other savings or investments?

Mr Lumley: I have some shares invested in the (7) .... ,
but their value has gone down to just a few hundred pounds.

Adviser: And last time we spoke, you were talking about maybe starting a new
(8) .... with a colleague.

Mr Lumley: No, that's fallen through. We couldn't (9) .... the
necessary .... to satisfy the bank manager.
Probably just as well. It will make filling in my
(10) .... a lot easier.

Adviser: Yes, that's certainly true. It all gets very complicated if you're
self-employed.

4 <u>Underline</u> the two most suitable options in each sentence.

1 Harry has a good salary. He *gains/gets/makes* over £20,000 a year.
2 Mary was awarded a *grant/scholarship/subsidy* to study child psychology.
3 How much did you *give/pay/take* for your new car?
4 Their house *fetched/produced/sold for* a lot more than they expected.
5 I'm going to the bank to *take out/remove/withdraw* the money for the rent.
6 The manager disappeared with the *receipts/takings/wages* from the concert.
7 By the time Kate retired she was a *fortunate/prosperous/wealthy* businesswoman.
8 We had a good holiday but it was rather *costly/expensive/valuable*.
9 Unfortunately the old painting I found turned out to be *priceless/valueless/worthless*.
10 We would appreciate it if you would *close/settle/pay* your bill as soon as possible.

5 Complete the text by writing a word from the box in each space which collocates with the words in **bold**.

credit	market	redundant	~~value~~	charge
fortune	investment	booming	retirement	bankrupt

Have your shares just **fallen in** (1) ......*value*...... and you don't know what to do? Or have you **come into a** (2) .... and don't know how to invest it? Well, whether you've been **made** (3) .... or **qualified for early** (4) .... , whether your **business is** (5) .... or you've just been **declared** (6) .... , we are the bank for you, the caring bank. We've got the account for you and can advise you accordingly. Take out a Premier Account with us and you will be **making a wise** (7) .... We offer some of the most competitive loans and mortgages **on the** (8) .... Provided you maintain your account **in** (9) .... , and at a minimum level of £1500, we will offer you financial advice completely **free of** (10) .... , whenever you request it. Can't be bad, can it?

6 **Complete each sentence with a word from the box.**

financial	company	enterprise	~~shares~~	price
claim	currency	figures	fund	credit

1 Sally became quite wealthy by investing in stocks and ...shares.... .
2 Our company receives a lot of payments in foreign ....
3 This government believes firmly in the value of free ....
4 I'd like to buy this property, but I find the asking .... too high.
5 Tom is near retirement and is putting a lot of money into his pension ....
6 After our house was damaged by fire, we put in an insurance ....
7 Everyone was impressed by the sales .... for the new product.
8 Margaret found it hard to raise a loan as she had a poor ....rating .
9 Susan's business is being taken over by a multinational ....
10 Before making an investment, consult an independent .... adviser.

7 **Replace the words underlined with a more formal word from the box.**

appreciate	~~concerning~~	deducting	delayed	dispatching
enclosed	endeavour	inconvenience	maintain	trust

Dear Mrs Carter

Thank you for your letter of 24th June about (1) ..concerning.. your order 3882. Please accept our apologies for any trouble (2) .... caused to you by the late delivery of this order. While we try (3) .... to ensure that deliveries take place within the time slot stated on the invoice, orders are sometimes made late (4) .... by matters beyond our control. In this particular case, the courier service failed to follow our instructions, and your delivery was returned to us in error.

We also apologize for not sending (5) .... your order correctly. The missing items have been sent by express delivery.

Our policy at ComputaDirect is to keep up (6) .... a high standard of service. As a goodwill gesture, we are taking off (7) .... the cost of the missing items from your invoice. Please find a cheque for this amount in the envelope in this letter (8) ....

We would like (9) .... an acknowledgement of the new delivery, and of this goodwill payment, using the freepost envelope.

We hope (10) .... that this matter has now been resolved to your satisfaction.

Yours sincerely

John Barr

John Barr
Customer Services Manager

9

People and relationships

1 Complete the text by writing a word or phrase from the box in each space.

struck out	interests	sheltered	hit it off	follow
domineering	live up to	commitment	plucked up	rebelled
pushy	trial	~~spoilt~~	pressure	patch

I guess I was what one might call a (1) ....*spoilt*.......... child, for I was an
only child and I got whatever I wanted. I had a rather weak-minded mother
and by contrast a very (2) .... father who had exceedingly high
expectations of me, expectations that I could not (3) .... You
see, my father was quite an eminent lawyer and wanted nothing more than for
me to (4) .... in his footsteps. He encouraged me to win at
everything and to be ultra-competitive. He just couldn't see that he was being
far too (5) .... and putting too much (6) ....
on me. He simply thought that he was acting in my best (7) ....
Not surprisingly, perhaps, I (8) .... against my upbringing by
becoming thoroughly apathetic at school. As soon as I turned 18, I
(9) .... on my own and went off on a trip to India. It was there
that I met Ingrid, a fellow traveller. It became clear that we came from very
similar backgrounds. She too was running away from something: in her case
a very (10) .... upbringing, caused by having two very over-
protective parents. We (11) .... immediately, and I
(12) .... courage and asked her to be my girlfriend. But I was
young and I needed space, and I guess I was too immature to handle the give
and take of a relationship. Or perhaps I was just afraid of
(13) .... Anyway, we went through a very bad
(14) .... and had a (15) .... separation for a
couple of months.

2 <u>Underline</u> the most suitable option in each sentence.

1 As I am officially <u>*an alien*</u>/*an outsider*/*a stranger* I have to register with the police.
2 Let me introduce you to my *betrothed*/*engaged*/*fiancée*. We're getting married next month.
3 Jim is just *an acquaintance*/*a colleague*/*a figure* I met on holiday.
4 Why not bring your child along to the Mothers and *Juveniles*/*Juniors*/*Toddlers* group? It's for one- and two-year-olds.
5 Local people are campaigning for better facilities for the *senior*/*ancient*/*elderly*.
6 Our *ancestors*/*descendants*/*predecessors* are all buried in the local churchyard.
7 Peter is 50 and unmarried and his friends call him 'an eligible *bachelor*/ *independent*/*single*'.
8 The bridegroom was handed the ring by the *assistant groom*/*best man*/*godfather*.
9 When I was a *bloke*/*chap*/*lad* I used to walk ten miles to school.
10 We call her 'Auntie Flo', though she is not really any *family*/*relation*/*relative* to us.

3 Complete each sentence with an adjective from the box.

aggressive	attentive	devoted	insensitive	solitary
apathetic	~~conscientious~~	extrovert	mature	prejudiced

1 Sharon works very hard and is extremely ...*conscientious*... .
2 David does everything alone. He is a rather .... person.
3 What a lovely couple! They seem totally .... to one another.
4 Jim has extreme views, and is .... against all immigrants.
5 Very few students wanted to join in the activities. They seemed rather ....
6 Simon is always getting into fights, he's so ....
7 Jane may look rather young, but she has a very .... attitude.
8 Pauline is a good teacher, and very .... to the needs of the students.
9 Bill is shy but his brother Mike is more ....
10 Mary doesn't realize how she hurts people. She is really ....

4 **Match each expression (1–10) with an explanation (a–j).**

1 nearest and dearest ...*g*.....

2 newlyweds ....

3 the nuclear family ....

4 adults ....

5 a community ....

6 a generation ....

7 contemporaries ....

8 the extended family ....

9 a household ....

10 outcasts ....

a people who are alive at the same time or for example attend the same school

b people who have only recently been (or are still) on their honeymoon

c all the people of approximately the same age

d the people in a family who live together under the same roof

e the entire range of relatives in one family

f all the people living together in the same area

g a person (or people) from your immediate family

h people who are no longer teenagers

i people abandoned by their families or by society in general

j parents and their children

5 **Complete each sentence with a verb from the box.**

abandoned	criticized	~~neglected~~	quarrelled	separated
adopted	humiliated	offended	retired	scolded

1 Keith's parents ....*neglected*...... him when he was a baby.

2 The small child was being .... by its mother for getting dirty.

3 Tom deeply .... Ann by ignoring her at the party.

4 David is not my real father. I was .... by him when I was small.

5 Ian and Fiona are .... and they may get divorced.

6 I .... with my boyfriend but we made it up in the end.

7 Jack .... on his 65th birthday and received his pension.

8 My parents .... me for having a ring in my nose.

9 Julie's parents .... her when she was a few months old and she grew up in a children's home.

10 My boss utterly .... me in front of important clients, so I resigned.

6 Replace the words underlined in each sentence with a phrase from the box.

> turned him down   went out together   got to know   kept in touch   moved in with
> got on well with   fell out   ran away from   stood him up   grew up

1 When Brian asked her to marry him, Ann <u>said no</u>. ...*turned him down*...

2 I <u>communicated regularly</u> with most of my old friends. ....

3 Ann <u>spent her childhood years</u> in London. ....

4 David and Jean <u>dated</u> for three months before they got engaged. ....

5 Kate <u>quarrelled</u> with her boyfriend and they stopped seeing each other.
....

6 Helen <u>had a good relationship with</u> her in-laws. ....

7 Harry <u>left</u> home <u>without his parents' permission</u>. ....

8 Sophia promised to meet Michael after work but <u>disappointed him</u>.
....

9 After a few weeks I <u>went to live in the house of</u> some friends. ....

10 I <u>grew friendly with</u> Pam when we worked together. ....

7 Complete the spaces with one word which fits in all three sentences.

1 Barry was a very complicated individual who easily ....*took*........ offence.
I ....*took*........ to the job immediately and felt like I'd been doing it all
my life.
After 36 days of fighting, the invading forces finally ....*took*........ the city.

2 After quarrelling with David, Martina was .... to tears.
It was a .... call, but I think Leupers just won it from Collins in second
place.
In such sweltering heat, it was unbearably .... and humid on the
Underground.

3 Jane's father .... with rage when she told him she was pregnant.
Events in oil-producing countries .... the confidence of investors.
The lion .... its magnificent mane and gave an almighty roar.

4 John and Mary met at university, and they've been going .... for almost
five years.
'........................ on – is that really what you want you to do?'
There has been a .... decline in the number of male applicants.

5 'I just can't imagine my Dad .... me down the aisle in church to get
married,' said Maggie.
Lewis Hamilton is currently .... the drivers' championship.
She emerged from the stable .... a beautiful black horse.

Social problems

1 Read the text and decide which option (A, B, C or D) best fits each space.

Ask most people for their Top Ten fears, and you'll be sure to find being burgled fairly high on the (1) ...D..... . An informal survey I (2) .... among friends at a party last week revealed that eight of them had had their homes broken into more than twice, and two had been burgled five times. To put the record (3) .... , none of my friends owns valuable paintings or a sideboard full of family silverware. Three of them are students, (4) .... The most typical burglary, it seems, (5) .... the theft of easily transportable items – the television, the video, even food from the freezer. This may have something to do with the fact that the (6) .... burglar is in his (or her) late teens, and probably wouldn't know what to do with a Picasso, (7) .... selling a personal stereo or a vacuum cleaner is a much easier (8) .... They are perhaps not so much professional criminals, as hard-up young people who need a few pounds and some excitement. Not that this makes having your house (9) .... upside down and your favourite things stolen any easier to (10) .... In most (11) .... , the police have no luck (12) .... any of the stolen goods. Unless there is definite evidence, they are probably unable to do anything at all. And alarms or special locks don't (13) .... to help either. The only advice my friends could (14) .... was 'Never live on the ground floor' and 'Keep two or three very fierce dogs', which reminded me of a case I read about, where the burglars' (15) .... included the family's pet poodle.

1	A rank	B rating	C grade	D list
2	A called up	B held with	C set about	D carried out
3	A straight	B right	C correct	D steady
4	A as well	B however	C in fact	D at any rate
5	A means	B involves	C affects	D covers
6	A common	B medium	C average	D middle
7	A whereas	B as yet	C much as	D as soon as
8	A concern	B event	C situation	D matter
9	A put	B turned	C stood	D pulled
10	A submit	B receive	C accept	D admit
11	A examples	B cases	C items	D occasions
12	A taking	B making	C tracking	D recovering
13	A sound	B look	C show	D seem
14	A come up with	B make do with	C go through with	D get off with
15	A takings	B profit	C loot	D receipts

2 Complete each sentence with a verb from the box.

blocked	failed	held	~~collapsed~~	sustained
evacuated	used	met	spread	sealed

1 The whole building ...collapsed.... but fortunately there were no casualties.

2 Throughout the flooded area, villages are being .... by helicopter.

3 The terrorists threatened to kill their hostages if their demands were not

   ....

4 Several buildings .... damage from the earthquake.

5 Trees were uprooted and many roads were ....

6 The two trains collided after one .... to stop at signals.

7 Rescue teams .... out little hope of finding other survivors.

8 The blaze rapidly .... to neighbouring buildings.

9 Police .... tear-gas in an attempt to disperse the mob.

10 Police .... off the town-centre for two hours while they searched for the
   bomb.

3 Complete the text by writing a form of the word in CAPITALS in each space.

One of the most (1) ...worrying... crime statistics in Europe is   WORRY
the rise in juvenile crime. Often the root cause is

(2) .... to drugs, an expensive habit which often   ADDICT

leads young (3) .... into a life of petty crime.   OFFENCE
Some parents, unable to cope with their children's addiction have

thrown them out of home, forcing them to live the lives of

(4) .... 'Kate' (not her real name) is one such   BEG

person. (5) .... since she was 18, Kate has had   HOME
various brushes with the law, most recently for

(6) .... , in order to raise cash to fuel a heroin   THIEF

habit. As a result of that transgression, Kate spent two months

in prison, rubbing shoulders with (7) .... criminals   HARD

and murderers. After drugs counselling, she is now trying to

put her life back together. 'I know the law has to be (8) .... ,'   FORCE

she says, 'but addicts need help more than punishment.' She

does agree, though, that most drugs should remain (9) ....   LEGAL

'I suppose that might stop kids trying drugs, though it wasn't a

(10) .... in my case. You have to realize that you can   DETER

get your life sorted out without drugs. And that can take time.'

4 Correct any errors of spelling or punctuation in each line of the text. Some lines
are correct.

After drinking a bottle of vodka, Alan and Richard Potter both 15, decided	1 Potter,
to go out and do some joyriding. The car they broke into belonged to	2 ✓
a Mrs McDiarmad. Having drivern the car at high speeds along country	3 driven
lanes, they abandonned it in a lay-by, and thumbed a lift home. Mercifully,	4 ....
no other drivers were hurt, although several had to swirve dangerously to	5 ....
avoid the Potter boys. In an experiment which is proveing to be remarkably	6 ....
sucessful, the two teenagers were obliged to meet the victim of their crime	7 ....
in person. Mrs McDiarmad told them in no uncertain terms that 20 years	8 ....
earlier she had lost a nephew in a car accident caused by a drinken driver.	9 ....
The Potters ended up in tears, and the younger, Alan, has since visited Mrs	10 ....
McDiarmad on two occassions to apologize for his actions. The scheme	11 ....
Alan and Richard took part in is known, as 'Face up to it'. It brings together	12 ....
young offenders' with those they have wronged. Naturally, the victim must	13 ....
agree to participate, and many find themselves simply unable to coperate.	14 ....
The scheme is being operated on a tryal basis in several major cities, and	15 ....
has the aproval of the social services. Early results suggest that young	16 ....
people who take part are considarably less likely to commit any further	17 ....
offences. It is to be hoped that this is indeed, the case with Alan and	18 ....
Richard Potter.	

5 <u>Underline</u> the most suitable option in each sentence.

1 The police arrested Jack and took him into <u>*custody*</u>/*detention*/*prison*.
2 In most countries, the *capital*/*death*/*execution* penalty has been abolished.
3 A man is said to be helping the police with their *arrests*/*detection*/*inquiries*.
4 The judge in the court was wearing a *hairpiece*/*head-dress*/*wig*.
5 Two football fans were later charged with *aggression*/*assault*/*attack*.
6 In some legal systems, the accused is presumed *honest*/*faultless*/*innocent* until
   proved guilty
7 I was given a light sentence because it was my first *case*/*charge*/*offence*.
8 A patrol car stopped me because I was *racing*/*running*/*speeding* in a built-up area.
9 The court case was dismissed for lack of *evidence*/*a jury*/*defence*.
10 'Members of the jury, what is your *answer*/*summary*/*verdict*?'

6 Complete each sentence with a suitable preposition.

1 The new law on dropping litter comes .... force next month.

2 Ann was released from prison and now she is .... probation.

3 Local students have been banned .... taking part in the demonstration.

4 Local people have called for an investigation .... the causes of the fire.

5 Football fans went .... the rampage in the centre of Norwich last night.

6 She claimed that the selling of habit-forming drugs was getting .... of control.

7 The car left the road and crashed .... a tree.

8 Several guests at the hotel were robbed .... jewellery and money.

9 David, 19, has been sleeping .... a park bench for the past six months.

10 The police have charged Helen .... driving without due care and attention.

7 Replace the words underlined in each sentence with a word from the box.

abolished	deported	neglected	rioted	swerved
cheated	~~dispersed~~	pardoned	squatted	swindled

1 At the end of the demonstration, the crowd <u>went off in different directions</u> peacefully. *dispersed*

2 The government has <u>done nothing about</u> this problem for years. ....

3 The employees were <u>cheated</u> out of their pensions by the managing director. ....

4 Hundreds of football fans <u>acted violently</u> in the city streets. ....

5 David was <u>officially released from prison</u> when the police discovered new evidence. ....

6 Brian was an illegal alien and when he was caught he was <u>made to leave the country</u>. ....

7 Jim and Sue <u>lived illegally without paying rent</u> in a house in South London for two years. ....

8 Jane was asked to leave the examination after she <u>acted dishonestly</u> and was caught. ....

9 Capital punishment was <u>brought to an end</u> some time ago in most countries. ....

10 The police car <u>turned suddenly</u> to avoid a pedestrian, and crashed. ....

VOCABULARY

Entertainment

1 Read the text and decide which option (A, B, C or D) best fits each space.

Until the early part of this century there was certainly a (1) ....B.... between popular music, the songs and dance tunes of the masses, and what we have (2) .... to call classical music. Up to that point, however, there were at least some points of contact between the two, and perhaps general recognition of what made a good voice, or a good song. With the development of (3) .... entertainment, popular music (4) .... away and has gradually developed a stronger life of its own to the point where it has become (5) .... with the classics. In some (6) .... , it is now dominated by the promotion of youth culture.

1	A contradiction	B distinction	C separation	D discrimination
2	A come	B become	C ended	D moved
3	A crowd	B majority	C quantity	D mass
4	A cut	B split	C cracked	D branched
5	A incongruous	B inconsistent	C incidental	D incompatible
6	A respects	B manners	C effects	D regards

2 Read the text and decide which option (A, B, C or D) best fits each space.

There is a new (1) ....C.... of classical musicians, led by the likes of Russell Watson and Vanessa Mae, who have achieved the (2) .... of rock stars, and have been marketed in the same way. This seems to suggest that many young people enjoy classical music but do not wish to be (3) .... with the lifestyle of those who are traditionally supposed to enjoy it. Or it may (4) .... be that recording companies have discovered that there is an insatiable desire for 'sounds', and that classical music is beginning to sound exciting to a generation (5) .... on rock but now (6) .... into affluent middle-age.

1	A line	B species	C breed	D pedigree
2	A grade	B degree	C rank	D status
3	A accompanied	B combined	C associated	D related
4	A simply	B clearly	C easily	D plainly
5	A fostered	B raised	C nurtured	D grown
6	A establishing	B settling	C lowering	D relaxing

3 Both options make sense. <u>Underline</u> the one which makes a common collocation.

1 Everyone clapped enthusiastically when the actors came on *screen/<u>stage</u>*.
2 Most critics agree that Celia gave the best *acting/performance*.
3 We bought some ice-cream during the *interlude/interval* of the play.
4 Jean has decided to join an amateur *dramatic/theatrical* society.
5 There was so much suspense that I was kept on the edge of my *place/seat*.
6 The leading lady unfortunately lost her voice during the *dress/stage* rehearsal.
7 Most modern plays don't need a lot of complicated *scenery/landscape*.
8 I thought it was a good film but it got terrible *previews/reviews*.
9 Quite honestly, I haven't much time for *horror/terror* films.

4 Match each person from the box with a description (1–9).

acrobat	cast	conductor	juggler	understudy
ballerina	~~clown~~	stuntman	vocalist	

1 someone who makes people laugh at the circus ....*clown*....
2 someone who sings ....
3 someone who is a member of this is an actor ....
4 someone who entertains others by throwing and catching things ....
5 someone who entertains others by performing gymnastics ....
6 someone who takes an actor's place in an emergency ....
7 someone who tells an orchestra what to do ....
8 someone who performs dangerous actions in place of an actor ....
9 someone who dances gracefully in a leading role ....

5 Complete each sentence with a word from the box.

brass	chorus	lyrics	organist	string
~~concert~~	opera	percussion	woodwind	

1 I went to a rock ....*concert*.... held in a large football stadium.
2 The .... section of the orchestra needs a new violinist.
3 Keith wanted to learn a .... instrument so took up the clarinet.
4 Their music is really great, but I can't understand the ....
5 As we entered the church, the .... began playing a solemn tune.
6 I used to play the trumpet in the local .... band.
7 You need a good voice and acting ability to perform in a/an ....
8 I'll sing the first verse, and everyone will join in for the ....
9 Nowadays it is possible to simulate most .... instruments electronically, so drums are not always needed.

6 Complete the text by writing a form of the word in CAPITALS in each space.

It's 8.30 at the headquarters of the Boogy Woogers dance group,
a (1) .....rehearsal.... studio in Geneva. Dancers of all shapes — REHEARSE
and sizes begin to tumble (2) .... through the doors. — ENERGY
Some begin limbering up, others splinter off into groups to try
out new moves. One woman, lost in her own (3) .... — THINK
sits with her headphones on, preparing for the punishing routines
to follow. A long-haired man with a goatee beard puts a tape in
the hi-fi, and rap music blares out of the (4) .... — SPEAK
Soon the room is alive with whirling, spinning bodies and
(5) .... fills the air. — LAUGH
The Boogy Woogers are the brainchild of Tomas Seeler, who
handpicked many of his troupe from local street dancers. Seeler's
own (6) .... was in gymnastics, but others come — BACK
from the worlds of martial arts, bodybuilding and ballet. Many
different (7) .... are represented in the group, — NATIONAL
including Chilean, Fijian and Senegalese dancers. The group
has been performing all over Europe, most notably in Paris,
where they became (8) .... celebrities. Famous — NIGHT
for their (9) .... and novel interpretations, the — CREATE
Boogy Woogers have made several (10) .... on TV, — APPEAR
and look set to remain the 'in' thing for many years to come.

7 Complete each sentence with a suitable preposition.

1 The clowns walked into the ring ....on......... stilts, looking about three metres tall!
2 The stadium was packed .... people for the athletics meeting.
3 Janet holds the world record .... long distance swimming.
4 During the match, a message came .... the loudspeakers.
5 There is a craze .... skateboarding at the moment.
6 Harry last appeared .... the role of King Lear at the National Theatre.
7 Have you got any tickets left .... the front stalls, please?
8 Alex accompanied Helen's singing .... the piano.
9 The play was so bad that the actors were booed .... the stage.
10 David challenged Cathy .... a game of chess.

8 Match each activity from the box with one of the sentences.

| jigsaw puzzle | table tennis | computer game | board game | pool |
| darts | cards | chess | television | draughts |

1 If you look at the picture on the box it's easier to decide where the pieces go.
.....jigsaw puzzle.....

2 Whenever you deal you seem to get at least three aces. ....

3 The white ball hit the red ball and went into the corner pocket. ....

4 I took all of his pieces in one move! I swept the board! ....

5 Pass the remote control – I want to get the weather report. ....

6 Throw the dice twice and then pick up a card. ....

7 The bulls-eye is worth fifty, but it's a bit hard to hit. ....

8 If the ball hits the net when you serve, it doesn't count. ....

9 You can easily put her in check if you make the next move with your queen.
....

10 I've been playing this for a month and I've got to Level Three. ....

9 Complete the spaces with one word which fits in all three sentences.

1 Briggs won the 100 metres in a new world.....record..... time.
It's difficult for anyone with a criminal .....record..... to get a job.
The police are keeping a .....record..... of all cars which enter the area.

2 The group have benefited from considerable media ....
Maria didn't find John attractive, but was rather flattered by his ....
It's been brought to my .... that there have been a number of thefts from the office.

3 Like all great opera singers, Pavarotti had an imposing ....
She showed great .... of mind and led the children calmly downstairs to safety.
There was a huge police .... at the football match.

4 My favourite .... in the play is where Uncle Toby breaks a priceless vase.
No thanks, discos are not really my ....
Reporting from the .... of the accident is Channel 4's Jeremy Charles.

5 Ford's latest .... is a collaboration with several other great pianists.
After his .... from prison, Golding promised to go straight.
Several workers were taken to hospital after the accidental .... of carbon dioxide in a local chemical factory.

Government and society

1 Read the text and decide which option (A, B, C or D) best fits each space.

Viewed from the outside (1) ...B.... , the Houses of Parliament look impressive. The architecture gives the place a traditional look, and the buildings are sandwiched between a busy square and the river, making them a (2) .... between the country house of an eccentric duke and a Victorian railway station. You have only to learn that the members (3) .... to each other as 'The Honourable Member' to (4) .... the picture of a dignified gentlemen's club, with of course a few ladies to (5) .... the numbers. Sadly, over the past few years first radio, and now television, have shown the (6) .... public, who are (7) .... the electorate, what in fact (8) .... when bills are discussed and questions are asked. The first obvious fact is that the chamber is very rarely full, and there may be only a handful of members present, some of whom are quite clearly asleep, telling jokes to their neighbour, or shouting like badly-behaved schoolchildren. There is not enough room for them all in the chamber in any (9) .... , which is a second worrying point. Of course, television does not follow the work of committees, which are the small discussion groups that do most of the real work of the House. But the (10) .... impression that voters receive of the workings of government is not a good one. To put it (11) .... , parliament looks disorganized, is clearly behind the (12) .... and seems to be (13) .... with bores and comedians. This is presumably why members (14) .... for so long the efforts of television companies to (15) .... parliamentary matters on television.

1	A	likewise	B	at least	C	nevertheless	D	as well
2	A	mixture	B	combination	C	cross	D	match
3	A	call	B	refer	C	speak	D	submit
4	A	finalize	B	end	C	conclude	D	complete
5	A	take away	B	bring about	C	make up	D	set in
6	A	average	B	ordinary	C	normal	D	general
7	A	after all	B	anyway	C	even	D	furthermore
8	A	comes up	B	turns up	C	goes on	D	lets on
9	A	point	B	way	C	matter	D	case
10	A	total	B	broad	C	overall	D	comprehensive
11	A	bluntly	B	shortly	C	directly	D	basically
12	A	ages	B	times	C	moments	D	years
13	A	full	B	filled	C	composed	D	comprised
14	A	prevented	B	checked	C	defied	D	resisted
15	A	circulate	B	beam	C	spread	D	broadcast

2 Complete the collocations in the text by writing a word from the box in each space.

candidate	~~vote~~	retirement	majority	asylum
campaign	poll	manifesto	election	line

Well, it's 9.30 at night, and by now almost everybody has cast their (1) .....*vote*..... . Very soon all our questions will be answered. Were the government right to hold the (2) .... so soon after the so-called 'dash for cash' scandal, in which certain applicants were apparently granted political (3) .... in exchange for financial favours? Will the opposition benefit from the decision of ex-Prime Minister David Howe to come out of (4) .... and stand as a (5) .... ? Will Mr Howe's famous refusal to toe the party (6) .... in matters of policy affect party unity? Will the vicious smear (7) .... which the government have mounted against Mr Howe backfire on them? Well, all will be revealed pretty soon. Interestingly, an opinion (8) .... conducted yesterday by 'Express Newspapers' put the government just two per cent ahead, while another, in the 'Daily Mirror', indicated they would be re-elected with an increased (9) .... According to the latter poll, people felt that the opposition's election (10) .... was poor and contained nothing new.

3 Complete each sentence with a word from the box.

conventional	~~diplomatic~~	oppressed	progressive	rebellious
courteous	notorious	privileged	radical	respectable

1 If you are ..*diplomatic*.. , you are tactful when dealing with people.
2 If you are .... , you have a good reputation in your community.
3 If you are .... , you are polite.
4 If you are .... , you have extreme or very strong views.
5 If you are .... , you are being ruled unjustly or cruelly.
6 If you are .... , you behave just like everyone else, perhaps too much so.
7 If you are .... , you are against authority and hard to control.
8 If you are .... , you have more advantages than other people.
9 If you are .... , you have gained a bad reputation.
10 If you are .... , you are in favour of new ideas.

4 Complete each sentence with a word from the box.

survey	bill	council	authorities	power
~~mayor~~	poll	motion	cabinet	reign

1 Mr Bradly has been elected ......*mayor*...... of Greenswold for the third time.
2 The government has introduced a .... outlining its plans for the coal industry.
3 Hello, I'm conducting a .... about leisure habits.
4 According to the latest opinion .... , the National Party are well ahead of their nearest rivals, the Co-operative Party.
5 Although there is an elected assembly, it is generally recognized that General Domenico wields the real ....
6 There is a locally elected .... which has responsibility for roads, street lighting, and other facilities.
7 The king enjoyed a long .... , and was eventually succeeded by his son, George.
8 The .... were slow to take control of the situation after the earthquake.
9 The Leader of the Opposition proposed a .... of no confidence in the government.
10 The Prime Minister called a top-level meeting with the Finance Minister, the Foreign Minister, and other members of the ....

5 Replace the word(s) underlined with a word from the box.

abolished	restricted	required	illegal	compulsory
permitted	voluntary	binding	barred	~~licensed~~

1 The proprietor is officially allowed to sell alcohol. .*licensed*..
2 The sale of drugs is <u>controlled by law</u> in most countries. ....
3 Education from the age of five is <u>obligatory</u> in Britain. ....
4 Students have been <u>banned</u> from using local pubs since the incident. ....
5 The law prohibiting the sale of fruit in the street has been <u>done away with</u>. ....
6 For both parties, the terms of this contract are <u>to be obeyed</u>. ....
7 With the application, a passport-sized photograph is <u>necessary</u>. ....
8 Smoking is not <u>allowed</u> in the classroom. ....
9 You don't have to stay after school to help; it's <u>your own decision</u>. ....
10 Parking in this street is <u>not allowed</u> on weekdays at certain times. ....

6 Match the words from the box with the explanations.

| ambassador | ~~president~~ | delegate | patriot | chairperson |
| ringleader | sovereign | terrorist | traitor | minister |

1 This person may be the elected head of state. ....president.....
2 This person is responsible for a government department. ....
3 This person leads others to make trouble. ....
4 This person represents their country abroad. ....
5 This person loves their country. ....
6 This person represents others at a meeting or conference. ....
7 This person betrays their country. ....
8 This person may be the head of state by birth. ....
9 This person uses violence rather than the political system for political ends.
   ....
10 This person is the head of a formal meeting. ....

7 Complete the spaces with a word which fits in all three sentences.

1 Channel 4 will, as ever, be ..following... the election as it happens.
   The Prime Minister was accused of .... a disastrous economic policy.
   Coverage of the sport is postponed .... the sudden death of President Gonzales.
2 It remains to be seen whether Signor Riva .... a controlling interest in his business empire if he becomes Prime Minister.
   As legal executor in this matter, Mr Tomlinson .... the right to claim compensation costs.
   And it's gold! Muller .... the title which he won in Sydney.
3 Yesterday's poll shows a significant .... of public opinion away from the Democrats.
   Workmen came to remove the faulty .... from the park.
   I've only been here for two days, so I haven't quite got back into the .... of things yet.
4 The .... to ban fox hunting was carried by a large majority.
   And now we'll see the goal again in slow ....
   The constant swaying .... of the ship made Jan feel sea sick.
5 You can rely on the Prime Minister to take .... of the situation.
   There was a long queue of people waiting to go through passport ....
   The police were accused of heavy-handed crowd .... tactics.

Health and the body

1 Read the text and decide which option (A, B, C or D) best fits each space.

Keeping fit and staying healthy have, not (1) ...D...... , become a growth (2) .... Quite apart from the amount of money spent each year on doctors' prescriptions and private medical (3) .... , huge sums are now spent on health foods and remedies of various kinds, from vitamin pills to mineral water, not to mention health clubs and keep-fit books and videos. We are more concerned than ever, it seems, about the water we drink and the air we breathe. But accidents can still befall even the fittest and most health-conscious of us. One of my friends, who is a keep-fit (4) .... , a non-smoker and teetotaller, and who is very (5) .... about what he eats, is at present languishing in bed with a wrist in plaster and a badly (6) .... ankle.

1	A strangely	B unusually	C evidently	D surprisingly
2	A business	B industry	C trade	D commerce
3	A attention	B curing	C treatment	D therapy
4	A fanatic	B activist	C extremist	D militant
5	A singular	B particular	C special	D peculiar
6	A torn	B scraped	C grazed	D sprained

2 Underline the most suitable option in each sentence.

1 After I drank a cup of black coffee I felt wide *awake/awoken/woken*.
2 These tablets may make you feel *dazed/dozy/drowsy* so don't drive.
3 I've been working for twelve hours and I feel *exhausting/tiresome/worn* out.
4 The doctor said I was *all in/run down/stale* and gave me some vitamins.
5 Bill's father is *impaired/immobile/invalid*, and needs a wheelchair to get around.
6 After walking for miles over the mountains, my feet were *limp/sore/sprained*.
7 Ann needs a holiday. She has been under a lot of *depression/pain/stress* lately.
8 The authorities are worried about the increase in drug *abuse/disuse/misuse*.
9 I told the doctor that climbing the stairs left me *catching/gasping/panting* for breath.
10 Mary spent a week in bed with *an attack/a case/an outbreak* of rheumatism.

3 Complete the texts by writing a form of the word in CAPITALS in each space.

Text 1

Bottled water is expensive, unreliable and has no health benefits
– at least, that's the view of Water Board chief Bill Tyson. To

(1) ....highlight........ what good value for money ordinary tap   HIGH

water still represents, Tyson is running a campaign promoting good
old-fashioned tap water and, by implication, criticizing bottled

water. He claims that there is little to (2) ....   DIFFER

bottled water from tap water, since there are often discrepancies

between the actual mineral (3) .... of bottled water   CONTAIN

and what's on the label. Furthermore, he claims some bottled water

(4) .... are blended from several sources and might   PRODUCE

even contain tap water. Furthermore, the health claims made for

bottled water are 'fairly (5) ....', he added, 'and   SCIENCE

have no experimental basis.'

Text 2

My interest in alternative medicine began when I learned

(6) .... techniques to help overcome stress. I was a   RELAX

student in those days, and I was impressed by the way these

techniques worked. My doctor had given me a (7) ....   PRESCRIBE

for tranquilizers, but I found these completely (8) ....   EFFECT

Now I'm a fully qualified alternative (9) .... , and I   PRACTICE

work on the fundamental principle that most (10)   ILL

stem from a disturbance of energy in the body.

4 Complete each sentence with a word from the box.

chin	~~heel~~	thumb	shoulder	throat	elbow	knee	neck	thigh	wrist

1 My left boot is too tight and now I've got a blister on my ....*heel*........

2 I can't talk today because I've got a really sore ....

3 Jean twisted her .... skiing and now she can't walk.

4 My arm is in plaster and so I can't bend my ....

5 Ann can't use her right hand because she's sprained her ....

6 I pulled a muscle in my .... when I was running, and now I can't walk.

7 Little Jimmy's mother tried to stop him sucking his ....

8 Tony injured his .... by always carrying a heavy bag on a strap.

9 Peter cut himself badly on the................... while shaving.

10 Pat put both arms round my .... and gave me a kiss.

5 Six people are talking about their medical experiences. Complete each space with a suitable word. The first letter of each space is given.

1 **David**
When I was playing football, I broke my ankle and was carried off the pitch on a s~~tretcher~~.... . I was taken to c.................. , where the doctor put a p....................... cast on my leg. For the next two months I needed c.................. to get around with.

2 **Maria**
I'm a hospital p.................. . You'll see me pushing trolleys or wheelchairs, or carrying supplies from one department to another. Typically, I collect people who've just come out of s.................. , where they've had an o.................. , and take them to their w.................. , where they stay and recover.

3 **Sue**
I was s.................. on the hand by a wasp, which may sound no big deal, but I'm a.................. to such things. The doctor gave me some cream and put my arm in a s.................. . She said I should keep the hand exposed to the air rather than put a p.................. on it.

4 **Kath**
I've never been fat, but recently I noticed I was getting a bit f................. round the waist, and I happened to read an article that said I was 10 kilos o.................. for my height, age and build. I wish I was 16 again. I had a lovely f.................. at that age. Now I really have to be selective about what I eat, although I don't believe in d.................. .

5 **Bob**
I've been having toothache and imagined I'd need to have a f................. at the dentist's. But when I went to get it checked out, she said the tooth would have to be e.................. . Well, after it was all over and the effect of the i.................. had worn off, I was in a.................. for two days and had to have painkillers.

6 **Match each sentence (1–10) with an explanation (a–j).**

1 I nodded. ...*i*......
2 I chuckled. ....
3 I grinned. ....
4 I shook my head. ....
5 I scowled. ....
6 I giggled. ....
7 I yawned. ....
8 I frowned. ....
9 I choked. ....
10 I stared. ....

a I moved my eyebrows together to show disapproval.
b I laughed uncontrollably, in a silly way.
c I looked with wide-open eyes at the same place for several moments.
d I laughed quietly under my breath.
e I opened my mouth uncontrollably to show boredom or tiredness.
f I gave a large smile.
g I moved my head from side to side meaning 'no'.
h I made a threatening expression with my lips.
i I moved my head up and down meaning 'yes'.
j I had trouble breathing because my throat was blocked.

7 **Replace the words underlined in each sentence with a word from the box.**

crawling	hobbling	marching	staggering	tiptoeing
dashing	limping	~~rambling~~	strolling	wandering

1 I really enjoy <u>walking for pleasure</u> in the countryside. ...*rambling*....

2 After about six months babies start <u>moving about on their hands and knees</u>. ....

3 My sister was <u>walking on the front part of her foot</u> so as to make no noise along the corridor. ....

4 The injured player began <u>walking with one leg more easily than the other</u> off the pitch. ....

5 The drunken man was <u>moving unsteadily</u> from one side of the street to the other. ....

6 Nowadays soldiers have motorized transport and do little <u>moving on foot</u>. ....

7 There is nothing more pleasant than <u>walking in a leisurely manner</u> along the sea front. ....

8 I've been <u>moving very rapidly</u> backwards and forwards all day, and I'm exhausted. ....

9 When I visit a new town I like <u>walking with no particular purpose</u> around looking at the sights. ....

10 I wasn't used to so much walking, and ended up <u>moving with difficulty</u> home, with blisters on both feet. ....

14

VOCABULARY

World issues

1 Read the text and decide which option (A, B, C or D) best fits each space.

Over the past fifty years or so, the methods used for collecting money from the public to (1) ....B.... the developing world have changed out of all recognition, along with the gravity of the problems (2) .... , and the increasing awareness among the population that something must be done. At the beginning of this period, it would have been common to put money in a collecting box, perhaps on the street or at church. The 1960s saw the (3) .... of shops which sold second-hand goods, donated by the public, and which also began to sell articles manufactured in the developing world in charitable projects set up to guarantee a fair income to local people. The next development was probably the charity 'event', in which participants were (4) .... to run, cycle, swim or what have you, and collected money from friends and relatives (5) .... how far or long they managed to keep going. The first hint of what was to become the most successful means of (6) .... money was the charity record, where the artists donated their time and talent, and the (7) .... from the sales went to a good (8) .... This was perhaps a (9) .... of the fact that young people felt increasingly concerned about the obvious differences between life in Europe and the United States, and that in most of Africa, for example. A feeling of frustration was building up. Why was so little being done? The huge success of Band Aid, and (10) .... televised concerts, showed the power of the media, and of music in particular, to inspire and shock. It differed significantly in style from other events. People phoned up in their thousands on the day and pledged money by (11) .... their credit card numbers. (12) .... , if you have enough money to buy an MP3 player, you can afford something for the world's starving children.

1	A finance	B aid	C pay	D loan
2	A faced	B covered	C opposed	D approached
3	A occurrence	B entrance	C happening	D advent
4	A supported	B funded	C sponsored	D promoted
5	A in as much as	B according to	C with reference to	D as regards
6	A increasing	B lifting	C boosting	D raising
7	A produce	B proceeds	C receipts	D returns
8	A agency	B enterprise	C cause	D movement
9	A consideration	B reflection	C view	D display
10	A subsequent	B consequent	C attendant	D relevant
11	A mentioning	B quoting	C affirming	D recalling
12	A Anyway	B After all	C Although	D At any rate

2 Match the words from the box with the explanations.

~~negotiation~~	organic	recycling	self-sufficiency
irrigation	subsidy	charity	immunization

1 This is the settling of a dispute through discussion. *negotiation*

2 This is the ability of a country or person to support themselves without outside help. ....

3 This is a means of protecting people against some diseases. ....

4 This describes food that is grown without the use of chemical fertilizers. ....

5 This is the collection of raw materials so that they can be used again. ....

6 This is money given by a government to lower the prices of e.g. basic foods. ....

7 This is a system of distributing water to places which need it for agriculture. ....

8 This is an organization which collects money from the public and uses it to help people in need. ....

3 Complete each text with a word formed from the word in CAPITALS.

1 The country's energy ...*consumption*... is some 30% higher   CONSUME
than a decade ago. At the same time we have seen an increase
in the use of .... energy sources such as wind   RENEW
power and solar power.

2 An entire month's average .... hit Bilbao   RAIN
yesterday, while across the border in France, it's the opposite
problem. The recent lack of rain is likely to lead to
water .... in some areas.   SHORT

3 The oil spill was described as 'an .... disaster'.   ECOLOGY
It is thought likely to affect .... within a   WILD
20-mile radius.

4 Numerous species face .... if nothing is done   EXTINCT
about the problem of ....   FOREST

5 Most of these .... species will only be saved   DANGER
as a result of .... by government agencies.   INTERVENE

6 Many .... products, such as cleaning liquids   HOUSE
and bleach, contain .... chemicals.   HARM

7 Many people prefer to eat food which has not been
sprayed with ....   PEST
although using such chemicals can increase
food ....   PRODUCE

8 Large cities can be affected by .... smog,   POISON
formed from car exhaust fumes, and made worse
by .... conditions.   CLIMATE

4 Complete each sentence by adding a word or part of a word from the box to the prefix given.

burdened	estimated	lying	~~populated~~	crowded
nourished	privileged	rated	simplified	joyed

1 Many countries with high birth rates are seriously over....populated...... .

2 I'm afraid I think President Lawson's contribution to reducing global famine has been over...................... .

3 When the United Nations relief supplies arrived, the people were over...................... .

4 The government has seriously under...................... the gravity of the situation in drought-stricken areas.

5 Those who say that developing countries simply need more money have over...................... the problem.

6 Most of the children in the camp were seriously under...................... .

7 Most third world economies are already over...................... with foreign debt.

8 Those of us who live in prosperous countries should try and help the under...................... peoples of the developing world.

9 The refugee camps are now seriously over...................... and more blankets and food are needed.

10 Sending aid to countries may help in the short term, but the under...................... causes of the problem must also be tackled.

5 Replace the word(s) underlined in each sentence with an adjective from the box.

impoverished	illiterate	essential	urban	densely
inadequate	traditional	sparsely	~~rural~~	wealthy

1 In many countries, there is a drift of population from <u>country</u> areas to the cities. ....rural.....

2 Education is desperately needed in many countries where a high percentage of the population is <u>unable to read and write</u>. ....

3 Remote villages usually lack <u>basic</u> services such as piped water and electricity. ....

4 <u>Rich</u> people often find it hard to understand how the poor become poor. ....

5 The mountain region of the country is <u>thinly</u> populated. ....

6 Many <u>poor</u> nations can no longer afford to run schools and hospitals. ....

7 Poor immigrants often end up living in shanty towns in <u>city</u> areas. ....

8 In <u>heavily</u> populated areas, unemployment may be a cause of poverty. ....

9 The diet of most children in this area is <u>poor</u>. ....

10 When villagers move to the city, they often lose touch with their <u>established</u> way of life. ....

6 Complete the texts by writing a form of the word in CAPITALS in each space.

Text 1

With (1) <u>humanitarian</u> aid now pouring into the country,	HUMAN
charitable agencies are still struggling to cope in a country	
where day to day life is a struggle for (2) .... In	EXIST
some areas agency workers have encountered (3)	RESIST
to their efforts from government forces. Meanwhile, in an	
attempt to (4) .... the economy, the Government	STABLE
has (5) .... the currency for the third time this year.	VALUE

Text 2

The United Nations has not ruled out the possibility of military	
(6) .... , although it is still hopeful of achieving a	INTERVENE
settlement by (7) .... means. The Secretary General	DIPLOMACY
roundly condemned the President's policy of ethnic	
(8) .... , and also criticized him for spending a	CLEAN
(9) .... amount of his country's money on weapons.	PROPORTION
This follows last week's 'reminder' to the President that	
(10) .... is now universally illegal, a fact he	SLAVE
continues to ignore.	

7 Both options make sense. <u>Underline</u> the one which forms a common collocation.

1 Many small houses and huts were *flooded away/<u>washed away</u>* when the river burst its banks.
2 Poor farming methods are responsible for soil *devaluation/erosion* in many areas of sub-Saharan Africa.
3 During the earthquake, many people were *buried/covered* alive.
4 The forest fire left a wide area of the mountainside blackened and *ablaze/ smouldering*.
5 Villagers are hoping for rain this month after nearly a year of *dry weather/drought*.
6 Before the hurricane struck, many people were *evacuated/shifted* to higher ground.
7 Thousands of children in the famine-stricken area are suffering from *malnutrition/ undernourishment*.
8 Heavy snow has fallen in the mountains and many villages have been *blocked out/ cut off* for the past two days.
9 The Aids *epidemic/plague* is having serious effects in some countries.
10 Many small islands in the Indian Ocean are threatened by rising sea *waters/levels*.

15

VOCABULARY

Thinking and feeling

1 Read the text and decide which option (A, B, C or D) best fits each space.

> Interpreting the feelings of other people is not always easy, as we all know, and we (1) ....B.... as much on what they seem to be telling us, as on the (2) .... words they say. Facial (3) .... and tone of voice are obvious ways of showing our (4) .... to something, and it may well be that we unconsciously (5) .... views that we are trying to hide. The art of being tactful lies in (6) .... these signals, realizing what the other person is trying to say, and acting so that they are not embarrassed in any way. For example, we may understand that they are (7) .... reluctant to answer our question, and so we stop pressing them. Body movements in general may also (8) .... feelings, and interviewers often (9) .... particular attention to the way a candidate for a job walks into the room and sits down. However, it is not difficult to present the right kind of appearance, while what many employers want to know relates to the candidate's character (10) .... , and psychological stability. This raises the (11) .... question of whether job candidates should be asked to complete psychological tests, and the further problem of whether such tests actually produce (12) .... results. For many people, being asked to take part in such a test would be an objectionable (13) .... into their private lives. Quite (14) .... from this problem, can such tests predict whether a person is likely to be a (15) .... employee or a valued colleague?

1	A estimate	B rely	C reckon	D trust
2	A other	B real	C identical	D actual
3	A looks	B expression	C image	D manner
4	A view	B feeling	C notion	D reaction
5	A express	B declare	C exhibit	D utter
6	A taking down	B putting across	C picking up	D going over
7	A at least	B above all	C anyhow	D in fact
8	A display	B indicate	C imply	D infer
9	A have	B show	C make	D pay
10	A quirks	B mannerisms	C traits	D points
11	A awkward	B risky	C unpleasant	D touchy
12	A faithful	B regular	C reliable	D predictable
13	A invasion	B intrusion	C infringement	D interference
14	A different	B apart	C away	D except
15	A pedantic	B particular	C laborious	D conscientious

243

2 <u>Underline</u> the most suitable option in each sentence.

1   As there is little hope of being rescued, I have *abandoned/decided/<u>resigned</u>* myself to the worst.

2   Tom didn't believe us, and it took a long time to *convince/establish/confirm* him.

3   I *define/regard/suppose* this project as the most important in my career.

4   In my *point of view/viewpoint/view*, this plan will not work.

5   Are you *aware/conscious/knowledgeable* that £10,000 has gone missing?

6   I haven't the faintest *sense/notion/opinion* of what you are talking about.

7   Mr Smith has appointed his best friend as the new director! It's a clear case of *favouritism/prejudice/subjectivity*.

8   Your new boyfriend *recollects/remembers/reminds* me of a cousin of mine.

9   Sue just can't stop thinking about football! She is *biased/concerned/obsessed* with her local team!

10 I just can't understand the *attitude/manner/mentality* of people who are cruel to animals.

3 Match each sentence opener (1–10) with an expression with 'feel' (a–j).

1   So, looking back, would you say you enjoyed your stay in Britain? .....e.....

2   Phew! I can't keep up with you any more. ....

3   Did the anaesthetic hurt? ....

4   If it's any consolation, ...

5   Well, just make yourself at home while you're waiting. ....

6   It's going to rain. ....

7   She's a very sensitive girl. ....

8   Now just relax and remember what I told you. ....

9   You should be really pleased with your daughter, Mrs Owen. ....

10 I'm really sorry I had to take this decision. ....

a   Feel free to have some tea or coffee.

b   Dawn clearly has a feel for languages.

c   I can feel it in my bones.

d   You'll soon get the feel of it.

e   I have mixed feelings about it.

f   I hope you have no hard feelings about it.

g   I don't want to hurt her feelings.

h   No, I didn't feel a thing!

i   I'm starting to feel my age.

j   I know just how you feel.

4 Complete each sentence with a word from the box.

spot	utter	follow	mislead	appreciate
~~put~~	imply	express	plead	wonder

1 I don't know how to ....put......... this, but I'm afraid the money has gone!

2 Could you say that again? I didn't quite .... you.

3 I would .... it if you could help me with this job.

4 I was so flabbergasted that I couldn't .... a single word.

5 I simply said we had lost the order. I didn't .... that it was your fault.

6 I was so overwhelmed that I just couldn't .... my feelings.

7 Whenever I ask you about damage to the car, you always .... ignorance.

8 I .... that you can get up at 6.00 after what you did last night.

9 Most of the clues in a detective story are there to .... the reader.

10 Did you .... the deliberate mistake on page two?

5 Match each expression to do with thinking (1–10) with a suitable ending (a–j).

1 It's just a thought, but maybe … ......f.....

2 I'll give it some thought … ....

3 Am I right in thinking … ....

4 He thinks very highly of you … ....

5 On second thoughts, ...

6 That's all I can think of … ....

7 That's a thought! ....

8 I thought as much! ....

9 I've thought long and hard about it … ....

10 Sorry, I wasn't thinking straight. ....

a … so don't break his heart!

b … and I've decided not to accept.

c … and get back to you tomorrow.

d I've written my old address at the top!

e David has taken the car again without my permission!

f … you could go by train.

g … you used to live in Manchester?

h … at the moment.

i … perhaps I'd better do it after all.

j Yes, maybe I should do that.

6 Replace the words underlined in each sentence with a word from the box.

cherished	dreaded	mourned	~~regretted~~	resented
deplored	loathed	offended	reproached	stressed

1 Peter was <u>very sorry about</u> leaving his old job. ...*regretted*....
2 The Prime Minister said he <u>strongly disapproved of</u> the behaviour of the demonstrators. ....
3 Lily <u>felt bitter about</u> the fact that everyone had been promoted except her. ....
4 David <u>felt extremely worried about</u> visiting the dentist. ....
5 Sally <u>held very dear</u> the memory of her childhood in the country. ....
6 Neil <u>grieved for</u> the death of his mother and father for many weeks. ....
7 I am sorry if I <u>hurt the feelings of</u> your sister. ....
8 Brenda really <u>felt a strong dislike for</u> her new boss. ....
9 Our teacher <u>laid emphasis on</u> the importance of regular study. ....
10 Jim <u>strongly criticized</u> me for not doing my fair share of the work. ....

7 Complete the spaces with a word which fits in all three spaces.

1 Let's go down to the river. It's a really nice ....*spot*........ for a picnic.
   I'm afraid I'm going to be late. I'm having a ....*spot*........ of bother with my car.
   The evening in Blackpool was the only bright ....*spot*......... in an otherwise disappointing holiday.
2 I'm so tired I'm finding it difficult to keep my .... on my work.
   If you can cast your .... back to lesson two, you'll remember we were talking about body posture.
   My daughter is very ill, so I've got a lot on my .... right now.
3 Perhaps I could talk to you later in private – it's a personal ....
   It's only a .... of time before the city falls to the rebels.
   Dealing with problems like that is all just a .... of being firm.
4 It's very upsetting news, as she was a very .... friend.
   It's rather .... for me – haven't you got anything cheaper?
   As the boat lurched from side to side, we held on for .... life.
5 Police suspect that the shopkeeper had a .... in the robbery.
   Come on, concentrate on the job in .... and don't get distracted.
   Do you think you could give me a .... with the decorating?
6 After her boss shouted at her, Maria felt too .... to stay in the job.
   I had to stay at home because my stomach was ....
   Jim .... the coffee pot, and the coffee made a mess of the white carpet.

16

Technology

1 Read the text and decide which option (A, B, C or D) best fits each space.

> Most people who have mobile phones say that having one is simply a matter
> of (1) ....D.... . As a techno-phobe who does not possess a mobile phone,
> still less an online connection, I am always flabbergasted when I hear people
> saying this. The (2) .... reason I do not have a mobile phone is that I refuse
> to be at someone else's beck and (3) .... 24 hours a day. But apparently
> there are plenty of sane adults out there who actually want to be in this
> position. Of course a lot of people say they only got a mobile on the (4) ....
> understanding that it was to be used for emergencies only. But sure enough
> the insidious thing soon took over their lives, to the (5) .... where it seems
> they can barely live without it. Giving a mobile phone to a child makes even less
> sense. Parents lose their freedom and the children lose the ability to (6) ....
> for themselves.

1	A ease	B handiness	C utility	D convenience
2	A sheer	B perfect	C very	D utter
3	A cry	B ring	C need	D call
4	A strict	B absolute	C severe	D precise
5	A mark	B point	C spot	D position
6	A support	B keep	C fend	D sustain

2 Complete each sentence with a word from the box.

appliance	component	automation	machinery	gadget
contraption	equipment	experiment	overhaul	system

1 What a peculiar ...*contraption*.... ! What on earth is that for?

2 A washing-machine is probably the most useful household ....

3 We will have to order a new .... to replace the damaged one.

4 The noise of .... filled the factory and nearly deafened me.

5 My new computer has a completely different operating ....

6 Scientists in this laboratory are conducting an interesting ....

7 When .... is introduced, the number of workers will be reduced.

8 Do you like this new .... I bought for peeling potatoes?

9 Every six months the nuclear reactor needs a complete ....

10 My brother has a shop selling photographic ....

3 Correct any errors in each line of the text. Some lines are correct.

When faced with some new and possibly bewildering tecnological | 1 technological
change, most people react, in one of two ways. They either recoil | 2 react in
from anything new, claiming that it is unnecessary or too complicated, | 3 ✓
or that it somehow makes life less personal. Or they learn to adapt to | 4 ....
the new invention, and eventually wonder, how they could possibly | 5 ....
have existed without it. Take computers as an example, for many of | 6 ....
us, they still represent a threat to our freedom, and give us a | 7 ....
frigtening sense of a future in which all decisions will be taken by | 8 ....
machines. This may be because they seem misterious, and difficult | 9 ....
to understand. Ask most people, what you can use a home computer | 10 ....
for, and you usually get vauge answers about how 'they give you | 11 ....
information'. In fact, even those of us who are familiar with computers', | 12 ....
and use them in our dayly work, have very little idea of how they | 13 ....
actually work? But it does not take long to learn how to operate a | 14 ....
bussiness programme, even if things occasionally go wrong for no | 15 ....
apparant reason. Presumably much the same happened when the | 16 ....
telephone and the television became widespred. What seems to | 17 ....
alarm most people is the speed of technological change, rather than | 18 ....
change itself. And the objections that are maid to new technology | 19 ....
may well have a point to them, since change is not always an | 20 ....
improvement. As we discover during power cuts there is a lot to be | 21 ....
said for the oil lamp, the cole fire, and forms of entertainment, such | 22 ....
as books or board games, that dont have to be plugged in to work. | 23 ....

4 Match each problem (1–10) with a solution (a–j).

1 The door squeaks. ....d....
2 The car battery is dead. ....
3 The pencil is blunt. ....
4 The screw is coming loose. ....
5 My watch has stopped. ....
6 The car seat is in the wrong position. ....
7 The light bulb is flickering. ....
8 The dishwasher is making odd noises. ....
9 This wire has come loose. ....
10 The piano sounds terrible!

a It needs servicing.
b It needs tightening.
c It needs reconnecting.
d The hinges need oiling.
e It needs tuning.
f It needs recharging.
g It needs sharpening.
h It needs winding up.
i It needs adjusting.
j It probably needs replacing.

5 Complete the texts by writing a form of the word in CAPITALS in each space.

Text 1

(1) ......_Installation_...... of your new energy-efficient domestic gas   INSTALL
boiler is free of charge, and will be performed within 5 days of
payment. Regular (2) .... from a qualified engineer   MAINTAIN
is advised. The system comes with an (3) ....   ADJUST
cover, which can be kept fully extended or half down. The cover
must be completely removed for repairs to be carried out. As with
all (4) .... equipment, please exercise great care if   ELECTRIC
you are attempting to repair the (5) .... yourself.   APPLY

Text 2

Attach the motor to the (6) .... outlet pipe.   CYLINDER
Screw the motor down into place. If the motor does not
engage, remove it and (7) .... the outlet-pipe. All   TIGHT
engineers installing or repairing this machinery must observe all
necessary (8) .... precautions. This includes the   SAFE
wearing of goggles, masks and other (9) ....   PROTECT
equipment. For instructions on how to remove the outlet valve,
please refer to the (10) .... described on page 28   PROCEED
of this manual.

6 <u>Underline</u> the most suitable option in each sentence.

1 The hair-drier is fitted with a three point *cable/<u>plug</u>/socket*.
2 Don't touch that wire! It's *live/lively/living*.
3 This small vacuum cleaner *runs/powers/works* on batteries.
4 The set wouldn't work because there was a faulty *connection/joint/link*.
5 I can't use my drill here. The *lead/plug/wire* isn't long enough.
6 Turn off the mains first in case you get *an impact/a jolt/a shock*.
7 Oh dear the lights have gone off! The *cable/fuse/safety* must have gone.
8 Can you lend me that DVD? I want to *record/transcribe/write* it.
9 The appliance is powered by a small electric *engine/machine/motor*.
10 Jim has just started work as an *electrical/electricity/electrician* engineer.
11 The electrician twisted the wires together using a pair of *hammers/chisels/pliers*.
12 I buy coffee beans and put them in a *grinder/mixer/blender*.
13 The good thing about this knife is that the *blade/point/edge* can be replaced.
14 I can't undo this nut. I need a larger *bolt/screwdriver/spanner*.
15 You can save electricity by using low energy light *globes/bulbs/glasses*.

17

Quality and quantity

1 Read the text and decide which option (A, B, C or D) best completes each collocation or fixed phase.

The quality of life these days is something most of us take for
(1) ....c....... . It takes some radically different experience to (2) .... this
fact home to people. In my (3) .... , it was spending three weeks
aboard a yacht with twelve other people, competing in a major sailing race.
Although I was officially a guest, it was made clear from the start that there was
to be no room for passengers, and that I'd have to (4) .... my weight.
For the first few nights, none us was able to sleep for more than a couple of
hours at a (5) .... before being rudely awoken by an aggressive command.
Then we'd do physically exhausting work in total darkness. Every few minutes
we'd be completely soaked to the (6) .... by a large wave we couldn't see
coming. I shared sleeping (7) .... with six other women, with barely enough
room to stretch my legs. Soon I found myself (8) .... for my comfortable
sheets back home, a hot chocolate and a warm bath.

1	A given	B accepted	C granted	D read
2	A bring	B push	C sweep	D carry
3	A example	B instance	C case	D experience
4	A offer	B move	C use	D pull
5	A piece	B time	C period	D moment
6	A flesh	B skin	C bones	D toes
7	A quarters	B premises	C dormitories	D digs
8	A desiring	B yearning	C dreaming	D craving

2 Both options make sense. <u>Underline</u> the one which forms a common collocation.

1 We advertised the house widely but only a *handful/minority* of people have shown any interest.
2 The surgeon told Sam that the operation had been only a *minor/partial* success.
3 The amount of parking space available here is no longer *adequate/passable*.
4 Sue has already written the *bulk/mass* of her third novel.
5 You have to use a magnifying glass to see some of the *miniature/minute* details.
6 I am glad to report that the company has made a *large-scale/sizeable* profit.
7 There has been quite a *dearth/want* of good biographies this year.
8 I suppose I have had a *fair/good* amount of experience in making speeches.
9 We can't afford such a lavish party with the *limited/narrow* means available.
10 There is really a *wide/vast* difference between the two plans.

3 Complete each sentence with a verb from the box.

| supplemented | declined | dwindled | faded | reduced |
| diminished | enlarged | ~~extended~~ | spread | contracted |

1 The old railway line has been ......*extended*.... as far as the new airport.
2 In an effort to increase sales, prices will be .... for a short period.
3 Hope has now .... for the two climbers missing since last Friday.
4 Helen .... her small salary by making shrewd share dealings.
5 The school playground has been .... by the addition of the old garden.
6 Unfortunately the fire has now .... to neighbouring buildings.
7 The team's enthusiasm was not at all .... by their early setbacks.
8 As a seaside resort, Mudford has .... a lot since its heyday in the 1920s.
9 The company has .... in size, and now employs only 300 people.
10 The number of students attending the class .... until only two remained.

4 Match each sentence (1–10) with a comment from the same speaker (a–j).

1 United are much better than City. ....
2 You threw the ball before I was ready. ....
3 These wines taste just the same to me. ....
4 Why don't I pick you up at the house? ....
5 Why bother waiting here when we've missed the last bus? ....
6 Congratulations on your promotion. ....
7 The hotel we are staying in is a bit disappointing. ....
8 There's no food in this cupboard. ....
9 Pauline has got a new Benson 500. ....
10 Our product is without doubt the best on the market. ....

a Personally, I don't think much of it.
b It would be more convenient.
c It doesn't count.
d There's no comparison.
e None whatsoever.
f I can't tell the difference.
g It has no equal.
h It doesn't come up to expectations.
i It's pointless.
j You deserve it.

5 Complete the text by writing a form of the word in CAPITALS in each space.

Ask any adult over forty to make a (1) ....*comparison*..... between   COMPARE
the past and the present and most will tell you that things have
been getting steadily worse for as long as they can remember.
Take the weather for example. Everyone remembers that in their
(2) .... the summers were considerably hotter,   YOUNG
and that winter always included (3) ....   ABOUND
falls of snow just when the school holidays had started.
Of course, the food in those days was far superior too, as nothing
was imported and everything was fresh. (4) ....   EMPLOY
was negligible, the money in your pocket really was worth
something, and you could afford a (5) .... house even   SIZE
if your means were limited. And above all, people were somehow
nicer in those days, and spent their free time on innocent
(6) .... making model boats and tending their   PURSUE
stamp (7) .... rather than gazing at the television   COLLECT
screen for hours on end. As we know, this image of the past simply
cannot be true, and there are plenty of statistics dealing with health
and (8) .... which prove that it is not true. So, why   PROSPER
is it that we all have a (9) .... to idealize the past   TEND
and to be so (10) .... of the present?   CRITICIZE

6 Replace the words <u>underlined</u> in each sentence with a phrase from the box.

> are not alike   completely different   similar   is not as good as we had hoped
> calculated in relation to   ~~nothing exactly the same as~~

1 There is <u>no equivalent to</u> this word in any other language.
...*nothing exactly the same as*...

2 I am afraid that your sales performance <u>has fallen short of expectations</u>.
....

3 These two cars are <u>alike</u>.
....

4 The problem can be divided into two <u>distinct</u> parts.
....

5 Although they are based on the same novel, the two films <u>differ</u>.
....

6 The salary given will be <u>commensurate with</u> experience.
....

7 Complete each sentence with an adjective from the box.

abundant	lavish	excessive	superior	inferior
negligible	major	middling	potential	ample

1 The guests were impressed by the ......*lavish*...... scale of the banquet.
2 Water is .... in this part of the country, owing to the heavy rainfall.
3 Make a list of .... clients, and then send them our brochure.
4 Response to our sales campaign was only .... , which was a little bit disappointing.
5 The government was accused of making .... demands on the taxpayers.
6 There is no need to rush. We have .... time before the meeting.
7 Since winning the pools, Helen and Joe have moved to a .... neighbourhood.
8 There's no need to take the car to a garage. The damage is ....
9 The signing of the peace treaty was an event of .... importance.
10 Just because you don't have your own desk in the office, you needn't feel ....

8 Replace the word(s) underlined in each sentence with a word from the box.

altogether	considerably	especially	practically	specifically
barely	effectively	moderately	respectively	thoroughly

1 United are <u>virtually</u> certain of a place in the final after this result. ...*practically*..
2 I'm <u>particularly</u> proud of Jan's contribution to the play. ....
3 Peter says he is <u>utterly</u> fed up with the government. ....
4 Be careful! I can <u>hardly</u> walk! ....
5 After finishing the decorating I felt <u>completely</u> exhausted. ....
6 Classes 3 and 4 scored 10 points and 15 points each <u>in that order</u>. ....
7 I am <u>fairly</u> satisfied with the results so far. ....
8 Since the revolution, the army has <u>to all intents and purposes</u> run the country. ....
9 We have been <u>greatly</u> heartened by the news from the surgeon in charge. ....
10 I told you clearly and <u>definitely</u> not to write your answers in pencil, Smith! ....

Education

1 **Complete each space in the text with a word formed from the word in CAPITALS.**

Last year I resigned my post as a Head of Department at a large comprehensive

school. After 23 years of teaching, I had simply had enough of a job which is becoming

increasingly (1) ...problematic... . As a Departmental Head,   PROBLEM

I saw at close hand the effect of the government's increased

(2) .... in educational matters; the job is now   INVOLVE

ten times more (3) .... than it was when I   BUREAU

started out. Not content with loading teachers down with

paperwork, the government has also imposed standard national

tests on pupils as young as six, a fact which has left many teachers

(4) .... with their profession. But that side of   ENCHANT

things is by no means all. There is also the growing

(5) .... of the pupils, including the girls.   AGGRESSIVE

There are the frequent little acts of (6) ....   RUDE

which teachers have become almost (7) .... to stop,   POWER

now that the right to discipline pupils has been all but taken

from them. There is the restlessness and sheer (8) ....   BORING

of children brought up on a diet of computer games and violent

videos. Some people dismiss any link between computer games

and a (9) .... in attention span, but few of them are   REDUCE

teachers. When I started out, I used to enjoy teaching history,

my chosen discipline, to (10) .... pupils; now I do so   RESPECT

every Tuesday evening, teaching local history to pensioners.

2 Both options make sense. <u>Underline</u> the one which forms a common collocation.

1 In my country we have to do nine *basic/<u>core</u>* subjects and then we can choose several others.

2 At this school we put a strong emphasis on *academic/scholarly* achievement.

3 In my country *bodily/corporal* punishment was abolished 40 years ago.

4 In my class we had a *helper/support* teacher who assisted pupils with learning difficulties.

5 On Friday afternoons we had lessons with the *trainee/apprentice* teacher.

6 In my country we have some end of year tests but most of our marks come from *progressive/continuous* assessment.

7 At 16 we have the choice of doing more *vocation/employment* oriented courses, such as Business Studies and Accounting.

8 When I was 15, I had a 2-week work *position/placement* with a local factory.

9 There were a number of *teenage/child* mothers in my class.

10 I was expelled from school for *playing/going* truant too many times.

3 Read the text and decide which option (A, B, C or D) best completes each collocation or fixed phrase.

A report on the notorious Fiveways School, visited recently by government (1) ....B.... , was published yesterday. The report (2) .... inadequate strategic planning, poor (3) .... of teaching, and semi-derelict building conditions as being largely to blame for the problems at Fiveways, the school branded 'the worst in Europe'. Our reporters entered the school by (4) .... arrangement, and witnessed at (5) .... hand the chaos that has heaped infamy on the school. On the day of their visit, our reporters learned that one disruptive pupil had been given a 3-week (6) .... for punching a teacher in the face. Our reporters saw pupils virtually (7) .... riot, throwing stones at passers-by and verbally (8) .... a teacher.

1 A authorities	B inspectors	C controllers	D examiners
2 A highlights	B illuminates	C features	D activates
3 A measures	B patterns	C standards	D specifications
4 A former	B earlier	C preceding	D prior
5 A original	B first	C immediate	D direct
6 A expulsion	B caution	C suspension	D ban
7 A running	B going	C making	D taking
8 A harming	B abusing	C damaging	D oppressing

4 Five people are speaking about their learning experiences. Complete each space with a suitable word. The first letter of each space is given.

1 **Emma**

I've just finished university, although I'll have to go back for my g.*raduation* .... ceremony in October. So now I'm the proud possessor of a d............................ . in Modern Languages. At last I can get down to earning some money and paying back my l............................ from the government. My friend is luckier than me in this respect – she's off to the States. She has a s............................ to study at Yale University.

2 **Jack**

I was known as a rather naughty, mischievous pupil, and I often used to get s............................ out of the lesson or put in d............................ after school. Little did the school know, however, that Dad was actually paying me to have extra Maths lessons at home with a private t............................ . And it paid off, for in my Maths exam, I surprised everyone by getting the top m............................ in the class.

3 **Sarah**

I left school without any q............................ , and with no real job p............................ . But then I started doing e............................ classes at the local f............................ education college. And now I'm a mechanic, and delighted with my job!

4 **Tom**

My problem was exams. I was never any good at them. Classwork fine, exams no go. For my A levels I r............................ solidly for three months, but despite all this preparation, I got disappointing g............................: D for Physics, E for Chemistry, and E for Biology. The school suggested that I r............................ the exams, but to be honest, I didn't fancy all that studying all over again. But I did win a p............................ at Sports Day, for the Senior Boys Long Jump.

5 **Mary**

When I was 28, I decided I wanted to go back into education, as I was getting more and more interested in English literature. One option was to become a m............................ student at a university, but I couldn't afford this full-time commitment. So in the end I signed up for a c............................ course, or 'distance learning', as it's called. I sent my essays and a............................ to a tutor by post and also communicated with her by email. I had to study English literature from 1300 to the present day, but I chose to s............................ in the twentieth-century novel.

5 Complete the extracts from two school reports by writing a word from the box in each space.

half-hearted	respect	mature	distracted	concentrate
contributes	applies	~~effort~~	insolent	participated

Report 1

Tracey has made a big (1) ....*effort*...... this term, showing herself to be very
(2) .... for her age. She (3) .... herself well and (4) ....
fully to class discussions. She shows a lot of (5) .... towards her teachers.

Report 2

On one occasion Derek was sent home for being (6) .... to a teacher. In terms
of effort, his work can sometimes be rather (7) .... He is easily
(8) .... and finds it hard to (9) .... in class. Also he has not
(10) .... in group work as well as he should.

6 Complete the spaces with one word which fits in all three sentences.

1 When we had finished acting, the teacher gave us all a ....*mark*...... out of ten.
   Elka has only been in the office for three months, but already she has really made
   her ....*mark*...... .
   The teacher told Jeremy off for making a ....*mark*...... on Emma's notebook.

2 We're pleased with Ann's work – she .... herself very well to the task in hand.
   The comment I have just made to Smith .... equally to all of you.
   I really hope my sister .... for that new job; she'd be so good at it.

3 I've virtually .... any ambition I ever had of becoming a teacher.
   I .... out of college after one term and went travelling around the world
   instead.
   On police advice, Mr Bortello has .... the charges he brought against his
   neighbours.

4 Mr Ross, our old history teacher .... his classes with a rod of iron!
   The judge .... that Newton had acted in self-defence, and instructed the
   jury to find him 'not guilty'.
   Police have not .... out the possibility of murder in this case.

5 The entire workforce at Holman Avionics downed tools today, in .... of
   two sacked colleagues.
   If you need help, put your hand up and I or Mrs Kent, the .... teacher,
   will come to you.
   I'll come along to your speech, if you like, and give you some moral ....

Word formation

Word formation has been practised throughout the vocabulary section. This unit gives further practice in greater detail.

1 Complete each sentence with a word beginning *over-* or *–under-* formed from the word in brackets.

1 The _underlying_ (lie) causes of the problem are widely known.

2 What a terrible film. It's really .... (rate) in my views.

3 The first time I tried out my new bike I .... (balance) and fell off.

4 Don't forget to give the door a/an .... (coat) as well as a coat of gloss paint.

5 The bath .... (flow) and the water dripped through into the living room.

6 It is not as easy as all that. I think you are .... (simplify) the problem.

7 I apologize for the delay in sending your order but we are .... (staff) at present.

8 You can cross the road by going down these steps and through the .... (pass) .

9 The garden has been neglected and was .... (grow) with weeds.

10 You should have turned the meat off before. It's .... (do) now.

2 Complete the word in each sentence with either *-able* or *-ible*. Make any necessary spelling changes.

1 Brenda's new book is really remark_able_ .

2 I don't find your new colleague very like........................ .

3 The pie looked very good, but it wasn't very easily digest........................ .

4 That was a really contempt........................ way of getting the boss on your side!

5 I think that anything is prefer........................ to having to tell so many lies.

6 The advantage of these chairs is that they are collapse........................ .

7 I do hope that you find your room comfort........................ .

8 Why don't you go to the police? It's the sense........................ thing to do.

9 John takes good care of the children and is very response........................ .

10 I find your aunt a very disagree........................ person I'm afraid.

3 Complete the word in each sentence by adding a suitable prefix.

1 I didn't pay the bill and now the electricity has been ....*dis*.connected.

2 There is a law against dropping litter, but it is rarely ....forced.

3 The government has decided not to ....introduce military service.

4 I thought the effects in the film were rather ....done.

5 The rumours about the minister's death were completely ....founded.

6 Anyone with a ....ability may qualify for a special pension.

7 I am ....debted to you for all the help you have given me.

8 When a currency is ....valued, it is worth less internationally.

9 I found the instructions you gave us very ....leading.

10 John rents the house and I ....let a room from him.

4 Replace the words underlined in each sentence with one word ending in -ly and beginning with the letter given.

1 The country imports over two million tons of rice every year. a*nnually*......

2 Harry's work has improved a great deal. c......................

3 By chance, I'm driving there myself tomorrow. C......................

4 I'll be with you straight away. d......................

5 The two sisters were dressed in exactly the same way. i......................

6 I'm afraid that Carol's writing is quite illegible. a......................

7 Tim only understands in a hazy manner what is going on. v......................

8 I think that this plan is downright ridiculous! t......................

9 Diana just wants to know the truth. m......................

10 The passengers only just escaped with their lives. b......................

5 Complete the word in each sentence with either in- or un-.

1 Why are you so ......*in*.sensitive to other people's problems?

2 The garden is divided into two ....equal parts.

3 I think you were ....justified in punishing both boys.

4 I am afraid that the world is full of ....justice.

5 This ticket is ....valid. You haven't stamped it in the machine.

6 Thank you for your help. It was ....valuable.

7 Quite honestly I find that argument ....tenable.

8 The government's ....action can only be explained as sheer neglect.

9 The amount of food aid the country has received is quite ....sufficient.

10 Her remarks were so rude they were frankly ....printable.

6 Complete the word in each sentence by adding a word from the box.

pour	dust	flake	mare	quake
hand	fire	~~shift~~	sick	goer

1 We used cushions and blankets as a make......*shift*...... bed.

2 I woke up screaming after having a terrible night...................... .

3 The house was severely damaged by an earth...................... .

4 We got soaked to the skin in a sudden down...................... .

5 Don't forget to tell everyone about the meeting before...................... .

6 The average theatre...................... will find this play incomprehensible.

7 After six months abroad, Angela was beginning to feel home...................... .

8 The floor of the workshop was covered in saw...................... and shavings of wood.

9 The children made a poster based on the shape of a snow...................... .

10 The United Nations tried to arrange a cease...................... but without success.

7 Complete the compound word in each sentence.

1 One of the draw......*backs*...... of this car is its high petrol consumption.

2 From the hotel there is a breath...................... view across the canyon.

3 Peter's gambling ability gave him a nice little wind...................... of £300.

4 We always lock the computer in this cupboard, just as a safe...................... .

5 If I were you, I'd spend a bit more and buy the hard...................... version of the book.

6 Michael's playboy life...................... was the envy of all his friends.

7 That building has been ear...................... for redevelopment by the council.

8 We cannot take off because the run...................... is rather icy.

9 From my stand...................... , this would not be a very profitable venture.

10 There is wide...................... dissatisfaction with the government's policies.

8 Complete the word in each sentence with a suitable suffix.

1 I object strongly to the commercial*ization* of sport.

2 Skateboarding is no longer very fashion...................... in this country.

3 Don't touch that glass vase! It's absolutely price...................... !

4 We decided to go to watch some tradition...................... dances in the next village.

5 Helen's uncle turned out to be a really remark...................... person.

6 We have not yet received confirm...................... of your telephone booking.

7 Driving on these mountain roads in winter is a bit hazard...................... .

8 I just couldn't put up with his relent...................... nagging.

9 The doctor will be available for a consult...................... on Thursday morning.

10 None of this work has been done properly. Don't you think you have been rather neglect...................... ?

9 Complete the text by writing a form of the word in CAPITALS in each space.

ROMFORDCOLLEGEALUMNICLUB

Hello all Romfordians!

Welcome to another edition of the club newsletter.

A list of (1) ......*forthcoming*...... events for the autumn is being	COME
prepared. It will be displayed on the club's	
(2) .... Sadly our intended celebrity guest, the	NOTICE
actor George Wells, has had to (3) .... from	DRAW
the summer fair. However, we are pleased to announce that we	
have lined up a (4) .... in the shape of Bethan	PLACE
Rogers, the folk-singer.	
Meanwhile, we are looking for (5) .... to help	VOLUNTARY
run both the cloakroom and the (6) .... stall.	FRESH
If you are interested please let me know as soon as possible.	
The cost of (7) .... to the fair for non-members	ADMIT
has been agreed at £5.00, but free, of course, for members.	
As you know, Professor Byatt, who has been associated with	
the club for 15 years, is retiring at the end of term. In	
(8) .... of his support and enthusiasm, we are	RECOGNIZE
planning to hold a little (9) .... for him.	PRESENT
Mrs Byatt has suggested we buy him a gold watch. Please send	
any (10) .... you would like to make to me	CONTRIBUTE
by Friday 30th.	

Multiple meaning

Multiple meaning has been practised throughout the vocabulary section. This unit gives further practice in greater detail.

1 **Replace the words <u>underlined</u> in each sentence with a verb from the box.**

withdrew	damaged	stopped	opened	~~started moving~~
produced	extracted	dragged	told off	succeeded

1 The lorry <u>pulled away</u> very slowly because of its heavy load. *started moving*
2 I think I must have <u>pulled</u> a muscle. ....
3 The man <u>pulled out</u> a gun and aimed it at the bank clerk. ....
4 It was still dark when I <u>pulled back</u> the curtains. ....
5 Surprisingly, when the dentist <u>pulled out</u> my tooth, I didn't feel a thing. ....
6 I think it's amazing that Jack <u>pulled it off</u> – I never thought he'd do it. ....
7 The United Nations <u>pulled out</u> their troops from the capital. ....
8 Mike was <u>pulled up</u> by his boss for making a joke about the Chairman. ....
9 They <u>pulled</u> the heavy sandbag along as it was too heavy to carry. ....
10 A police car <u>pulled up</u> outside the Burtons' house. ....

2 **Decide whether *run* in each sentence is correct or not. If it is correct, write a tick. If not, correct it.**

1 I'll run your message to John and see what he thinks. *pass/give*
2 Would you like me to run you to the bus station? ....
3 I can't stand all the chlorine in the pool – it makes my eyes run. ....
4 Your home address isn't run correctly in our records. ....
5 They sometimes run an extra train if they know it's going to be busy. ....
6 It is thought that the total cost will run 50% higher than the estimate. ....
7 Well I'm extremely busy, but, at a run, I might be able to do it for you. ....
8 The run of the matter is, we've decided to get married in August. ....
9 My contract still has six months to run. ....
10 Karen hasn't decided yet if she wants to run for the Presidency again this year. ....

3 **Which word completes each set of collocations or fixed phrases?**

1   an instrument .....*panel*.......

 a ....*panel*.....of experts

 a control .....*panel*.......

 a wooden .....*panel*.....

2   a .... ballot

 a .... agent

 keep it a ....

 meet in ....

 the .... of success

3   take .... of the situation

 it's out of ....

 the .... exchange

 the .... market

4   a .... sheet

 a .... zone

 only .... will tell

 long .... no see

 for the .... being

5   a .... minder

 .... abuse

 .... care facilities

 a .... prodigy

 behaving like a ....

4 **Decide whether *odd* in each sentence is correct or not. If it is correct, write a tick. If not, correct it.**

1   There are some very odd characters living in this street. ....✓.......

2   Come on Jack, one odd glass of beer before you leave! ....

3   It's odd to think that this time yesterday we were on the other side of the world. ....

4   I think this software is odd with my computer. ....

5   I'm getting odd feet about this – it's all a bit dangerous. ....

6   Look I can't wear odd socks – everyone will laugh at me. ....

7   The match was mediocre – apart from the odd flash of genius from Lupeto. ....

8   Put your odd finger over the hole as you blow. ....

9   Look, I'd like to lend you the money, but you're putting me in an odd position. ....

10   The question master tells you three things, and you have to say which is the odd one out. ....

5 Underline the two words which collocate best with the words around the space.

1 Please .... this receipt, as it means we can identify your photographs more quickly. (*maintain/retain/keep*)

2 Ok, if you can just .... still while I take the photograph. (*stay/stop/stand*)

3 The final .... will be shown here on Channel 3 at 8.30 on Tuesday. (*part/ programme/series*)

4 The doctor said I had a .... skin condition. (*mild/weak/slight*)

5 Her work gives a sense of .... to her life. (*aim/purpose/direction*)

6 He even had the .... to ask me to do his photocopies for him. (*cheek/ brain/nerve*)

7 Thanks to that wretched mosquito, my ankle .... to twice its normal size. (*swelled/grew/rose*)

8 I couldn't stand any more, so I left early, but John stayed to the .... end. (*far/very/bitter*)

9 Today's not a good day for a meeting. I'm rather .... for time. (*tight/ pushed/pressed*)

10 Come on Elly, concentrate on the game; it's your .... (*turn/go/take*)

6 Replace the underlined words in each sentence with one word which fits in all three sentences.

1 It would <u>require</u> a lot of strength to lift that boulder.
I find his views on foreigners very hard to <u>accept</u>.   *take*
I hope the burglars didn't <u>steal</u> anything valuable.

2 Sue has not really been <u>challenged</u> at school this term.
The pullover <u>expanded</u> when I washed it.   ....
I <u>reached</u> out my arm as far as it would go.

3 I <u>intend</u> to leave as early as possible.
I <u>nominate</u> Sally Field for the post of Chairperson.   ....
I <u>suggest</u> setting up another meeting for next Thursday.

4 I hope you've got enough <u>room</u> to work at that desk.
There's a large storage <u>area</u> under the stairs.   ....
There's a <u>place</u> here for you Emma, if you want to sit down.

5 Erica thought for a <u>while</u> and then dropped the ring over the bridge.
From that <u>point</u> on, their relationship was never quite the same.   ....
At the last <u>minute</u>, they decided to pull out of the competition.

1

Words and phrases

These units also revise items from earlier units.

1 *Come*

Complete each sentence with a word from the box.

~~expectation~~	fortune	world	useful	force
pressure	undone	strike	realize	light

1 I'm afraid that Jim's new play didn't come up to ....*expectation*........ .
2 The building workers have voted to come out on ....
3 The government is coming under .... to change the law.
4 When her uncle died, Susan came into a ....
5 The truth of the matter came to .... during the investigation.
6 Oh bother! My shoelaces have come ....
7 Bring the torch with you. It might come in ....
8 Ted used to be quite wealthy, but he's come down in the ....
9 Recently I've come to .... that you were right all the time.
10 The new traffic regulations come into .... tomorrow.

2 *In*

Complete each sentence with a word from the box.

advance	comparison	earnest	doubt	response
~~detention~~	sympathy	practice	charge	way

1 All the pupils who misbehaved have been kept in ....*detention*........ .
2 I'm not joking. I'm speaking in ....
3 Your rent is, of course, payable in ....
4 The bus drivers are on strike, and the railway workers have come out in ....
5 This city makes London seem quite small in ....
6 It's a depressing book, but I enjoyed it in a ....
7 Everyone else is away, so I am in .... of the office.
8 Theoretically term ends at 4.00 on Friday, but in .... everyone leaves at lunchtime.
9 If in .... , do not hesitate to contact our representative.
10 We decided to show the film again in .... to public demand.

3 *Hand*

Match each expression (1–10) with an explanation (a–j).

1 She did it single-handedly. .....g.....
2 You have to hand it to her. ....
3 She can turn her hand to just about anything. ....
4 Her behaviour was rather high-handed. ....
5 She played right into their hands. ....
6 She's an old hand at this kind of thing. ....
7 At the end they gave her a big hand. ....
8 I think her behaviour is getting out of hand. ....
9 She has managed to keep her hand in. ....
10 She was given a free hand. ....

a She unsuspectingly gave them an advantage.
b She took advantage of her position to use her power wrongly.
c She was allowed to do whatever she wanted.
d She is becoming uncontrollable.
e She was applauded loudly.
f She has practised so as not to lose her skill.
g She did it on her own.
h She can learn any skill very easily.
i She has to be congratulated.
j She has a lot of past experience.

4 Wood and metal

Complete each sentence with a word from the box.

beam	pole	plank	stick	trunk
girder	post	rod	~~twig~~	wand

1 A small bird was carrying a ....twig........ in its beak back to its nest.
2 The wall was supported by a thick metal ....
3 Wasps had made a hole in the .... of the old fruit tree.
4 A workman pushed the wheelbarrow along a ....
5 The magician waved the .... and the rabbit vanished.
6 We have to replace an old oak .... which supports the ceiling.
7 I use a long piece of bamboo as a fishing ....
8 Our neighbour crashed his car into our gate ....
9 After I left hospital I could only walk with a ....
10 We hoisted the flag to the top of the ....

5 Prefix *un-*

Rewrite each sentence so that it contains a form of the word <u>underlined</u> beginning *un-*.

1 I don't <u>envy</u> his position.
   His position .... *is unenviable* ....

2 Philip flew to New York without the <u>company</u> of his parents.
   Philip flew to New York ....

3 Margaret has no <u>inhibitions</u> at all.
   Margaret is completely ....

4 There is no <u>foundation</u> to the rumour that I have been dismissed.
   The rumour that I have been dismissed ....

5 I just can't <u>bear</u> this heat!
   For me, this heat ....

6 There's no <u>doubt</u> that Schwartz is the best skier around at the moment.
   Schwartz is ....

7 The sound of Jenny's voice cannot be <u>mistaken</u>.
   The sound of Jenny's voice ....

8 There is no <u>justification</u> for your behaviour.
   Your behaviour is quite ....

9 There is no <u>precedent</u> for such action.
   Such action ....

10 Ian teaches but has no teaching <u>qualifications</u>.
   Ian is an ....

6 Verbs of movement

<u>Underline</u> the most suitable option in each sentence.

1 The drunken soldier was *marching/<u>staggering</u>/scrambling* crazily from one side of the street to the other.
2 George suddenly *dashed/slunk/rambled* into the room waving a telegram.
3 Sue found it very difficult to *pass/overtake/cross* the busy street.
4 Passengers who wish to *alight/leave/descend* at the next station should travel in the front four coaches.
5 The runner with the injured foot *flashed/limped/trundled* across the finishing line.
6 Kate spent the morning *rambling/strolling/crawling* along the sea-front.
7 Harry *strode/tiptoed/trudged* along the landing, trying not to make any noise.
8 The road was icy, and I *skidded/skated/slipped* as I was walking along.
9 I managed to *creep/slink/strut* up to the burglar before he noticed me.
10 After the meal we *lounged/loitered/lingered* over our coffees for an hour or so.

2

Words and phrases

1 Get

Replace the words <u>underlined</u> with an expression from the box.

get you down	get your own back	~~get the sack~~	get it straight
get hold of	get the idea across	get up speed	get rid of
	get away with murder	there's no getting away from it	

1 If you're not careful, you're going to be <u>dismissed</u>. ..*get the sack*....
2 Doesn't this gloomy winter weather <u>depress</u> you? ....
3 You're going to grow old one day. <u>You can't ignore it</u>. ....
4 Willie treated you really badly. How are you going to <u>take revenge</u>? ....
5 These trains start very slowly but they soon <u>accelerate</u>. ....
6 Ann talks well but she doesn't always <u>communicate what she wants to say</u>.

   ....
7 The pipes have burst. We must try to <u>find</u> a plumber. ....
8 Let's <u>understand each other</u>. I don't want to go out with you! ....
9 Philip is the teacher's favourite. She lets him <u>do whatever he wants</u>. ....
10 I feel awful. I can't seem to <u>shake off</u> this cold. ....

2 Colour

Complete each sentence with a colour, in a suitable form of the word.

1 When Bill saw my new car he was ......*green*...... with envy.
2 Tina never comes here now. We only see her once in a .... moon.
3 When the visitors from Japan arrived, the company gave them the ....
   carpet treatment.
4 I'm fed-up with this job. I feel completely .... off.
5 Julie's letter was unexpected. It arrived completely out of the ....
6 The ....-collar workers received a rise, but the workers on the shop floor
   were told they had to wait.
7 We decided to celebrate by going out and painting the town ....
8 Tony can't be trusted yet with too much responsibility, he's still ....
9 You can talk until you're .... in the face, but he still won't listen.
10 They fell deeper and deeper into the .... and then went bankrupt.

3 Common phrases

Match each sentence (1–10) with a comment from the same speaker, (a–j).

1 Gosh, it's incredibly hot today. .....*f*.....

2 I'm really terribly sorry about damaging your car. ....

3 I feel that proof of Smith's guilt has now been established. ....

4 Well, that's the last item we had to discuss. ....

5 Why didn't you phone me at all? ....

6 It's a good plan, I suppose. ....

7 You may be the office manager … ....

8 The search has gone on now for three days. ....

9 Don't worry about the missing money. ....

10 Haven't you heard about Gordon and Eileen then? ....

a But that doesn't give you the right to speak to me like that.

b Chances are it's just an administrative error.

c Beyond a shadow of doubt, in my opinion.

d For all you know, I might be dead!

e I thought it was common knowledge.

f I could really do with a cold drink.

g As far as it goes, that is.

h So I think that covers everything.

i And hope appears to be fading, I'm afraid.

j All I can say is that it certainly won't happen again.

4 *See*

Complete each sentence with a word or phrase from the box.

better days	my way	the last	things	~~it through~~
eye to eye	red	the light	a lot	the funny side

1 I started this project, and I intend to see ....*it through*..... .

2 If you ask me, this restaurant has seen .... The décor is very old.

3 Well, so much for Jack. I think we've seen .... of him for a while.

4 I don't think we really see .... over this matter, do we?

5 Come on, laugh! Can't you see .... ?

6 When Brenda told me I had been dismissed, I saw ....

7 I don't think I can see .... to lending you the money after all.

8 Mark and Ellen have been seeing .... of each other lately.

9 At last! Rob has seen .... and come round to my way of thinking.

10 Ghosts! Don't be silly! You're seeing .... !

5 Suffix *-ful*

Rewrite each sentence, so that it contains a form of the word <u>underlined</u> ending in *-ful*.

1 Martin did his <u>duty</u> as a son.
   Martin .... *was a dutiful son* ....

2 You didn't show much <u>tact</u>, did you?
   You .... ?

3 I think the whole idea is a flight of <u>fancy</u>.
   I think the whole idea ....

4 We have a relationship which <u>means</u> something.
   We have ....

5 I have my <u>doubts</u> about this plan.
   I ....

6 I can only <u>pity</u> his performance, I'm afraid.
   His performance ....

7 Smoking definitely <u>harms</u> the health.
   Smoking ....

8 It would be of some <u>use</u> to know what they intend to do.
   It would be ....

9 Jim doesn't show any <u>respect</u> to his teachers.
   Jim ....

10 I'm afraid your directions weren't much <u>help</u>.
   I'm afraid ....

6 *Out*

Complete each sentence with a phrase from the box.

| of the way | on strike | of sight | of my control | of all proportion |
| and about | of range | of breath | of character | of order |

1 I don't spend all my time in the office, I get out ...*and about*... quite a lot.

2 She doesn't usually behave like that. It's completely out ....

3 I wish you'd get out .... ! I can't get past.

4 After running up the stairs I was quite out ....

5 The gunners couldn't fire at the castle because it was out ....

6 This was a small problem which has been exaggerated out ....

7 Don't bother trying the lift, it's out .... again.

8 The railway workers are out .... again.

9 I can't do anything, I'm afraid, it's out ....

10 The riders went over the top of the hill and were soon out ....

3

Words and phrases

1 *On*

Complete each sentence with a word or phrase from the box.

his retirement	average	the premises	the market	a permanent basis
~~its own merits~~	purpose	good terms	the verge of	loan

1 Each of the five peace plans will be judged on ..*its own merits*.. .
2 The company gave George a gold watch on ....
3 We have decided to employ Sue on .... from now on.
4 This is easily the best type of outboard motor on ....
5 This Rembrandt is on .... to the National Gallery at present.
6 There should be at least five fire extinguishers on ....
7 Mary has remained on .... with her ex-husband.
8 Paul's doctor says he is on .... a nervous breakdown.
9 We serve ten thousand customers on .... every week.
10 I don't think that was an accident. I think you did that on ....

2 *One*

Complete each sentence with a word or phrase from the box.

one at a time	~~for one~~	one another	one-time	one-way
one by one	all in one	one-off	one-sided	one in three

1 You may disagree, but I ..*for one*....... think the play is a ghastly failure.
2 The match was a .... affair, with United dominating throughout.
3 Irene Woods, the .... singing star, has written her third musical.
4 According to a survey, ... students are unable to pay tuition fees.
5 We are willing to make you a .... payment of £1,000 as compensation.
6 Not all together please! Can you come out to the front ....
7 Jim is trainer, manager and driver ....
8 .... the weary soldiers fell exhausted along the side of the road.
9 We can't turn left here. It's a .... street.
10 I wish you kids would stop pushing .... and start behaving yourselves.

3 Break

Match each sentence (1–10) with an explanation (a–j).

1 They have broken down several miles from home. .....i.....
2 They worked on without a break. ....
3 They took the corner at breakneck speed. ....
4 They got on well as soon as they broke the ice. ....
5 Their marriage is about to break up. ....
6 They have made a breakthrough at last. ....
7 They broke off at that point. ....
8 There has been a break-in at their house. ....
9 They broke the news to Pauline gently. ....
10 They broke her heart in the end. ....

a They have made an important discovery.
b They have been burgled.
c They got over their initial shyness.
d They were interrupted.
e They went on without stopping
f They made her very unhappy.
g They are on the verge of separating.
h They revealed what had happened.
i They have had trouble with their car.
j They were going extremely fast.

4 Sounds

Underline the most suitable option in each sentence.

1 A bee was *humming/buzzing/crashing* angrily against the window pane, unable to get out.
2 The crowd *banged/rustled/booed* in disagreement as the politician left the platform.
3 The bus stopped at the traffic lights with a *screech/howl/grind* of brakes.
4 I had to put some oil on the hinges to stop the door *whining/squeaking/whimpering*.
5 The sack of potatoes fell from the lorry with a heavy *crunch/splash/thud*.
6 The helicopter passed overhead with a *grinding/chirping/whirring* sound, like a giant insect.
7 The mirror fell from the wall with a *whoosh/crash/screech*.
8 Air was escaping from the punctured tyre with a *hissing/bubbling/puffing* sound.
9 The tiny bells on the Christmas tree were *clanging/ringing/tinkling* in the draught.
10 The saucepans fell onto the floor with a great *clatter/crunch/ping*.

5 Memory

Complete the second sentence so that it has a similar meaning to the first sentence, using the word given. Do not change the word given.

1   This house makes me think of the place where I grew up.

   reminds

   This house ....*reminds me of*................. the place where I grew up.

2   I used to remember things a lot better.

   memory

   My .... it was.

3   Please say hello to your mother for me.

   remember

   Please .... to your mother.

4   Edward couldn't remember anything about the crash.

   memory

   Edward .... the crash.

5   I'm sorry, but I've forgotten your name.

   slipped

   I'm sorry but .... my mind.

6   Remind me to put the rubbish out.

   forget

   Don't .... put the rubbish out.

7   That makes me think of something that happened to me.

   brings

   That .... something that happened to me.

8   I can never remember anything.

   forgetful

   I am .... my old age.

9   I will never forget seeing Nureyev dance.

   unforgettable

   Seeing .... experience.

10 Brenda is very good at memorizing phone numbers.

   by

   Brenda is very good at ....

4

Words and phrases

1 Formality

Replace each word or phrase <u>underlined</u> with a more formal word from the box.

abandoned	scrutinized	~~dismissed~~	beneficial	investigated
commensurate	discrepancy	rudimentary	inopportune	lucrative

1 George was <u>given the sack</u> yesterday. ..*dismissed*..
2 I am afraid I have only a/an <u>basic</u> knowledge of physics. ....
3 The whole matter is being <u>looked into</u> by the police. ....
4 I'm looking for a job <u>on a level</u> with my abilities. ....
5 The actual voting is <u>carefully watched over</u> by special officers. ....
6 Terry was <u>left somewhere</u> by her parents when she was a baby. ....
7 I must apologize if I have arrived at a/an <u>bad</u> moment. ....
8 There is a/an <u>difference</u> between the sum of money sent, and the sum received.
    ....
9 Carol's new catering business turned out to be very <u>profitable</u>. ....
10 I am sure that a month's holiday would be <u>good for you</u>. ....

2 *No*

Complete each phrase in bold with one of the words from the box.

likelihood	~~choice~~	wonder	trace	matter
knowing	means	concern	point	use

1 It's unfortunate, but I'm afraid you **give me no** ..*choice*.. .
2 By the time the police arrived, there was **no** .... of the burglars.
3 It's **no** .... asking me the way, I'm only a visitor here.
4 If you will smoke so much it's **no** .... you have a bad cough.
5 You go home, there's **no** .... **in** both of us waiting.
6 Mind your own business, it is **no** .... **of yours**.
7 As far as we know, the old man has **no** .... **of** support.
8 **There is really no** .... what Eric will do next.
9 I couldn't solve the puzzle, **no** .... **how** hard I tried.
10 At the moment there is **no** .... **of** the Prime Minister resigning.

3 *Head*

Match each sentence (1–10) with an explanation (a–j).

1 I never even thought of it. ....b......

2 I avoid attracting attention. ....

3 I made sure that something had to be decided. ....

4 I'm not a practically minded person. ....

5 I'm involved so far that it's out of my control. ....

6 I don't understand it at all. ....

7 I've gone mad. ....

8 I've let my feelings get out of control. ....

9 I never lose control of my emotions. ....

10 I find it really easy. ....

a I always keep my head.

b It never entered my head.

c I brought matters to a head.

d My head is in the clouds.

e I can't make head or tail of it.

f I'm in way over my head.

g I could do it standing on my head.

h It's completely gone to my head.

i I'm off my head.

j I keep my head down.

4 People

Underline the most suitable option in each sentence.

1 I thought that Wendy's action was rather out of *personality/character/role*.

2 Paul was easy to manage when he was crawling, but now he is a *youngster/brat/toddler* it's a little more difficult.

3 Tim has been visiting some distant *relatives/family/parents* in the country.

4 She's not a teenager any more. She looks quite *outgrown/overgrown/grown up* now.

5 I can't understand Keith, he's a strange *figure/human/individual*.

6 Good heavens, it's you, Tom. You are the last *person/personality/character* I expected to see here.

7 Mary later became a *figure/being/character* of some importance in the academic world.

8 With the end of childhood, and the onset of *teenage/youth/adolescence* young people experience profound changes.

9 Do you think that *masses/humans/beings* will ever be able to live on other planets?

10 Jean has a very easy-going *reputation/characteristic/personality* which is why she is so popular.

5 Make

Complete each sentence with a word from the box.

impression	provision	~~sense~~	effort	time
difference	inquiries	point	offer	way

1 Don't be silly. What you are saying just doesn't make ......*sense*...... .

2 If you made more .... , you would succeed.

3 Although the police made .... about the missing car, it was never found.

4 I don't know how much I want. Why don't you make me a/an .... ?

5 What .... are you trying to make, exactly?

6 You may not care one way or the other, but it makes a .... to me.

7 Jack made ample .... for his family in his will.

8 Well, it's time we started making our .... home, I think.

9 I'm afraid the play didn't make much of a/an .... on me.

10 You may think you're too busy to read, but you should make .... for it.

6 Compound words

Rewrite each sentence so that it contains a compound word formed from the two words in bold. Some changes can be made to the words. The word may or may not be hyphenated.

1 A girl with **fair hair** answered the door.
.............*A fair-haired girl answered the door.*.............

2 When we **set out** on this project, you knew the risks.

....

3 Jack loses his **temper** after just a **short** time.

....

4 I am not sure which **point** of **view** you are taking on this problem.

....

5 You have to **serve** yourself in this restaurant.

....

6 We have certainly had **some trouble** from our neighbours.

....

7 The people upstairs have a child who is five **years old**.

....

8 I stood on the **step** outside the **door** at the back of the house.

....

9 The sight of the waterfall **took** my **breath** away.

....

10 Tony has contracted a disease which **threatens** his **life**.

....

5

Words and phrases

1 Size – adjectives

Complete each sentence with an adjective from the box. More than one adjective may fit.

considerable	~~sheer~~	mere	well over	minor
substantial	slight	bare	widespread	good

1. The soldiers held out for a while, but in the end were overwhelmed by ....*sheer*........ numbers.
2. There were .... ten thousand people shouting outside the parliament building.
3. Jack was given a .... part in the play. He only had one line.
4. There were a .... thousand people at last week's hockey match.
5. A .... number of people have reported seeing a UFO over Exmoor.
6. Wendy had a .... cold, but thought it wouldn't get any worse.
7. The company suffered .... losses after the stock market crash and found it difficult to recover.
8. I'm not hurt, it's a .... scratch, nothing serious.
9. We expected a good turn-out for the meeting, but a .... handful of people turned up.
10. There is a .... belief that the economic situation will improve.

2 Suffixes

Complete the word in each sentence with a suitable suffix.

1. The customs official was accused of bribe*ry*............... and corruption.
2. This painting has a certain charming child....................... quality.
3. Long leather boots were extremely fashion....................... at one time.
4. A shelf fell on Jim's head and knocked him sense....................... .
5. Helen served her apprentice....................... as a reporter on a local paper.
6. The Prime Minister handed in his resign....................... yesterday.
7. The film didn't live up to my expect....................... at all.
8. Every employ....................... will be given an electric badge for entrance and exit purposes.
9. Paul doesn't just like to be clean, he is obsessed with clean....................... .
10. We have no plans to move house for the foresee....................... future.

3 Headlines

The headlines (a–j) contain special 'headline words'. Each of these has a more common equivalent in 1–27. Match the 'headline words' with their common equivalents.

a ARMS SWOOP: TWO HELD
b NUMBER TEN TO BACK CITY PROBE
c PEACE TALKS HEAD FOR SPLIT
d NUCLEAR SCARE RIDDLE
e GO-AHEAD FOR SCHOOLS RETHINK
f ROYAL TO RE-WED PUZZLE
g PM HITS OUT IN JOBLESS ROW
h DEATH TOLL RISES IN DISCO BLAZE
i PRESIDENT OUSTED IN COUP DRAMA
j SMOKING BAN STAYS: OFFICIAL

1 disagreement ....row......
2 discussions ....
3 raid ....
4 confusing news ....
5 approval ....
6 revolution ....
7 prohibition ....
8 the unemployed ....
9 investigation ....
10 the government ....
11 financial institutions ....
12 criticizes ....
13 arrested ....
14 number killed ....
15 removed by force ....
16 mystery ....
17 marry again ....
18 fire ....
19 the Prime Minister ....
20 remains ....
21 alarm ....
22 reorganization ....
23 dispute ....
24 weapons ....
25 with legal authority ....
26 member of the royal family ....
27 support ....

4 Body movements

Underline the most suitable option in each sentence.

1 I *grabbed/clutched/cuddled* the bag of money tightly so no one could steal it.
2 Several people came forward to congratulate me and *held/grasped/shook* me by the hand.
3 Pauline was only wearing a thin coat and begin *trembling/vibrating/shivering* in the cold wind.
4 With a violent movement, the boy *eased/snatched/dashed* the purse from Jane's hand.
5 Could you *extend/catch/hand* me that file on your desk, please?
6 The barman began to *fold/bundle/clench* his fists in a threatening manner so I left.
7 If you really *lengthen/stretch/expand* can you reach that book on the top shelf?
8 Please don't *lean/curl/tumble* against the wall. It dirties the new paint.
9 Harry *crept/crouched/reclined* down behind the desk, trying to hide.
10 I can't control this movement. My arm keeps *ticking/twitching/revolving* like this. What do you recommend doctor?

5 At

Rewrite each sentence so that the underlined words are replaced by an expression containing *at*.

1 <u>Suddenly</u> there was a knock at the door.
   .... *All at once there was a knock at the door.* ....
2 I could see <u>just from looking quickly</u> that Sam was ill.
   I could see ....
3 The captain is <u>on the ship</u> at the moment, in the middle of the Atlantic.
   The captain is ....
4 Harry is a <u>very skilful tennis player</u>.
   Harry is ....
5 I thought this book was rather dull <u>originally</u>, but I've changed my mind.
   I thought ....
6 A new carpet will cost <u>not less than</u> £500.
   A new carpet ....
7 Paul shot <u>in the direction of</u> the duck, but missed it.
   Paul shot ....
8 Brenda ran up the stairs <u>taking three stairs in one step</u>.
   Brenda ran ....
9 Tim won the 100 metres gold medal <u>when he tried for the second time</u>.
   Tim won ....
10 <u>Anyway</u>, whatever happens the government will have to resign.
   ....

6

Words and phrases

1 *Set*

Match each sentence (1–10) with an explanation (a–j).

1 I don't set much store by it. .....9.......   a I've arranged the meal.

2 I've set my mind on it. ....   b I am strongly opposed to it.

3 I've had a set-back. ....   c I have operated the timer.

4 I'm dead set against her marriage. ....   d I've decided for certain.

5 I've set up the meeting for next week. ....   e I have had a reversal of fortune.

6 I've set the table in the living-room. ....   f I've made the arrangements.

7 I've got the whole set. ....   g I don't consider it very important.

8 I set you two exercises for today. ....   h I don't like the bitter taste.

9 It sets my teeth on edge. ....   i I have a complete collection.

10 I've set it to turn on at seven. ....   j I gave you some homework.

2 Places

Complete each sentence with an adjective from the box. More than one adjective may fit.

post	location	site	venue	~~whereabouts~~
plot	position	spot	haunt	point

1 The missing girl's exact .....whereabouts..... is still uncertain.

2 The sculpture cannot be appreciated unless you stand in the right
....

3 Don't go to that part of town. It is a well-known .... of muggers.

4 The film was made on .... in West Africa.

5 There is an empty .... opposite the church where a school could be built.

6 The precise .... of the ancient temple is a matter of scholarly dispute.

7 We had our picnic at a local beauty ....

8 The .... where these two lines meet gives us our position on the map.

9 The .... for our next concert has been changed to Wembley Stadium.

10 Helen was the first past the winning ....

3 Words with more than one meaning

Replace the words <u>underlined</u> with a word from the box.

sound	dead	~~fast~~	bare	run	live
rare	clean	even	late	light	slim

1 We tied the boat <u>securely</u> to the tree, and went for a walk. ...*fast*....
2 I only take the <u>absolute</u> essentials with me when I go camping. ....
3 The sales campaign is <u>exactly</u> on target so far. ....
4 Did you know that Bob and Tina <u>manage</u> the local pub? ....
5 The robbers got <u>completely</u> away from the police in a sports car. ....
6 I'd like my steak <u>underdone</u>, please. ....
7 Mr Jones erected a memorial to his <u>recently dead</u> wife. ....
8 Don't touch that wire. It's <u>carrying an electric current</u>. ....
9 He dropped my drink and I dropped his, so now we are <u>equal</u>. ....
10 I think that the idea of investing the money is very <u>reliable</u> advice. ....
11 There were no delays. The traffic was really <u>minimal</u>, for a change. ....
12 Unfortunately, our chance of success are <u>very small</u>. ....

4 Speaking

<u>Underline</u> the most suitable option in each sentence.

1 The accused sat silently throughout the proceedings and did not *emit/pronounce/utter* a word.
2 I forgot to *announce/mention/narrate* earlier that I'll be home late this evening.
3 We were just having a friendly *gossip/chat/whisper* about football.
4 I'm sorry to *cut/butt/rush* in but did you happen to mention the name 'Fiona'?
5 The police officer *addressed/argued/lectured* the children for ten minutes about the dangers of throwing stones, but then let them off with a warning.
6 John was *muttering/whispering/swallowing* something under his breath, but I didn't catch what he said.
7 It is difficult for me to *speak/tell/say* exactly what I mean in a foreign language.
8 The two people involved in the accident were both *pronounced/defined/stated* dead on arrival at Kingham Hospital.
9 My boss didn't say it in so many words, but she *clarified/declared/implied* that I would get a promotion before the end of the year.
10 After we saw the film, we stayed up half the night *disputing/arguing/criticizing*.
11 When all the votes had been counted, Julia was *declared/announced/stated* the winner.
12 I don't think you should have *accused/named/called* her a nuisance. That was a bit rude!

5 Within

Complete each sentence with a word from the box.

| the law | means | sight | reason | ~~power~~ | the hour | reach | enquire |

1 The police promised to do everything within their ....*power*..... to help us.

2 The notice on the door said '...................... within.'

3 Provided you live within your .... , you won't get into debt.

4 As long as we stay within .... , we won't have any legal problems.

5 There are several shops within easy .... of the house.

6 The ship sank when it was within .... of land.

7 You can have anything you want for your birthday, within ....

8 Hurry up! The president will be here within ....

6 Suffix -ing

Rewrite each sentence so that it contains a form of the word in CAPITALS ending in -ing.

1 There was a very strong smell coming from the lab.
   There was an overpowering smell coming from the lab.   POWER

2 Oh dear, we don't seem to have understood each other.
   ....   UNDERSTAND

3 I was really frightened by that horror film.
   ....   TERROR

4 The root cause of the problem is an economic one.
   ....   LIE

5 Building the hydro-electric dam is of supreme importance.
   ....   RIDE

6 The plane appears to be breaking up in mid-air.
   ....   INTEGRATE

7 The operation will not leave you with an ugly scar.
   ....   FIGURE

8 The government is intent on basing the country's economy on industry.
   ....   INDUSTRY

9 They will be cutting off the electricity in the morning.
   ....   CONNECT

10 I think you are making this problem seem simpler than it is.
   ....   SIMPLE

7

Words and phrases

1 By

Complete each sentence with a word or phrase from the box.

the way	profession	chance	all means	~~far~~
and large	the time	myself	no means	rights

1 This digital camera is brilliant; it's by ....far.......... the best available at this price.
2 By .... , I should give you a parking ticket, but I'll let you off this time.
3 Williams was a doctor by .... , but is more famous as a poet.
4 It is by .... certain that the bill will become law.
5 We met the other day at the supermarket by ....
6 There was not total agreement, but by .... the members agreed that the new rules were necessary.
7 I don't really like going to the cinema all by ....
8 By .... , are you coming to the union meeting next week?
9 By .... wait here if you have got nowhere else to wait.
10 By .... I got back to the bus-stop, the bus had already passed.

2 Other uses for names of parts of the body

Complete each sentence with a word from the box.

foot	head	arm	cheek	neck
chest	hand	~~leg~~	heart	spine

1 My football team won the first ....leg.......... of the two-match tie.
2 You can't fool me, I'm an old .... at this game!
3 The hotel lies in the .... of the English countryside.
4 Absolutely right! You've hit the nail right on the ....
5 The trouble with paperback books is that the .... often breaks.
6 I sat on the .... of the chair because there was nowhere else to sit.
7 The village lay at the .... of the mountain beside the lake.
8 You've got a lot of .... to speak to me like that!
9 We didn't have a corkscrew so we broke the .... of the bottle.
10 We packed all our clothes into a strong .... and sent it by rail.

3 Adjective-noun collocations

Complete each sentence with an adjective from the box.

high	significant	blunt	calculated	sound
~~sole~~	common	scattered	heavy	standing

1 Jenny was the ....sole.......... survivor of the air crash in the Brazilian jungle.
2 The island has only a .... population of less than a thousand.
3 Terry's old car is a .... joke among the people at her office.
4 It is .... knowledge that the director has applied for another job.
5 The management bears a .... responsibility for this strike.
6 The college expects a .... standard of behaviour from its students.
7 Janet has a .... grasp of theoretical nuclear physics.
8 The victim was hit on the head from behind with a .... object.
9 Buying the shares was a .... risk, but luckily it came off.
10 There has been a .... increase in the number of unemployed.

4 *Have*

Rewrite each sentence so that it contains an expression which includes the verb *have* in a suitable form.

1 There are still a few days until the end of our holiday.
   We still .... *have a few days left* .... of our holiday.
2 Old Mrs Jones can't climb stairs very easily.
   Old Mrs Jones .... climbing stairs.
3 I don't want to hear you complaining any more!
   I've .... your complaining!
4 I do not intend to call the police.
   I .... calling the police.
5 I don't wish to be a nuisance.
   I .... to be a nuisance.
6 I really don't know where we are.
   I .... where we are.
7 Give me the spanner and I'll try to do it.
   Here, let me .... , I'm very good with a spanner.
8 I don't recollect posting the letter.
   I .... posting the letter.
9 I went to the hairdresser's this afternoon.
   I .... this afternoon.
10 There's a rumour going around that a new Director is going to be appointed.
   Rumour .... a new Director is going to be appointed.

5 Verbs of seeing

Underline the most suitable option in each sentence.

1 She *noticed/watched/eyed* her daughter's boyfriend up and down, and then asked him in.
2 Jack *stared/glimpsed/glanced* at the map for a while, unable to believe his eyes.
3 Would you like to *regard/observe/view* the house that is for sale this afternoon?
4 Police *faced/gazed/spotted* the wanted man in the crowd outside a football ground.
5 I *checked/glanced/faced* at my watch. It was already well after three.
6 The burglar turned to *view/regard/face* me and said, 'Don't you recognize me?'
7 I only *beheld/witnessed/noticed* we were running low on petrol after we had passed the last filling station.
8 Tony was *noticing/glimpsing/scanning* the page, looking for his name in print.
9 I only *peered/glimpsed/squinted* the Queen from a distance before her car drove away.
10 Sally was sitting by the sea, *glancing/gazing/facing* at the shape of the distant island.

6 Do

Match each sentence (1–10) with an explanation (a–j).

1 He'll do you a favour. ....c....
2 It does him credit. ....
3 He's having a do. ....
4 He just won't do. ....
5 He was doing over a hundred. ....
6 He does go on. ....
7 He'll make do. ....
8 He likes do-it-yourself. ....
9 He won't do you any harm. ....
10 He could do with one. ....

a He is unsatisfactory for the job.
b The dog is quite safe.
c He will help you.
d He can manage, don't worry.
e He talks all the time.
f He needs one of those.
g It's his party on Saturday.
h His hobby is fixing his own house.
i It shows how good he is.
j He was driving extremely fast.

7 Time expressions

Complete each sentence with a word or phrase from the box.

for the time being	before too long	this minute	while	shortly
~~any minute now~~	by then	now and again	as of today	not long

1 Hurry up! They'll be arriving ....*any minute now*...., and we're not ready yet.
2 Sophia and I do meet .... , but I wouldn't say it was very often.
3 .... , no mobile phones will be allowed in the building.
4 We're meant to start at 8.00, but we won't be ready ....
5 The government will .... be announcing its new tax proposals .
6 I can put you up .... , but you'll have to move out next month.
7 Come and clear up this mess .... , or there'll be trouble!
8 Fancy seeing you again so soon! It's .... since we met at Dave's party.
9 You mark my words, ... Carol will be the boss of this company!
10 I'll be a little .... yet, so would you mind waiting?

8

Words and phrases

1 Collocations: nouns linked by *of*

Complete each sentence with a word from the box.

matter	slip	offer	waste	right
difference	~~lapse~~	price	fact	term

1 As people get older they often suffer from this kind of ......**lapse**...... of memory.

2 No, I don't think he's weird. As a matter of .... , I'm rather attracted to him.

3 The two leaders had a .... of opinion over the right course of action.

4 She said that her use of the word 'Baldy' was a .... of endearment.

5 The .... of failure in this case will be the loss of 2,000 jobs.

6 The authorities have had to turn down our .... of help.

7 As far as I am concerned, the meeting was a .... of time.

8 I feel that we should treat this as a .... of importance.

9 Our neighbours claim that this footpath is a public .... of way.

10 I'm sorry I said that, it was just a .... of the tongue.

2 Size and amount

<u>Underline</u> the option that best completes the collocation.

1 The results of the two experiments varied only by a <u>*negligible*</u>/*petty* amount.

2 You can travel from one end of the park to the other on a *minute/miniature* railway.

3 It's a smallish town, but it has a *sizeable/middling* park near the centre.

4 The cost of building a tunnel under the Atlantic would be *vast/astronomical*.

5 Exeter is a *medium-/standard-*sized city in the west of the country.

6 Travel to other planets involves covering *vast/monstrous* distances.

7 It's a small flat with rooms of *medium/neutral* size.

8 We have made a *considerable/plentiful* amount of progress towards negotiating a cease-fire.

9 One has to admire the *minute/tiny* attention to detail in Rodin's paintings.

10 You could make *reasonable/substantial* savings by transferring your bank account to us, Mr Jones.

3 Bring

Match each sentence (a–10) with an explanation (a–j).

1 She couldn't bring herself to do it. .....f.....

2 This brought her quite a lot. ....

3 She brought all her powers to bear on it. ....

4 It brought her to her knees. ....

5 It brought it home to her. ....

6 Eventually she was brought to book. ....

7 It brought it all back to her. ....

8 She brought the house down. ....

9 She brought him into the world. ....

10 She brought it about. ....

a It nearly defeated her.

b She was punished.

c She did everything she could to find a solution.

d She gave birth to him.

e She remembered.

f She couldn't bear the idea.

g She made it happen.

h She was applauded enthusiastically.

i It fetched a good price.

j It made her realize.

4 Feelings

<u>Underline</u> the most suitable option in each sentence.

1 I didn't go to the party as I felt a bit under the *water/clouds/<u>weather</u>*.

2 When he called me those names I just *went/took/saw* red and hit him.

3 Peter agreed reluctantly to sign the form but looked extremely ill-at-*ease/heart/ soul*.

4 When I saw the door begin to open I was scared out of my *bones/wits/blood*.

5 I feel very nervous; I've got *birds/butterflies/bees* in my stomach.

6 You look rather out of *order/tune/sorts*. Why don't you see a doctor?

7 When Ellen told me I was going to become Manager I was pleased as *powder/pigs/ punch*.

8 Hearing about people who mistreat animals makes me go hot under the *sleeves/ collar/shirt*.

9 When Sally told me she was my lost sister I was completely taken *aback/awash/ aware*.

10 Sam is a happy-*over-heels/go-lucky/may-care* kind of person, and worries about nothing.

5 Well-

Complete each sentence with a word from the box.

nigh	meaning	~~informed~~	advised	to-do
done	groomed	founded	chosen	worn

1 Carol reads a lot and is extremely well-*informed* about the world.
2 Her attempts to help were well-...................... but rather ineffective.
3 You would be well-...................... to take out travel insurance before you leave.
4 'Let's go for it' is becoming a rather well-...................... expression.
5 Ann doesn't spend much on clothes but is always well-...................... .
6 Peter brought the meeting to an end with a few well-...................... words.
7 The rumour about Sarah's engagement turned out to be well-...................... .
8 We found the climb up the cliff to the castle well-...................... impossible.
9 I prefer my steak well-...................... , please. I can't stand the sight of blood.
10 Harry lives in a large house in a well-...................... neighbourhood.

6 From

Complete each sentence with a word from the box.

memory	home	appearance	today	scratch
another	~~heart~~	exhaustion	head	now

1 What I am saying to you now comes truly from the .... *heart* .
2 George can repeat whole pages of books from ....
3 The houses are so much alike that we couldn't tell one from ....
4 We decided to abandon all the work we had done and start again from ....
5 Two members of the expedition died from ....
6 She was dressed completely in white from .... to foot.
7 From .... on, we're going to study really hard and make sure we pass the exams.
8 From .... , the price of petrol is rising by ten per cent.
9 I think he will feel much more relaxed once he is away from ....
10 From Carol's .... you wouldn't guess that she was over fifty.

9

Words and phrases

1 Adverbs

Decide how many of the words from the box will go into each sentence.

extensively	broadly	largely	practically	invariably
widely	considerably	effectively	~~literally~~	relatively

1   The music from the four loudspeakers was ....literally.... deafening.

2   The factory is now .... given over to the manufacture of spare parts.

3   It has been .... rumoured that Mr Murwell is about to be arrested.

4   The weather .... changes for the worse whenever we go on holiday.

5   .... speaking, I would agree with Jane Bowling, though not entirely.

6   The decorating is .... finished, and we should have everything ready soon.

7   The theatre was .... damaged in the explosion and will have to close.

8   We thought that this year's exam paper was .... easy.

9   Her career .... ended after her injury, although she did play again.

10   The government will be .... encouraged by these latest figures.

2 Expressions with *think*

Complete each sentence with a word formed from *think* or *thought*.

1   Russell was one of the greatest ....thinkers.... of the last century.

2   How kind of you. That was very ....

3   We cannot possibly surrender. The idea is ....

4   I don't like that idea. It doesn't bear .... about.

5   You might have phoned to say you'd be late. It was a bit ....

6   This plan won't work. We'll have to .... the whole idea.

7   Thanks for sending a card. It was a very kind ....

8   I'm having second .... about marrying Gavin.

9   Jack is very generous, and very .... brought us some champagne.

10   I wasn't paying attention and .... I threw the receipt away.

3 *Give*

Rewrite each sentence so that it contains an expression including the verb *give* in an appropriate form.

1 Why don't you phone me tomorrow?

   Why not .... *give me a call/ring tomorrow* .... ?

2 Can you assure me that the money will be paid?

   Can you .... ?

3 What makes you think you can just come in here like that?

   What .... ?

4 She made me think that she would vote for me.

   She... that she would vote for me.

5 All right, officer, I'll come quietly.

   All right officer, ... ?

6 How much did that car cost you?

   How much .... ?

7 The old wooden floor collapsed under their weight.

   The old wooden floor ....

8 If you want to leave this job, you have to tell us two weeks in advance.

   If you want ....

9 I'd rather have old-fashioned dance music any day.

   Give ....

10 Julia had a baby last week.

   Julia ....

4 Modifiers

<u>Underline</u> the most suitable word or phrase in each sentence.

1 It is <u>*by no means*</u>/*without doubt* certain whether the plan will go ahead.
2 To all intents and *reasons/purposes* the matter has been settled.
3 The minister has, in a *form/manner* of speaking, resigned.
4 There has *hardly/apparently* been no sighting of the ship for a week or more.
5 As a matter of *coincidence/fact* I bought my fridge at the same shop.
6 Some people *truthfully/actually* still believe that the Earth is flat.
7 The plan is a very good one, as far as it *goes/seems*.
8 The police are *in some ways/more or less* certain who the culprit is.
9 In some *aspects/respects* it was one of the cleverest crimes of the century.
10 The work is beyond the shadow of a *suspicion/doubt* one of the best she has written.

5 Words with more than one meaning

Complete each sentence with the most appropriate word from the box.

blow	drop	bay	~~deal~~	plain
burst	hand	minutes	post	set

1 We have been seeing a good ......*deal*........ of each other lately.

2 I don't want too much milk in my tea, just a .... will do.

3 I managed to keep the cold at .... by drinking lemon juice.

4 We decided to buy them a .... of saucepans as a wedding present.

5 The victim was killed by a .... to the back of the head.

6 More than a hundred people applied for this ....

7 My watch needs to be repaired. The hour .... has fallen off.

8 After you cross the mountains you come to a wide ....

9 Fifty metres from the end Carol put on a .... of speed and took first place.

10 Sam was secretary and so he took down the .... of the meeting.

6 *But*

Match each sentence (1–10) with one of the explanatory sentences (a–j).

1 We couldn't help but lose our way. ....*f*.....

2 But for you we would have lost our way. ....

3 Everyone but us lost their way. ....

4 We tried, but we lost our way. ....

5 You have but to ask, and you won't lose your way. ....

6 But for losing our way, we would have found you. ....

7 We had nothing but trouble and lost our way. ....

8 We've done everything but lose our way. ....

9 We all but lost our way. ....

10 Nothing but losing our way would have stopped us. ....

a We had a lot of problems.

b We managed not to.

c That is the only thing which would have prevented us coming.

d It happened despite our efforts.

e We have had other problems.

f It was bound to happen.

g We took the wrong road.

h It nearly happened.

i Thanks for your help.

j If you get some advice everything will be all right.

10

Words and phrases

1 *Put*

Complete each sentence with a word from the box.

vote	flight	stop	test	expense
ease	~~blame~~	foot	bed	market

1 The real culprits managed to put the ......blame...... on us.

2 When I asked her if she was Phil's mother, I realized I had put my .... in it.

3 In Saturday's violent storm, the new sea defences were put to the ....

4 When the policeman saw the boys fighting, he soon put a .... to it.

5 After the second attack, the troops were easily put to ....

6 We've found a new house and so we have put this one on the ....

7 Having to repair the car put us to considerable ....

8 When the proposal was put to the .... , it was passed easily.

9 The sick man was examined by the nurse and then put to ....

10 Carol soon put the candidate at .... by chatting about the weather.

2 *Run*

Complete each sentence with a word from the box.

luck	~~police~~	feeling	riot	money
bank	house	family	eye	play

1 Peter has been on the run from the ......police...... for three months.

2 In the second half the team ran .... and invaded the pitch.

3 During the recent financial crisis there was a run on the ....

4 Do you think you could just run your .... over this for me?

5 Having a good singing voice runs in the ....

6 I would have won easily but I had a run of bad ....

7 They gave us the complete run of the .... while they were away.

8 You can't really complain, you've had a good run for your ....

9 After recent pay cuts and redundancies, ... among the work force is running high.

10 The .... had an extremely long run in the West End.

3 Prefix *under-*

Rewrite each sentence so that the <u>underlined</u> words are replaced by an expression containing a word beginning *under-*.

1 We <u>thought</u> our opponents <u>were worse</u> than they actually were.
...... *We underestimated our opponents.* ......

2 Fiona is <u>having</u> treatment for a back condition.
....

3 There are <u>not enough people</u> working in this hotel.
....

4 Harry's father <u>arranges funerals</u>.
....

5 The shop <u>didn't ask me for enough</u> money.
....

6 I managed to hide in the <u>grass and bushes</u>.
....

7 Edward got his promotion in a rather <u>dishonest</u> fashion.
....

8 The children had clearly <u>not been fed properly</u>.
....

9 The <u>wheels</u> of the plane fell off as it was about to land.
....

10 We have not yet discovered what <u>really caused</u> the accident.
....

4 Names

<u>Underline</u> the most suitable option in each sentence.

1 What does your middle *letter/initial/name* stand for?
2 I'd rather not be called 'Miss' or 'Mrs', so please call me *Mr/Messrs/Ms*.
3 Her first book was published under a *homonym/synonym/pseudonym*.
4 Many people think that *prefixes/addresses/titles* such as Lord or Sir are out of date.
5 People are often surprised that the British do not carry *identity/identifying/identification* cards.
6 Her married name is Dawson, but Graham is her *virgin/spinster/maiden* name.
7 At school we gave all our teachers *namesakes/nicknames/pen-names*. We called the maths teacher 'Fido'.
8 William Bonney, *versus/ergo/alias* Billy The Kid, was a famous Wild West gunman.
9 It's a small black dog and *belongs/obeys/answers* to the name of 'Emily'.
10 I *entitle/register/name* this ship 'Titanic'. May God bless all who sail in her.

5 Call

Complete each sentence with a word from the box.

question	~~names~~	halt	bar	mind
attention	blame	duty	box	close

1 The children were calling each other .....*names*..... in the playground.
2 The police called a .... to the investigation after they found the letter.
3 I found a call ...., but I didn't have the right change.
4 David studied the law for ten years before being called to the ....
5 After the loss of our supplies, the whole expedition was called into ....
6 That was a .... call! We nearly hit that lamp-post!
7 Well, I must be going. .... calls, I'm afraid.
8 This new scandal calls to .... last year's collapse of Green's Bank.
9 Don't feel guilty. You have no call to .... yourself.
10 I would like to call your .... to something you may have overlooked.

6 Verbs with *up*

Complete each sentence with a word from the box.

dream	slip	sell	hang	dig
cheer	~~take~~	end	link	tot

1 I didn't expect anyone to ......*take*......... up such an unsatisfactory offer.
2 Whoever it was on the phone decided to .... up when I answered.
3 A journalist managed to .... up some interesting facts about John.
4 If you're not careful, you'll .... up paying twice as much.
5 When they find out who has managed to .... up, there will be trouble!
6 The Russian expedition is hoping to .... up with the Americans.
7 Of course it's not true! He managed to .... up the whole thing.
8 If you .... up the figures again, I think you'll find I'm right.
9 Why don't you .... up! Things could be worse!
10 The company was not doing well so we decided to .... up.

INDEX

VOCABULARY WORDLIST

Unit 1

allegedly	əˈledʒɪdli
amateur	ˈæmətə
appeal to	əˈpiəl tə
armbands	ˈɑːmbændz
aspects	ˈæspekts
aspiring	əˈspaɪərɪŋ
association	əˌsəʊsiˈeɪʃ(ə)n
beneficial	ˌbenɪˈfɪʃ(ə)l
capability	ˌkeɪpəˈbɪləti
compass	ˈkʌmpəs
confederation	kənˌfedəˈreɪʃ(ə)n
confidence	ˈkɒnfɪd(ə)ns
contribute	kənˈtrɪbjuːt
dedication	ˌdedɪˈkeɪʃ(ə)n
diversion	daɪˈvɜːʃ(ə)n
do-it-yourself	ˌduː ɪt jəˈself
exhaustion	ɪgˈzɔːstʃ(ə)n
facilities	fəˈsɪlɪtɪz
flipper	ˈflɪpə
flourish	ˈflʌrɪʃ
forbidden	fəˈbɪd(ə)n
goggle	ˈgɒg(ə)l
heat (race)	hiːt
helmet	ˈhelmɪt
highlights	ˈhaɪlaɪts
ideal (n)	aɪˈdɪəl
jog	dʒɒg
lap	læp
laze about	ˈleɪz əˈbaʊt
leisure	ˈleʒə
lens	lenz
mask	mɑːsk
mood swings	ˈmuːd swɪŋz
novice	ˈnɒvɪs
nutritional	njuːˈtrɪʃən(ə)l
occurrences	əˈkʌrənsəz
opponents	əˈpəʊnənts
performance-enhancing drugs	pəˈfɔːməns ɪnˌhɑːnsɪŋ ˈdrʌgz
peter out	ˌpiːtə ˈaʊt

positive	ˈpɒzətɪv
psychological	ˌsaɪkəˈlɒdʒɪk(ə)l
pump	pʌmp
ratio	ˈreɪʃɪəʊ
rucksack	ˈrʌkˌsæk
scuba diving	ˈskuːbə ˌdaɪvɪŋ
sponsor	ˈspɒnsə
stress	stres
striving	ˈstraɪvɪŋ
surpassed	səpɑːst
thrive	θraɪv
tripod	ˈtraɪpɒd
trying	ˈtraɪŋ
turn a blind eye	tɜːn ə blaɪnd ˈaɪ
undergo	ˌʌndəˈgəʊ
water chute	ˈwɔːtə ˌʃuːt

Unit 2

abandon	əˈbændən
accelerate	əkˈseləreɪt
aground	əˈgraʊnd
air pollution	ˈeə pəˌluːʃn
alight	əˈlaɪt
alternative	ɔːlˈtɜːnətɪv
argument	ˈɑː(r)gjʊmənt
ascend	əˈsend
circumstance	ˈsɜːkəmstəns
civic	ˈsɪvɪk
collide	kəˈlaɪd
common	ˈkɒmən
compensate	ˈkɒmpənseɪt
completion	kəmˈpliːʃ(ə)n
conductor (transport)	kənˈdʌktə
congested	kənˈdʒestɪd
cram	kræm
current (tide)	ˈkʌrənt
deadline	ˈdedˌlaɪn
deserted	dɪˈzɜːtɪd
dismount	dɪsˈmaʊnt
document (vb)	ˈdɒkjʊˌment
domestic	dəˈmestɪk

dune	djuːn	authority	ɔːˈθɒrəti
endanger	ɪnˈdeɪndʒə	baffled	ˈbæfld
enormous	ɪˈnɔːməs	basis	ˈbeɪsɪs
eternal	ɪˈtɜːn(ə)l	bear out	beə(r) ˈaʊt
financial	faɪˈnænʃ(ə)l	boost	buːst
gracefully	ˈgreɪsfli	chaos	ˈkeɪɒs
grizzly bear	ˌgrɪzli ˈbeə	closure	ˈkləʊʒə
haunt (n)	hɔːnt	combination	ˌkɒmbɪˈneɪʃ(ə)n
heyday	ˈheɪdeɪ	common knowledge	ˌkɒməm ˈnɒlɪʤ
initiative	ɪˈnɪʃətɪv	concerned	kənˈsɜːnd
justified	ˈdʒʌstɪfaɪd	concrete (adj)	ˈkɒŋkriːt
mound	maʊnd	confidence	ˈkɒnfɪd(ə)ns
(non-) peak periods	nɒn piːk ˈpɪərɪədz	controversial	ˌkɒntrəˈvɜːʃ(ə)l
occasional	əˈkeɪʒ(ə)nəl	debatable	dɪˈbeɪtəb(ə)l
passer-by	ˌpɑːsəˈbaɪ	decline	dɪˈklaɪn
permanently	ˈpɜːmənəntli	detain	dɪˈteɪn
rambler	ˈræmblə	disclaim	dɪsˈkleɪm
rarely	ˈreəli	disguise	dɪsˈgaɪz
refuge	ˈrefjuːdʒ	disposal	dɪˈspəʊz(ə)l
relatively	ˈrelətɪvli	doubtful	ˈdaʊtf(ə)l
remotely	rɪˈməʊtli	dwellers	ˈdweləz
resemble	rɪˈzemb(ə)l	electorate	ɪˈlekt(ə)rət
restriction	rɪˈstrɪkʃ(ə)n	event	ɪˈvent
saturate	ˈsætʃəreɪt	exaggerated	ɪgˈzædʒəˌreɪtɪd
schedule	ˈʃedjuːl	expansion	ɪkˈspænʃ(ə)n
skid	skɪd	extensively	ɪkˈstensɪvli
static	ˈstætɪk	foreseeable	fɔːˈsiːəb(ə)l
stationary	ˈsteɪʃ(ə)n(ə)ri	further to	ˈfɜːðə tə
steward	ˈstjuːəd	go-ahead	gəʊ əˈhed
stranded	ˈstrændɪd	hazardous	ˈhæzədəs
swarms	swɔːmz	headquarters	hedˈkwɔːtəz
throngs	θrɒŋz	incident	ˈɪnsɪd(ə)nt
undergrowth	ˈʌndəˌgrəʊθ	justify	ˈdʒʌstɪfaɪ
underpass	ˈʌndəˌpɑːs	likelihood	ˈlaɪklihʊd
vehicles	ˈviːɪkl	loom	luːm
virgin snow	ˈvɜːdʒɪn ˈsnəʊ	mislead	mɪsˈliːd
vital	ˈvaɪt(ə)l	moreover	mɔːrˈəʊvə
wastes (n)	weɪsts	negotiation	nɪˌgəʊʃiˈeɪʃn
widespread	ˈwaɪdˌspred	notorious	nəʊˈtɔːrɪəs
wilderness	ˈwɪldənəs	occupant	ˈɒkjʊpənt
		overpowered	ˌəʊvəˈpaʊəd
Unit 3		pay deal	ˈpeɪ diːl
		perilous	ˈperələs
according to	əˈkɔːdɪŋ ˌtuː	potential	pəˈtenʃ(ə)l
advocate	ˈædvəkeɪt	press (n)	pres
assurance	əˈʃɔːrəns	prided (vb)	ˈpraɪdɪd
assure	əˈʃɔː		

prominent	ˈprɒmɪnənt	edition	ɪˈdɪʃ(ə)n
proportion	prəˈpɔːʃ(ə)n	estuary	ˈestjuəri
prospect (n)	ˈprɒspekt	eventually	ɪˈventʃuəli
pull off	pʊl ˈɒf	exclusively	ɪkˈskluːsɪvli
quote	kwəʊt	experts	ˈekspɜːt
refugee	ˌrefjʊˈdʒiː	focus	ˈfəʊkəs
reject (vb)	rɪˈdʒekt	furnished	ˈfɜːnɪʃt
resident	ˈresɪd(ə)nt	habitation	ˌhæbɪˈteɪʃ(ə)n
restore	rɪˈstɔː	hinges	ˈhɪndʒɪz
resume	rɪˈzjuːm	horizon	həˈraɪz(ə)n
rip apart	rɪp əˈpɑːt	impassable	ɪmˈpɑːsəb(ə)l
runway	ˈrʌnweɪ	inspiring	ɪnˈspaɪərɪŋ
scandal	ˈskænd(ə)l	lease	liːs
secure (vb)	sɪˈkjʊə	lodging	ˈlɒdʒɪŋ
severe	sɪˈvɪə	mantelpiece	ˈmænt(ə)lˌpiːs
speculation	ˌspekjʊˈleɪʃ(ə)n	medieval	ˌmediˈiːv(ə)l
spokesperson	ˈspəʊksˌpɜːs(ə)n	patch	pætʃ
stand by	stænd ˈbaɪ	paused	pɔːzd
strain	streɪn	pedestrian zone	pəˈdestrɪən ˌzəʊn
suicide	ˈsuːɪsaɪd	permanent	ˈpɜːmənənt
survivor	səˈvaɪvə	persuade	pəˈsweɪd
terminal	ˈtɜːmɪn(ə)l	physical	ˈfɪzɪk(ə)l
toll	təʊl	porch	pɔːtʃ
transform	trænsˈfɔːm	possession	pəˈzeʃ(ə)n
verge	vɜːdʒ	premises	ˈpremɪsɪz
victim	ˈvɪktɪm	residence	ˈrezɪd(ə)ns
vow	vaʊ	rusty	ˈrʌsti
		scenery	ˈsiːnəri
Unit 4		self-study	ˈself ˈstʌdi
accumulation	əˌkjuːmjʊˈleɪʃ(ə)n	sheer	ʃɪə
activate	ˈæktɪveɪt	site	saɪt
adequate	ˈædɪkwət	skip (n)	skɪp
advantage	ədˈvɑːntɪdʒ	sparsely	ˈspɑːsli
afford (a view)	əˈfɔːd	spectacular	spekˈtækjʊlə
approximately	əˈprɒksɪmətli	squatter	ˈskwɒtə
bay window	beɪ ˈwɪndəʊ	strait	streɪt
bush	bʊʃ	streets ahead	striːts əˈhed
capacity	kəˈpæsəti	tenancy	ˈtenənsi
cathedral	kəˈθiːdrəl	tower above	ˌtaʊə əˈbʌv
cluttered	ˈklʌtəd	undoubtedly	ʌnˈdaʊtɪdli
cramped	kræmpt	(un) inviting	ʌnɪnvˈaɪtɪŋ
cultivate	ˈkʌltɪveɪt	vertical	ˈvɜːtɪk(ə)l
damp	dæmp	vicinity	vəˈsɪnəti
domestic	dəˈmestɪk		
dune	djuːn	**Unit 5**	
economic	ˌiːkəˈnɒmɪk	action hero	ˈækʃn ˌhɪərəʊ

autobiographical	ˌɔːtəʊbaɪə'græfɪk(ə)l	overweight	ˌəʊvə'weɪt
blatant	'bleɪt(ə)nt	passive	'pæsɪv
bombard	bɒm'baːd	political unrest	pə'lɪtɪkl ʌn'rest
booklet	'bʊklət	promote	prə'məʊt
brain-washing	'breɪnˌwɒʃɪŋ	prose	prəʊz
brochure	'brəʊʃə	restrict	rɪ'strɪkt
bulletin	'bʊlətɪn	sceptical	'skeptɪk(ə)l
campaign	kæm'peɪn	sensationalize	sen'seɪʃ(ə)nəlaɪz
cartoon character	ˌkaːtuːn 'kærɪktə	sensible	'sensəb(ə)l
censorship	'sensəʃɪp	sheer	ʃɪə
circulation	ˌsɜːkjʊ'leɪʃ(ə)n	situation comedy	sɪtʃu'eɪʃn 'kɒmədi
compensate	'kɒmpənseɪt	subliminal	sʌb'lɪmɪn(ə)l
conclude	kən'kluːd	substance	'sʌbstəns
conscious	'kɒnʃəs	surreal	sə'rɪəl
consumer	kən'sjuːmə	suspicious	sə'spɪʃəs
correspondent	ˌkɒrɪ'spɒndənt	swirling (adj)	'swɜːlɪŋ
couch potato	ˌkaʊtʃ pə'teɪtəʊ	target (vb)	'taːgɪt
coverage	'kʌv(ə)rɪdʒ	unprintable	ʌn'prɪntəb(ə)l
damning (adj)	'dæmɪŋ	variety	və'raɪəti
data	'deɪtə	vast	vaːst
depict	dɪ'pɪkt	visual	'vɪʒʊəl
digital camera	'dɪdʒɪtl 'kæm(ə)rə	whatsoever	ˌwɒtsəʊ'evə
dominated	'dɒmɪneɪtɪd		
edition	ɪ'dɪʃ(ə)n	**Unit 6**	
excessively	ɪk'sesɪvli	abound	ə'baʊnd
exposure	ɪk'spəʊʒə	assert	ə'sɜːt
fiction	'fɪkʃ(ə)n	atmosphere	'ætməsˌfɪə
gist	dʒɪst	binoculars	bɪ'nɒkjʊləz
glamorous	'glæmərəs	born and bred	'bɔːn ənd 'bred
grounds (reasons)	graʊndz	cancerous	'kænsərəs
hallucinate	hə'luːsɪneɪt	captivity	kæp'tɪvəti
handicap (vb)	'hændiˌkæp	climate	'klaɪmət
humble	'hʌmb(ə)l	cub	kʌb
hype (vb)	haɪp	current (n)	'kʌrənt
illegible	ɪ'ledʒəb(ə)l	defunct	dɪ'fʌŋkt
illiterate	ɪ'lɪtərət	destruction	dɪ'strʌkʃ(ə)n
imitation	ˌɪmɪ'teɪʃ(ə)n	dire	'daɪə
inane	ɪ'neɪn	diverse	daɪ'vɜːs
insulting	ɪn'sʌltɪŋ	doom	duːm
journalist	'dʒɜːnəlɪst	draught	draːft
literature	'lɪtrətʃə	epitomize	ɪ'pɪtəmaɪz
manuscript	'mænjuˌskrɪpt	era	'ɪərə
media	'miːdɪə	extent	ɪk'stent
nag	næg	falconer	'fɔːlkənə
negate	nɪ'geɪt	glacier	'glæsɪə
obvious	'ɒbvɪəs	global warming	'gləʊb(əl) 'wɔːmɪŋ

hawk	hɔːk
imminent	ˈɪmɪnənt
influential	ˌɪnfluˈenʃ(ə)l
insofar as	ˌɪnsəʊˈfɑːr æz
interaction	ˌɪntərˈækʃ(ə)n
issue	ˈɪʃuː
ivory	ˈaɪvəri
mature	məˈtʃʊə
millennium	mɪˈleniəm
nigh	naɪ
nocturnal	nɒkˈtɜːn(ə)l
off-shore	ˈɒf ʃɔː
prediction	prɪˈdɪkʃ(ə)n
prey	preɪ
prophet	ˈprɒfɪt
proportion	prəˈpɔːʃ(ə)n
race (type)	reɪs
resource	rɪˈzɔːs
revolution	ˌrevəˈluːʃ(ə)n
savannah	səˈvænə
species	ˈspiːʃiːz
squeak	skwiːk
stalk	stɔːk
substantial	səbˈstænʃ(ə)l
survive	səˈvaɪv
time-honoured	ˈtaɪm ˈɒnəd
torrent	ˈtɒrənt
tusk	tʌsk
virus	ˈvaɪrəs
vital	ˈvaɪt(ə)l
voluntary	ˈvɒlənt(ə)ri
warrior	ˈwɒriə
wildebeest	ˈvɪldəˌbiːst
wilderness	ˈwɪldənəs

Unit 7

administrative assistant	ədˈmɪnɪstrətɪv əˈsɪstənt
appalling	əˈpɔːlɪŋ
bonus	ˈbəʊnəs
client	ˈklaɪənt
commence	kəˈmens
complacent	kəmˈpleɪs(ə)nt
conference	ˈkɒnf(ə)rəns
constant	ˈkɒnstənt
consult	kənˈsʌlt
content (adj)	kənˈtent

contract	ˈkɒntrækt
convince	kənˈvɪns
creation	kriˈeɪʃ(ə)n
curiosity	ˌkjʊəriˈɒsəti
driving licence	ˈdraɪvɪŋ ˌlaɪsəns
eligible	ˈelɪdʒəb(ə)l
end of one's tether	ˌend əv wʌnz ˈteðə
eventually	ɪˈventʃuəli
executive	ɪgˈzekjʊtɪv
forefront	ˈfɔːfrʌnt
headhunt	ˈhedˌhʌnt
in respect of	ɪn rɪsˈpekt əv
inspiration	ˌɪnspəˈreɪʃ(ə)n
intention	ɪnˈtenʃ(ə)n
lack	læk
mechanization	ˌmekənaɪˈzeɪʃ(ə)n
motivation	ˌməʊtɪˈveɪʃ(ə)n
multinational	ˌmʌltiˈnæʃ(ə)nəl
negotiate	nɪˈgəʊʃieɪt
nose to the grindstone	ˈnəʊz tə ðə ˈgraɪndˌstəʊn
notification	ˌnəʊtɪfɪˈkeɪʃ(ə)n
nowadays	ˈnaʊəˌdeɪz
on one's toes	ɒn wʌnz ˈtəʊz
opportunity	ˌɒpəˈtjuːnəti
pay dispute	ˈpeɪ dɪsˌpjuːt
permanent	ˈpɜːmənənt
praise	preɪz
productivity	ˌprɒdʌkˈtɪvəti
reimburse	ˌriːɪmˈbɜːs
right up your street	ˌraɪt ʌp jə ˈstriːt
scheme	skiːm
sheer	ʃɪə
substantial	səbˈstænʃ(ə)l
supplementary	ˌsʌplɪˈment(ə)ri
(un) necessary	ʌnˈnesəs(ə)ri
vocation	vəʊˈkeɪʃ(ə)n
worthwhile	ˌwɜːθˈwaɪl

Unit 8

accordingly	əˈkɔːdɪŋli
acknowledgement	əˈknɒlɪdʒmənt
apparently	əˈpærəntli
appreciate	əˈpriːʃiˌeɪt
bankrupt	ˈbæŋkrʌpt
booming	ˈbuːmɪŋ
capability	ˌkeɪpəˈbɪləti

capacity	kə'pæsəti	rattle	'ræt(ə)l
capital (money)	'kæpɪt(ə)l	redundant	rɪ'dʌndənt
cease	siːs	request	rɪ'kwest
code	kəʊd	resolve	rɪ'zɒlv
commission	kə'mɪʃ(ə)n	scholarship	'skɒləʃɪp
complicated	'kɒmplɪˌkeɪtɪd	self-employed	ˌself ɪm'plɔɪd
conclude	kən'kluːd	settle (pay)	'set(ə)l
courier	'kʊriə	shares (money)	ʃeəz
currency	'kʌrənsi	sheer	ʃɪə
current account	ˌkʌrənt ə'kaʊnt	subsidy	'sʌbsədi
decade	'dekeɪd	takings	'teɪkɪŋz
deceit	dɪ'siːt	technological	ˌteknə'lɒdʒɪk(ə)l
declare	dɪ'kleə	thrifty	'θrɪfti
deduct	dɪ'dʌkt	time slot	'taɪm ˌslɒt
dispatch	dɪ'spætʃ	trickery	'trɪkəri
downright	'daʊnˌraɪt	vanish	'vænɪʃ
endeavour	ɪn'devə	venture	'ventʃə
ensure	ɪn'ʃɔː	wealthy	'welθi
enterprise	'entəˌpraɪz	whether	'weðə
entire	ɪn'taɪə	wise	waɪz
expenditure	ɪk'spendɪtʃə	within	wɪð'ɪn
express delivery	ɪk'spres dɪ'lɪv(ə)ri		
fall through	fɔːl 'θruː	**Unit 9**	
fetch	fetʃ		
fraud	frɔːd	abandon	ə'bændən
fund	fʌnd	acquaintance	ə'kweɪntəns
further to	'fɜːðə tə	adopt	ə'dɒpt
gesture	'dʒestʃə	aisle	aɪl
grant (n)	grɑːnt	alien	'eɪliən
haggle	'hæg(ə)l	almighty	ɔːl'maɪti
(in) convenience	kən'viːniəns	ancestor	'ænsestə
(in) dependent	dɪ'pendənt	ancient	'eɪnʃ(ə)nt
instalment	ɪn'stɔːlmənt	apathetic	ˌæpə'θetɪk
instance	'ɪnstəns	approximately	ə'prɒksɪmətli
interest (money)	'ɪntrəst	attentive	ə'tentɪv
key (in)	kiː 'ɪn	attitude	'ætɪˌtjuːd
maintain	meɪn'teɪn	betrothed	bɪ'trəʊðd
matter	'mætə	bloke	bləʊk
minimum	'mɪnɪməm	boss	bɒs
multinational	ˌmʌlti'næʃ(ə)nəl	bridegroom	'braɪdˌgruːm
nest-egg	'nest eg	campaign (vb)	kæm'peɪn
potential	pə'tenʃ(ə)l	chap	tʃæp
priceless	'praɪsləs	churchyard	'tʃɜːtʃˌjɑːd
provided (that)	prə'vaɪdɪd	client	'klaɪənt
psychology	saɪ'kɒlədʒi	communicate	kə'mjuːnɪkeɪt
qualify	'kwɒlɪfaɪ	community	kə'mjuːnəti
		complicated	'kɒmplɪˌkeɪtɪd

contemporary	kən'temp(ə)r(ə)ri	prejudice (vb)	'predʒʊdɪs
contrast	'kɒntrɑːst	pushy	'pʊʃi
criticize	'krɪtɪsaɪz	rage	reɪdʒ
date (vb)	deɪt	rebel	'reb(ə)l
decline	dɪ'klaɪn	scold	skəʊld
deeply	'diːpli	solitary	'sɒlət(ə)ri
descendant	dɪ'sendənt	spoilt	spɔɪlt
devoted	dɪ'vəʊtɪd	stable	'steɪb(ə)l
divorce (vb)	dɪ'vɔːs	stand (someone) up	'stænd sʌmwʌn 'ʌp
domineering	ˌdɒmɪ'nɪərɪŋ	sweltering	'swelt(ə)rɪŋ
elderly	'eldəli	upbringing	'ʌpˌbrɪŋɪŋ
eligible	'elɪdʒəb(ə)l	utterly	'ʌtəli
emerge	ɪ'mɜːdʒ		
eminent	'emɪnənt	**Unit 10**	
exceedingly	ɪk'siːdɪŋli		
extended family	ɪk'stendɪd 'fæmili	abandon	ə'bændən
extreme	ɪk'striːm	addiction	ə'dɪkʃ(ə)n
extrovert	'ekstrəˌvɜːt	alien	'eɪliən
facilities	fə'sɪlətiz	blaze	bleɪz
forces	'fɔːsiz	break into	breɪk 'ɪntə
godfather	'gɒdˌfɑːðə	brush with the law	'brʌʃ wɪð ðə 'lɔː
groom	gruːm	built-up area	'bɪlt ʌp 'eəriə
hit it off	ˌhɪt ɪt 'ɒf	collapse	kə'læps
honeymoon	'hʌniˌmuːn	cope with	'kəʊp wɪð
humid	'hjuːmɪd	counsel	'kaʊns(ə)l
humiliate	hjuː'mɪlieɪt	custody	'kʌstədi
(im) mature	mə'tʃʊə	deport	dɪ'pɔːt
immediate	ɪ'miːdiət	detection	dɪ'tekʃ(ə)n
immigrant	'ɪmɪgrənt	detention	dɪ'tenʃ(ə)n
in someone's footsteps	ɪn ˌsʌmwʌnz 'fʊtsteps	disperse	dɪ'spɜːs
independent	ˌɪndɪ'pendənt	evacuate	ɪ'vækjueɪt
individual	ˌɪndɪ'vɪdʒuəl	execution	ˌeksɪ'kjuːʃ(ə)n
insensitive	ɪn'sensətɪv	expensive	ɪk'spensɪv
invading	ɪn'veɪdɪŋ	fierce	fɪəs
juvenile	'dʒuːvənaɪl	hairpiece	'heəˌpiːs
keep in touch	kiːp ɪn 'tʌtʃ	head-dress	'hed dres
live up to	lɪv 'ʌp tə	helicopter	'helɪˌkɒptə
magnificent	mæg'nɪfɪs(ə)nt	hostage	'hɒstɪdʒ
neglect	nɪ'glekt	(in) formal	'fɔːm(ə)l
newlyweds	'njuːliˌwedz	investigation	ɪnˌvestɪ'geɪʃ(ə)n
nuclear family	ˌnjuːkliə 'fæmɪli	joyride	'dʒɔɪˌraɪd
officially	ə'fɪʃ(ə)li	juvenile	'dʒuːvənaɪl
outcast	'aʊtˌkɑːst	loot	luːt
pluck up	plʌk 'ʌp	murderer	'mɜːdərə
predecessor	'priːdɪˌsesə	neglect	nɪ'glekt
pregnant	'pregnənt	patrol car	pə'trəʊl kɑː
		penalty	'pen(ə)lti

petty	'peti	collaboration	kə,læbə'reɪʃ(ə)n
presume	prɪ'zju:m	complicated	'kɒmplɪ,keɪtɪd
probation	prə'beɪʃ(ə)n	contradiction	,kɒntrə'dɪkʃ(ə)n
(on the) rampage	ræm'peɪdʒ	craze	kreɪz
reveal	rɪ'vi:l	dice	daɪs
riot (vb)	'raɪət	discrimination	dɪ,skrɪmɪ'neɪʃ(ə)n
root cause	'ru:t 'kɔ:z	distinction	dɪ'stɪŋkʃ(ə)n
rub shoulders with	rʌb 'ʃəʊldəz ,wɪð	dominate	'dɒmɪneɪt
sideboard	'saɪd,bɔ:d	electronically	,elek'trɒnɪkli
silverware	,sɪlvə,weə	enthusiastically	ɪn,θju:zi'æstɪkli
squat	skwɒt	establish	ɪ'stæblɪʃ
statistics	stə'tɪstɪks	flatter	'flætə
submit	səb'mɪt	foster	'fɒstə
summary	'sʌməri	goatee beard	gəʊti: 'bɪəd
survey	'sɜ:veɪ	gymnastics	dʒɪm'næstɪks
survivor	sə'vaɪvə	handpick	,hænd'pɪk
sustain	sə'steɪn	headphones	'hed,fəʊnz
swerve	swɜ:v	headquarters	hed'kwɔ:təz
swindle	'swɪnd(ə)l	incidental	,ɪnsɪ'dent(ə)l
tear-gas	'tɪə ,gæs	incompatible	,ɪnkəm'pætəb(ə)l
thumb a lift	,θʌm ə 'lɪft	incongruous	ɪn'kɒŋgruəs
transgression	trænz'greʃ(ə)n	(in) consistent	kən'sɪstənt
uproot	ʌp'ru:t	insatiable	ɪn'seɪʃəb(ə)l
vacuum cleaner	'vækjʊəm ,kli:nə	instrument	'ɪnstrʊmənt
whereas	weər'æz	interlude	'ɪntə,lu:d
wig	wɪg	interpretation	ɪn,tɜ:prɪ'teɪʃ(ə)n
		jigsaw puzzle	'dʒɪgsɔ:

Unit 11

		juggler	'dʒʌglə
(in) check (chess)	tʃek	landscape	'læn(d),skeɪp
accompany	ə'kʌmp(ə)ni	limber (up)	'lɪmbə
acrobat	'ækrə,bæt	loudspeaker	,laʊd'spi:k
affluent	'æflu:ənt	lyrics	'lɪrɪks
associate	ə'səʊsi,eɪt	manners	'mænəz
athletics	æθ'letɪks	market (vb)	'ma:kɪt
benefit (from)	'benɪfɪt	martial arts	,ma:'ʃ(ə)l 'a:ts
blare	bleə	(the) masses	ðə 'mæsɪz
bodybuilding	'bɒdibɪldɪŋ	notably	'nəʊtəbli
brainchild	'breɪn,tʃaɪld	novel (adj)	'nɒv(ə)l
branch (vb)	bra:ntʃ	nurture	'nɜ:tʃə
bulls-eye	'bʊlzaɪ	pedigree	'pedɪgri:
carbon dioxide	,ka:bən daɪ'ɒksaɪd	percussion	pə'kʌʃ(ə)n
celebrity	sə'lebrəti	pool (game)	pu:l
century	'sentʃəri	popular	'pɒpjʊlə
chemical	'kemɪk(ə)l	preview	'pri:vju:
chess	tʃes	priceless	'praɪsləs
clarinet	,klærə'net	quantity	'kwɒntəti

rap music	ˈræp ˌmjuːzɪk	community	kəˈmjuːnəti
recognition	ˌrekəgˈnɪʃ(ə)n	compensation	ˌkɒmpənˈseɪʃ(ə)n
remote control	rɪˌməʊt kənˈtrəʊl	compose	kəmˈpəʊz
represent	ˌreprɪˈzent	comprehensive	ˌkɒmprɪˈhensɪv
routine	ruːˈtiːn	comprise	kəmˈpraɪz
scenery	ˈsiːnəri	conclude	kənˈkluːd
simulate	ˈsɪmjʊleɪt	constant	ˈkɒnstənt
skateboarding	ˈskeɪtbɔːdɪŋ	conventional	kənˈvenʃ(ə)nəl
solemn	ˈsɒləm	council	ˈkaʊns(ə)l
species	ˈspiːʃiːz	courteous	ˈkɜːtiəs
splinter (off)	ˈsplɪntə	coverage	ˈkʌv(ə)rɪdʒ
stadium	ˈsteɪdiəm	cruel	ˈkruːəl
stilts	stɪlts	defy	dɪˈfaɪ
stuntman	ˈstʌntˌmæn	delegate	ˈdeləgət
suspense	səˈspens	dignified	ˈdɪgnɪfaɪd
theft	θeft	diplomatic	ˌdɪpləˈmætɪk
troupe	truːp	disastrous	dɪˈzɑːstrəs
tumble	ˈtʌmb(ə)l	disorganized	dɪsˈɔːgənaɪzd
understudy	ˈʌndəˌstʌdi	eccentric	ɪkˈsentrɪk
vase	vɑːz	election	ɪˈlekʃ(ə)n
verse	vɜːs	electorate	ɪˈlekt(ə)rət
vocalist	ˈvəʊkəlɪst	executor	ɪgˈzekjʊtə
whirl	wɜːl	extreme	ɪkˈstriːm
woodwind	ˈwʊdˌwɪnd	furthermore	ˈfɜːðəˌmɔː
		head of state	ˌhed əv ˈsteɪt

Unit 12

		heavy-handed	ˌhevi ˈhændɪd
ambassador	æmˈbæsədə	honourable	ˈɒn(ə)rəb(ə)l
assembly	əˈsembli	in exchange for	ɪn ɪksˈtʃeɪndʒ
asylum	əˈsaɪləm	indicate	ˈɪndɪkeɪt
backfire	ˌbækˈfaɪə	latter	ˈlætə
barred (from)	ˈbɑːd frəm	licensed	ˈlaɪs(ə)nst
basically	ˈbeɪsɪkli	majority	məˈdʒɒrəti
beam	biːm	manifesto	ˌmænɪˈfestəʊ
betray	bɪˈtreɪ	mayor	meə
binding	ˈbaɪndɪŋ	minister	ˈmɪnɪstə
bluntly	ˈblʌntli	motion	ˈməʊʃ(ə)n
bore (n)	bɔː	mount	maʊnt
cabinet	ˈkæbɪnət	nevertheless	ˌnevəðəˈles
campaign	kæmˈpeɪn	notorious	nəʊˈtɔːriəs
candidate	ˈkændɪdeɪt	obligatory	əˈblɪgət(ə)ri
cast (a vote)	kɑːst	opinion	əˈpɪnjən
chairperson	ˈtʃeəˌpɜːs(ə)n	oppressed	əˈprest
chamber	ˈtʃeɪmbə	parliament	ˈpɑːləmənt
circulate	ˈsɜːkjʊleɪt	patriot	ˈpætriət
combination	ˌkɒmbɪˈneɪʃ(ə)n	permit	pəˈmɪt
committee	kəˈmɪti	policy	ˈpɒləsi

poll	pəʊl	concerned	kən'sɜːnd
postpone	pəʊs'pəʊn	corridor	'kɒrɪdɔː
president	'prezɪdənt	crawl	krɔːl
presumably	prɪ'zjuːməbli	cure	kjʊə
pretty (very)	'prɪti	dazed	deɪzd
privilege	'prɪvəlɪdʒ	depression	dɪ'preʃ(ə)n
proprietor	prə'praɪətə	disapproval	ˌdɪsə'pruːv(ə)l
radical	'rædɪk(ə)l	discrepancy	dɪs'krepənsi
rebellious	rɪ'beljəs	disturbance	dɪ'stɜːbəns
reign	reɪn	disuse	dɪs'juːs
reputation	ˌrepjʊ'teɪʃ(ə)n	dizzy	'dɪzi
require	rɪ'kwaɪə	dozy	'dəʊzi
resist	rɪ'zɪst	drowsy	'draʊzi
respectable	rɪ'spektəb(ə)l	drunken	'drʌŋkən
restrict	rɪ'strɪkt	evidently	'evɪd(ə)ntli
reveal	rɪ'viːl	expose	ɪk'spəʊz
ringleader	'rɪŋˌliːdə	extremist	ɪk'striːmɪst
sandwiched (between)	'sændwɪtʃt bɪ'twiːn	fanatic	fə'nætɪk
scandal	'skænd(ə)l	frown	fraʊn
significant	sɪg'nɪfɪkənt	fundamental	ˌfʌndə'ment(ə)l
smear	smɪə	furthermore	'fɜːðəˌmɔː
sovereign	'sɒvrɪn	giggle	'gɪg(ə)l
submit	səb'mɪt	graze	greɪz
succeed (in power)	sək'siːd	health-conscious	'helθ ˌkɒnʃəs
tactful	'tæk(t)f(ə)l	highlight	'haɪˌlaɪt
terrorist	'terərɪst	hobble	'hɒb(ə)l
toe the line	təʊ ðə 'laɪn	immobile	ɪ'məʊbaɪl
traditional	trə'dɪʃ(ə)nəl	impaired	ɪm'peəd
traitor	'treɪtə	implication	ˌɪmplɪ'keɪʃ(ə)n
unity	'juːnəti	invalid	ɪn'vælɪd
vicious	'vɪʃəs	languish	'læŋgwɪʃ
voluntary	'vɒlənt(ə)ri	leisurely	'leʒəli
vote	vəʊt	limp	lɪmp
wield	wiːld	mention	'menʃ(ə)n
		militant	'mɪlɪtənt

Unit 13

		mineral water	'mɪn(ə)rəl ˌwɔːtə
abuse	ə'bjuːs	misuse (n)	mɪs'juːs
activist	'æktɪvɪst	morning sickness	'mɔːnɪŋ ˌsɪknəs
alternative medicine	ɔːl'tɜːnətɪv 'medsɪn	motorized	'məʊtəraɪzd
befall	bɪ'fɔːl	outbreak	'aʊtˌbreɪk
benefits	'benɪfɪts	painkiller	'peɪnˌkɪlə
blister	'blɪstə	peculiar	pɪ'kjuːliə
boredom	'bɔːdəm	principle	'prɪnsəp(ə)l
campaign	kæm'peɪn	ramble	'ræmb(ə)l
choke	tʃəʊk	remedy	'remədi
chuckle	'tʃʌk(ə)l	represent	ˌreprɪ'zent

rheumatism	ˈruːməˌtɪz(ə)m	drift	drɪft
scowl	skaʊl	ecology	ɪˈkɒlədʒi
selective	sɪˈlektɪv	encounter	ɪnˈkaʊntə
shave	ʃeɪv	enterprise	ˈentəˌpraɪz
singular	ˈsɪŋɡjʊlə	epidemic	ˌepɪˈdemɪk
smelling salts	ˈsmelɪŋ ˌsɔːlts	erosion	ɪˈrəʊʒ(ə)n
sprain	spreɪn	essential	ɪˈsenʃ(ə)l
stagger	ˈstæɡə	estimate	ˈestɪmeɪt
stale	steɪl	ethnic	ˈeθnɪk
stroll	strəʊl	evacuate	ɪˈvækjueɪt
sum	sʌm	fertilizer	ˈfɜːtəlaɪzə
technique	tekˈniːk	frustration	frʌˈstreɪʃ(ə)n
teetotaller	tiːˈtəʊt(ə)lə	global	ˈɡləʊb(ə)l
therapy	ˈθerəpi	gravity	ˈɡrævəti
tiptoe	ˈtɪpˌtəʊ	guarantee	ˌɡærənˈtiː
tiresome	ˈtaɪəs(ə)m	humanitarian	hjuːˌmænɪˈteəriən
tranquilizer	ˈtræŋkwɪlaɪzə	illiterate	ɪˈlɪtərət
treatment	ˈtriːtmənt	immigrant	ˈɪmɪɡrənt
typically	ˈtɪpɪkli	immunization	ˌɪmjʊnaɪˈzeɪʃ(ə)n
unsteadily	ʌnˈstedɪlɪ	impoverished	ɪmˈpɒvərɪʃt
vitamin pill	ˈvɪtəmɪn ˌpɪl	inadequate	ɪnˈædɪkwət
wander	ˈwɒndə	intervene	ˌɪntəˈviːn
		irrigation	ˌɪrɪˈɡeɪʃ(ə)n
Unit 14		lack	læk
ablaze	əˈbleɪz	malnutrition	ˌmælnjuˈtrɪʃ(ə)n
affirm	əˈfɜːm	media	ˈmiːdiə
agency	ˈeɪdʒ(ə)nsi	method	ˈmeθəd
agriculture	ˈæɡrɪˌkʌltʃə	military	ˈmɪlɪt(ə)ri
average	ˈæv(ə)rɪdʒ	nourish	ˈnʌrɪʃ
awareness	əˈweənəs	numerous	ˈnjuːmərəs
bleach	bliːtʃ	organic	ɔːˈɡænɪk
burden	ˈbɜːd(ə)n	participant	pɑːˈtɪsɪpənt
cause	kɔːz	percentage	pəˈsentɪdʒ
chemical	ˈkemɪk(ə)l	plague	pleɪɡ
consequent	ˈkɒnsɪkwənt	pledge	pledʒ
consumption	kənˈsʌmpʃ(ə)n	population	ˌpɒpjʊˈleɪʃ(ə)n
contribution	ˌkɒntrɪˈbjuːʃ(ə)n	privilege	ˈprɪvəlɪdʒ
decade	ˈdekeɪd	proportion	prəˈpɔːʃ(ə)n
densely	ˈdensli	quote	kwəʊt
devaluation	diːˌvæljuˈeɪʃ(ə)n	radius	ˈreɪdiəs
developing world	dɪˌveləpɪŋ ˈwɜːld	raw material	ˌrɔː məˈtɪəriəl
diet	ˈdaɪət	recall	rɪˈkɔːl
diplomacy	dɪˈpləʊməsi	recycling	riːˈsaɪklɪŋ
disease	dɪˈziːz	refugee	ˌrefjʊˈdʒiː
dispute	dɪˈspjuːt	relevant	ˈreləv(ə)nt
donate	dəʊˈneɪt	remote	rɪˈməʊt

roundly	'raʊndli	establish	ɪ'stæblɪʃ
self-sufficiency	ˌself sə'fɪʃənsɪ	estimate	'estɪmət
settlement	'set(ə)lmənt	exhibit	ɪg'zɪbɪt
shift	ʃɪft	extract	ɪk'strækt
significantly	sɪg'nɪfɪkəntli	favouritism	'feɪv(ə)rətɪzəm
simplify	'sɪmplɪfaɪ	flabbergasted	'flæbəˌgɑːstɪd
slave	sleɪv	folio number	'fəʊliəʊ ˌnʌmbə
smoulder	'sməʊldə	grieve	griːv
solar power	ˌsəʊlə 'paʊwə	handbook	'hæn(d)ˌbʊk
sparsely	'spɑːsli	hard feelings	ˌhɑːd 'fiːlɪŋz
species	'spiːʃiːz	identical	aɪ'dentɪk(ə)l
sponsor	'spɒnsə	ignorance	'ɪgnərəns
stricken	'strɪkən	image	'ɪmɪdʒ
struggle	'strʌg(ə)l	imply	ɪm'plaɪ
subsequent	'sʌbsɪkwənt	indicate	'ɪndɪkeɪt
subsidy	'sʌbsədi	infer	ɪn'fɜː
talent	'tælənt	infringement	ɪn'frɪndʒmənt
third world	'θɜːd 'wɜːld	interpret	ɪn'tɜːprɪt
undernourishment	ˌʌndə'nʌrɪʃmənt	intrusion	ɪn'truːʒ(ə)n
universally	ˌjuːnɪ'vɜːsli	knowledgeable	'nɒlɪdʒəb(ə)l
		laborious	lə'bɔːriəs
		loathe	ləʊð

Unit 15

abandon	ə'bændən	lurch	lɜːtʃ
anaesthetic	ˌænəs'θetɪk	manner	'mænə
appreciate	ə'priːʃiˌeɪt	mannerism	'mænəˌrɪz(ə)m
attitude	'ætɪˌtjuːd	mentality	men'tæləti
awkward	'ɔːkwəd	mourn	mɔːn
biased	'baɪst	notion	'nəʊʃ(ə)n
bitter	'bɪtə	obsessed	əb'sest
candidate	'kændɪdeɪt	overwhelmed	ˌəʊvə'welmd
cherish	'tʃerɪʃ	particular	pə'tɪkjʊlə
clue	kluː	pedantic	pɪ'dæntɪk
concerned	kən'sɜːnd	picnic	'pɪknɪk
confirm	kən'fɜːm	plead	pliːd
conscientious	ˌkɒnʃi'enʃəs	posture	'pɒstʃə
consolation	ˌkɒnsə'leɪʃ(ə)n	predict	prɪ'dɪkt
convince	kən'vɪns	prejudice	'predʒʊdɪs
decorate	'dekəreɪt	psychological	ˌsaɪkə'lɒdʒɪk(ə)l
define	dɪ'faɪn	quirk	kwɜːk
deplore	dɪ'plɔː	reaction	ri'ækʃ(ə)n
detective	dɪ'tektɪv	rebel (vb)	rɪ'bel
display	dɪ'spleɪ	recollect	ˌrekə'lekt
distract	dɪ'strækt	regard	rɪ'gɑːd
dread	dred	regret	rɪ'gret
drop shadow	ˌdrɒp 'ʃædəʊ	reluctant	rɪ'lʌktənt
emphasis	'emfəsɪs	remind	rɪ'maɪnd

reproach	rɪˈprəʊtʃ	nuclear reactor	ˌnjuːklɪə riˈæktə
resent	rɪˈzent	overhaul	ˌəʊvəˈhɔːl
risky	ˈrɪski	peculiar	pɪˈkjuːliə
robbery	ˈrɒbəri	pliers	ˈplaɪəz
sensitive	ˈsensətɪv	precaution	prɪˈkɔːʃ(ə)n
signal	ˈsɪgn(ə)l	precise	prɪˈsaɪs
spot (vb)	spɒt	react	riˈækt
stability	stəˈbɪləti	recoil	rɪˈkɔɪl
stressed	strest	severe	sɪˈvɪə
subjectivity	ˌsʌbdʒekˈtɪvəti	sheer	ʃɪə
tactful	ˈtæk(t)f(ə)l	squeak	skwiːk
touchy	ˈtʌtʃi	sustain	səˈsteɪn
trait	treɪt	techno-phobe	ˈteknəʊfəʊb
unconsciously	ʌnˈkɒnʃəsli	transcribe	trænˈskraɪb
utter (vb)	ˈʌtə	utility	juːˈtɪləti
wonder	ˈwʌndə	utter (adj)	ˈʌtə
		widespread	ˈwaɪdˌspred
		wonder	ˈwʌndə

Unit 16

adapt	əˈdæpt
adjust	əˈdʒʌst
appliance	əˈplaɪəns
automation	ˌɔːtəˈmeɪʃ(ə)n
beck and call	ˌbek ənd ˈkɔːl
bewildering	bɪˈwɪld(ə)rɪŋ
blade	bleɪd
blender	ˈblendə
bolt (n)	bəʊlt
chisel	ˈtʃɪz(ə)l
component	kəmˈpəʊnənt
contraption	kənˈtræpʃ(ə)n
convenience	kənˈviːniəns
cylinder	ˈsɪlɪndə
fend	fend
flabbergasted	ˈflæbəˌgɑːstɪd
flicker	ˈflɪkə
fuse	fjuːz
goggles	ˈgɒg(ə)lz
grinder	ˈgraɪndə
hinge	hɪndʒ
impact (n)	ˈɪmpækt
insidious	ɪnˈsɪdiəs
install	ɪnˈstɔːl
jolt	dʒəʊlt
manual	ˈmænjʊəl
mask	mɑːsk
mysterious	mɪˈstɪəriəs

Unit 17

abound	əˈbaʊnd
abundant	əˈbʌndənt
adequate	ˈædɪkwət
ample	ˈæmp(ə)l
augment	ɔːgˈment
banquet	ˈbæŋkwɪt
brochure	ˈbrəʊʃə
bulk	bʌlk
calculate	ˈkælkjʊleɪt
campaign	kæmˈpeɪn
commensurate	kəˈmenʃərət
comparison	kəmˈpærɪs(ə)n
contract (vb)	kənˈtrækt
contribution	ˌkɒntrɪˈbjuːʃ(ə)n
convenient	kənˈviːniənt
crave	kreɪv
dearth	dɜːθ
decline	dɪˈklaɪn
decorate	ˈdekəreɪt
desire	dɪˈzaɪə
diminish	dɪˈmɪnɪʃ
dormitory	ˈdɔːmɪtri
dwindle	ˈdwɪnd(ə)l
enlarge	ɪnˈlɑːdʒ
enthusiasm	ɪnˈθjuːziˌæzəm
equivalent	ɪˈkwɪvələnt

especially	ɪˈspeʃ(ə)li	branded	ˈbrændɪd
excessive	ɪkˈsesɪv	bureau	ˈbjʊərəʊ
extend	ɪkˈstend	caution	ˈkɔːʃ(ə)n
fade	ˈfeɪd	chaos	ˈkeɪɒs
flesh	fleʃ	communicate	kəˈmjuːnɪkeɪt
guest	gest	comprehensive school	ˈkɒmprɪˌhensɪv ˈskuːl
heartened	ˈhɑːtnd	concentrate	ˈkɒns(ə)nˌtreɪt
inferior	ɪnˈfɪərɪə	continuous assessment	kənˌtɪnjʊəs əˈsesmənt
lavish	ˈlævɪʃ	contribute	kənˈtrɪbjuːt
magnifying glass	ˈmægnɪfaɪŋ ˌglɑːs	core	kɔː
mass	mæs	derelict	ˈderəlɪkt
means (n)	miːnz	discipline	ˈdɪsəplɪn
miniature	ˈmɪnətʃə	disruptive	dɪsˈrʌptɪv
minute (small) (adj)	maɪˈnjuːt	effort	ˈefət
negligible	ˈneglɪdʒəb(ə)l	emphasis	ˈemfəsɪs
novel	ˈnɒv(ə)l	expulsion	ɪkˈspʌlʃ(ə)n
partial	ˈpɑːʃ(ə)l	feature (vb)	ˈfiːtʃə
passable	ˈpɑːsəb(ə)l	frequent	ˈfriːkwənt
peace treaty	ˈpiːs ˌtriːti	half-hearted	ˌhɑːf ˈhɑːtɪd
personally	ˈpɜːs(ə)nəli	highlight	ˈhaɪˌlaɪt
physically	ˈfɪzɪkli	illuminate	ɪˈluːmɪneɪt
potential	pəˈtenʃ(ə)l	impose	ɪmˈpəʊz
premises	ˈpremɪsɪz	inadequate	ɪnˈædɪkwət
quarters	ˈkwɔːtəz	incidentally	ˌɪnsɪˈdent(ə)li
radically	ˈrædɪkli	infamy	ˈɪnfəmi
respectively	rɪˈspektɪvli	insolent	ˈɪnsələnt
revolution	ˌrevəˈluːʃ(ə)n	literature	ˈlɪtrətʃə
setback	ˈsetˌbæk	matter	ˈmætə
shrewd	ʃruːd	mature	məˈtʃʊə
soaked	səʊkt	measure (n)	ˈmeʒə
specifically	spəˈsɪfɪkli	mischievous	ˈmɪstʃɪvəs
speech	spiːtʃ	moral	ˈmɒrəl
statistics	stəˈtɪstɪks	notorious	nəʊˈtɔːrɪəs
superior	sʊˈpɪərɪə	oppress	əˈpres
vast	vɑːst	oriented	ˈɔːrɪentɪd
virtually	ˈvɜːtʃʊəli	participate	pɑːˈtɪsɪpeɪt
whatsoever	ˌwɒtsəʊˈevə	placement	ˈpleɪsmənt
yacht	jɒt	precede	prɪˈsiːd
yearn	jɜːn	problematic	ˌprɒbləˈmætɪk
		progressive	prəʊˈgresɪv

Unit 18

		scholarly	ˈskɒləli
abuse	əˈbjuːs	specification	ˌspesɪfɪˈkeɪʃ(ə)n
academic	ˌækəˈdemɪk	strategic	strəˈtiːdʒɪk
apprentice	əˈprentɪs	suspension	səˈspenʃ(ə)n
authorities	ɔːˈθɒrɪtɪz	tell (someone) off	ˌtel sʌmwʌn ˈɒf
basic	ˈbeɪsɪk	trainee	ˌtreɪˈniː

truant	ˈtruːənt	sufficient	səˈfɪʃ(ə)nt
verbally	ˈvɜːbəli	suggest	səˈdʒest
virtually	ˈvɜːtʃʊəli	venture	ˈventʃə
vocation	vəʊˈkeɪʃ(ə)n	version	ˈvɜːʃ(ə)n
witness (vb)	ˈwɪtnəs	voluntary	ˈvɒlənt(ə)ri
		weed	wiːd

Unit 19

advantage	ədˈvɑːntɪdʒ
alumni	əˈlʌmnaɪ
associate (vb)	əˈsəʊsiˌeɪt
available	əˈveɪləb(ə)l
canyon	ˈkænjən
cease	siːs
celebrity	səˈlebrəti
cloakroom	ˈkləʊkˌruːm
commercialization	kəˌmɜːʃəlaɪˈzeɪʃ(ə)n
consult	kənˈsʌlt
consumption	kənˈsʌmpʃ(ə)n
contempt	kənˈtempt
contribute	kənˈtrɪbjuːt
digest	daɪˈdʒest
enthusiasm	ɪnˈθjuːziˌæzəm
envy	ˈenvi
flake	fleɪk
forthcoming	fɔːθˈkʌmɪŋ
gloss paint	ˌglɒs ˈpeɪnt
guest	gest
hazard	ˈhæzəd
hazy	ˈheɪzi
illegible	ɪˈledʒəb(ə)l
(in) comprehensible	ˌkɒmprɪˈhensəb(ə)l
(in) sensitive	ˈsensətɪv
makeshift	ˈmeɪkˌʃɪft
manner	ˈmænə
military	ˈmɪlɪt(ə)ri
nag	næg
neglect	nɪˈglekt
playboy	ˈpleɪˌbɔɪ
policies	ˈpɒlɪsɪz
profitable	ˈprɒfɪtəb(ə)l
redevelopment	ˌriːdɪˈveləpmənt
remarkable	rɪˈmɑːkəb(ə)l
response	rɪˈspɒns
rumour	ˈruːmə
sheer	ʃɪə
simplify	ˈsɪmplɪfaɪ

Unit 20

ballot	ˈbælət
boulder	ˈbəʊldə
capital (city)	ˈkæpɪt(ə)l
chlorine	ˈklɔːriːn
contract (n)	ˈkɒntrækt
estimate (n)	ˈestɪmət
exchange	ɪksˈtʃeɪndʒ
expand	ɪkˈspænd
extract	ˈekstrækt
extremely	ɪkˈstriːmli
facilities	fəˈsɪlətɪz
foreigner	ˈfɒrɪnə
genius	ˈdʒiːniəs
identify	aɪˈdentɪfaɪ
lorry	ˈlɒri
maintain	meɪnˈteɪn
mediocre	ˌmiːdiˈəʊkə
nominate	ˈnɒmɪneɪt
prodigy	ˈprɒdədʒi
pullover	ˈpʊləʊvə
retain	rɪˈteɪn
sandbag	ˈsæn(d)ˌbæg
software	ˈsɒf(t)ˌweə
tell (someone) off	ˌtel sʌmwʌn ˈɒf
withdraw	wɪðˈdrɔː
wretched	ˈretʃɪd

GRAMMAR ANSWERS

Every effort has been made to make the answer key as all-inclusive as possible.

Where students provide their own answers, verbs are given in the full form or contracted following their use in the question.

Grammar 1

1 1 *I'm thinking about it.*
 2 I hope
 3 I visit
 4 It's getting
 5 I recognize
 6 It lasts
 7 do you do
 8 doesn't fit
 9 happens
 10 are you looking

2 1 *all the time*
 2 currently
 3 these days
 4 now
 5 Normally
 6 now
 7 at present
 8 until
 9 forever
 10 now

3 1 *hear*
 2 are drinking
 3 am depending
 4 are forever interrupting
 5 do you think
 6 want
 7 is handling
 8 doubt
 9 are you getting on
 10 is just being

4 1 *know*
 2 spend

3 am thinking
4 Take
5 runs
6 is going out
7 seem
8 knows
9 fancies
10 happen
11 dislikes
12 stop
13 is deceiving
14 is seeing
15 are currently going on
16 are experiencing
17 realize
18 upsets
19 am also trying
20 suspect

5 1 *looks just/exactly like*
 2 that belongs to you
 3 am really enjoying working
 4 means I take
 5 cycling group consists of
 6 you think is going to
 7 I am measuring (the width of)
 8 never remembers
 9 survival depends on its ability
 10 are you thinking about

6 1 ✓
 2 *Does this total include the new students?*
 3 are you waiting
 4 taste
 5 ✓
 6 ✓
 7 is going/is
 8 ✓
 9 Do you hear
 10 ✓

7 1 *trying*
 2 shooting
 3 listening
 4 talking
 5 asking
 6 coming
 7 taking
 8 making

a 2
b 4
c 5

Grammar 2

1 1 *I will be relaxing*
 2 will be
 3 will have left
 4 will be
 5 are you doing/are you going to do
 6 will have decided
 7 won't be
 8 finish/have finished
 9 am going to faint
 10 are you giving/are you going to give

2 1 *will have been*
 2 he's finally retiring
 3 we're going to take
 4 We'll be leaving
 5 We're flying
 6 we'll be stopping over
 7 We'll probably spend
 8 we're thinking
 9 We'll know
 10 we'll be researching.
 11 we'll have
 12 won't be
 13 we'll really have to
 14 we'll be travelling
 15 you won't recognize

3 1 *B* 6 A
 2 A 7 C
 3 C 8 A
 4 A 9 A
 5 B 10 B

4 1 *won't have heard*
 2 believes his party will win
 3 I will have been
 4 I will have written/finished
 5 about to make
 6 going to have/having another
 7 won't be home until
 8 who is going to win

9 will be (here) on
10 are getting married

5 1 *B, C*   6 A, C
  2 A, B   7 B, C
  3 A, B   8 A, B
  4 A, C   9 A, C
  5 B, C 10 A, B

6 1 *in a few minutes*
  2 in the end
  3 the moment
  4 by the time
  5 before long
  6 by then
  7 This time tomorrow
  8 soon
  9 from now on
  10 in two weeks' time

7 1 *see*
  2 have
  3 give
  4 let
  5 go
  6 go
  7 see
  8 be
  9 be
  10 come

  a 1
  b 6
  c 7

Grammar 3

1 1 *did you notice*
  2 were shouting
  3 did you use to travel
  4 were dancing
  5 hadn't eaten
  6 went
  7 was staring
  8 had decided
  9 was trying
  10 didn't realize

2 1 *Once*
  2 before
  3 as
  4 until
  5 whenever
  6 at the time
  7 later
  8 in his day
  9 the moment
  10 by

3 Text 1: *1* ✓ 2 ✓ 3 ✓
  4 got 5 waited
  6 turned up
  Text 2: *1* ✓ 2 had received/
  received
  3 ✓
  4 was considering
  5 had discovered
  6 ✓

4 1 *was cycling*
  2 had decided
  3 had been
  4 knew
  5 had managed
  6 were wondering
  7 had made
  8 had planned
  9 had forgotten
  10 had rained/had been raining
  11 ended up
  12 were riding/rode
  13 skidded
  14 fell off
  15 realized
  16 had broken
  17 caught
  18 were not expecting/did not expect
  19 had gone
  20 spent

5 1 *was going to*
  2 me more pudding I said I had had
  3 to have sung the solo
  4 did not use to be so/that
  5 were intending to go to Rome but
  6 used to cycle to work every
  7 was wondering about
  8 was passing your house
  9 the time the bus (finally) arrived there were
  10 the explosion occurred

6 1 *B*
  2 O: was waiting
  3 O: would always have
  4 B
  5 O: used to own
  6 O: didn't mean
  7 B, but *ate* is colloquial in this context
  8 B
  9 B

10 O: didn't always use to look

7 1 *spent*
  2 would
  3 used
  4 was
  5 happened
  6 was
  7 came
  8 wondering
  9 had
  10 was
  11 had
  12 took
  13 got
  14 seen/noticed
  15 had

8 1 *was stealing, felt*
  2 phoned, was washing
  3 offered, had had
  4 was watching, took, put
  5 did not realize, had left, started
  6 disliked, was always picking/ always picked
  7 found, knew, had gone/been
  8 found out, had been writing/ had written, had been opening
  9 did not understand, was going on, were shouting/shouted, was waving/waved
  10 knew, had done, received

Grammar 4

1 1 *has been stealing*
  2 have you been doing, left
  3 didn't you tell, tripped
  4 saw, has he been doing
  5 have eaten, only brought
  6 haven't seen, has been waiting
  7 did you think, Did you stay
  8 have been weeding, haven't rested
  9 has been calling, telling
  10 have you been having, have you taken

2 1 *e, h*
  2 i
  3 b, h
  4 j
  5 c
  6 g, h, i
  7 a
  8 b, c, d, f, h
  9 h
  10 d

3 1 *haven't noticed,* have not been paying
2 have not come/have not been coming
3 have been working
4 has reached, left
5 has announced, escaped, have given themselves up
6 Have you made up, have you decided
7 left, have not heard
8 has shown, did not discover, landed
9 have become, have improved/ have been improving
10 Has something happened, have been trying
11 got, has been complaining

4 1 *have lived here/in this house*
2 have never eaten Korean food
3 the first time Tony has been
4 ages since we went/we have been
5 has been learning French for
6 have written ten pages
7 been married for more
8 seen Dick since
9 your work has definitely
10 second time I have visited

5 1 *has risen*
2 You have been eating
3 I've been reading
4 I've put
5 I've been counting
6 Have you taken it?
7 has been wearing
8 It's been making
9 has asked
10 I've been phoning

6 1 *moved*
2 arrived
3 have been wondering
4 heard/had heard
5 has made
6 have spent/have been spending
7 grew up
8 have not
9 always wanted/have always wanted
10 offered
11 jumped
12 have actually started
13 came across

14 have chosen
15 have secretly been hoping

7 1 *since*
2 lately
3 already
4 for years
5 now
6 since then
7 so far
8 at last
9 ever since
10 yet

8 1 *d*
2 g
3 i
4 a
5 c
6 h
7 e
8 j
9 b
10 f

Consolidation 1

1 1 *know*
2 have been having/have had
3 have been turning/have turned/are turning
4 involves
5 did hear/heard
6 holds
7 have turned up
8 was passing
9 thought
10 didn't believe
11 has already studied
12 has heard
13 find
14 stayed
15 found
16 race
17 is waiting
18 run
19 have not eaten
20 were obviously enjoying/ obviously enjoyed

2 1 *is of no concern to/does not concern*
2 we will have completed
3 time is the train supposed to
4 day 30 years ago, Liz and John got were
5 means getting up
6 does this watch belong

7 is the first time Cathy has been
8 appointment to see the dentist on/next
9 time the team has played (a match)
10 attended the fair than we had
11 a month before I received
12 have not returned their

3 1 ✓
2 time
3 do
4 himself
5 will
6 it
7 is
8 ✓
9 had
10 that
11 never
12 much
13 ✓
14 was
15 ✓
16 ✓
17 been
18 ✓
19 having
20 ✓

4 1 *ages*
2 recently
3 since
4 ago
5 yet
6 moment/minute
7 by/for
8 had
9 before
10 soon/directly/presently/ shortly

5 1 *do you think*
2 live
3 have you done/did you do
4 meant/was meaning/have been meaning
5 do you do
6 depends
7 felt
8 were talking
9 have been expecting

6 1 *plan/are planning*
2 will be
3 ask

4 belong
5 died
6 have met/have been meeting
7 love/loved
8 has visited
9 suffered
10 borrowed
11 was not working
12 got
13 have worked/have been working
14 went
15 are thinking
16 have always wanted
17 performed
18 has been
19 was
20 owns

7 1 *hadn't received*, spoke
2 was considering/had been considering, have changed
3 feel, are feeling, will bring
4 found, had lost
5 was, have been dying
6 have had, will send
7 happens, will meet
8 have finished/finish, will have missed
9 was not expecting/did not expect, are you doing

8 1 ✓
2 rented, went
3 ✓
4 ✓
5 explored, went
6 built
7 ✓
8 finds
9 tastes really

Grammar 5

1 1 *have been broken into*
2 was being rebuilt
3 ✓
4 being interrupted
5 was given/has been given
6 had/has disappeared/disappeared
7 ✓
8 has been decided

2 1 *was slowly being filled*
2 was invented, has been
3 has been suggested
4 was advised to

5 will be brought (to you)
6 was opened with
7 has been dealt with
8 was announced
9 was ever heard of
10 was paid to

3 1 *The phone was left off the hook all night.*
2 It has been announced that petrol prices will rise tomorrow.
3 Our house was broken into last week.
4 I was asked the way three times.
5 The apples are picked early in the morning.
6 It's time something was done about this problem.
7 Lots of cars had been parked on the pavement.
8 The government agreed with the report and so the law was changed.
9 An application form has to be filled in.
10 It is not known what happened to the ship.
11 The group's leader has not been seen since his arrest last month.

4 1 *have not been packed*
2 is still being prepared
3 will be launched/is being launched
4 had not been sold
5 was being decorated
6 has been cancelled/is cancelled
7 will have been sold/will be sold
8 are served
9 was scored
10 was built
11 is being repaired
12 would be delivered

5 1 *Unfortunately your letter has been mislaid.*
2 Harry is being questioned at the police station.
3 The remains of an old Roman villa have been discovered nearby.
4 After six months your salary will be raised.

5 The match was abandoned after half an hour.
6 Traffic was banned from (using) the centre.
7 Chris was prosecuted for dangerous driving.
8 This fish is usually served with a white sauce.
9 We have not been introduced.

6 1 *has been seen*, was found
2 is being/is going to be delivered, has not been/was not damaged
3 is (being) sold, is fitted
4 have been working, is being redecorated
5 has been announced, will not now be built
6 has been discovered, is thought
7 were received, was launched
8 was raised, has still not been reached
9 will be made, have been interviewed

7 1 *by a thief*
2 by the authorities
3 by someone standing next to him
4 ✓
5 by someone
6 by the selectors
7 by post
8 ✓
9 by everyone
10 ✓

8 1 *have been selected*
2 answered
3 was entered
4 has chosen
5 are invited
6 is made
7 have been offered
8 are asked
9 are interested
10 detach

9 1 *has been announced*
2 have been discovered
3 has been called
4 have been taken
5 have been/will be displayed
6 was written
7 was printed

8 was assumed/had been assumed
9 had been destroyed
10 is offered

10 1 *It has been decided to adopt a flexi-time system for a trial period of three months.*
2 The details are here below, and a formal document will be sent out in due course.
3 All members of staff will be consulted through their line manager,
4 and feedback will be sought.
5 Comments will be collected and analysed.
6 before a decision is made
7 as to whether the system will be adopted permanently or not.
8 It is also possible that the trial period may be extended for a further month.
9 All employees will be required to arrive between the hours of 8.00 and 10.00, and to leave after their contractual obligations of eight hours have been fulfilled
10 It is hoped that this arrangement meets with your approval.

Grammar 6

1 1 *I've just had my hair cut.*
2 We are having our house painted.
3 same
4 same
5 same
6 I'll have this wrapped for you/ I'll have someone wrap this for you.
7 same
8 We're having a new water-heater put in next week.
9 same

2 1 *with*
2 by
3 in
4 by
5 with
6 by
7 by
8 with

9 with
10 with

3 1 *is thought to date*
2 need to get your hair
3 is being made to study hard by
4 appears not to have sustained
5 are thought to have been repairing
6 is rumoured to be
7 been agreed that we will
8 decided that we would
9 confirmed that Mr Jackson intends
10 not to be a viable solution

4 1 *Our company has been taken over.*
2 Your complaint is being dealt with.
3 Not all the missing passengers have been accounted for./The missing passengers have not all been accounted for.
4 The lock of the front door had been tampered with.
5 We don't know how the body was disposed of.
6 I must insist that the rules are kept to.
7 This allegation is being looked into.
8 Any attempts to cheat in the exam will be frowned upon.
9 The youngest student complained that he was being picked on.
10 The second pizza hasn't been paid for.
11 I think the whole story has been made up.

5 1 *with*
2 in
3 in/with
4 with
5 with
6 by
7 by
8 with
9 in
10 with
11 in
12 by

6 1 *is known to have experienced*
2 is thought to have been
3 is not known
4 was seen
5 was brought
6 was obliged to
7 are believed to have been
8 was packed
9 were made to
10 are thought to be

7 It is not known exactly when gunpowder was invented. It is known for a fact that rockets and fireworks were made by the Chinese long before gunpowder was used in Europe, which occurred at about the beginning of the thirteenth century. It is generally believed that the 'Age of Chivalry' was brought to an end by gunpowder, since a mounted knight could be brought down by anyone with a firearm. In fact, efficient firearms were not developed until the sixteenth century. When it was first introduced, gunpowder was used mainly in siege cannon. Later it was used in engineering work and mining, but it was found to be extremely dangerous. Gunpowder has now been replaced by modern explosives, but it is still used for making fireworks, just as it was by the Chinese.

Grammar 7

1 1 *had written down*, would not have happened
2 lived, would be
3 do not punish, will only commit
4 had not been/were not/was not, would be
5 had, would lend
6 touch, won't bite
7 had, were
8 decide, calls
9 had not missed, would have been killed
10 have finished, will clear away

2 1 ✓
2 If it wasn't for David, we

would have missed the bus.

3 ✓

4 If you hadn't lent us the money …

5 ✓

6 ✓

7 ✓

8 If I had known you were coming …

9 But for your help/If you hadn't helped us…

10 ✓

3 1 *B*   5 B

2 A 6   C

3 C   7 A

4 A

4 1 *to say I*

2 had not rained/had not been raining

3 would not have said

4 could not have done it

5 would have had

6 Unless you pay/If you do not pay

7 had not had

8 I would not touch them

9 it was not/were not for/it had not been for

5 1 *We'll go away unless the weather is bad./We won't go away unless the weather improves.*
We will only go away if the weather improves.
We will stay at home if the weather is bad.

2 If you don't hurry up you will be late.
Hurry up, or you will be late.
If you do not want to be late, hurry up.

3 If they were to offer you the job, would you accept?
If they should offer you the job, would you accept?
If they happened to offer you the job, would you accept?

4 If it hadn't been for your help, I would have given up years ago.
But for your help, I would have given up years ago.
If you hadn't helped (me), I would have given up years

ago.

5 I'll lend you the money, provided (that) you pay it back next week.
I'll lend you the money, as long as you pay it back next week.
I'll only lend you the money if you pay it back next week.

6 1 *condition*

2 do

3 in

4 Unless

5 find/land

6 unable

7 but

8 have

9 not

10 have

7 1 *had had the money I would have bought*

2 happen to be in London

3 will do everything yourself

4 will (just) take a seat

5 do the shopping and

6 for Pauline's interest

7 been for the night-watchman, the fire would have

8 be in prison if a detective had not

9 was/were (a bit) taller I could/ would be able to

10 was/were not for Helen's wonderful acting

11 will (still) win, even if

12 I get up early it

8 1 *had fallen*

2 have finished with my pen

3 tries harder

4 wouldn't make

5 would have drowned

6 would have bought

7 had not been

8 I am

9 would not have gone

10 Finish the painting

9 1 *if*

2 unless

3 not

4 Should

5 Providing/Provided

6 be

7 will

8 would

9 may/might

10 so

Grammar 8

1 1 *hope*

2 hope

3 wish

4 wish

5 wish

6 hope

7 wish

8 hope

9 hope

10 wish

2 1 *would stop*

2 did not turn/switch

3 I paid/gave you (back)

4 you don't/won't

5 had gone/could go

6 essential/imperative that

7 started

8 made/got/prepared/cooked

9 was/went

10 not to

3 1 *didn't watch*

2 started

3 had spent

4 owned/owns

5 did/would not keep

6 left

7 had gone/had not gone

8 sat/did not sit

9 (should) be

10 was/were going/could go

4 1 *high*

2 would

3 would

4 Be

5 could

6 were

7 look

8 Suppose/Supposing

9 were

10 hope

5 1 *I wish I had bought that old house.*

2 I'd rather you didn't eat all the bread.

3 It's time I went.

4 I wish I owned a motorbike.

5 I wish we were not leaving in the morning.

6 Sue would rather read than
watch television.
7 Come what may, I'll be on
your side.
8 I hope it (will) stop(s)
raining/I wish it would stop
raining.
9 I'd prefer you not to wait/I'd
rather you didn't wait./I'd
prefer it if you didn't wait.
10 I wish I hadn't listened to you
before.

6 1 *wish you had gone*
2 time I was going/went
3 prefer not to
4 acts as if/though he knows/
knew
5 wish I could
6 a pity I sold
7 would be better if you didn't
8 insisted on our wearing/that
we wear
9 wish you would stop/wouldn't
keep
10 wish I was/were sitting

7 1 *put your things away*
2 take/show more interest in
your school work
3 speak more languages
4 afford to buy a car
5 get/buy (some) more chess
books
6 put some soap in the
bathroom
7 be a bit more romantic

8 1 *be*
2 had
3 enjoy
4 didn't
5 sleep
6 weren't
7 can't
8 been
9 met
10 may

Consolidation 2

1 1 *was revealed*
2 are employed
3 is being transferred
4 are expected
5 were we not informed
6 were only told
7 started

8 are affected
9 knew
10 been made
11 has been made
12 questioned
13 were not told/had not been
told
14 was promised/had been
promised
15 (had) decided

2 1 *gets*
2 having/taking
3 by
4 gave
5 only
6 Even
7 did/does
8 But
9 would
10 happened/were/decided

3 1 *thought to have been*
2 was being bent
3 being interrogated about
4 help I won't be able
5 if the salary is doubled
6 wish you were going
7 you were to find the money
which has
8 was banned from playing
9 you will come this way
10 is being helped by the
discovery of

4 1 *Mushrooms are usually picked/
gathered in the early morning.*
2 It is time the economy was
brought under control.
3 Several coats were stolen from
the cloakroom.
4 It has been decided to reduce
the workforce by 10%.
5 Our house was decorated in
only a day.
6 It is not known what caused
the accident/The cause of the
accident is not known.
7 An application for a visa has
to be made in advance.
8 Tickets are collected on the
train on this line.
9 Lots of luggage had been left
on the platform.
10 Sally was directed to the
wrong address.

5 1 *Be*
2 had
3 unless
4 started/began
5 were
6 hope
7 Suppose
8 could
9 would
10 thought/considered

6 1 *had gone*
2 was done
3 to have been
4 had not caught, would not
have met
5 is being dealt
6 would not have passed
7 are served
8 have been sold
9 had studied
10 to tell

7 1 *was directed/had been directed*
2 had known, would arrive/were
arriving, would have come
3 had not eaten
4 tease, will scratch
5 had not helped, would not
have finished
6 will have been taken/will be
taken
7 has been decided/was decided
8 had been/got married
9 was/were/had not been, would
still be
10 has been/is called off

8 1 *have/get your trousers pressed*
2 is known to be
3 has been suggested that
4 have been asked to
5 have been successfully
accounted
6 been seen of Sue since
7 it if you sat
8 shown the way
9 is being made to
10 (high) time I was

Grammar 9

1 1 *should*
2 couldn't
3 can't
4 can
5 could
6 shouldn't

7 may
8 might
9 would
10 shall

2 1 *must*
2 better
3 might/may
4 need/have
5 can't/won't
6 could
7 wouldn't
8 need
9 would/should
10 should
11 can
12 bound/got
13 shall/can
14 have/need
15 couldn't

3 1 *happy as (I) could be*
2 as I might
3 is bound to be
4 (that) you and I should have
5 were you, I would/should
6 could be one of
7 won't let you
8 cannot (possibly) be the
9 may as well
10 may be summer, but

4 1 *A*
2 B
3 B
4 B
5 A
6 B
7 A
8 A
9 B
10 B
11 A
12 B

5 1 *don't have to*
2 couldn't possibly
3 couldn't be
4 must like
5 may be
6 might as well
7 wouldn't be
8 must be
9 need to
10 I might

6 1 *might/may*
2 would

3 can't/cannot
4 must
5 could/might/may
6 may/might
7 have
8 may/might
9 can
10 if
11 rather
12 than
13 can/may/might
14 must
15 wouldn't

Grammar 10

1 1 *can't have been*
2 might have given
3 had to see
4 might have lost
5 would have been
6 could have been
7 should have bought
8 wouldn't
9 could have helped
10 shouldn't have

2 1 *shouldn't have*
2 ought to have
3 can't have
4 must have
5 can't have
6 shouldn't have
7 may have
8 shouldn't have
9 didn't need to
10 may not have

3 1 *couldn't have left you to do*
2 might not have noticed (that)
3 needn't have gone to
4 seems to have borrowed
5 might have backed
6 needn't have worried
7 can't possibly have opened
8 could have given
9 to leave might have left
10 didn't have to wear

4 1 *could*
2 should
3 couldn't
4 could/might/should
5 should/could
6 might/could
7 should/must
8 couldn't
9 shouldn't

10 would/should

5 1 *can't*
2 ✓
3 ✓
4 ✓
5 could/might have won
6 should/could have told
7 needn't have gone
8 shouldn't have been
9 ✓
10 could/might have been

6 1 *can't have*
2 could have
3 couldn't have
4 might/may not have
5 could/might have been
6 didn't have to
7 might/could have
8 must have been
9 should have
10 needn't have

7 1 *obviously*
2 easily
3 well
4 really
5 simply
6 just
7 Surely
8 simply
9 still
10 well

8 1 *might have heard*
2 would have meant
3 would have had
4 should have resigned
5 might have found
6 must have thought
7 needn't have worried
8 can't have been
9 must be
10 might have known

Grammar 11

1 1 *That pudding was so nice that ...*
2 ✓
3 ✓
4 If you fancy a pizza ...
5 I've never seen this film/I haven't seen this film before.
6 ✓
7 If I had the time ...
8 We had scarcely been

introduced when ...
9 ✓
10 ✓

2 1 *the office phoned me did I find out*
2 later were the facts
3 was the response
4 did Harry break his leg but he
5 did the police suspect the judge
6 no way can the bus driver be held
7 the government to raise
8 had I got home than
9 I asked a passer-by, did I realize
10 had the minister started his speech when

1 1 *Hardly had*
2 Under no circumstances are
3 Little did
4 Were you
5 as do
6 Rarely have
7 Not only did
8 Under no circumstances will
9 No sooner had
10 Rarely have

4 1 *you need*
2 to have taken off
3 I studied
4 you be
5 you gone
6 has/had she spent
7 you feel
8 we to offer
9 you/we/they/the government taken
10 had we got

5 1 *he would never*
2 did I remember
3 when
4 was I
5 was I aware
6 passed
7 Pete has arrived
8 than

6 1 *No sooner*
2 Seldom
3 along
4 Not only
5 Little
6 Scarcely

7 Such
8 Had
9 under no circumstances
10 as

7 1 *am I (ever) to be interrupted*
2 has anyone from this school
3 was so great
4 no circumstances is the money
5 three days had passed did we arrive
6 had no idea
7 when I stopped did I realize
8 no time did the accused express
9 exhausted were the runners that none
10 do we see/does one see

Grammar 12

1 1 *do think*
2 by no means
3 none at all
4 time and time again
5 the least bit
6 as it may seem
7 what we did
8 waited and waited
9 not at all
10 can't have been

2 1 *at*
2 utter
3 Why
4 What
5 is
6 whatever
7 All
8 again
9 as
10 whatsoever

3 1 *the car needs is*
2 least bit worried
3 was Keith who
4 absolutely no money left
5 though it may seem
6 cannot stand is
7 did was go
8 must have been a ghost that
9 was the very last car
10 carelessness caused the accident to

4 1 *not at all*
2 utter
3 because
4 So I am!

5 even
6 Whatever
7 quite
8 very own
9 do expect
10 nothing whatsoever

5 1 *B*
2 A
3 C
4 C
5 A
6 B
7 A
8 C
9 B
10 A

6 1 *d*
2 i
3 g
4 e
5 b
6 j
7 a
8 h
9 f
10 c

7 1 *own*
2 So
3 do
4 means
5 What
6 searched
7 Where
8 did
9 All
10 least

Consolidation 3

1 1 *must*
2 should
3 can
4 must
5 had
6 might
7 should
8 had
9 could
10 need/would
11 can
12 would
13 might/could/may
14 should
15 ought/need

2 1 *better*
2 Rarely/Never/Seldom
3 may
4 might/could/should
5 until
6 What
7 must
8 very
9 Little
10 bound

3 1 *no circumstances are you to*
2 two weeks had passed did
3 was her popularity
4 did not need to re-take/re-sit
5 I could do was
6 was midnight before
7 did Paul smash a window but he also
8 have to be worn by
9 over and over
10 as it may seem
11 shouldn't have brought
12 may as well

4 1 *should have*
2 bound
3 may be
4 not have been
5 might/may be
6 should not
7 can't be
8 was sure/might have known
9 would not
10 doubt

5 1 *A*
2 B
3 A
4 B
5 B

6 1 *Three policemen came*
2 ✓
3 Hardly had I sat down
4 ✓
5 under any circumstances.
6 ✓
7 Strange as it may seem, I enjoy
8 ✓
9 ✓
10 ✓

7 1 *would*
2 did
3 had
4 Little

5 himself
6 would
7 whatsoever
8 should
9 least
10 only
11 sooner
12 when
13 should
14 must
15 might/may

8 1 *can't have finished*
2 might have been
3 as it may seem
4 have I seen
5 should have left
6 you should have
7 as I might
8 does snow fall
9 needn't have taken/didn't need
10 can't have been

9 1 *have*
2 it
3 had
4 really/quite
5 needs/needed
6 as
7 the
8 very
9 when
10 down

Grammar 13

1 1 *denied*
2 told me
3 persuaded me
4 advised me
5 warned me
6 reminded us
7 answered them
8 announced
9 accepted
10 confirmed

2 1 *The customer decided to take the brown pair.*
The customer decided (that) he/she would take the brown pair.
The customer said (that) he/she would take the brown pair.
2 Bob denied taking Sue's calculator.
Bob denied that he had taken Sue's calculator.

3 Clare reminded Andy to buy some milk.
Clare said (that) Andy should not forget to buy some milk.
Clare reminded Andy that they needed/he needed to buy some milk.
4 David said he was sorry (that) he couldn't come on Saturday.
David said he was sorry (that) he had not been able to come on Saturday.
David apologized for not being able to come on Saturday.
5 I asked Brian why he didn't go back to Singapore.
I suggested that Brian should go back to Singapore.
I suggested going back to Singapore./I suggested that Brian go back to Singapore.
6 Jack said Tim should not leave too late.
Jack warned Tim not to leave too late.
Jack warned Tim against leaving too late.

3 1 *asked Helen if she wanted/ would like*
2 forbade him from smoking
3 advised me to
4 suggested that the committee
5 that the police do
6 said I could
7 on not staying
8 threatened to call off the football match unless
9 promised (her mother) that she would
10 congratulated Sue on her

4 1 *mention*
2 remarked
3 estimated
4 complained
5 predicted
6 rumoured
7 claimed
8 ordered
9 suggested
10 gave

5 1 *could*
2 to
3 accused

4 time
5 was
6 suffering
7 had
8 him
9 about
10 that

6 1 *Tom not to stay out in the cold for too long*
2 Andy to buy some milk
3 Jack not to go back into the house
4 to stay near the airport
5 me that I would make a complete recovery
6 that he was getting married to Ann Jones
7 me round to his house for a meal
8 that she was expecting a baby

7 1 *apologize*
2 assure
3 anticipate/estimate
4 estimate/anticipate
5 reporting
6 announce
7 mention/mentioned
8 confirm
9 request
10 advised

Grammar 14

1 1 *the*
2 a
3 the
4 –
5 the
6 The
7 the/–
8 –
9 a
10 the
11 –
12 the
13 the
14 –
15 –
16 the
17 –
18 –
19 the
20 the
21 –
22 the
23 –

24 a/–
25 the
26 a
27 the
28 the
29 a
30 –

2 1 *the*, the
2 –, a
3 the, –
4 a, a
5 a, –, the
6 the, –, an
7 The, –
8 The, the
9 the, the
10 the, –

3 1 *It's not first-class accommodation unless it has a private bathroom.*
2 On this record the twins play a piano duet.
3 Halfway through the meal we realized what the waiter had said.
4 If a/– Mrs Hillier phones, say I'm away on a trip.
5 There is wonderful scenery in the eastern part of Turkey.
6 The cocker spaniel is one of the most popular pet dogs.
7 There is going to be fog and cold weather all next week.
8 I spent a very interesting holiday at Lake Coniston in England.
9 We are against war in general, so of course we are against a war like this between a superpower and a developing country.
10 Burglaries are definitely on the increase.

4 1 *the*
2 the, a/the, a, a
3 a, –
4 The, –
5 –, the, the, the/–, the
6 the, the
7 the/–, –
8 a, a, the
9 The, The
10 The, the, the

5 1 *the*, the, a
2 the, –
3 the, the
4 –, –
5 the, a, –, the
6 The, a, –
7 a, the
8 the, a
9 the, a
10 a, the

6 Word processing and the calculator are without a shadow of doubt here to stay, and in *the* many respects our lives are the much richer for them. But the teachers and other academics are claiming that we are now starting to feel the first significant wave of their effects on a generation of the users. It seems nobody under the age of 20 can spell or add up any more. Even several professors at leading universities have commented on the detrimental effect the digital revolution has had on the most intelligent young minds in the country. At the root of one part of the problem, evidently, lies the automatic spellcheck now widely available on the word processing software. Professor John Silver of the Sydney University, Australia, said: 'Why should we bother to learn how to spell correctly, or for that matter to learn even the most basic of the mathematical sums, when at the press of a button we have our problem answered for us? The implications are enormous. Will the adults of the future look to the computer to make the decisions for them, to tell them who to marry or what kind of the house to buy? Are we heading for a future individual incapable of the independent human thought?'

7 1 *the*, the, the
2 –, the
3 –, a, a
4 a, –
5 –, the, the

6 a, The
7 the, the
8 –, the
9 an, the
10 –, the, the

8 1 –, the, a, –
2 –, –, a
3 The, the
4 the, the
5 –, –, the
6 a, –
7 an, a, –
8 The, –, a
9 –, –, a, –
10 The, –, –

Grammar 15

1 Having just spent three weeks of my life sitting on an uncomfortable saddle, pounding the roads of France, I am in no fit state *that* to do anything except sit and write, which suits me fine. For I have cycled some 1,500 kilometres, a figure which includes some extremely hilly routes, and frankly the thought of mounting a bicycle again <u>which</u> is not one that I can face for a good few days yet. The journey, which I undertook alone for most of the way, was all in the name of charity – Help the Aged, a cause which I support whenever <u>that</u> I can. Having organized my sponsorship, <u>which</u> I arrived in France armed only with a tiny map of the Tour de France route, <u>which</u> hastily removed from last month's 'Cycling World' magazine. My intention <u>which</u> was to try and follow the route that the professionals take, but after three days in which I pushed my body to extremes that it had never experienced before, <u>that</u> I rapidly abandoned this plan and returned to flatter ground. On the flat <u>which</u> I was able to keep to about 120 kilometres a day, which is respectable. I did have to rest my weary limbs at the weekends, though, which enabled me to recharge my batteries, by which I mean my bodily ones, not the ones <u>that</u> inside my bike lights. I am pleased to say that after three tortuous weeks <u>which</u> I ended up in Marseilles, but what pleased me all the more is that I managed to raise over £2,000 for Help the Aged.

2 1 *which*
2 whom
3 which
4 Whoever
5 which
6 which
7 who
8 when
9 whose
10 who

3 1 *at which point I*
2 we suggested was
3 who can understand this application form is
4 is the last time I will
5 which made a
6 what he is
7 the person who (had) committed
8 one of her books that/one book of hers that
9 when it last rained
10 the person who

4 1 *The train we eventually caught was one that stops at every station.*
2 Slamming the door, Carol drove off in the car her father had given her as a present.
3 At the end of the street, which was crowded with shoppers, (there) was a building Tom had not noticed before.
4 The people who have just moved in next door have the same surname as the people who have just moved out.
5 Noticing the door was open, I decided to go in, which turned out to be a mistake.
6 Flora Benstead, the Popular Party candidate, who is expected to win the election, has announced that she will cut income tax by 10% if elected.
7 I listened to George patiently until he started insulting me, at which point I told him a few home truths he didn't like.
8 Pauline asked me a question to which I had no reply.
9 Shouting at the top of his voice, which was typical, he rushed out the room.
10 By the end of the week, which was the deadline, everyone who wanted travel scholarships had applied (for them).

5 1 *Taking my life in*
2 who to address
3 which took us
4 Whoever he spoke
5 is one which
6 in which case I'll
7 person everyone looks
8 gang whose identity has

6 1 *planet, which*
2 man I
3 remember which
4 party was
5 friends who
6 ball must

Grammar 16

1 1 *to do*
2 to be
3 to wake me
4 to tell you
5 to find
6 to take/taking
7 telling
8 buying
9 to pick up
10 to be

2 1 *do*
2 dare
3 considered
4 grew
5 intend
6 looking forward to
7 arranged
8 appears
9 dying
10 face

3 1 *appreciate you giving*
2 the job will mean

3 not permitted/allowed to park
4 offered to carry Pauline's
5 enabled us to
6 risks missing the plane
7 led me to believe
8 pay (extra) to use
9 appears to be
10 managed to finish

4 1 *invited me to*
2 use calling Jim
3 are required to
4 waste time copying
5 you to ask David if he will come/go
6 not to leave him on his
7 resents being treated
8 to bring the matter
9 not to use
10 involves a lot

5 1 *to tell you*
2 hope to
3 will mean
4 you feel like
5 said to be
6 would not keep
7 can/could you suggest

6 1 *to be*
2 to talk
3 to have
4 to combine
5 making
6 to appear
7 travelling
8 doing
9 to have
10 to exploit
11 to tell
12 to confess
13 to become
14 standing
15 to learn

Consolidation 4

1 1 *happen to have seen*
2 of things, all of
3 is reported to be
4 enabled her to
5 which was a stupid
6 warned (that) we should
7 smoking you risk becoming
8 to do the job without leaving

9 is no point (in) worrying
10 to be related

2 1 *the*, a
2 the, a
3 a, –, the
4 a, the
5 The, the, the
6 The, The, –, –
7 a, a, –, –
8 The, the, –
9 the, the, the, the
10 The, the, the

3 1 *to send*
2 not try/don't you try
3 had won
4 would mean
5 do you fancy
6 seeing
7 made me
8 is (being)/has been denied
9 to be
10 to believe

4 1 *to pay for parking/to park*
2 managed to find
3 agreed (that) she could/ agreed to let her
4 spent a long time looking for the book
5 those who visit the town
6 threatened Tom with
7 the last place I expected
8 seeing each other a long time
9 did the washing up didn't make a
10 was surprised when

5 1 *The*
2 –
3 –
4 the
5 –
6 –
7 –
8 the
9 the
10 –
11 –
12 the
13 the
14 –
15 the
16 the
17 the
18 the

19 –
20 –

6 1 *whom*
2 whose
3 Whoever
4 try
5 fancy
6 would
7 made/had
8 should/–
9 forward
10 who

7 1 *which was good of them.*
2 refused to say
3 I regret to say
4 whose voices could be clearly heard
5 I don't suppose you'd like
6 the customers should be searched
7 is take a long holiday
8 Whatever happens
9 congratulated me on passing
10 at which time
11 made the manager hand over/ forced the manager to hand over
12 looking forward to seeing you

8 1 *that/which*
2 the
3 where
4 in
5 means
6 that/which
7 risk/are
8 the
9 to
10 consider

Grammar 17

1 1 *to*
2 with
3 against
4 from
5 at
6 for
7 with
8 about
9 with
10 from

2 1 *suffering*
2 attributed
3 blamed

4 subjected
5 discussed
6 suggested
7 benefit
8 resign
9 account
10 referred
11 specialized
12 refrain
13 hinted
14 suspected
15 met

3 1 *always confides in*
2 is based on
3 marvelled at Jane's ability
4 was packed with
5 dreamed/dreamt about you
6 expelled from the school
7 reminds me of
8 translated the book from French
9 is associated with
10 would benefit from

4 1 *appeal*
2 succeeded
3 resort
4 accounted
5 confronted/faced
6 apply
7 prides/prided
8 distracted
9 apologize
10 paid
5 1 *of*
2 with
3 of
4 to
5 for
6 from
7 of
8 in
9 from
10 to
11 with
12 from
13 to
14 on
15 for

6 1 *when faced with*
2 derive a lot of pleasure from
3 answer to the description of
4 was acquainted with
5 resulted in over fifty people being

6 have been provided with
7 the wedding coincides with our holiday
8 does not really account for the disappearance
9 are/have been attributed to
10 to taking care of

Grammar 18

1 1 *on (very) good terms with*
2 is much in demand
3 in good/high spirits
4 was conscious of
5 out of luck
6 no access to
7 in all probability
8 the time being
9 way or another
10 cover of darkness

2 1 *for*
2 with
3 in
4 under
5 to
6 for
7 with
8 to
9 in
10 with
11 without
12 in
13 out
14 on
15 under

3 1 *capable*
2 serious
3 regular
4 stages
5 view
6 attempt
7 afraid
8 time
9 different
10 room

4 1 *behalf of my colleagues*
2 under the impression
3 the exception of Sally
4 be out of doors/be outdoors
5 serious about
6 of the ordinary
7 the solution was/is to
8 within (easy) walking distance

9 in recognition of
10 are liable for

5 1 *of*
2 out
3 without
4 under
5 to
6 in
7 beyond
8 for
9 of
10 for
11 in
12 on
13 of
14 to
15 for

6 1 *for*
2 by
3 at
4 under
5 on
6 of
7 for
8 to
9 at
10 by

Grammar 19

1 1 *story*
2 meeting
3 problem
4 six o' clock
5 what Peter had said
6 my homework
7 plan
8 standard
9 at 11.30
10 laughing

2 1 *carried*
2 down
3 come
4 add
5 get
6 comes
7 asking
8 dropping
9 bring
10 follow

3 1 *A*
2 C
3 C
4 B

5 D

6 D

4 1 C

2 A

3 C

4 B

5 D

6 B

5 1 *got off with*

2 you getting on

3 ended up walking

4 than I bargained for

5 fallen out with

6 broke down

7 came up with

8 getting on for

9 was borne out

10 getting/putting her ideas

Grammar 20

1 1 *it*

2 the matter

3 this kind of thing

4 we'll need them later

5 the pressure

6 put it in the fridge

7 the second paragraph

8 to Tom's report

9 confessed

10 behind my back

2 1 *playing*

2 grow

3 laid

4 picking

5 put

6 gave

7 made

8 go

9 make

10 look

3 1 *B*

2 A

3 D

4 A

5 C

6 A

4 1 C

2 B

3 C

4 D

5 A

6 C

5 1 *go in for*

2 back for being rude

3 put you up

4 let off with a

5 pointed out (that) the

6 was given away by

7 be put down to

8 gave off a faint smell

9 has (got) it in for

10 live up to our

Grammar 21

1 1 *turned him down*

2 Initially

3 it

4 a committee

5 the pace

6 its new owner

7 The good news

8 told her off

9 difficulties

10 you off

2 1 *D*

2 C

3 B

4 A

5 D

6 D

3 1 *D*

2 B

3 A

4 D

5 D

6 B

4 1 *down*

2 on/upon

3 up

4 over/through

5 up

6 up

7 out

8 about

9 by

10 out

5 1 *stand in for me*

2 turned out to

3 sending up

4 talked me out of selling

5 takes off

6 wears off after/in

7 would stand by

8 taken out a

9 tracked down the thief

10 work out the total without

Consolidation 5

1 1 *at*

2 to

3 After

4 to

5 under

6 of

7 up

8 for

9 up

10 in

11 in

12 from

13 under

14 for

15 without

2 1 *with*

2 in

3 to/for

4 of

5 in

6 of

7 for

8 for

3 1 *confusing me with*

2 himself on always

3 no access to

4 does nuclear fission differ from

5 blamed the fire on

6 comes down to money

7 not taken in by

8 worked out at

9 sunk in yet that I (have)

10 ended up having to walk

4 1 *tampered*

2 about

3 grateful

4 charged

5 commit

6 cater

7 refrain

8 benefit

5 1 *collided with*

2 it out on me

3 me out of selling

4 is based on

5 blamed the accident on

6 is on (very) good terms

7 out of the ordinary

8 out of work

6 1 *away*
2 off
3 up
4 down
5 off
6 on
7 out
8 off
9 off
10 off

7 1 *D*
2 A
3 C
4 B
5 D
6 C
7 A
8 B
9 D
10 A

8 1 *comes*
2 get
3 let
4 put
5 go
6 set
7 fallen
8 make
9 given
10 run

9 1 *rejected*
2 compensates
3 disappointed
4 established
5 resigning
6 specialize in
7 coincides with
8 was under the impression
9 take place
10 abolished
11 are under no obligation to
12 draw your attention

Grammar 22

1 1 *to be honest*
2 For that reason
3 By and large, Having said that
4 As a result
5 To start with
6 Anyway
7 Even so
8 whereas

9 On the whole
10 On the contrary

2 1 *Nevertheless*
2 In contrast
3 For one thing
4 as opposed to
5 as well as
6 to a large extent
7 as opposed to
8 however
9 despite the fact that
10 Even so

3 1 *C* 6 C
2 A 7 A
3 C 8 B
4 B 9 C
5 B 10 C

4 1 *B* 6 C
2 A 7 C
3 C 8 A
4 B 9 B
5 A 10 B

Grammar 23

1 **Text 1**
I've been to the following Italian cities: Rome, Florence, Genoa(,) and Pisa. I thought Rome was incredible: the food was great, the views were fantastic(,) and I will never forget the vivacious people. The Italians' legendary hospitality was nowhere more evident than in the capital city. But my all-time favourite is probably Genoa, with its fabulous hill-top houses and its dusty mountains, reverberating to the sound of grasshoppers. I spent many a happy hour looking down on the seething city below and the sea beyond. Best of all, the city's location at the heart of the Italian Riviera meant that fabulous resorts like Portofino and Camogli were only a train ride away.

Text 2
Water is becoming a more and more precious commodity, so save as much as you can. Flushing the toilet accounts for a third of all household water use, so don't flush wastefully. If you are only getting rid of a tissue, for example, resist the habit of reaching for the handle or chain. Take a shower rather than a bath; it uses about a third of the water. And don't keep the water running all the time when you wash or clean your teeth. If you have a garden, try to find ways of saving water outside, such as using a water butt to collect rain water, rather than using a hosepipe to water your flowers. A simple pipe connecting external gutters to a water butt can save an awful lot of water.

2 1 *bear, bare*
2 sight, site
3 waist, waste
4 sees, seize
5 paste, paced

3 1 ✓
2 *better than*
3 *naturally*
4 cent
5 ✓
6 whether
7 piece
8 cutting it, instead of ...
9 ✓
10 you; otherwise ...
11 business
12 know whether
13 ✓
14 today's
15 juice
16 ✓
17 forgotten
18 much upon
19 ✓
20 shoppers

21 There
22 by
23 foods
4 1 *affecting*
   2 ✓
   3 recommended
   4 ✓
   5 counsellor
   6 ✓
   7 guarantee
   8 separate
   9 disappeared
  10 ✓

5 1 *technically*
   2 ✓
   3 *suggests,*
   4 ✓
   5 know
   6 others,
   7 Shaking
   8 believed
   9 viruses,
  10 body's
  11 resistance
  12 whose
  13 susceptible
  14 ✓
  15 soaked
  16 permit
  17 ✓
  18 ✓
  19 studies
  20 colds
  21 their
  22 produce
  23 effective

6 1 ✓
   2 *Otter', has*
   3 *losing*
   4 ✓
   5 Williamson's
   6 ✓
   7 1927,
   8 has, however,
   9 pesticides
  10 led
  11 eighties
  12 valleys
  13 eliminated
  14 effects
  15 ✓
  16 designed
  17 borne
  18 pessimistic

19 ✓
20 population
21 ✓
22 sightings
23 widespread

Consolidation 6

1 1 *which*   9 For
   2 whose   10 since
   3 like   11 when
   4 they   12 instead
   5 or   13 their
   6 For   14 all
   7 why   15 what
   8 so

2 1 *sooner had I arrived home than*
   2 you do, don't
   3 put you up
   4 known to have been
   5 had read the book, he
   6 said there should be
   7 you would benefit from
   8 need to get/have
   9 knew who Miss Rutherford
  10 worried/worrying about something

3 Tina: Well Martin, pleased to meet *with* you, and congratulations on getting the job. I'm going to show you round the department, so that you know a bit more before you will start work next week. I gather you're coming with me to the Paris conference.
Martin: Yes, in two weeks' time. Is the job going to be involve a lot of travel to abroad?
Tina: A fair bit – Korea mainly. You'd better to get yourself a Korean phrasebook!
Martin: I've ever been to Korea once before, so I know a few words.
Tina: Good. We have contacts with most of Asian countries in fact. Well, here's the office you'll be working in. As you can see in this room has a photocopier, your computer … by the way, are you familiar with PowerPoint?
Martin: Well, to be perfectly

honest, no. I've never really had needed it up to now.
Tina: You really need to spend a few hours in studying this book, then, if you don't mind. I'm sure it'll explain you how the system works.
Martin: May I ask who that man was who was leaving the office when we came in?
Tina: Oh that's Mike. I'm surprised he wasn't at your interview. He's probably the nicest one of the managers.
Martin: He looks like very cheerful.
Tina: As I say it, he's a very nice guy. He's my immediate boss. The only thing is, he does tend to make me to do more jobs than I can cope with. Still, he's letting me to go home early today, so I'm not complaining!
Martin: And on to the subject of leaving, I didn't really understand what they were saying about this 'finish your task' system.
Tina: Oh, well it's just one of the systems you can choose. Basically, it means that the sooner you do finish the sooner you can go to home. But if you finish your task, say, three hours over normal time, you can come in three hours of late the next day.

4 1 *can*
   2 in
   3 with
   4 looking
   5 against
   6 could
   7 did
   8 Can
   9 on
  10 should

5 1 *of*
   2 ✓
   3 so
   4 both
   5 family
   6 ✓
   7 as

8 much
9 and
10 either
11 thus
12 up
13 ✓
14 to
15 ✓
16 a
17 on
18 of
19 the
20 from
21 ✓
22 there
23 as

Grammar 24

1 1 *of*
2 *they*
3 ✓
4 and
5 the
6 which
7 ✓
8 as
9 they
10 to
11 are
12 make
13 once
14 not
15 of
16 ✓
17 if
18 are
19 as
20 ✓
21 not
22 it
23 the

2 1 C
2 B
3 B
4 A
5 D
6 D
7 A
8 B
9 A
10 C
11 B
12 C
13 A
14 C
15 B

3 1 *no circumstances am I*
2 the (very) last person I
expected
3 doesn't concern you
4 time for me to
5 which was a foolish thing
6 what to do
7 did I notice (that) I had
8 is no instant solution to
9 talked me into going
10 the weather picks up

4 1 *to*
2 ✓
3 of
4 ✓
5 she
6 ✓
7 ✓
8 that (second)
9 to
10 with
11 than
12 is
13 a
14 for
15 ✓
16 the (first)
17 is
18 not
19 rather
20 ✓
21 it
22 did

5 1 *which*
2 these
3 under
4 who
5 no
6 who
7 it
8 in
9 despite
10 from
11 are
12 However
13 own
14 for
15 that

6 1 *can't have been*
2 wouldn't have won
3 will have been married
4 have I seen
5 as it may
6 would have gone to
7 as I might
8 shouldn't have
9 did I realize
10 go through with

7 1 *say*
2 for
3 and
4 some
5 What
6 these/such
7 which
8 be
9 into
10 as
11 a
12 another
13 to
14 does/should
15 have

VOCABULARY ANSWERS

Vocabulary 1

1 1 *C*
    2 A
    3 C
    4 D
    5 D
    6 B
    7 A
    8 C

2 1 *horse, bars*
    2 flippers, mask
    3 rod, bait
    4 rucksack, compass
    5 tripod, lens
    6 hammer, spanner
    7 goggles, armbands
    8 helmet, pump

3 1 *took part in*
    2 appeal to me
    3 cut out for
    4 beneficial
    5 raise
    6 sponsor
    7 gasping
    8 stragglers
    9 crossed
   10 suffering from
   11 personal best
   12 broke
   13 on standby
   14 stations
   15 catch up with

4 1 *expectations*
    2 handful
    3 remarkable
    4 invariably
    5 exception
    6 equipment
    7 accessible
    8 distinguish
    9 increasing
   10 foreseeable

5 1 *C*
    2 D
    3 D
    4 A
    5 A

    6 D
    7 B
    8 D
    9 B
   10 C

6 1 *oar*
    2 draw
    3 lap
    4 fan
    5 dive
    6 whistle
    7 board
    8 round
    9 referee
   10 runner-up

7 1 *took*
    2 board
    3 low
    4 tread
    5 turn

Vocabulary 2

1 1 *C*
    2 D
    3 A
    4 B
    5 A
    6 C
    7 B
    8 C

2 1 *rambler*
    2 steward
    3 hitchhiker
    4 passer-by
    5 driver
    6 cyclist
    7 traffic warden
    8 pedestrian
    9 passenger
   10 commuter

3 1 *outward*
    2 package
    3 flight
    4 maintenance
    5 assistance
    6 unacceptable
    7 compensation
    8 operator(s)

4 1 *ahead of*
    2 broke
    3 single
    4 collided, injured
    5 opposition
    6 skidded
    7 room
    8 goods
    9 limit
   10 flying

5 1 *D*
    2 C
    3 A
    4 C
    5 A
    6 B
    7 D
    8 B

6 1 *dismounted*
    2 accelerated
    3 reversed
    4 disembark
    5 alight
    6 fasten
    7 endanger
    8 ascended
    9 collided
   10 board

7 1 *hold*
    2 save
    3 set
    4 line
    5 track

Vocabulary 3

1 1 *C*
    2 D
    3 A
    4 A
    5 B
    6 C
    7 D
    8 A
    9 C
   10 D
   11 A
   12 C
   13 B

14 D
15 A

2 1 *disguised*
2 sole
3 extensively
4 critical
5 comment on
6 detained
7 findings
8 tackled
9 sensitive
10 baffled

3 1 *prospect*
2 conditions
3 knowledge
4 incident
5 place
6 verge
7 opinion
8 confidence
9 evidence
10 responsibility

4 1 *f*
2 c
3 j
4 h
5 a
6 e
7 i
8 d
9 b
10 g

5 1 *have no intention*
2 It is common knowledge
3 brought about
4 raised fears
5 little prospect of success
6 say for certain
7 argue that there should be
8 explained the cause as

6 1 *vows*
2 boost
3 set
4 cleared
5 bid
6 held
7 toll
8 looms
9 clash

7 1 *speculation*
2 announcement
3 analysts
4 survival

5 assurances
6 unthinkable
7 political
8 downfall
9 criticism
10 disastrous
11 failure
12 unemployment
13 unity
14 divisions
15 justification

Vocabulary 4

1 1 C
2 C
3 B
4 A
5 D
6 C
7 D
8 A
9 B
10 C
11 A
12 A
13 D
14 D
15 A

2 1 *summit*
2 key
3 state
4 view
5 press
6 wind

3 1 *sparsely*
2 tenancy
3 household
4 rights
5 property
6 storey
7 entrance
8 sharp
9 barely
10 sheer

4 1 *spring*
2 horizon
3 tide
4 cliff
5 strait
6 pass
7 bay
8 slope
9 landscape
10 plain

5 1 *e*
2 i
3 a
4 d
5 j
6 g
7 b
8 h
9 f
10 c

6 1 *scenery*
2 architecture
3 summit
4 desert
5 valley
6 shore
7 site
8 range
9 estuary
10 square

7 1 *large number*
2 was much taller than
3 undecided
4 gathering of national leaders
5 a long way
6 puzzled
7 reach the highest point
8 focus exclusively on
9 managed to get
10 situation has changed

Vocabulary 5

1 1 *booklet*
2 novel
3 forecast
4 broadcast
5 bulletin
6 coverage
7 edition
8 media
9 campaign
10 brochure

2 1 *D*
2 B
3 A
4 C
5 D
6 A

3 1 C
2 C
3 D
4 A
5 B
6 C

4 1 *fiction*
2 illegible
3 gist
4 unprintable
5 literature
6 shorthand
7 illiterate
8 prose
9 manuscript
10 outline

5 1 C
2 A
3 D
4 C
5 A
6 D
7 D
8 B
9 C
10 A
11 A
12 C
13 D
14 B
15 C

6 1 *coverage*
2 out of print
3 correspondent
4 circulation
5 edition
6 censorship
7 target
8 projects
9 public
10 blankly

7 1 *spoonful*
2 headlong
3 terrifying
4 controversial
5 unacceptable
6 implication
7 interpretation
8 intended
9 subconscious
10 encouragement

Vocabulary 6

1 1 C
2 D
3 A
4 C
5 D
6 B

2 1 *draught*
2 downpour
3 prey
4 extinct
5 peel
6 tame
7 resources
8 issues
9 off-shore
10 breed

3 1 *hoof, saddle, stable*
2 hive, buzz, sting
3 cub, stripe, roar
4 whine, net, spray
5 bark, kennel, lead
6 flock, lamb, wool
7 ivory, trunk, tusks
8 squeak, hole, trap
9 blind, nocturnal, wing
10 purr, kitten, scratch

4 1 *captivity*
2 survival/surviving
3 volunteers
4 endangered
5 Environmentalists
6 maternal/mothering
7 abundant
8 maturity
9 handful
10 diversity

5 1 *change*
2 occupy
3 lump
4 drowned
5 straight

6 1 *lightning*
2 blossom
3 wildlife
4 the countryside
5 the land
6 horizon
7 young
8 species
9 downpour
10 stone

Vocabulary 7

1 1 *covering letter*
2 career path
3 promotion prospects
4 claims form
5 travel expenses
6 working conditions
7 job description
8 trial period
9 sick pay
10 pension scheme

2 1 C
2 A
3 D
4 A
5 D
6 B
7 C
8 D
9 D
10 A

3 1 *productivity*
2 investments
3 qualifications
4 expertise
5 action
6 representatives
7 economize
8 consultants
9 streamlined
10 clarified

4 1 *executive*
2 foreman
3 manufacturer
4 trainee
5 agent
6 industrialist
7 competitor
8 labourer
9 dealer
10 client

5 1 *e*
2 i
3 g
4 c
5 h
6 j
7 a
8 d
9 f
10 b

6 1 *eligible*
2 entitled
3 negotiable
4 dressed
5 working
6 overtime
7 absence(s), certificate/letter/note
8 terminated, notice

7 1 *work*
2 earned
3 conditions
4 satisfaction
5 achievement
6 case
7 congratulate
8 contributed
9 employs
10 bonus
11 provides
12 busy

Vocabulary 8

1 1 *B*
2 C
3 A
4 C
5 C
6 D
7 D
8 D
9 B
10 C
11 D
12 A

2 1 *e*
2 i
3 a
4 h
5 b
6 d
7 g
8 c
9 f

3 1 *current account*
2 household bills
3 savings account
4 earns interest
5 down payment
6 monthly instalments
7 stock market
8 business venture
9 raise capital
10 tax return

4 1 *gets, makes*
2 grant, scholarship
3 give, pay
4 fetched, sold for
5 take out, withdraw
6 receipts, takings
7 prosperous, wealthy
8 costly, expensive
9 valueless, worthless
10 settle, pay

5 1 *value*
2 fortune
3 redundant
4 retirement
5 booming
6 bankrupt
7 investment
8 market
9 credit
10 charge

6 1 *shares*
2 currency
3 enterprise
4 price
5 fund
6 claim
7 figures
8 credit
9 company
10 financial

7 1 *concerning*
2 inconvenience
3 endeavour
4 delayed
5 dispatching
6 maintain
7 deducting
8 enclosed
9 appreciate
10 trust

Vocabulary 9

1 1 *spoilt*
2 domineering
3 live up to
4 follow
5 pushy
6 pressure
7 interests
8 rebelled
9 struck out
10 sheltered
11 hit it off
12 plucked up
13 commitment
14 patch
15 trial

2 1 *alien*
2 fiancée
3 an acquaintance
4 Toddlers
5 elderly
6 ancestors
7 bachelor
8 best man

9 lad
10 relation

3 1 *conscientious*
2 solitary
3 devoted
4 prejudiced
5 apathetic
6 aggressive
7 mature
8 attentive
9 extrovert
10 insensitive

4 1 *g*
2 b
3 j
4 h
5 f
6 c
7 a
8 e
9 d
10 i

5 1 *neglected*
2 scolded
3 offended
4 adopted
5 separated
6 quarrelled
7 retired
8 criticized
9 abandoned
8 humiliated

6 1 *turned him down*
2 kept in touch
3 grew up
4 went out together
5 fell out
6 got on well with
7 ran away from
8 stood him up
9 moved in with
10 got to know

7 1 *took*
2 close
3 shook
4 steady
5 leading

Vocabulary 10

1 1 *D*
2 D
3 A
4 C
5 B

6 C
7 A
8 D
9 B
10 C
11 B
12 D
13 D
14 A
15 C

2 1 *collapsed*
2 evacuated
3 met
4 sustained
5 blocked
6 failed
7 held
8 spread
9 used
10 sealed

3 1 *worrying*
2 addiction
3 offenders
4 beggars
5 Homeless
6 theft
7 hardened
8 enforced
9 illegal
10 deterrent

4 1 *Potter,*
2 ✓
3 driven
4 abandoned
5 swerve
6 proving
7 successful
8 ✓
9 drunken
10 ✓
11 occasions
12 known as
13 offenders
14 co-operate
15 trial
16 approval
17 considerably
18 indeed the

5 1 *custody*
2 death
3 inquiries
4 wig
5 assault
6 innocent

7 offence
8 speeding
9 evidence
10 verdict

6 1 *into*
2 on
3 from
4 into
5 on
6 out
7 into
8 of
9 on
10 with

7 1 *dispersed*
2 neglected
3 swindled
4 rioted
5 pardoned
6 deported
7 squatted
8 cheated
9 abolished
10 swerved

Vocabulary 11

1 1 *B*
2 A
3 D
4 B
5 D
6 A

2 1 C
2 D
3 C
4 A
5 B
6 B

3 1 *stage*
2 performance
3 interval
4 dramatic
5 seat
6 dress
7 scenery
8 reviews
9 horror

4 1 *clown*
2 vocalist
3 cast
4 juggler
5 acrobat
6 understudy

7 conductor
8 stuntman
9 ballerina

5 1 *concert*
2 string
3 woodwind
4 lyrics
5 organist
6 brass
7 opera
8 chorus
9 percussion

6 1 *rehearsal*
2 energetically
3 thoughts
4 speakers
5 laughter
6 background
7 nationalities
8 overnight
9 creative
10 appearances

7 1 *on*
2 with
3 for
4 over/through
5 for
6 in
7 for
8 on
9 off/from
10 to

8 1 *jigsaw puzzle*
2 cards
3 pool
4 draughts
5 television
6 board game
7 darts
8 table tennis
9 chess
10 computer game

9 1 *record*
2 attention
3 presence
4 scene
5 release

Vocabulary 12

1 1 *B*
2 C
3 B
4 D

5 C
6 D
7 A
8 C
9 D
10 C
11 A
12 B
13 B
14 D
15 D

2 1 *vote*
2 election
3 asylum
4 retirement
5 candidate
6 line
7 campaign
8 poll
9 majority
10 manifesto

3 1 *diplomatic*
2 respectable
3 courteous
4 radical
5 oppressed
6 conventional
7 rebellious
8 privileged
9 notorious
10 progressive

4 1 *mayor*
2 bill
3 survey
4 poll
5 power
6 council
7 reign
8 authorities
9 motion
10 cabinet

5 1 *licensed*
2 restricted
3 compulsory
4 barred
5 abolished
6 binding
7 required
8 permitted
9 voluntary
10 illegal

6 1 *president*
2 minister

3 ringleader
4 ambassador
5 patriot
6 delegate
7 traitor
8 sovereign
9 terrorist
10 chairperson

7 1 *following*
2 retains
3 swing
4 motion
5 control

Vocabulary 13

1 1 *D*
2 B
3 C
4 A
5 B
6 D

2 1 *awake*
2 drowsy
3 worn out
4 run down
5 immobile
6 sore
7 stress
8 abuse
9 gasping
10 an attack

3 1 *highlight*
2 differentiate
3 content
4 products
5 unscientific
6 relaxation
7 prescription
8 ineffective/ineffectual
9 practitioner
10 illnesses

4 1 *heel*
2 throat
3 knee
4 elbow
5 wrist
6 thigh
7 thumb
8 shoulder
9 chin
10 neck

5 1 *stretcher,* casualty, plaster,
crutches

2 porter, surgery, operation,
ward(s)
3 stung, allergic, sling, plaster
4 flabby, overweight, figure,
dieting/diets
5 filling, extracted, injection,
agony

6 1 *i*
2 d
3 f
4 g
5 h
6 b
7 e
8 a
9 j
10 c

7 1 *rambling*
2 crawling
3 tiptoeing
4 limping
5 staggering
6 marching
7 strolling
8 dashing
9 wandering
10 hobbling

Vocabulary 14

1 1 *B*
2 A
3 D
4 C
5 B
6 D
7 B
8 C
9 B
10 A
11 B
12 B

2 1 *negotiation*
2 self-sufficiency
3 immunization
4 organic
5 recycling
6 subsidy
7 irrigation
8 charity

3 1 *consumption,* renewable
2 rainfall, shortages
3 ecological, wildlife
4 extinction, deforestation
5 endangered, intervention

6 household, harmful
7 pesticide(s), production
8 poisonous, climatic

4 1 *overpopulated*
2 overrated
3 overjoyed
4 underestimated
5 oversimplified
6 undernourished
7 overburdened
8 underprivileged
9 overcrowded
10 underlying

5 1 *rural*
2 illiterate
3 essential
4 Wealthy
5 sparsely
6 impoverished
7 urban
8 densely
9 inadequate
10 traditional

6 1 *humanitarian*
2 existence
3 resistance

4 stabilize
5 devalued
6 intervention
7 diplomatic
8 cleansing
9 disproportionate
10 slavery

7 1 *washed away*
2 erosion
3 buried
4 smouldering
5 drought
6 evacuated
7 malnutrition
8 cut off
9 epidemic
10 levels

Vocabulary 15

1 1 *B*
2 D
3 B
4 D
5 A
6 C
7 D
8 B
9 D

10 C
11 A
12 C
13 B
14 B
15 D

2 1 *resigned*
2 convince
3 regard
4 view
5 aware
6 notion
7 favouritism
8 reminds
9 obsessed
10 mentality

3 1 *e*
2 i
3 h
4 j
5 a
6 c
7 g
8 d
9 b
10 f

4 1 *put*
2 follow
3 appreciate
4 utter
5 imply
6 express
7 plead
8 wonder
9 mislead
10 spot

5 1 *f*
2 c
3 g
4 a
5 i
6 h
7 j
8 e
9 b
10 d

6 1 *regretted*
2 deplored
3 resented
4 dreaded
5 cherished
6 mourned
7 offended
8 loathed

9 stressed
10 reproached

7 1 *spot*
2 mind
3 matter
4 dear
5 hand
6 upset

Vocabulary 16

1 1 *D*
2 C
3 D
4 A
5 B
6 C

2 1 *contraption*
2 appliance
3 component
4 machinery
5 system
6 experiment
7 automation
8 gadget
9 overhaul
10 equipment

3 1 *technological*
2 *react in*
3 ✓
4 ✓
5 wonder how
6 example. For
7 ✓
8 frightening
9 mysterious
10 people what
11 vague
12 computers and
13 daily
14 work. But
15 business
16 apparent
17 widespread
18 ✓
19 made
20 ✓
21 cuts, there
22 coal
23 don't

4 1 *d*
2 f
3 g
4 b
5 h

6 i
7 j
8 a
9 c
10 e

5 1 *Installation*
2 maintenance
3 adjustable
4 electrical
5 appliance
6 cylindrical
7 tighten
8 safety
9 protective
10 procedure

6 1 *plug*
2 live
3 runs
4 connection
5 lead
6 a shock
7 fuse
8 record
9 motor
10 electrical
11 pliers
12 grinder
13 blade
14 spanner
15 bulbs

Vocabulary 17

1 1 C
2 A
3 C
4 D
5 B
6 B
7 A
8 B

2 1 *handful*
2 partial
3 adequate
4 bulk
5 minute
6 sizeable
7 dearth
8 fair
9 limited
10 vast

3 1 *extended*
2 reduced
3 faded
4 augmented

5 enlarged
6 spread
7 diminished
8 declined
9 contracted
10 dwindled

4 1 *d*
2 c
3 f
4 b
5 i
6 j
7 h
8 e
9 a
10 g

5 1 *comparison*
2 youth
3 abundant
4 Unemployment
5 sizeable
6 pursuits
7 collection
8 prosperity
9 tendency
10 critical

6 1 *nothing exactly the same as*
2 is not as good as we had hoped
3 similar
4 completely different
5 are not alike
6 calculated in relation to

7 1 *lavish*
2 abundant
3 potential
4 middling
5 excessive
6 ample
7 superior
8 negligible
9 major
10 inferior

8 1 *practically*
2 especially
3 altogether
4 barely
5 thoroughly
6 respectively
7 moderately
8 effectively
9 considerably
10 specifically

Vocabulary 18

1 1 *problematic*
2 involvement
3 bureaucratic
4 disenchanted
5 aggression, aggressiveness
6 rudeness
7 powerless
8 boredom
9 reduction
10 respectful

2 1 *core*
2 academic
3 corporal
4 support
5 trainee
6 continuous
7 employment
8 placement
9 teenage
10 playing

3 1 *B*
2 A
3 C
4 D
5 B
6 C
7 A
8 B

4 1 *graduation*, degree, loan, scholarship
2 sent, detention, tutor (teacher), mark(s)
3 qualifications, prospects, evening, further
4 revised, grades, retake/resit, prize
5 mature, correspondence, assignments, specialize

5 1 *effort*
2 mature
2 applies
4 contributes
5 respect
6 insolent
7 half-hearted
8 distracted
9 concentrate
10 participated

6 1 *mark*
2 applies
3 dropped
4 ruled
5 support

Vocabulary 19

1 1 *underlying*
2 overrated
3 overbalanced
4 undercoat
5 overflowed
6 oversimplifying
7 understaffed
8 underpass
9 overgrown
10 overdone

2 1 *remarkable*
2 likeable
3 digestible
4 contemptible
5 preferable
6 collapsible
7 comfortable
8 sensible
9 responsible
10 disagreeable

3 1 *disconnected*
2 enforced
3 reintroduce
4 overdone
5 unfounded
6 disability
7 indebted
8 devalued
9 misleading
10 sublet

4 1 *annually*
2 considerably
3 Coincidentally
4 directly
5 identically
6 absolutely
7 vaguely
8 totally
9 merely
10 barely

5 1 *insensitive*
2 unequal
3 unjustified
4 injustice
5 invalid
6 invaluable
7 untenable
8 inaction
9 insufficient
10 unprintable

6 1 *makeshift*
2 nightmare
3 earthquake
4 downpour
5 beforehand
6 theatregoer
7 homesick
8 sawdust
9 snowflake
10 ceasefire

7 1 *drawbacks*
2 breathtaking
3 windfall
4 safeguard
5 hardback
6 lifestyle
7 earmarked
8 runway
9 standpoint
10 widespread

8 1 *commercialization*
2 fashionable
3 priceless
4 traditional
5 remarkable
6 confirmation
7 hazardous
8 relentless
9 consultation
10 neglectful

9 1 *forthcoming*
2 noticeboard
3 withdraw
4 replacement
5 volunteers
6 refreshment
7 admittance
8 recognition
9 presentation
10 contribution(s)

Vocabulary 20

1 1 *started moving*
2 damaged
3 produced
4 opened
5 extracted
6 succeeded
7 withdrew
8 told off
9 dragged
10 stopped

2 1 *pass/give*
2 ✓
3 ✓
4 recorded/written
5 ✓
6 be
7 pinch/push
8 fact
9 ✓
10 ✓

3 1 *panel*
2 secret
3 stock
4 time
5 child

4 1 ✓
2 more
3 ✓
4 not compatible
5 cold
6 ✓
7 ✓
8 index
9 awkward/difficult
10 ✓

5 1 *retain, keep*
2 stay, stand
3 part, programme
4 mild, slight
5 purpose, direction
6 cheek, nerve
7 swelled, grew
8 very, bitter
9 pushed, pressed
10 turn, go

6 1 *take*
2 stretched
3 propose
4 space
5 moment

WORDS AND PHRASES ANSWERS

Words and phrases 1

1 1 *expectation*
 2 strike
 3 pressure
 4 fortune
 5 light
 6 undone
 7 useful
 8 world
 9 realize
 10 force

2 1 *detention*
 2 earnest
 3 advance
 4 sympathy
 5 comparison
 6 way
 7 charge
 8 practice
 9 doubt
 10 response

3 1 *g*
 2 i
 3 h
 4 b
 5 a
 6 j
 7 e
 8 d
 9 f
 10 c

4 1 *twig*
 2 girder
 3 trunk
 4 plank
 5 wand
 6 beam
 7 rod
 8 post
 9 stick
 10 pole

5 1 *is unenviable*
 2 unaccompanied
 3 uninhibited
 4 is unfounded
 5 is unbearable

 6 undoubtedly the best skier
   around at the moment
 7 is unmistakable
 8 unjustifiable
 9 is unprecedented
 10 unqualified teacher

6 1 *staggering*
 2 dashed
 3 cross
 4 alight
 5 limped
 6 strolling
 7 tiptoed
 8 slipped
 9 creep
 10 lingered

Words and phrases 2

1 1 *get the sack*
 2 get you down
 3 there's no getting away from it
 4 get your own back
 5 get up speed
 6 get the idea across
 7 get hold of
 8 get it straight
 9 get away with murder
 10 get rid of

2 1 *green*
 2 blue
 3 red
 4 browned
 5 blue
 6 white
 7 red
 8 green
 9 blue
 10 red

3 1 *f*
 2 j
 3 c
 4 h
 5 d
 6 g
 7 a
 8 i

 9 b
 10 e

4 1 *it through*
 2 better days
 3 the last
 4 eye to eye
 5 the funny side
 6 red
 7 my way
 8 a lot
 9 the light
 10 things

5 1 *was a dutiful son*
 2 were not very tactful, were you
 3 is fanciful
 4 a meaningful relationship
 5 am doubtful about this plan
 6 was pitiful, I'm afraid
 7 is definitely harmful to the
   health
 8 useful to know what they
   intend to do
 9 is disrespectful towards his
   teachers
 10 your directions weren't very
   helpful

6 1 *and about*
 2 of character
 3 of the way
 4 of breath
 5 of range
 6 of all proportion
 7 of order
 8 on strike
 9 of my control
 10 of sight

Words and phrases 3

1 1 *its own merits*
 2 his retirement
 3 a permanent basis
 4 the market
 5 loan
 6 the premises
 7 good terms
 8 the verge of

9 average
10 purpose

2 1 *for one*
2 one-sided
3 one-time
4 one in three
5 one-off
6 one at a time
7 all in one
8 One by one
9 one-way
10 one another

3 1 *i*
2 e
3 j
4 c
5 g
6 a
7 d
8 b
9 h
10 f

4 1 *buzzing*
2 booed
3 screech
4 squeaking
5 thud
6 whirring
7 crash
8 hissing
9 tinkling
10 clatter

5 1 *reminds me of*
2 memory is a lot worse than
3 remember me
4 had no memory of
5 your name has slipped
6 forget to tell me to/let me forget to
7 brings to mind
8 very forgetful in
9 Nureyev dance was an unforgettable
10 learning/remembering phone numbers by heart

Words and phrases 4

1 1 *dismissed*
2 rudimentary
3 investigated
4 commensurate
5 scrutinized
6 abandoned

7 an inopportune
8 a discrepancy
9 lucrative
10 beneficial

2 1 *choice*
2 trace
3 use
4 wonder
5 point
6 concern
7 means
8 knowing
9 matter
10 likelihood

3 1 *b*
2 j
3 c
4 d
5 f
6 e
7 i
8 h
9 a
10 g

4 1 *character*
2 toddler
3 relatives
4 grown up
5 individual
6 person
7 figure
8 adolescence
9 humans
10 personality

5 1 *sense*
2 effort
3 inquiries
4 an offer
5 point
6 difference
7 provision
8 way
9 an impression
10 time

6 1 *A fair-haired girl answered the door.*
2 You knew the risks at the outset of this project.
3 Jack is short-tempered.
4 I am not sure what your viewpoint on this problem is.
5 This restaurant is self-service.

6 Our neighbours are certainly troublesome.
7 The people upstairs have a five-year-old child.
8 I stood on the back doorstep.
9 The sight of the waterfall was breathtaking.
10 Tony has contracted a life-threatening disease.

Words and phrases 5

1 1 *sheer*
2 well over
3 minor
4 good
5 considerable/good/ substantial
6 slight
7 substantial/considerable
8 mere/minor/slight
9 bare/mere
10 widespread

2 1 *bribery*
2 childlike
3 fashionable
4 senseless
5 apprenticeship
6 resignation
7 expectations
8 employee
9 cleanliness
10 foreseeable

3 1 *row*
2 talks
3 swoop
4 puzzle
5 go-ahead
6 coup
7 ban
8 jobless
9 probe
10 Number 10
11 city
12 hits out
13 held
14 death toll
15 ousted
16 riddle
17 re-wed
18 blaze
19 PM
20 stays
21 scare
22 rethink
23 split

24 arms
25 official
26 royal
27 back

4 1 *clutched*
2 shook
3 shivering
4 snatched
5 hand
6 clench
7 stretch
8 lean
9 crouched
10 twitching

5 1 *All at once there was a knock at the door.*
2 at a glance that Sam was ill
3 at sea (at the moment in the middle of the Atlantic)
4 very good at tennis
5 this book was rather dull at first, but I've changed my mind
6 will cost at least £500
7 at the duck, but missed it
8 up the stairs three at a time
9 the 100 metres gold medal at the second attempt
10 At any rate, whatever happens the government will have to resign.

Words and phrases 6

1 1 *g*
2 d
3 e
4 b
5 f
6 a
7 i
8 j
9 h
10 c

2 1 *whereabouts*
2 position/spot
3 haunt
4 location
5 plot/site/spot
6 site/whereabouts/location/position
7 spot
8 point
9 venue
10 post

3 1 *fast*
2 bare
3 dead
4 run
5 clean
6 rare
7 late
8 live
9 even
10 sound
11 light
12 slim

4 1 *utter*
2 mention
3 chat
4 butt
5 lectured
6 muttering
7 say
8 pronounced
9 implied
10 arguing
11 declared
12 called

5 1 *power*
2 Enquire
3 means
4 the law
5 reach
6 sight
7 reason
8 the hour

6 1 *There was an overpowering smell coming from the lab.*
2 Oh dear, there seems to have been a misunderstanding.
3 I found that horror film terrifying.
4 The underlying cause of the problem is economic.
5 Building the hydro-electric dam is of over-riding importance.
6 The plane appears to be disintegrating in mid-air.
7 The operation will leave no/not leave any disfiguring marks.
8 The government is intent on industrializing the country.
9 They will be disconnecting the electricity in the morning.
10 I think you are oversimplifying this problem.

Words and phrases 7

1 1 *far*
2 rights
3 profession
4 no means
5 chance
6 and large
7 myself
8 the way
9 all means
10 the time

2 1 *leg*
2 hand
3 heart
4 head
5 spine
6 arm
7 foot
8 cheek
9 neck
10 chest

3 1 *sole*
2 scattered
3 standing
4 common
5 heavy
6 high
7 sound
8 blunt
9 calculated
10 significant

4 1 *have a few days left*
2 has difficulty
3 had enough of
4 have no intention of
5 have no wish/desire
6 have no idea
7 have a go
8 have no recollection/memory of
9 had my hair cut
10 has it (that)

5 1 *eyed*
2 stared
3 view
4 spotted
5 glanced
6 face
7 noticed
8 scanning
9 glimpsed
10 gazing

6 1 *c*
   2 i
   3 g
   4 a
   5 j
   6 e
   7 d
   8 h
   9 b
  10 f

7 1 *any minute now*
   2 now and again
   3 as of today
   4 by then
   5 shortly
   6 for the time being
   7 this minute
   8 not long
   9 before too long
  10 while

Words and phrases 8

1 1 *lapse*
   2 fact
   3 difference
   4 term
   5 price
   6 offer
   7 waste
   8 matter
   9 right
  10 slip

2 1 *negligible*
   2 miniature
   3 sizeable
   4 astronomical
   5 medium–
   6 vast
   7 medium
   8 considerable
   9 minute
  10 substantial

3 1 *f*
   2 i
   3 c
   4 a
   5 j
   6 b
   7 e
   8 h
   9 d
  10 g

4 1 *weather*

   2 saw
   3 ease
   4 wits
   5 butterflies
   6 sorts
   7 punch
   8 collar
   9 aback
  10 go-lucky

5 1 *informed*
   2 meaning
   3 advised
   4 worn
   5 groomed
   6 chosen
   7 founded
   8 nigh
   9 done
  10 to-do

6 1 *heart*
   2 memory
   3 another
   4 scratch
   5 exhaustion
   6 head
   7 now
   8 today
   9 home
  10 appearance

Words and phrases 9

1 1 *literally*
   2 largely/effectively/ practically
   3 widely
   4 invariably
   5 Broadly/Relatively
   6 practically/largely
   7 extensively
   8 relatively
   9 effectively
  10 considerably

2 1 *thinkers*
   2 thoughtful
   3 unthinkable
   4 thinking
   5 thoughtless
   6 rethink
   7 thought
   8 thoughts
   9 thoughtfully
  10 thoughtlessly
3 1 *give me a call/ring tomorrow*
   2 give me an assurance/your word that the money will be

   paid
   3 gives you the right to think/ the idea that you can just come in here like that
   4 gave me the impression
   5 I won't give you any trouble
   6 did you give for that car
   7 gave way under their weight
   8 to leave/give up this job, you have to give (us) two weeks' notice
   9 me old-fashioned dance music any day
  10 gave birth last week

4 1 *by no means*
   2 purposes
   3 manner
   4 apparently
   5 fact
   6 actually
   7 goes
   8 more or less
   9 respects
  10 doubt

5 1 *deal*
   2 drop
   3 bay
   4 set
   5 blow
   6 post
   7 hand
   8 plain
   9 burst
  10 minutes

6 1 *f*
   2 i
   3 b
   4 d
   5 j
   6 g
   7 a
   8 e
   9 h
  10 c

Words and phrases 10

1 1 *blame*
   2 foot
   3 test
   4 stop
   5 flight
   6 market
   7 expense
   8 vote

9 bed
10 ease

2 1 *police*
2 riot
3 bank
4 eye
5 family
6 luck
7 house
8 money
9 feeling
10 play

3 1 *We underestimated our opponents.*
2 Fiona is undergoing treatment for a back condition.
3 This hotel is understaffed.
4 Harry's father is an undertaker.
5 The shop undercharged me.
6 I managed to hide in the undergrowth.
7 Edward got his promotion in rather an underhand fashion.
8 The children were clearly undernourished/had clearly been underfed.
9 The plane's undercarriage fell off as it was about to land.
10 We have not yet discovered the underlying cause of the accident.

4 1 *initial*
2 Ms
3 pseudonym
4 titles
5 identity
6 maiden
7 nicknames
8 alias
9 answers
10 name

5 1 *names*
2 halt
3 box
4 bar
5 question
6 close
7 Duty
8 mind
9 blame
10 attention

6 1 *take*
2 hang
3 dig
4 end
5 slip
6 link
7 dream
8 tot
9 cheer
10 sell